CLYMER®

HONDA

TRX250R/FOURTRAX 250R & ATC 250R • 1985-1989

The world's finest publisher of mechanical how-to manuals

INTERTEC PUBLISHING

P.O. Box 12901, Overland Park, Kansas 66282-2901

Copyright ©1990 Intertec Publishing

FIRST EDITION
First Printing April, 1988
Second Printing November, 1989

SECOND EDITION
First Printing December, 1990
Second Printing May, 1992
Third Printing November, 1993
Fourth Printing May, 1995
Fifth Printing November, 1996
Sixth Printing April, 1998
Seventh Printing July, 1999
Eighth Printing December, 2000

Printed in U.S.A.

CLYMER and colophon are registered trademarks of Intertec Publishing.

ISBN: 0-89287-540-2

Library of Congress: 90-55699

MEMBER

MOTORCYCLE
INDUSTRY
COUNCIL, INC.

Technical photography by Ed Scott.

Technical and photographic assistance by Curt Jordan, Jordan Engineering, Santa Ana, California.

Technical illustrations by Mitzi McCarthy.

COVER: Photographed by Mark Clifford, Mark Clifford Photography, Los Angeles, California. Fourtrax 250R courtesy of Honda Santa Monica, Santa Monica, California.

CLYMER PUBLICATIONS
Intertec Directory & Book Division
President Cameron Bishop
Executive Vice President of Operations/CFO Dan Altman
Vice President, Directory & Book Division Rich Hathaway

EDITORIAL

Senior Editor
Mark Jacobs

Associate Editor
James Grooms

Technical Writers
Ron Wright
Ed Scott
George Parise
Mark Rolling
Michael Morlan
Jay Bogart
Ronney Broach

Inventory and Production Manager
Shirley Renicker

Editorial Production Supervisor
Dylan Goodwin

Editorial Production Assistants
Greg Araujo
Dennis Conrow
Susan Hartington
Holly Messinger
Shara Meyer

Technical Illustrators
Steve Amos
Robert Caldwell
Mitzi McCarthy
Bob Meyer
Michael St. Clair
Mike Rose

MARKETING/SALES AND ADMINISTRATION

General Manager, Technical and Specialty Books
Michael Yim

Advertising & Promotions Manager
Elda Starke

Marketing Assistant
Melissa Abbott

Associate Art Directors
Chris Paxton
Tony Barmann

Sales Manager/Marine
Dutch Sadler

Sales Manager/Motorcycles
Matt Tusken

Sales Coordinator
Paul Cormaci

Customer Service Supervisor
Terri Cannon

Fulfillment Coordinator
Susan Kohlmeyer

Customer Service Representatives
Ardelia Chapman
Donna Schemmel
Kim Jones
April LeBlond

The following books and guides are published by Intertec Publishing.

CLYMER SHOP MANUALS
Boat Motors and Drives
Motorcycles and ATVs
Snowmobiles
Personal Watercraft

ABOS/INTERTEC/CLYMER BLUE BOOKS AND TRADE-IN GUIDES
Recreational Vehicles
Outdoor Power Equipment
Agricultural Tractors
Lawn and Garden Tractors
Motorcycles and ATVs
Snowmobiles and Personal Watercraft
Boats and Motors

AIRCRAFT BLUEBOOK-PRICE DIGEST
Airplanes
Helicopters

AC-U-KWIK DIRECTORIES
The Corporate Pilot's Airport/FBO Directory
International Manager's Edition
Jet Book

I&T SHOP SERVICE MANUALS
Tractors

INTERTEC SERVICE MANUALS
Snowmobiles
Outdoor Power Equipment
Personal Watercraft
Gasoline and Diesel Engines
Recreational Vehicles
Boat Motors and Drives
Motorcycles
Lawn and Garden Tractors

CONTENTS

QUICK REFERENCE DATA

ANTIFREEZE PROTECTION

Temperature	Antifreeze-to-water ratio
Above -25° F (-32° C)	45:55
Above -34° F (-37° C)	50:50
Above -48° F (-44.5° C)	55:45

FRONT FORK OIL CAPACITY AND DIMENSION (3-WHEELED MODELS)

Model	Capacity		Dimension	
	cc	oz.	mm	in.
ATC250R				
1985	400	13.56	186	7.3
1986	465	15.5	113	4.4

TIRE INFLATION PRESSURE (COLD)*

Model	Tire pressure				Circumference	
	Minimum		Maximum			
	kPa	psi	kPa	psi	mm	in.
ATC250R						
Front	27	3.9	33	4.7	1,844	72.6
Rear	22	3.2	28	4.0	1,565	61.6
TRX250R/						
Fourtrax 250R						
1986-1987						
Front	24.5	3.6	30.5	4.4	—	—
Rear	17	2.5	23	3.3	—	—
1988-on						
Front	24.5	3.6	30.5	4.4	—	—
Rear	19.5	2.9	25.5	3.7	—	—

*Tire inflation pressure for factory equipped tires. Aftermarket tires may require different
inflation pressure.

DRIVE CHAIN REPLACEMENT NUMBERS

Model	Number	
	Diado	Takasago
ATC250R	S20VS-96	RK520HMOX 96RJ
TRX250R/Fourtrax 250R		
1986	DID520V4 96L	RK520HMO 96L
1987	DID520V6 96L	RK520SMO 96L
1988-on	DID520V6 92RJ	RK520SMOZ 92RJ

TUNE-UP SPECIFICATIONS

Spark plug type	
ATC250R	
Standard heat range	Champion RN-2C, NGK BR9ES
Cold weather	Champion RN-3C, NGK BR8ES
TRX250R/Fourtrax 250R	
Standard heat range	
1986, 1989	Champion RN-3C, NGK BR8ES
1987-1988	Champion RN-2C, NGK BR9ES
Spark plug gap	0.7-0.8 mm (0.028-0.031 in.)
Ignition timing	"F" mark @ 1,500 ±100 rpm
Carburetor air screw initial screw setting*	
ATC250R	
1985	2 turns out
1986	2 1/4 turns out
TRX250R/Fourtrax 250R	
1986-1987	1 7/8 turns out
1988	1 3/4 turns out
1989	1 1/2 turns out
Idle speed	
ATC250R	
1985	1,400 ±150 rpm
1986	1,580 ±150 rpm
TRX250R/Fourtrax 250R	1,500 ±150 rpm

*Number of turns out from a lightly seated position.

REPLACEMENT BULBS

Item/model	Voltage/wattage
Headlight	
ATC250R	
1985	12V 45/45W
1986	12V 60/55W
TRX250R/Fourtrax 250R	12V 45/45W
Taillight	
ATC250R	12V 5W
TRX250R/Fourtrax 250R	
1986	12V 8W
1987-on	12V 5W

MAINTENANCE AND TUNE-UP TORQUE SPECIFICATIONS

Item	N·m	ft.-lb.
Oil drain plug	25-35	18-25
Rear axle bearing holder lockbolts	20-23	14-17
Parking brake adjuster bolt locknut	15-20	11-14
Spark plug	15-20	11-14

FUEL AND OIL MIXTURE RATIO (20:1)

Gasoline Quantity* Liters or U.S. qt.	Oil cc	U.S. oz.
0.5	25	0.8
1.0	50	1.6
1.5	75	2.4
2.0	100	3.2
2.5	125	4.0
3.0	150	4.8
3.5	175	5.6
4.0	200	6.4
4.5	225	7.2
5.0	250	8.0
5.5	275	8.8
6.0	300	9.6
6.5	325	10.4
7.0	350	11.2
7.5	375	12.0
8.0	400	12.8
8.5	425	13.6
9.0	450	14.4
9.5	475	15.2
10.0	500	16.0

* If gasoline is measured in liters, use oil quantity from **cc** column. If gasoline is measured in U.S. quarts, use oil quantity from **U.S. oz.** column.

COOLING SYSTEM SPECIFICATIONS

Coolant capacity (total system)	
ATC250R	
Coolant change	0.91 liters (0.97 U.S. qt., 0.802 Imp. qt.)
Disassembly	1.32 liters (1.4 U.S. qt., 1.632 Imp. qt.)
TRX250R/Fourtrax 250R	
Coolant change	1.16 liters (1.23 U.S. qt., 1.02 Imp. qt.)
Disassembly	1.52 liters (1.61 U.S. qt., 1.34 Imp. qt.)
Freezing point (hydrometer test)	
Water-to-antifreeze ratio	
55:45	−32° C (−25° F)
50:50	−37° C (−34° F)
45:55	−44.5° C (−48° F)

CDI TROUBLESHOOTING

Symptoms	Probable cause
Weak spark	Poor connections in circuit (clean and retighten all connections)
	High voltage leak (replace defective wire)
	Defective ignition coil (replace coil)
No spark	Broken wire (replace wire)
	Defective ignition coil (replace coil)
	Defective pulse generator (replace alternator stator assembly)
	Defective CDI unit (replace CDI unit)
	Faulty engine kill switch (replace switch)
	Defective ignition switch (models so equipped) (replace ignition switch)

IGNITION SYSTEM TEST POINTS

Item	Terminal	Standard resistance values
Ignition coil primary circuit	Green and black/yellow wires	0.1-0.3 ohms*
Ignition coil secondary circuit with spark plug cap installed	Green wire and spark plug cap	7.4-11K ohms*
Alternator exciter coil	Black/red and green wires	50-250 ohms*
Pulse generator	Green/white and blue/yellow wires	50-200 ohms*
Engine stop switch (in RUN position)	Black/white and green wires	Infinity
Ignition switch (in ON position)	Black/white and green wires	Infinity

* For accurate readings the components must be at approximate temperature of 20° C (68° F).

CLYMER®

HONDA

TRX250R/FOURTRAX 250R & ATC 250R · 1985-1989

CHAPTER ONE

GENERAL INFORMATION

This detailed, comprehensive manual covers the Honda ATC250R, TRX250R and Fourtrax 250R from 1985-on. The expert text gives complete information on maintenance, tune-up, repair and overhaul. Hundreds of photos and drawings guide you through every step. The book includes all you need to know to keep your Honda running right.

A shop manual is a reference. You want to be able to find information fast. As in all Clymer books, this one is designed with you in mind. All chapters are thumb tabbed. Important items are extensively indexed at the rear of the book. All procedures, tables, photos, etc., in this manual are for the reader who may be working on the vehicle for the first time or using this manual for the first time. All the most frequently used specifications and capacities are summarized in the *Quick Reference Data* pages at the front of the book.

Keep the book handy in your tool box or tow vehicle. It will help you better understand how your bike runs, lower repair costs and generally improve your satisfaction with the bike.

Tables 1-3 are at the end of this chapter.

MANUAL ORGANIZATION

All dimensions and capacities are expressed in English units familiar to U.S. mechanics as well as in metric units.

This chapter provides general information and discusses equipment and tools useful both for preventive maintenance and troubleshooting.

Chapter Two provides methods and suggestions for quick and accurate diagnosis and repair of problems. Troubleshooting procedures discuss typical symptoms and logical methods to pinpoint the trouble.

Chapter Three explains all periodic lubrication and routine maintenance necessary to keep the Honda running well. Chapter Three also includes recommended tune-up procedures, eliminating the need to constantly consult chapters on the various assemblies.

Subsequent chapters describe specific systems such as the engine, clutch, transmission, fuel, exhaust, cooling, suspension and brakes. Each chapter provides disassembly, repair and assembly procedures in simple step-by-step form.

If a repair is impractical for a home mechanic, it is so indicated. It is usually faster and less expensive to take such repairs to a dealer or competent repair shop. Specifications concerning a particular system are included at the end of the appropriate chapter.

Some of the procedures in this manual specify special tools. In most cases, the tool is illustrated either in actual use or alone. Well equipped mechanics may find they can substitute similar tools already on hand or can fabricate their own.

NOTES, CAUTIONS AND WARNINGS

The terms NOTE, CAUTION and WARNING have specific meanings in this manual. A NOTE provides additional information to make a step or procedure easier or clearer. Disregarding a NOTE could cause inconvenience, but would not cause equipment damage or personal injury.

A CAUTION emphasizes areas where equipment damage could occur. Disregarding a CAUTION could cause permanent mechanical damage. However, personal injury is unlikely.

A WARNING emphasizes areas where personal injury or even death could result from negligence. Mechanical damage may also occur. WARNINGS are to be taken *seriously*. In some cases, serious injury or death has resulted from disregarding similar warnings.

SERVICE HINTS

Most of the service procedures covered are straightforward and can be performed by anyone reasonably handy with tools. However, you should consider your own capabilities carefully before attempting any operation involving major disassembly of the engine.

Some operations require, for example, the use of a press. It would be wiser to have these performed by a shop equipped for such work, rather than trying to do the job yourself with makeshift equipment. Other procedures require precise measurements. Unless you have the skills and equipment required, it would be better to have a qualified repair shop make the measurements for you.

Throughout this manual keep in mind 2 conventions. "Front" refers to the front of the vehicle. The front of any component, such as the engine, is the end which faces toward the front of the vehicle. The "left-" and "right-hand" sides refer to the position of the parts as viewed by a rider sitting on the seat facing forward. For example, the throttle control is on the right-hand side and the clutch lever is on the left-hand side. These rules are simple, but even experienced mechanics occasionally become disoriented.

There are many items available that can be used on your hands before and after working on your vehicle. A little preparation before getting "all greased up" will help when cleaning up later.

Before starting out, work Vaseline, soap or a product such as Pro-Tek Invisible Glove (**Figure 1**)

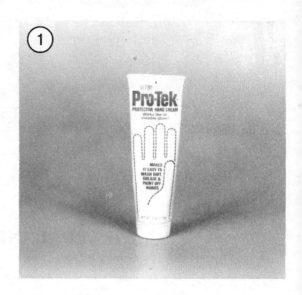

onto your forearms, into your hands and under your fingernails and cuticles. This will make cleanup a lot easier.

For cleanup, use a waterless hand soap such as Sta-Lube and then finish up with powdered Boraxo and a fingernail brush.

Repairs go much faster and easier if the vehicle is clean before you begin work. There are special cleaners, such as Gunk or Bel-Ray Degreaser (**Figure 2**), for washing the engine and related parts. Just spray or brush on the cleaning solution, let it stand, then rinse it away with a garden hose. Clean all oily or greasy parts with cleaning solvent as you remove them.

> *WARNING*
> *Never use gasoline as a cleaning agent. It presents an extreme fire hazard. Be sure to work in a well-ventilated area when using cleaning solvent. Keep a fire extinguisher, rated for gasoline fires, handy in any case.*

Special tools are required for some repair procedures. These may be purchased from a dealer or motorcycle shop, rented from a tool rental dealer or fabricated by a mechanic or machinist, often at a considerable savings.

Much of the labor charged for by mechanics is to remove and disassemble other parts to reach the defective unit. It is usually possible to perform the preliminary operations yourself and then take the defective unit in to the dealer for repair.

Once you have decided to tackle the job yourself, read the entire section in this manual which pertains to it, making sure you have identified the proper one. Study the illustrations and text until

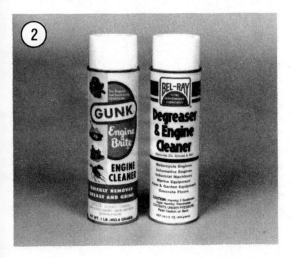

you have a good idea of what is involved in completing the job satisfactorily. If special tools or replacement parts are required, make arrangements to get them before you start. It is frustrating and time-consuming to get partly into a job and then be unable to complete it.

Simple wiring checks can be easily made at home, but knowledge of electronics is almost a necessity for performing tests with complicated electronic testing gear.

During disassembly of parts keep a few general cautions in mind. Force is rarely needed to get things apart. If parts are a tight fit, such as a bearing in a case, there is usually a tool designed to separate them. Never use a screwdriver to pry parts with machined surfaces such as crankcase halves. You will mar the surfaces and end up with leaks.

Make diagrams or take a Polaroid picture wherever similar-appearing parts are found. For instance, crankcase bolts are often not the same length. You may think you can remember where everything came from, but mistakes are costly. There is also the possibility you may be sidetracked and not return to work for days or even weeks, in which interval carefully laid out parts may have become disturbed.

Tag all similar internal parts for location and mark all mating parts for position. Record number and thickness of any shims as they are removed. Small parts such as bolts can be identified by placing them in plastic sandwich bags. Seal and label them with masking tape.

Wiring should be tagged with masking tape and marked as each wire is removed. Again, do not rely on memory alone.

Protect finished surfaces from physical damage or corrosion. Keep gasoline and hydraulic brake fluid off plastic parts and painted surfaces.

Frozen or very tight bolts and screws can often be loosened by soaking with penetrating oil, such as WD-40 or Liquid Wrench, then sharply striking the bolt head a few times with a hammer and punch (or screwdriver for screws). Avoid heat unless absolutely necessary, since it may melt, warp or remove the temper from many parts.

No parts, except those assembled with a press fit, require unusual force during assembly. If a part is hard to remove or install, find out why before proceeding.

Cover all openings after removing parts to keep dirt, small tools, etc., from falling in.

When assembling 2 parts, start all fasteners, then tighten evenly.

Electrical wire connectors and brake components should be kept clean and free of grease and oil.

When assembling parts, be sure all shims and washers are installed exactly as they came out.

Whenever a rotating part butts against a stationary part, look for a shim or washer. Use new gaskets if there is any doubt about the condition of the old ones. A thin coat of oil on gaskets may help them seal effectively.

Cold heavy grease can be used to hold small parts in place if they tend to fall out during assembly. However, keep grease and oil away from electrical and brake components.

High spots may be sanded off a piston with sandpaper, but fine emery cloth and oil will do a much more professional job.

Carbon can be removed from the head, the piston crown and the exhaust ports with a dull screwdriver. Do *not* scratch machined surfaces. Wipe off the surface with a clean cloth when finished.

The carburetor is best cleaned by disassembling it and soaking the parts in a commercial carburetor cleaner. Never soak gaskets and rubber parts in these cleaners. Never use wire to clean out jets and air passages; they are easily damaged. Use compressed air to blow out the carburetor *after* the float has been removed.

A baby bottle makes a good measuring device for adding oil to the front forks (3-wheeled models). Get one that is graduated in fluid ounces and cubic centimeters. After it has been used for this purpose, do not let a small child drink out of it as there will always be an oil residue in it.

Take your time and do the job right. Do not forget that a newly rebuilt engine must be broken in the same as a new one. Keep the rpm within the limits given in your owner's manual when you get back on the road.

TORQUE SPECIFICATIONS

Torque specifications throughout this manual are given in Newton meters (N•m) and foot-pounds (ft.-lb.). Newton meters have been adopted in place of meter kilograms (mkg) in accordance with the international modernized metric system. Tool manufacturers offer torque wrenches calibrated in Newton meters and foot-pounds and Sears has a Craftsman line calibrated in both values.

Existing torque wrenches calibrated in meter kilograms can be used by performing a simple conversion. All you have to do is move the decimal point one place to the right; for example, 4.7 mkg = 47 N•m. This conversion is accurate enough for mechanical work even though the exact mathematical conversion is 3.5 mkg = 34.3 N•m.

Refer to **Table 1** for standard torque specifications for various size screws, bolts and nuts that may not be covered in the various chapters and tables.

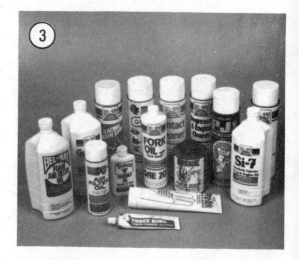

SAFETY FIRST

Professional mechanics can work for years and never sustain a serious injury. If you observe a few rules of common sense and safety, you can enjoy many hours servicing your own machine. If you ignore these rules you can hurt yourself or damage the vehicle.

1. Never use gasoline as a cleaning solvent.
2. Never smoke or use a torch in the vicinity of flammable liquids such as cleaning solvent in open containers.
3. If welding or brazing is required on the machine, remove the fuel tank to a safe distance, at least 50 feet away.
4. Use the proper sized wrenches to avoid damage to nuts and injury to yourself.
5. When loosening a tight or stuck nut, think about what would happen if the wrench should slip. Be careful. Protect yourself accordingly.
6. Keep your work area clean and uncluttered.
7. Wear safety goggles during all operations involving drilling, grinding or the use of a cold chisel.
8. Never use worn tools.
9. Keep a fire extinguisher handy and be sure it is rated for gasoline and electrical fires.

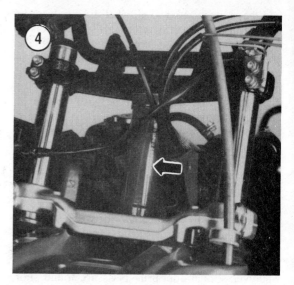

SPECIAL TIPS

Because of the extreme demands placed on the vehicle several points should be kept in mind when performing service and repair. The following items are general suggestions that may improve the overall life of the machine and help avoid costly failures.

1. Use a locking compound such as Loctite Lock N' Seal No. 2114 (blue Loctite) on all bolts and nuts, even if they are secured with lockwashers. This type of Loctite does not harden completely and allows easy removal of the bolt or nut. A screw or bolt lost from an engine cover or bearing retainer could easily cause serious and expensive damage before its loss is noticed. Make sure the threads are clean and free of grease and oil. Clean with contact cleaner before applying the Loctite.

CAUTION
When applying Loctite, use a small amount. If too much is used, it can work its way down the threads and stick parts together not meant to be stuck.

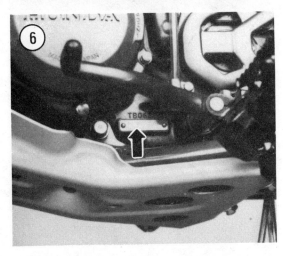

NOTE
Keep a tube of Loctite in your tool box;
when used properly it is cheap
insurance.

2. Use a hammer-driven impact tool to remove and install all bolts, particularly engine cover screws. These tools help prevent the rounding off of bolt and screw heads and ensure a tight installation.

3. When replacing missing or broken fasteners (bolts, nuts and screws), especially on the engine or frame components, always use Honda replacement parts. They are specially hardened for each application. The wrong fastener could easily cause serious and expensive damage, not to mention rider injury.

4. When installing gaskets in the engine, always use Honda replacement gaskets *without* sealer, unless designated. These gaskets are designed to swell when they come in contact with oil. Gasket

sealer will prevent the gaskets from swelling as intended, which can result in oil leaks. These Honda gaskets are cut from material of the precise thickness needed. Installation of a too thick or too thin gasket in a critical area could cause engine damage.

EXPENDABLE SUPPLIES

Certain expendable supplies are required during maintenance and repair work. These include grease, oil, gasket cement, wiping rags and cleaning solvent. Ask your dealer for the special locking compounds, silicone lubricants and other products (**Figure 3**) which make vehicle maintenance simpler and easier. Cleaning solvent or kerosene is available at some service stations or hardware stores.

PARTS REPLACEMENT

Honda makes frequent changes during a model year; some minor, some relatively major. When you order parts from the dealer or other parts distributor, always order by engine and frame number. Write the numbers down and carry them with you. Compare new parts to old before purchasing them. If they are not alike, have the parts manager explain the difference to you.

SERIAL NUMBERS

You must know the model serial number (frame and/or engine) for registration purposes and when ordering replacement parts.

The frame serial number (and VIN) is located as follows.

    a. 3-wheeled models—stamped on the left-hand side of the steering head (**Figure 4**).

    b. 4-wheeled models—stamped on the left-hand side of the frame (**Figure 5**) just behind the engine.

The engine serial number is stamped on the lower left-hand surface of the crankcase behind the alternator (**Figure 6**).

The carburetor identification number is stamped on the small raised pad on the side of the carburetor body (**Figure 7**) just above the float bowl.

BASIC HAND TOOLS

A number of tools are required to maintain the vehicle in top riding condition (**Figure 8**). You may already have some of these tools for home, motorcycle or car repairs. There are also tools made especially for vehicle repairs. These you will have to purchase. In any case, a wide variety of quality tools will make vehicle repairs easier and more effective.

Top quality tools are essential. They are also more economical in the long run. If you are now starting to build your tool collection, stay away from the "advertised specials" featured at some parts houses, discount stores and chain drug stores. These are usually a poor grade tool that can be sold cheaply and that is exactly what they are—*cheap*. They are usually made of inferior material and are thick, heavy and clumsy. Their rough finish makes them difficult to clean and they usually don't last very long. Quality tools are made of alloy steel and are heat treated for greater strength. They are lighter and better balanced than cheap ones. Their surface is smooth, making them a pleasure to work with and easy to clean. The initial cost of good quality tools may be more but it is cheaper in the long run. Don't try to buy everything in all sizes in the beginning; buy a little at a time until you have the necessary tools.

Keep your tools clean and in a tool box. Keep them organized with the sockets and related drives together and the open end and box wrenches together, etc. After using a tool, wipe off dirt and grease with a clean cloth and place the tool in its correct place. Doing this will save a lot of time you would have spent trying to find a socket buried in a bunch of clutch parts.

The following tools are required to perform virtually any repair job on a vehicle. Each tool is described and the recommended size given for starting a tool collection. **Table 2** includes the tools that should be on hand for simple home repairs or major overhaul. Additional tools and some duplicates may be added as you become more familiar with the vehicle. Almost all ATV's and motorcycles, with the exception of the U.S. built Harley and some English vehicles, use metric size bolts and nuts. If you are starting your collection now, buy metric sizes.

Screwdrivers

The screwdriver is a very basic tool, but if used improperly it will do more damage than good. The slot on a screw has a definite dimension and shape. A screwdriver must be selected to conform with that shape. Use a small screwdriver for small screws and a large one for large screws or the screw head will be damaged.

Two basic types of screwdriver are required to repair the vehicle—a common (flat blade) screwdriver and the Phillips screwdriver.

Screwdrivers are available in sets which often include an assortment of common and Phillips

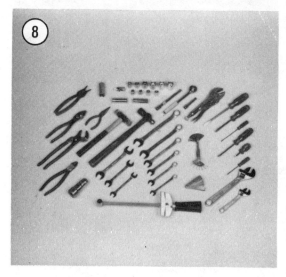

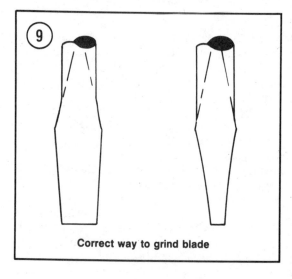

Correct way to grind blade

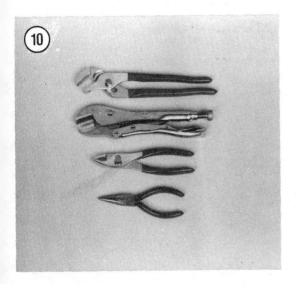

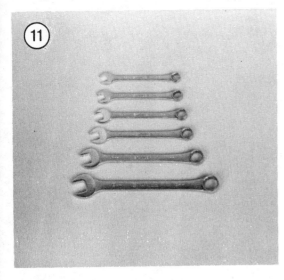

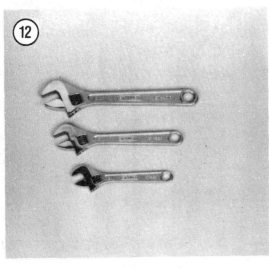

blades. If you buy them individually, buy at least the following:

   a. Common screwdriver—5/16×6 in. blade.
   b. Common screwdriver—3/8×12 in. blade.
   c. Phillips screwdriver—size 2 tip, 6 in. blade.

Use screwdrivers only for driving screws. Never use a screwdiver for prying or chiseling. Do not try to remove a Phillips or Allen head screw with a common screwdriver; you can damage the head so that the proper tool will be unable to remove it.

Keep screwdrivers in the proper condition and they will last longer and perform better. Always keep the tip of a common screwdriver in good condition. **Figure 9** shows how to grind the tip to the proper shape if it becomes damaged. Note the symmetrical sides of the tip.

Pliers

Pliers come in a wide range of types and sizes. Pliers are useful for cutting, bending and crimping. They should never be used to cut hardened objects or to turn bolts or nuts. **Figure 10** shows several pliers useful in vehicle repairs.

Each type of pliers has a specialized function. Gas pliers are general purpose pliers and are used mainly for holding things and for bending. Locking pliers, such as Vise Grips, are used as pliers or to hold objects very tight like a vise. Needlenose pliers are used to hold or bend small objects. Channel lock pliers can be adjusted to hold various sizes of objects; the jaws remain parallel to grip around objects such as pipe or tubing. There are many more types of pliers. The ones described here are most suitable for vehicle repairs.

Box and Open-end Wrenches

Box and open-end wrenches are available in sets or separately in a variety of sizes. The size number stamped near the end refers to the distance between 2 parallel flats on the hex head bolt or nut.

Box wrenches are usually superior to open-end wrenches. Open-end wrenches grip the nut on only 2 flats. Unless it fits well, it may slip and round off the points on the nut. The box wrench grips all 6 flats. Both 6-point and 12-point openings on box wrenches are available. The 6-point gives superior holding power; the 12-point allows a shorter swing.

Combination wrenches (**Figure 11**) which are open on one side and boxed on the other are also available. Both ends are the same size.

Adjustable (Crescent) Wrenches

An adjustable wrench, also called crescent wrench, can be adjusted to fit nearly any nut or bolt head. See **Figure 12**. However, it can loosen and

slip, causing damage to the nut and injury to your
knuckles. Use an adjustable wrench only when
other wrenches are not available.

Crescent wrenches come in sizes ranging from
4-18 in. overall. A 6 or 8 in. wrench is
recommended as an all-purpose wrench.

Socket Wrenches

This type is undoubtedly the fastest, safest and
most convenient to use. See **Figure 13**. Sockets
which attach to a ratchet handle are available with
6-point or 12-point openings and 1/4, 3/8, 1/2 and
3/4 inch drives. The drive size indicates the size of
the square hole which mates with the ratchet
handle.

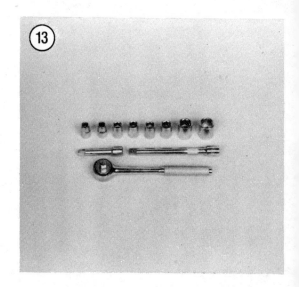

Torque Wrench

A torque wrench is used with a socket to
measure how tightly a nut or bolt is installed. They
come in a wide price range and with either 3/8 or
1/2 in. square drive. The drive size indicates the
size of the square drive which mates with the
socket. Purchase one that measures 0-140 N•m
(0-100 ft.-lb.).

Impact Driver

This tool might have been designed with the
vehicle in mind. See **Figure 14**. It makes removal
of engine and clutch parts easy and eliminates
damage to bolts and screw slots. This tool is
available at most large hardware, motorcycle or
auto parts stores.

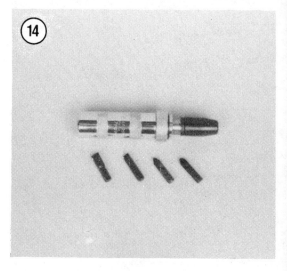

Circlip Pliers

Circlip pliers, sometimes referred to as snap-ring
pliers, are necessary to remove the circlips used on
the transmission shaft assemblies. See **Figure 15**.

Hammers

The correct hammer is necessary for vehicle
repairs. Use only a hammer with a face (or head) of
rubber or plastic or the soft-faced type that is filled
with buck shot. These are sometimes necessary in
engine tear-downs. *Never* use a metal-faced
hammer on the vehicle as severe damage will result
in most cases. You can always produce the same
amount of force with a soft-faced hammer.

Ignition Gauge

This tool (**Figure 16**) has both flat and wire
measuring gauges and is used to measure spark
plug gap. This device is available at most auto or
motorcycle supply stores.

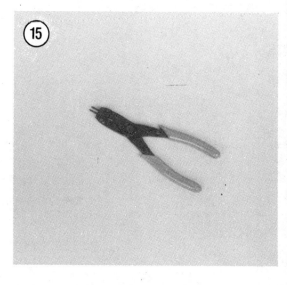

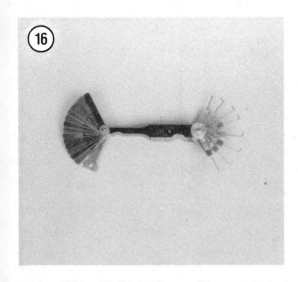

Other Special Tools

A few other special tools may be required for major service. These are described in the appropriate chapters and are available either from a Honda dealer or other manufacturers as indicated.

TUNE-UP AND TROUBLESHOOTING TOOLS

Multimeter or Volt-ohm Meter

This instrument (**Figure 17**) is invaluable for electrical system troubleshooting and service. A few of its functions may be duplicated by homemade test equipment, but for the serious mechanic it is a must. Its uses are described in the applicable sections of the book.

Portable Tachometer

A portable tachometer is necessary for tuning (**Figure 18**). Carburetor adjustments must be performed at the specified engine speed. The best instrument for this purpose is one with a low range of 0-1,000 or 0-2,000 rpm and a high range of 0-4,000 rpm. Extended range (0-6,000 or 0-8,000 rpm) instruments lack accuracy at lower speeds. The instrument should be capable of detecting changes of 25 rpm on the low range.

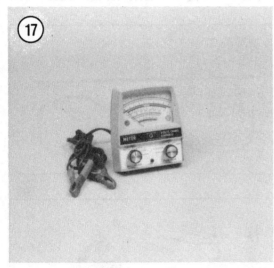

MECHANIC'S TIPS

Removing Frozen Nuts and Screws

When a fastener rusts and cannot be removed, several methods may be used to loosen it. First, apply penetrating oil such as Liquid Wrench or WD-40 (available at any hardware or auto supply store). Apply it liberally and let it penetrate for 10-15 minutes. Rap the fastener several times with a small hammer. Do not hit it hard enough to cause damage. Reapply the penetrating oil if necessary.

For frozen screws, apply penetrating oil as described, then insert a screwdriver in the slot and rap the top of the screwdriver with a hammer. This loosens the rust so the screw can be removed in the normal way. If the screw head is too chewed up to use a screwdriver, grip the head with Vise Grips and twist the screw out.

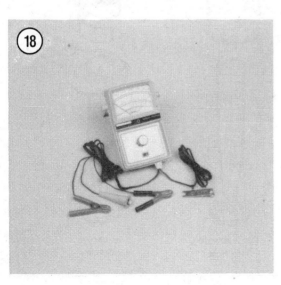

Remedying Stripped Threads

Occasionally, threads are stripped though carelessness or impact damage. Often the threads can be cleaned up by running a tap (for internal threads on nuts) or die (for external threads on bolts) through threads. See **Figure 19**.

Removing Broken Screws or Bolts

When the head breaks off a screw or bolt, several methods can be used to remove the remaining portion.

If a large portion of the remainder projects out, try gripping it with Vise Grips. If the projecting portion is too small, file it to fit a wrench or cut a slot in it to fit a screwdriver. See **Figure 20**.

If the head breaks off flush, use a screw extractor. To do this, centerpunch the remaining portion of the screw or bolt. Drill a small hole in the screw and tap the extractor into the hole. Back the screw out with a wrench on the extractor. See **Figure 21**.

"OFF THE ROAD" RULES

Areas set aside by the federal government, state or local agencies for off-road riding are continuing to disappear. The loss of many of these areas is usually due to the few who really don't care and therefore ruin the sport of off-road fun for those who do. Many areas are closed off to protect wildlife habitat, vegetation and geological structures. Do not enter into these areas as it can result in an expensive citation and adds to the anti-off-road vehicle sentiment that can result in further land closures. By following these basic rules

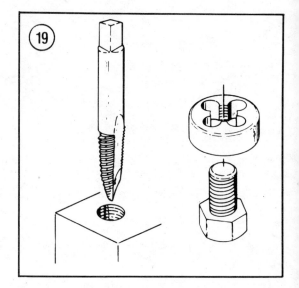

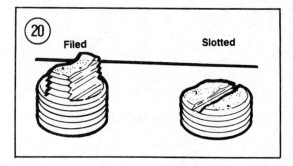

Filed   Slotted

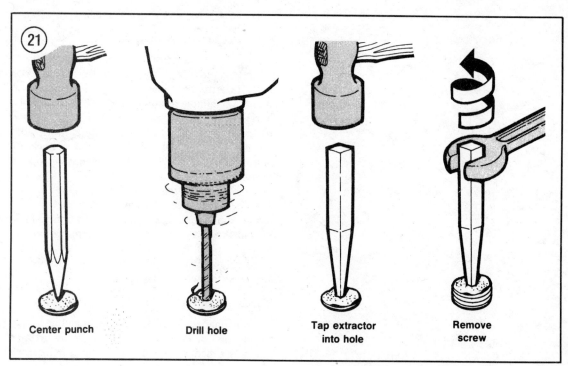

Center punch   Drill hole   Tap extractor into hole   Remove screw

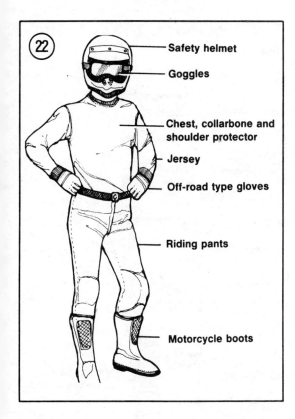

㉒

— Safety helmet

— Goggles

— Chest, collarbone and shoulder protector

— Jersey

— Off-road type gloves

— Riding pants

— Motorcycle boots

you and others will always have an area open for this type of recreational use.

1. When riding, always observe the basic practice of good sportsmanship and recognize that other people will judge all off-road vehicle owners by your actions.
2. Don't litter the trails or camping areas. Leave the area cleaner than it was before you came.
3. Don't pollute lakes, streams or the ocean.
4. Be careful not to damage living trees, shrubs or other natural terrain.
5. Respect other people's rights and property.
6. Help anyone in distress.
7. Make yourself and your vehicle available for assistance in any search and rescue parties.
8. Don't harass other people using the same area as you are. Respect the rights of others enjoying the recreation area.
9. Be sure to obey all federal, state, provincial and other local rules regulating the operation of the ATV.
10. Inform public officials when using public lands.
11. Don't harass wildlife and stay out of areas posted for the protection and feeding of wildlife.
12. Keep your exhaust noise to a minimum.
13. When riding in the snow, stay away from carefully   groomed   snowmobile   trails.

Snowmobilers get pretty upset, and rightfully so, when ATV's spoil the trails that they have worked hard to make.

SAFETY

General Tips

1. Read your owner's manual and know your machine.
2. Check the throttle and brake controls before starting the engine.
3. Know how to make an emergency stop.
4. Know all state, federal and local laws concerning the ATV. Respect private property.

> *NOTE*
> *The Honda ATV is designed and manufactured for off-road use **only**. It does not conform to federal motor vehicle safety standards and it is illegal to operate it on public streets, roads or highways.*

5. Never add fuel while anyone is smoking in the area or when the engine is running.
6. Never wear loose scarves, belts or boot laces that could catch on moving parts or tree limbs.
7. Always wear protective clothing to protect your *entire* body. **Figure 22** shows a well equipped off-road rider who is ready for almost any riding condition. Today's riding apparel is very stylish and you will be ready for action as well as being well protected.
8. Riding in the winter months requires a good set of clothes to keep your body dry and warm, otherwise your entire trip may be miserable. If you dress properly, moisture will evaporate from your body. If you become too hot, and if your clothes trap the moisture, you will become cold. **Figure 23** shows some recommended inner and outer layers of cold weather clothing. Even mild temperatures can be very uncomfortable and dangerous when combined with a strong wind or travel at high speed. See **Table 3** for wind chill factors. Always dress according to what the wind chill factor is, not the ambient temperature.
9. Never allow anyone to operate the ATV without proper instruction. This is for their bodily protection and to keep your machine from damage or destruction.
10. Use the "buddy system" for long trips, just in case you have a problem or run out of gas.
11. Never carry a passenger. The ATV is designed to carry only one person.
12. Never attempt to repair your machine with the engine running except when necessary for certain tune-up procedures.

13. Check all of the machine components and hardware frequently, especially the wheels and the steering.

14. Push the ATV onto a truck or trailer bed; *never* ride it on. Secure it firmly to the truck or trailer and if towing a trailer be sure that the trailer lights operate properly.

Operating Tips

1. Never operate the machine in crowded areas or steer toward people.

2. Avoid dangerous terrain.

3. Cross highways (where permitted) at a 90° angle after looking in both directions. Post traffic guards if crossing in groups.

4. Do not ride the vehicle on or near railroad tracks. The ATV engine and exhaust noise can drown out the sound of an approaching train.

5. Keep the headlight and taillight free of dirt and never ride at night without the headlight and taillight on.

6. Do not ride the ATV without the seat and fenders in place.

7. Always steer with both hands.

8. Be aware of the terrain and avoid operating the ATV at excessive speed.

9. Do not panic if the throttle sticks. Turn the engine stop switch to the OFF position.

10. Do not speed through wooded areas. Hidden obstructions, hanging tree limbs, unseen ditches and even wild animals and hikers can cause injury and damage to the ATV.

11. Do not tailgate. Rear end collisions can cause injury and machine damage.

12. Do not mix alcoholic beverages or drugs with riding; ride straight and sober.

13. Keep both feet on the foot pegs. Do not permit your feet to hang out to stabilize the machine when

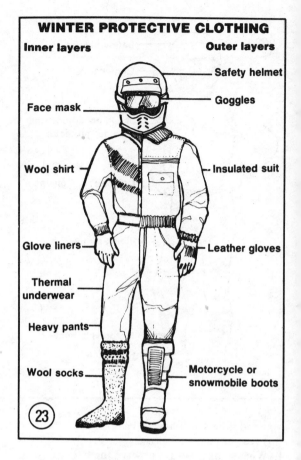

making turns or in near spill situations. Broken limbs could result.

14. Check your fuel supply regularly. Do not travel farther than your fuel supply will permit you to return.

15. Check to make sure that the parking brake is *completely* released while riding. If left on, the rear brake pads will be damaged.

Tables are on the following pages.

Table 1 MISCELLANEOUS TORQUE SPECIFICATIONS

Item	N·m	ft.-lb.
5 mm bolt and nut	4.5-6	3-4
6 mm bolt and nut	8-12	6-9
8 mm bolt and nut	18-25	13-18
10 mm bolt and nut	30-40	22-29
12 mm bolt and nut	50-60	36-43
5 mm screw	3.5-5	2-4
6 mm screw and 6 mm bolt with 8 mm head	7-11	5-8
6 mm flange bolt and nut	10-14	7-10
8 mm flange bolt and nut	24-30	17-22
10 mm flange bolt and nut	35-45	25-33

Table 2 WORKSHOP TOOLS

Tool	Size or Specifications
Screwdriver	
Common	5/16×8 in. blade
Common	3/8×12 in. blade
Phillips	Size 2 tip, 6 in. overall
Pliers	
Gas pliers	6 in. overall
Vise Grips	10 in. overall
Needlenose	6 in. overall
Channel lock	12 in. overall
Snap ring	–
Wrenches	
Box-end set	5-17 mm (24 and 28 mm)
Open-end set	5-17 mm (24 and 28 mm)
Crescent	6 in. and 12 in. overall
Socket set	1/2 in. drive ratchet with 5-17 mm sockets
Other special tools	
Strap wrench	–
Impact driver	1/2 in. drive with assorted bits
Torque wrench	1/2 in. drive 0-100 ft.lb.
Ignition gauge	–

Table 3 WIND CHILL FACTOR

Estimated Wind Speed in MPH	Actual Thermometer Reading (° F)											
	50	40	30	20	10	0	—10	—20	—30	—40	—50	—60
	Equivalent Temperature (° F)											
Calm	50	40	30	20	10	0	—10	—20	—30	—40	—50	—60
5	48	37	27	16	6	—5	—15	—26	—36	—47	—57	—68
10	40	28	16	4	—9	—21	—33	—46	—58	—70	—83	—95
15	36	22	9	—5	—18	—36	—45	—58	—72	—85	—99	—112
20	32	18	4	—10	—25	—39	—53	—67	—82	—96	—110	—124
25	30	16	0	—15	—29	—44	—59	—74	—88	—104	—118	—133
30	28	13	—2	—18	—33	—48	—63	—79	—94	—109	—125	—140
35	27	11	—4	—20	—35	—49	—67	—82	—98	—113	—129	—145
40	26	10	—6	—21	—37	—53	—69	—85	—100	—116	—132	—148

Little Danger (for properly clothed person)   **Increasing Danger**   **Great Danger**

• Danger from freezing of exposed flesh •

*Wind speeds greater than 40 mph have little additional effect.

CHAPTER TWO

TROUBLESHOOTING

Diagnosing mechanical problems is relatively simple if you use orderly procedures and keep a few basic principles in mind.

The troubleshooting procedures in this chapter analyze typical symptoms and show logical methods of isolating causes. These are not the only methods. There may be several ways to solve a problem, but only a systematic, methodical approach can guarantee success.

Never assume anything. Do not overlook the obvious. If you are riding along and the engine suddenly quits, check the easiest, most accessible problems first. Is there gasoline in the tank? Is the fuel shutoff valve in the ON position? Has the spark plug wire fallen off?

If nothing obvious turns up in a quick check, look a little further. Learning to recognize and describe symptoms will make repairs easier for you or a mechanic at the shop. Describe problems accurately and fully. Saying that "it won't run" isn't the same as saying "it quit at high speed and won't start" or that "it sat in my garage for 3 months and then wouldn't start."

Gather as many symptoms together as possible to aid in diagnosis. Note whether the engine lost power gradually or all at once. Remember that the more complicated a machine is, the easier it is to troubleshoot because symptoms point to specific problems.

After the symptoms are defined, areas which could cause the problems are tested and analyzed. Guessing at the cause of a problem may provide the solution, but it can easily lead to frustration, wasted time and a series of expensive, unnecessary parts replacements.

You do not need fancy equipment or complicated test gear to determine whether repairs can be attempted at home. A few simple checks could save a large repair bill and time lost while the bike sits in a dealer's service department. On the other hand, be realistic and don't attempt repairs beyond your abilities. Service departments tend to charge a lot for putting together a disassembled engine that may have been abused. Some dealers won't even take on such a job. Use common sense and don't get in over your head.

OPERATING REQUIREMENTS

An engine needs 3 basics to run properly; correct fuel-air mixture, compression and a spark at the correct time. If one or more are missing, the engine just won't run. The electrical system is the weakest link of the 3 basics. More problems result from electrical breakdowns than from any other source.

Keep that in mind before you begin tampering with carburetor adjustments and the like.

If the vehicle has been sitting for any length of time and refuses to start, check and clean the spark plug and then look to the gasoline delivery system. This includes the fuel tank, fuel shutoff valve (and integral fuel filter) and the fuel line to the carburetor. Be sure to shake the vehicle to re-mix the fuel/oil mixture in the fuel tank. Gasoline deposits may have formed and gummed up the carburetor's jets and air passages. Gasoline tends to lose its potency after standing for long periods. Condensation may contaminate the fuel with water. Drain the old fuel and try starting with a fresh tankful.

EMERGENCY TROUBLESHOOTING

When the vehicle is difficult to start or won't start at all, it does not help to wear out your leg on the kickstarter. Check for obvious problems even before getting out your tools. Go down the following list step by step. You may be embarrassed to find your kill switch is stuck in the OFF position, but that is better than wearing down your leg. If it still will not start, refer to the appropriate troubleshooting procedure which follows in this chapter.

1. Is there fuel in the tank? Open the filler cap and rock the vehicle. Listen for fuel sloshing around. Also make sure the vent tube is clear. Disconnect it and blow it out.

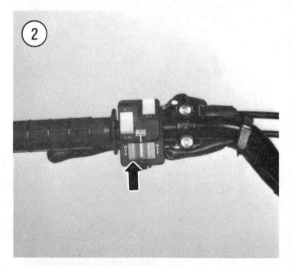

> *WARNING*
> *Do not use an open flame to check in the tank. A serious explosion is certain to result.*

2. Is the fuel shutoff valve (**Figure 1**) in the ON position?
3. Make sure the kill switch (**Figure 2**) is not stuck in the OFF position.
4. Is the spark plug wire (**Figure 3**) on tight? Push it on and slightly rotate it to clean the electrical connection between the plug and the connector.
5. Is the choke lever (**Figure 4**) in the right position? The knob or lever should be moved up for a cold engine and down for a warm engine.

ENGINE STARTING

An engine that refuses to start or is difficult to start is very frustrating. More often than not, the

WARNING
If it is necessary to hold the high voltage lead during the next step, do so with an insulated pair of pliers. The high voltage generated by the ignition pulse generator and CDI unit could produce serious or fatal shocks.

3. Crank the engine over with the kickstarter. A fat blue spark should be evident across the plug's electrodes.
4. If the spark is good, check for one or more of the following possible malfunctions.
   a. Obstructed fuel line.
   b. Leaking head gasket.
   c. Choke not operating properly.
   d. Throttle not operating properly.
5. If spark is not good, check for one or more of the following.
   a. Weak ignition coil.
   b. Weak CDI pulse generator.
   c. Broken or shorted high tension lead to the spark plug.
   d. Loose electrical connections.
   e. Loose or broken ignition coil ground wire.

Engine Is Difficult to Start

Check for one or more of the following possible malfunctions.
   a. Fouled spark plug.
   b. Improperly adjusted choke.
   c. Contaminated fuel system.
   d. Improperly adjusted carburetor.
   e. Incorrect fuel/air mixture.
   f. Weak ignition coil.
   g. Weak CDI pulse generator.
   h. Incorrect type ignition coil.

Engine Will Not Crank

Check for one or more of the following possible malfunctions:
   a. Defective or broken kickstarter mechanism.
   b. Seized piston.
   c. Seized crankshaft bearings.
   d. Broken connecting rod.
   e. Locked-up transmission or clutch assembly.

ENGINE PERFORMANCE

In the following checklist, it is assumed that the engine runs, but is not operating at peak performance. This will serve as a starting point from which to isolate a performance malfunction.

problem is very minor and can be found with a simple and logical troubleshooting approach.
   The following items show a beginning point from which to isolate engine starting problems.

Engine Fails to Start

Perform the following spark test to determine if the ignition system is operating properly.
1. Remove the spark plug from the cylinder.
2. Connect the spark plug wire and connector to the spark plug and touch the spark plug's base to a good ground such as the engine cylinder head (**Figure 5**). Position the spark plug so you can see the electrodes.

The possible causes for each malfunction are listed in a logical sequence and in order of probability.

Engine Will Not Start Or Is Hard To Start

a. Fuel tank empty.
b. Obstructed fuel line or fuel shutoff valve.
c. Sticking float valve in carburetor.
d. Carburetor incorrectly adjusted.
e. Improper choke operation.
f. Incorrect fuel/air mixture.
g. Fouled or improperly gapped spark plug.
h. Weak CDI pulse generator.
i. Ignition timing incorrect (faulty component in system).
j. Broken or shorted ignition coil.
k. Clogged air filter element.
l. Contaminated fuel.

Engine Will Not Idle or Idles Erratically

a. Carburetor incorrectly adjusted.
b. Fouled or improperly gapped spark plug.
c. Leaking head gasket or vacuum leak.
d. Weak CDI pulse generator.
e. Ignition timing incorrect (faulty component in system).
f. Obstructed fuel line or fuel shutoff valve.
g. Incorrect fuel/air mixture.

Engine Misses at High Speed

a. Fouled or improperly gapped spark plug.
b. Improper ignition timing (faulty component in system).
c. Improper carburetor main jet selection.
d. Clogged jets in the carburetor.
e. Weak ignition coil.
f. Weak CDI pulse generator.
g. Incorrect fuel/air mixture.
h. Obstructed fuel line or fuel shutoff valve.

Engine Continues to Run with Ignition Off

a. Excessive carbon build-up in engine.
b. Vacuum leak in intake system.
c. Contaminated or incorrect fuel octane rating.
d. Incorrect fuel/air mixture.

Engine Overheating

a. Coolant level low.

b. Faulty radiator cap.
c. Passages blocked in the radiator, hoses or water jackets in the engine.
d. Faulty water pump.
e. Improper ignition timing (faulty component in system).
f. Improper spark plug heat range.

Engine Misses at Idle

a. Fouled or improperly gapped spark plug.
b. Spark plug cap faulty.
c. Ignition cable insulation deteriorated (shorting out).
d. Dirty or clogged air filter element.
e. Carburetor incorrectly adjusted (too lean or too rich).
f. Choke valve stuck.
g. Cloged jet(s) in the carburetor.
h. Carburetor float height incorrect.
i. Incorrect fuel/air mixture.

Engine Backfires— Explosions in Mufflers

a. Fouled or improperly gapped spark plug.
b. Spark plug cap faulty.
c. Ignition cable insulation deteriorated (shorting out).
d. Ignition timing incorrect.
e. Incorrect fuel/air mixture.
f. Contaminated fuel.

Pre-ignition (Fuel Mixture Ignites Before Spark Plug Fires)

a. Hot spot in combustion chamber (piece of carbon).
b. Overheating engine.

Engine Runs Roughly

a. Carburetor mixture too rich.
b. Choke not operating correctly.
c. Water or other contaminants in fuel.
d. Clogged fuel line.
e. Incorrect fuel/air mixture.
f. Clogged air filter element.
g. Balancer system faulty.

Engine Loses Power at Normal Riding Speed

a. Carburetor incorrectly adjusted.
b. Engine overheating.

c. Improper ignition timing (faulty component in system).
d. Weak CDI pulse generator.
e. Incorrectly gapped spark plug.
f. Weak ignition coil.
g. Incorrect fuel/air mixture.
h. Obstructed muffler.
i. Dragging brake(s).

Engine Lacks Acceleration

a. Carburetor mixture too lean.
b. Clogged fuel line.
c. Improper ignition timing (faulty component in system).
d. Incorrect fuel/air mixture.
e. Dragging brake(s).

ENGINE NOISES

1. *Knocking or pinging during acceleration—* Caused by using a lower octane fuel than recommended. May also be caused by poor fuel. Pinging can also be caused by spark plugs of the wrong heat range. Refer to *Spark Plug Selection* in Chapter Three.

2. *Slapping or rattling noises at low speed or during acceleration—* May be caused by piston slap (excessive piston to cylinder wall clearance).

3. *Knocking or rapping while decelerating—* Usually caused by excessive rod bearing clearance.

4. *Persistent knocking and vibration—* Usually caused by excessive main bearing clearance. May be caused by faulty balancer system.

5. *Rapid on-off squeal—* Compression leak around cylinder head gasket or spark plug.

EXCESSIVE VIBRATION

Usually this is caused by loose engine mounting hardware or faulty balancer system. Otherwise it can be difficult to find without disassembling the engine.

FRONT SUSPENSION AND STEERING

Poor handling may be caused by improper tire pressure, a damaged or bent frame or front steering components, a worn front fork assembly (3-wheeled models), worn wheel bearings or dragging brakes.

BRAKE PROBLEMS

A sticking disc brake may be caused by a stuck piston in a caliper assembly or a warped pad shim. Glazed pads will cause loss of stopping power.

CHAPTER THREE

LUBRICATION, MAINTENANCE AND TUNE-UP

If this is your first experience with an ATV or motorcycle, you should become acquainted with products that are available in auto or motorcycle parts and supply stores. Look into the tune-up tools and parts and check out the different lubricants such as motor oil, locking compounds and greases. Also check engine degreasers, like Gunk or Bel-Ray Degreaser, for cleaning your engine before working on it.

The more you get involved in your ATV the more you will want to work on it. Start out by doing simple tune-up, lubrication and maintenance. Tackle more involved jobs as you gain experience.

The Honda ATV is a relatively simple machine but to gain the utmost in safety, performance and useful life from it, it is necessary to make periodic inspections and adjustments. Minor problems are often found during such inspections that are simple and inexpensive to correct at the time, but which could lead to major problems if not corrected.

This chapter explains lubrication, maintenance and tune-up procedures required for the Honda ATV covered in this book. **Table 1** is a suggested factory maintenance schedule. **Table 2** lists parts that require frequent replacement especially if the vehicle is used in competition. **Tables 1-9** are located at the end of this chapter.

PRE-CHECKS

The following checks should be performed before the first ride of the day.
1. Inspect the fuel line and fittings for wetness.
2. Make sure the fuel tank is full with the correct 20:1 fuel-oil mixture.
3. Make sure the transmission/clutch oil level is correct. Add oil if necesaary.
4. Inspect the coolant level. With the engine cool, the coolant must be up to the neck of the radiator

filler neck and to the "F" line on the coolant reserve tank. Refer to **Figure 1** for 3-wheeled models or **Figure 2** for 4-wheeled models.

5. Make sure the air filter element is clean.

6. Make sure the spark plug heat range is correct and that it is not carbon fouled. Inspect the spark plug lead for tightness at both the spark plug and the ignition coil.

7. Check the operation of the clutch and adjust if necessary.

8. Check the throttle and the brake levers. Make sure they operate properly with no binding.

9. Check the brake fluid level in each master cylinder reservoir. Add fluid if necessary.

10. Inspect the front and rear suspensions. Make sure they have a good solid feel with no looseness.

11. Inspect the drive chain for wear, correct tension and proper lubrication.

12. Check the drive chain roller and buffer for wear or damage; replace if necessary.

13. Check tire pressure as listed in **Table 3**.

14. Check the exhaust system for damage.

15. Check the tightness of all fasteners, especially engine mounting hardware.

16. Make sure the headlight and taillight work.

ENGINE LUBRICATION

The engine is a 2-stroke type that requires a combination gasoline-oil mixture. The oil mixed with the gasoline lubricates the internal components of the engine.

> *WARNING*
> *Serious fire hazards always exist around gasoline. Do **not** allow anyone to smoke where fuel is being mixed or when fueling the vehicle. Always have a fire extinguisher rated for gasoline fires (Class B) close by.*

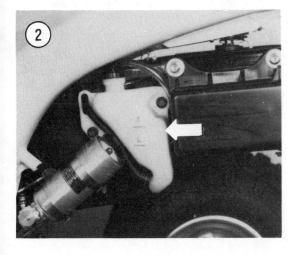

> *NOTE*
> *Mix the fuel at home so the gasoline and oil will mix thoroughly while towing the vehicle to your riding destination. Always mix fresh gasoline. Mix only the amount that will be used for that day's ride. Gasoline loses its potency after sitting for a period of time. The oil also loses some of its lubricating ability when mixed with the gasoline and then not used for a period of time.*

Fuel Mixing

Proper fuel mixing is very important for the life and efficiency of the engine. All engine lubrication is provided by the oil mixed with the gasoline. Always mix fuel in the exact proportions. A too-lean mixture can cause serious and expensive engine damage. A too-rich mixture can cause poor performance and a fouled spark plug, which can make engine starting difficult, if not impossible.

> *CAUTION*
> *Do not use gasoline containing methanol (methyl or wood alcohol) even if it contains cosolvents and corrosion inhibitors for methanol. If used, it may damage the fuel system and lead to performance problems. Using a gasoline/methanol mixture will also void any applicable Honda warranty.*

Use a premium grade of unleaded or low-lead gasoline with a Research octane rating of 89 or more. Use a good grade of 2-stroke oil in a 20:1 mixture. Never use more than one brand or type of 2-stroke oil when mixing a batch of fuel. The different brands of oil may not be compatible with each other, resulting in a lack of lubrication or excessive carbon deposits. Once you are satisfied with a particular brand of oil, don't change brands without a reason. Avoid using more than one type of pre-mix in a fuel tank at one time.

Use a graduated measuring device such as a baby bottle or a Ratio Rite container to ensure a precise measurement of oil. Always measure the quantities exactly. Refer to **Table 4** for a guide to determine the correct volumes of gasoline and oil to mix together to obtain a 20:1 ratio.

Be careful when using a vegetable based 2-stroke oil in cold weather. After the oil and gasoline are mixed together, vegetable based oils tend to separate from the gasoline more quickly than a 2-stroke mineral oil. Use a mineral based 2-stroke oil if the ambient temperature is expected to be 32° F (0° C) or lower in the area where you will be riding.

If there is fuel left in the fuel tank from a previous day's ride, shake the vehicle sideways and up and down to re-mix the fuel in the fuel tank.

1. Pour 1/2 of the required gasoline into a clean sealable container.

2. Add the required amount of 2-stroke oil (for the total amount of the fuel to be mixed) and mix thoroughly.

3. Add the remainder of the gasoline and mix the entire contents thoroughly.

4. Even though the fuel tank is equipped with a filter screen, always use a funnel equipped with a fine screen when adding the fuel mixture to the vehicle's tuel tank.

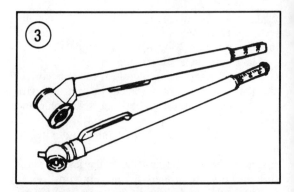

SERVICE INTERVALS

The services and intervals shown in **Table 1** are recommended by the factory. Strict adherence to these recommendations will ensure long service from your Honda ATV. However, if the vehicle is run in an area of high humidity, the lubrication and services must be done more frequently to prevent possible rust damage. This is especially true if you have run the ATV through water, particularly salt water.

For convenience when maintaining your vehicle, most of the services shown in **Table 1** are described in this chapter. However, some procedures which require more than minor disassembly or adjustment are covered elsewhere in the appropriate chapter.

TIRES AND WHEELS

Tire Pressure

Tire pressure should be checked and adjusted to maintain tire smoothness, good traction and handling and to get the maximum life out of the tire. A simple, accurate gauge (**Figure 3**) can be purchased for a few dollars and should be carried in your tool box in the tow vehicle. The appropriate tire pressures are shown in **Table 3**.

> *WARNING*
> *Always inflate both rear tires to the same pressure. If the ATV is run with unequal air pressures it will cause the vehicle to always run toward one side and cause poor handling.*

> *CAUTION*
> *Do not overinflate the stock tires as they will be permanently distorted and damaged. If overinflated, they will bulge out similar to inflating an inner tube that is not within the constraints of a tire. If this happens the tire will **not** return to its original contour.*

Tire Inspection

The tires take a lot of punishment due to the variety of terrain they are subject to. Inspect them periodically for excessive wear, cuts, abrasions, etc. If you find a nail or other object in the tire, mark its location with a light crayon before removing it. This will help locate the hole for repair. Refer to Chapter Nine for tire changing and repair information.

Rim Inspection

Frequently inspect the condition of the wheel rims, especially the outer side. If the wheel has hit a tree or large rock, rim damage may be sufficient

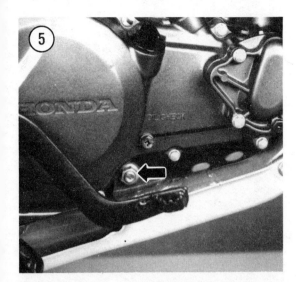

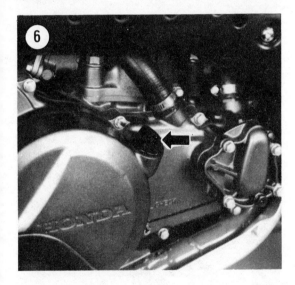

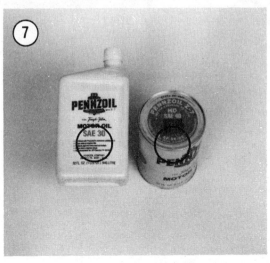

to cause an air leak or knock it out of alignment. Improper wheel alignment can cause severe vibration and result in an unsafe riding condition.

On models so equipped, make sure that the cotter pin (**Figure 4**) is securely in place on the wheel hubs. If they are lost and the castellated nut works loose—it's good-bye wheel.

PERIODIC LUBRICATION

Transmission/Clutch Oil Level Check

1. Start the engine and ride the ATV for 5-10 minutes to allow the oil to circulate throughout the transmission and clutch.
2. Shut off the engine and let the oil settle.
3. Place the ATV on level ground.
4. Unscrew the oil level check bolt (**Figure 5**) located on the left-hand side of the engine behind the clutch cover.
5. A small amount of oil should run out. The ATV must be level for a correct reading. If oil *does* run out, the oil level is correct. Reinstall the oil level check bolt.
6. If oil does *not* run out, the oil level is low. Remove the oil filler cap (**Figure 6**) and add SAE 10W-40 engine oil until oil starts to run out of the oil level check bolt hole. Install the oil level check bolt and the oil filler cap. Tighten both securely.

Transmission/Clutch Oil Change

Regular oil changes will contribute more to transmission and clutch longevity than any other maintenance performed. The factory recommended oil change is listed in **Table 1**. This assumes that the vehicle is operated in moderate climates. If it is raced or is operated under dusty conditions, the oil will get dirty more quickly and should be changed more frequently than recommended.

Use only a high quality detergent motor oil with an API rating of SE or SF. The quality rating is stamped or printed on top of the can or label on plastic bottles (**Figure 7**).

> *CAUTION*
> *Do not add any friction-reducing additives to the oil as they will cause clutch slippage. Also, do not use an engine oil with graphite added. The use of graphite oil will void any applicable Honda warranty. It is not established at this time if graphite will build up on the clutch friction plates and cause clutch problems. Until further testing is done by the oil and motorcycle industries, do not use this type of oil.*

To change the transmission and clutch oil you will need the following.

a. Drain pan.

b. Funnel.

c. Can opener or pour spout.

d. 17 mm wrench for drain plug.

e. One quart of oil.

NOTE
*Never dispose of motor oil in the trash, on the ground, or down a storm drain. Many service stations accept used motor oil and waste haulers provide curbside used motor oil collection. Do not combine other fluids with motor oil to be recycled. To locate a recycler, contact the American Petroleum Institute (API) at **www.recycleoil.org**.*

1. Start the engine and ride the ATV for 5-10 minutes to allow the oil to warm up. Shut off the engine.

2. Place the ATV on level ground and set the parking brake.

3. Place a drain pan under the engine.

4. Remove the 17 mm drain bolt (**Figure 8**) accessible through the hole in the skid plate.

5. Remove the oil filler cap (**Figure 6**) to speed up the flow of oil.

6. Let the oil drain for at least 15-20 minutes.

7. Inspect the sealing washer on the drain plug; replace if necessary.

8. Install the drain plug and tighten to the torque specification listed in **Table 5**.

9. Insert a funnel into the oil filler hole and fill with SAE 10W-40 weight motor oil.

NOTE
The capacity is approximately 600 cc (0.63 U.S. qt./0.53 Imp. qt.) for an oil change. If the engine has been disassembled the capacity is approximately 700 cc (0.74 U.S. qt./0.62 Imp. pt.).

10. Screw in the oil filler cap securely.

11. Start the engine and let the engine run at moderate speed and check for leaks.

12. Shut off the engine and check for correct oil level as described in this chapter. Adjust as necessary.

Front Fork Oil Change (3-Wheeled Models)

Change the fork oil at the interval indicated in **Table 1** or when it becomes contaminated.

1. Place the ATV on level ground and set the parking brake.

WARNING
Always bleed off all air pressure. Failure to do so may cause personal injury when disassembling the fork.

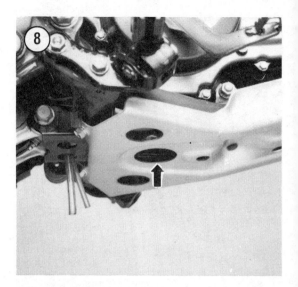

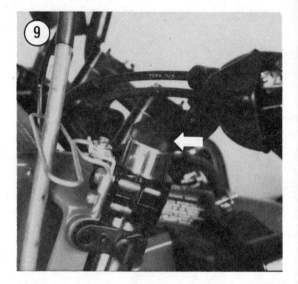

WARNING
Release air pressure gradually. If released too fast, fork oil will spurt out with the air. Protect your eyes and clothing accordingly.

2. Remove each fork top cover (**Figure 9**) and *bleed off all air pressure* from each fork by depressing the valve stem.

3. Place a drain pan under the drain screw (**Figure 10**) and remove the drain screw from each fork leg. Allow the oil to drain for at least 5 minutes. *Never reuse the oil.*

CAUTION
Do not allow the fork oil come in contact with any of the brake components.

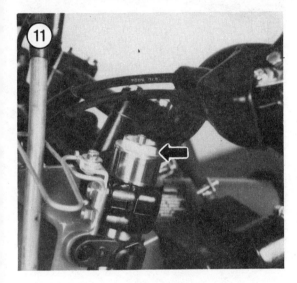

4. Apply the front brake, push down on the handlebar and pump the forks up and down 20 times or more. This will expel most of the old fork oil.

5. Place wood blocks under the frame to support the ATV with the front wheel off the ground.

6. Slowly unscrew the fork top cap/air valve assembly (**Figure 11**) as it is under spring pressure from the fork spring(s).

7. Inspect the gasket on the drain screw; replace if necessary. Install the drain screw and gasket and tighten securely.

8. Wrap a shop cloth around the top of the fork tube to catch any remaining fork oil as the fork spring(s) is withdrawn.

9A. On 1985 models, perform the following.
   a. Remove the upper fork spring "A" from the fork tube. The spring seat may stick to the bottom of the fork spring and come out with the spring. If so, don't lose it.
   b. If not already removed, remove the spring seat.
   c. Remove the lower fork spring "B" from the fork tube.

9B. On 1986 models, remove the fork spring from the fork tube.

10. Repeat Steps 6-9 for the other fork.

11. Remove the wood blocks from under the frame and set the front wheel on the ground. Gradually lower the front of the ATV until the front forks are totally compressed (bottomed out at the end of their travel).

12. Refill each fork leg with the specified quantity of Dexron automatic transmission fluid or 10W fork oil. Refer to **Table 6** for specified quantity and level and to **Figure 12**. Different fork damping characteristics can be produced by varying the amount of fork oil in the fork tube.

NOTE
To measure the correct amount of fluid, use a plastic baby bottle. These have measurements in cubic centimeters (cc) and fluid ounces (oz.) on the side.

13. Inspect the O-ring seal (**Figure 13**) on the fork top cap/air valve assembly; replace if necessary.

14. Place wood blocks under the frame to support the ATV with the front wheel off the ground.

15A. On 1985 models, perform the following.
   a. Install the lower fork spring "B" into the fork tube with the tapered end going in first.

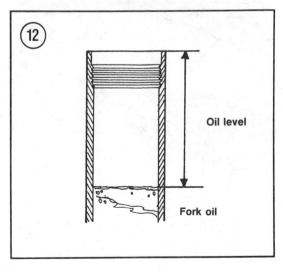

Oil level

Fork oil

b. Install the spring seat.

c. Install the upper fork spring "A" into the fork tube.

15B. On 1986 models, install the fork spring into the fork tube with the tapered end going in first.

16. Install the fork top cap/air valve assembly while pushing down on the fork spring(s). Start the fork cap bolt slowly. Don't crossthread it. Tighten to 15-30 N•m (11-22 ft.-lb.).

17. Repeat Step 15 and Step 16 for the other fork.

18. If you are using air assist in the front forks, inflate to the desired air pressure of 0-70 kPa (0-1.0 psi). Do not exceed the maximum air pressure or damage will occur to the fork seals. Do not use compressed air; use only a small hand-operated air pump.

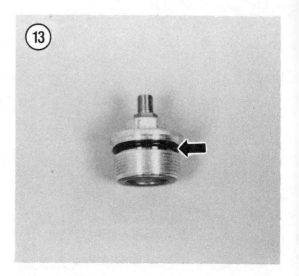

> *WARNING*
> *Never use any type of compressed gas as an explosion may be lethal. Never heat the fork assembly with a torch or place it near an open flame or extreme heat as this will also result in an explosion.*

19. Install the air valve caps.

20. Remove the wood blocks from under the frame. Road test the ATV and check for oil leaks.

Pro-link Suspension

The Pro-link suspension bushings should be lubricated at the intervals indicated in **Table 1**.

Use a hand-held grease gun and molybdenum disulfide grease to the Pro-link linkage fittings. Refer to **Figure 14**, **Figure 15**, **Figure 16** and **Figure 17**. Apply grease until it runs out of the bushing surrounds, then wipe off all excess. Use MoS2 (containing more than 40% molybdenum) type grease manufactured by the following.

a. Molykote G-N paste: Dow Corning

b. Honda Moly 45

c. Bel-Ray Moly-Lube MC-8

Control Cables

The control cables (throttle, clutch and parking brake) should be lubricated at the interval indicated in **Table 1**. They should be also inspected at this time for fraying and the cable sheath should be checked for chafing. The cables are relatively inexpensive and should be replaced when found to be faulty.

The control cables can be lubricated either with oil or with any of the popular cable lubricants and

a cable lubricator. The first method requires more time and the complete lubrication of the entire cable is less certain.

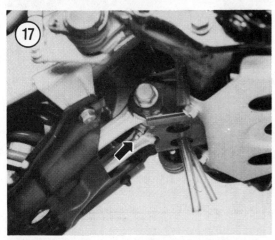

Oil method

1. Disconnect the cable from the control lever(s).
2. Make a cone of stiff paper and tape it to the end of the cable sheath.

> *NOTE*
> *To avoid a mess, place a shop cloth at the end of the cable to catch the oil as it runs out.*

3. Hold the cable upright and pour a small amount of light oil (SAE 10W/30) into the cone. Work the cable in and out of the sheath for several minutes to help the oil work its way down to the end of the cable.
4. Remove the cone, reconnect the control cable(s) and adjust as described in this chapter.

Lubricator method

1. Disconnect the cable from the control lever(s).
2. Attach a lubricator following the manufacturer's instructions.
3. Insert the nozzle of the lubricant can in the lubricator, press the button on the can and hold it down until the lubricant begins to flow out of the other end of the cable.

> *NOTE*
> *Place a shop cloth at the end of the cable(s) to catch all excess lubricant that will flow out.*

4. Remove the lubricator, reconnect the control cable and adjust the cable(s) as described in this chapter.

PERIODIC MAINTENANCE

Drive Chain Adjustment

The drive chain should be checked whenever fuel is added or at the beginning of each riding day. Clean, lubricate and adjust the drive chain at the interval indicated in **Table 1**. A properly lubricated and adjusted drive chain will provide maximum service life and reliability.

The correct amount of drive chain free play, when pushed up midway on the upper chain run, is 30-40 mm (1 1/4-1 1/2 in.). See **Figure 18**.

> *NOTE*
> *Drive chain removal, cleaning, inspection, lubrication and installation are covered in Chapter Ten.*

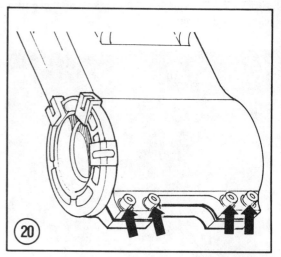

1. Place the ATV on level ground and set the parking brake.

2. Shift the transmission into NEUTRAL.

3A. On 3-wheeled models and 1985 4-wheeled models, adjust the tension as follows.

   a. Loosen the rear axle bearing holder clamping bolts (**Figure 19**).

   b. Attach the spanner wrench, furnished in the factory tool kit, to the axle adjuster.

   c. Rotate the axle holder on the swing arm in either direction until the correct amount of free play is achieved.

3B. On 1986-on 4-wheeled models, adjust the tension as follows:

   a. Loosen the rear axle bearing holder clamping bolts. Refer to **Figure 19** for 1986-1987 models or **Figure 20** for 1988-on models.

   b. Insert a drift or punch into one of the receptacles in the rear axle bearing holder adjuster (**Figure 21**).

   c. Rotate the axle holder on the swing arm in either direction until the correct amount of free play is achieved.

4. Release the parking brake and push the ATV forward to move the drive chain to another position and recheck the adjustment; chains rarely wear or stretch evenly and, as a result, the free play will not remain constant over the entire drive chain. If the drive chain cannot be adjusted when the axle holder is moved to the limit of adjustment, the drive chain is excessively worn and stretched and should be replaced as described in Chapter Ten. Drive chain replacement numbers are listed in **Table 7**. Always replace both sprockets when replacing the drive chain. Never install a new chain over worn sprockets.

> *WARNING*
> *Excess free play can result in chain breakage which could cause a serious accident.*

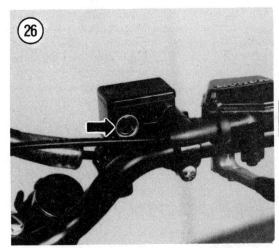

3

5. Tighten the rear axle bearing holder lockbolts to the torque specification listed in **Table 5**.

6. After the drive chain has been adjusted, the rear brake pedal free play must be adjusted as described in this chapter.

Drive Chain Slider and Rollers

Inspect the drive chain upper slider (**Figure 22**) on the swing arm and the lower slider (**Figure 23**) on the frame for wear at the interval indicated in **Table 1**. There is no visible wear line but if a groove is worn 2.0 mm (1/8 in.) down into the top surface of either slider, it should be replaced. To remove the upper slider, remove the swing arm as described in Chapter Ten.

Inspect the drive chain roller on the frame for wear at the interval indicated in **Table 1**. Refer to **Figure 24** for 3-wheeled models or **Figure 25** for 4-wheeled models. There is no visible wear line but if a groove is worn 2.0 mm (1/8 in.) into the surface of the roller, it should be replaced. To remove the roller, remove the bolt and nut securing the roller and remove the roller. Install a new roller and tighten the bolt securely.

Disc Brakes

The hydraulic brake fluid in each disc brake master cylinder should be checked at the interval listed in **Table 1**. The brake pads should also be checked for wear at the same time. Bleeding the system, servicing the brake system components and replacing the brake pads are covered in Chapter Eleven.

Disc Brake Fluid Level

The hydraulic brake fluid in the reservoir should be up to the upper line. Refer to **Figure 26** for the

front brake. For the rear brake, refer to **Figure 27** for 3-wheeled models or **Figure 28** for 4-wheeled models. If necessary, correct the level by adding fresh brake fluid. Clean any dirt from the area around the cover before removing the cover. Remove the screws securing the cover and remove the cover and the diaphragm.

> *WARNING*
> *Use brake fluid marked DOT 3 or DOT 4. Others may vaporize and cause brake failure. Do not intermix different brands or types of brake fluid as they may not be compatible. Do not intermix silicone based (DOT 5) brake fluid as it can cause brake component damage leading to brake system failure.*

> *CAUTION*
> *Be careful when adding brake fluid. Do not spill it on plastic, painted or plated surfaces as it will destroy the finish. Wash off the area immediately with soapy water and thoroughly rinse it off with clean water.*

Reinstall the diaphragm and cover. Tighten the cover screws securely.

Disc Brake Lines

Check the brake lines between the master cylinder and each brake caliper assembly. If there is any leakage, tighten the connections and bleed the brakes as described under *Bleeding the System* in Chapter Eleven. If tightening the connection does not stop the leak or if the brake line is obviously damaged, cracked or chafed, replace the brake line(s) and bleed the system as described in Chapter Eleven.

Disc Brake Pad Wear

Inspect the brake pads for excessive or uneven wear or scoring of the disc. If the pads are worn to the wear groove the pads must be replaced. If pad replacement is necessary, refer to Chapter Eleven.

> *NOTE*
> *Always replace both pads in each caliper at the same time to maintain even pressure on the brake disc.*

Disc Brake Fluid Change

Every time the reservoir cap is removed, a small amount of dirt and moisture enters the brake fluid system. The same thing happens if a leak occurs or any part of the hydraulic brake system is loosened or disconnected. Dirt can clog the system and

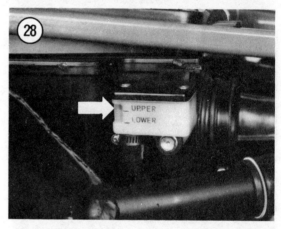

cause unnecessary wear. Water in the brake fluid vaporizes at high temperature, impairing the hydraulic action and reducing the brake's stopping ability.

To maintain peak braking efficiency, change the brake fluid at the interval listed in **Table 1**. To change brake fluid, follow the *Bleeding the System* procedure in Chapter Eleven. Continue adding new brake fluid to the master cylinder(s) and bleed the fluid out at the caliper(s) until the brake fluid leaving the caliper(s) is clean and free of contaminants.

> *WARNING*
> *Use brake fluid marked DOT 3 or DOT 4. Others may vaporize and cause brake failure. Do not intermix different brands or types of brake fluid as they may not be compatible. Do not intermix silicone based (DOT 5) brake fluid as it can cause brake component damage leading to brake system failure.*

2. Check that the brake pedal is in the at-rest position.

3. At the rear master cylinder, loosen the locknut (A, **Figure 29**) and turn the master cylinder pushrod (B, **Figure 29**) in either direction to achieve the correct brake pedal height. Tighten the locknut securely.

Parking Brake Adjustment

Apply the parking brake and push the ATV in either direction. The ATV should not move. If it does, adjust as follows.

1. Block the front wheel so the vehicle will not roll in either direction.

2. Disconnect the clutch cable at the clutch housing.

3. Press the parking brake button down and hold it in this position.

4. Pull in on the clutch/parking brake lever. The lever should move the following amount.
   a. 3-wheeled models: 31-39 mm (1 1/4-1 1/2 in.).
   b. 1986 4-wheeled models: 31-39 mm (1 1/4-1 1/2 in.).
   c. 1987 4-wheeled models: 25-30 mm (1-1 1/4 in.).

5. Release the clutch/parking brake lever.

6. If adjustment is necessary, perform the following at the rear brake caliper assembly.
   a. Loosen the locknut (A, **Figure 30**) on the brake lever arm.

NOTE
Loosen the locknut sufficiently so the locknut will not touch the caliper mounting bracket during the next step. If the locknut touches the mounting bracket it will give a false resistance reading and the adjustment will be incorrect.

   b. Screw the adjuster bolt on the brake lever arm, (B, **Figure 30**) in until resistance is felt, then stop. Back the adjuster bolt out 1/8 turn.
   c. Hold onto the adjuster bolt so it will not turn, then tighten the locknut to the torque specification listed in **Table 5**.

7. To adjust the lever, perform the following.
   a. Slide the rubber boot (**Figure 31**) away from the clutch/parking brake lever.

**Rear Brake Pedal Height Adjustment
(3-Wheeled Models)**

NOTE
Honda does not provide any height specifications nor adjustment procedure for 4-wheeled models.

Pedal height is correct when the top surface of the brake pedal is below the top surface of the footpeg by the following amount.
   a. 1985 models: 20 mm (3/4 in.).
   b. 1986 models: 0 mm (0 in.).

This height adjustment is really rider preference as to what feels comfortable.

1. Place the ATV on level ground and set the parking brake.

b. Loosen the locknut (A, **Figure 32**) on the cable adjuster.

c. Turn the adjuster (B, **Figure 32**) in either direction until the lever travel is as specified in Step 4.

d. Tighten both locknuts (A, **Figure 32**) on the parking brake cable.

e. Slide the rubber boot back into position on the clutch/parking brake lever.

> *WARNING*
> *Raise the rear wheels off the ground, rotate the rear wheels and make sure that the parking brake is not dragging; readjust if necessary. Also apply the parking brake and make sure that the rear wheels are locked with the brake applied; readjust if necessary.*

Clutch Adjustment

The clutch free play adjustment should be checked at the interval indicated in **Table 1**.

Clutch adjustment is limited to clutch lever free play. The cable adjustment takes up slack caused by cable stretching and clutch component wear. There is no provision for adjusting the clutch mechanism.

If the proper amount of free play cannot be achieved by using this adjustment procedure, either the cable has stretched to the point that it needs to be replaced or clutch components are worn and need replacing. Refer to Chapter Five for these service procedures.

1. Slide back the rubber boot (**Figure 31**) on the hand lever.

2. For *minor* adjustments, perform the following at the clutch hand lever.

a. Loosen the locknut (A, **Figure 33**) on the clutch hand lever.

b. Screw the adjuster barrel (B, **Figure 33**) in or out until there is 10-20 mm (3/8-3/4 in.) of free play at the tip of the lever.

c. Tighten the locknut.

3. For *major* adjustments, perform the following at the clutch cable lower adjuster.

a. Loosen the locknut (A, **Figure 34**) and turn the adjuster (B, **Figure 34**) in or out until the correct amount of lever free play is obtained.

b. Tighten the locknut.

4. After adjustment is completed, check that the locknuts are tight at both the hand lever and at the cable lower adjuster.

5. Test ride the ATV and make sure the clutch is operating correctly; readjust if necessary.

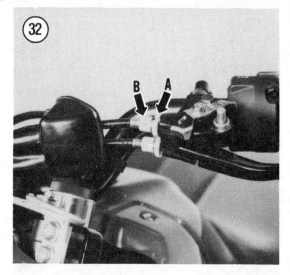

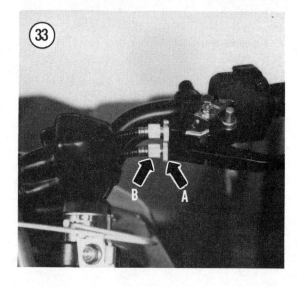

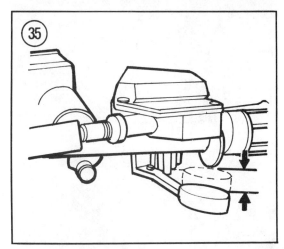

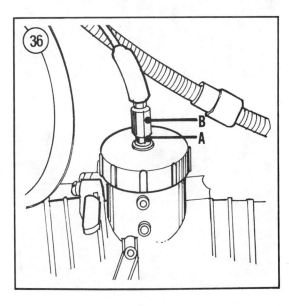

Throttle Lever Operation

The throttle operation should be checked at the interval indicated in **Table 1**.

Check for smooth throttle operation from fully closed to fully open and then return to automatic fully closed position. The throttle lever should return to the full closed position without any hesitation.

Check the throttle cable for damage, wear or deterioration. Make sure the throttle cable is not kinked at any place.

If the throttle lever does not return to the fully closed position smoothly and the exterior of the cable sheath appears to be in good condition, lubricate the throttle cable as described in this chapter.

If cable lubrication does not solve the problem, the throttle cable must be replaced as described in Chapter Six.

Throttle Lever Adjustment

The throttle cable free play should be checked at the interval indicated in **Table 1**. The throttle cable should have 3-8 mm (1/8-5/16 in.) of free play measured at the tip of the throttle lever (**Figure 35**).

If the proper amount of free play cannot be achieved by using this adjustment procedure, the cable has stretched to the point that it needs to be replaced. Refer to Chapter Six for this service procedure.

1985 3-wheeled models

1. At the top of the carburetor where the throttle cable enters, slide back the rubber boot.
2. Loosen the locknut (A, **Figure 36**) and turn the adjuster (B, **Figure 36**) until the correct amount of free play is achieved.
3. Tighten the locknut (A, **Figure 36**) and slide back the rubber boot.
4. Check the throttle cable from grip to carburetor. Make sure it is not kinked or chafed. Replace as necessary.

All other models

1. At the throttle lever, slide back the rubber boot.
2. Loosen the locknut (A, **Figure 37**) and turn the adjuster (B, **Figure 37**) in or out until the correct amount of free play is achieved. Tighten the locknut.
3. Slide the rubber boot back onto the throttle lever.

4. Check the throttle cable from grip to carburetor. Make sure it is not kinked or chafed. Replace as necessary.

Air Filter Element Cleaning

The air filter element should be removed and cleaned at the interval indicated in **Table 1** and replaced whenever it is damaged or starts to deteriorate.

The air filter removes dust and abrasive particles before the air enters the carburetor and engine. Without the air filter, very fine particles could enter into the engine and cause rapid wear of the piston rings, cylinder and bearings. They also might clog small passages in the carburetor. Never run the ATV without the element installed.

Proper air filter servicing can ensure long service from your engine.

1. Place the ATV on level ground and set the parking brake.

2. Remove the seat/rear fender assembly as described in Chapter Twelve.

3A. On 3-wheeled models, perform the following.

  a. Unhook the clips securing the air filter case cover and remove the cover (**Figure 38**).

  b. Remove the screw and bracket on the right-hand side of the element holder.

  c. Loosen the clamping screw securing the air filter assembly to the air box.

  d. Remove the air filter assembly (**Figure 39**) from the air box.

  e. Carefully slide the foam element (A, **Figure 40**) off the element holder (B, **Figure 40**).

3B. On 4-wheeled models, perform the following.

  a. Unhook the clips securing the air filter case cover and remove the cover (**Figure 41**).

  b. Loosen the clamping screw securing the air filter assembly to the air box.

  c. Remove the air filter assembly from the air box.

  d. Carefully slide the foam element (A, **Figure 42**) off the element holder (B, **Figure 42**).

> *CAUTION*
> *Do not wring or twist the element as it will be torn or the individual foam cells will be damaged. Squeeze the element during the cleaning and oiling procedures.*

4. Carefully clean the element gently in cleaning solvent until all dirt is removed. Squeeze out the

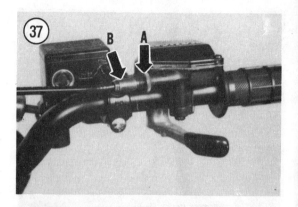

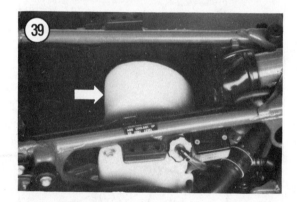

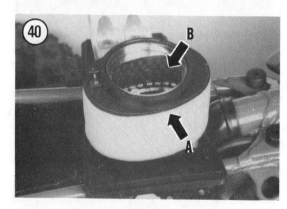

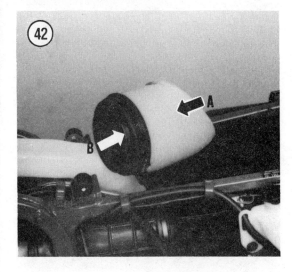

solvent and dry thoroughly in a clean shop cloth until all solvent residue is removed. Let it dry for about one hour.

> *CAUTION*
> *Inspect the element. If it is torn or broken in any area it should be replaced. Do not run with a damaged element as it may allow dirt to enter the engine.*

5A. On 3-wheeled models, perform the following:
    a. Pour Honda 2-stroke oil or special foam air filter oil onto the element and work into the porous foam material.
    b. Gently squeeze the element to remove the oil from the element, leaving it slightly wet with the oil. Do not oversaturate the element as too much oil will restrict air flow.

5B. On 1986-1987 4-wheeled models, perform the following:
    a. Pour a small amount of SAE 80W-90 gear oil or special foam air filter oil onto the element and work into the porous foam material.
    b. Gently squeeze the element to remove the oil from the element, leaving it slightly wet with the oil. Do not oversaturate the element as too much oil will restrict air flow.

5C. On 1988-on models, perform the following:
    a. Pour Honda 2-stroke oil or special foam air filter oil into the divided front top portion of the air filter cover. Completely fill this portion of the cover with the oil.
    b. Pour this measured amount of oil into the interior surfaces of the air filter element.
    c. Gently squeeze the element to work **all** of the oil into the element.

6. When the oil is distributed evenly, the element will be evenly discolored by the oil and should have the same color throughout.

7. Let the element dry for an hour after oiling before installation. If installed too soon, the chemical carrier in the special foam air filter oil will be drawn into the engine and may cause engine damage.

8. Wipe out the interior of the air box with a shop cloth dampened in cleaning solvent. Remove any foreign matter that may have passed through a broken element.

9. Inspect the seal (**Figure 43**) around the perimeter of the cover; replace if necessary.

10. Assemble and install the element by reversing these steps while noting the following.

11. Apply a light coat of multipurpose grease to the sealing edge of the element. This will ensure a good air-tight seal between the air filter element and the air box.

12. On 4-wheeled models, position the air filter element with the UP mark (**Figure 44**) facing up.

Fuel Shutoff Valve and Filter
Removal/Installation

The integral fuel filter in the fuel shutoff valve removes particles in the fuel which might otherwise enter the carburetor. This could cause the float needle to stay in the open position or clog one of the jets.

1. Remove the fuel tank as described in Chapter Six.

2A. On 3-wheeled models, remove the screws and collars (**Figure 45**) securing the fuel shutoff valve to the fuel tank and remove the valve and the gasket.

2B. On 4-wheeled models, perform the following.

   a. Remove the bolts (A, **Figure 46**) securing the fuel hose bracket and remove the bracket.

   b. Remove the screws and collars (B, **Figure 46**) securing the fitting to the fuel tank and remove the fitting, gasket, fuel lines and shutoff valve.

3. After removing the valve or fitting, insert a corner of a clean shop rag into the opening in the tank to stop the dribbling of fuel.

4. Remove the fuel filter from the shutoff valve or fitting. Clean it with a medium soft toothbrush and blow out with compressed air. Replace the filter if it is defective.

5. Install by reversing these removal steps, noting the following.

6. Do not forget to install the gasket between the valve or fitting and the tank and be sure to use the collars with the screws.

7. On 4-wheeled models, if the shutoff valve was disconnected from the fuel lines going to the fitting on the fuel tank, route the fuel hoses as shown in **Figure 47**.

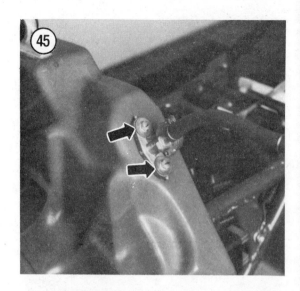

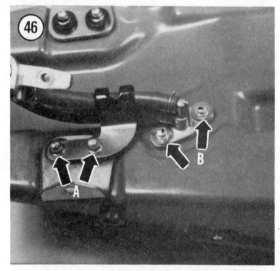

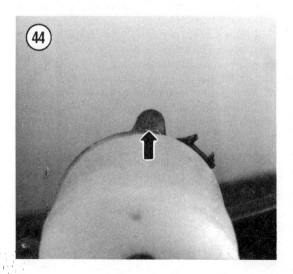

8. Check for fuel leakage after installation is completed.

Fuel Line Inspection

Inspect the fuel line (**Figure 48**) from the fuel shutoff valve to the carburetor. On 4-wheeled models, also inspect the fuel lines (**Figure 47**) from the shutoff valve to the fitting on the fuel tank.

If any are cracked or starting to deteriorate they must be replaced. Make sure the small hose clamps are in place and holding securely.

> *WARNING*
> *A damaged or deteriorated fuel line presents a very dangerous fire hazard to both the rider and the vehicle if fuel should spill onto a hot engine or exhaust pipe.*

Cooling System Inspection

The cooling system should be checked at the interval indicated in **Table 1**.

1A. On 3-wheeled models, perform the following.
   a. Remove the bolts securing the fuel tank side panel (**Figure 49**) and remove the side panel.
   b. Unscrew the radiator cap (**Figure 50**).

1B. On 4-wheeled models, perform the following.
   a. Remove the front fender assembly as described in Chapter Twelve.
   b. Remove the fuel tank as described in Chapter Six.
   c. Unscrew the radiator cap (**Figure 51**).

2. Insert an antifreeze tester into the coolant following the manufacturer's instructions. Test the specific gravity of the coolant to ensure adequate temperature and corrosion protection. The system

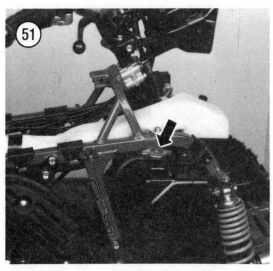

must have at least a 50/50 mixture of coolant (antifreeze) and purified water. Never let the mixture become less than 40 percent coolant or corrosion will occur.

3. Check all coolant system hoses for damage or deterioration. Replace any hose that is questionable. Make sure all hose clamps are tight.

4. Carefully clean any road dirt, bugs, mud, etc., from the radiator core. Use a whisk broom, compressed air or low-pressure water. If the radiator has been hit by a small rock or other item, *carefully* straighten out the fins with a screwdriver. If the radiator has been damaged across approximately 20 percent or more of the frontal area, the radiator should be replaced as described in Chapter Eight.

5. Install all items removed.

Coolant Change

The cooling system should be completely drained and refilled at the interval listed in **Table 1**.

It is sometimes necessary to drain the coolant from the system to perform a service procedure on some part of the engine. If the coolant is still in good condition, the coolant can be reused if it is kept clean. Drain the coolant into a *clean* drain pan and pour the coolant into a *clean* sealable container like a plastic milk or bleach bottle and screw on the cap. This coolant can then be reused.

> *CAUTION*
> *Use only a high-quality ethylene glycol coolant (antifreeze) specifically labeled for use with aluminum engines. Do not use an alcohol-based coolant.*

In areas where freezing temperatures occur, add a higher percentage of coolant to protect the system to ambient temperatures far below those likely to occur. **Table 8** lists the recommended amount of coolant for protection at various ambient temperatures.

> *CAUTION*
> *Do not use a higher percentage of coolant-to-water than recommended for the ambient temperature. A higher concentration of coolant (60 percent or greater) will actually **decrease** the performance of the cooling system.*

1. Set the ATV on a level surface and set the parking brake.

2A. On 3-wheeled models perform the following.

   a. Remove the bolts securing the fuel tank side panel (**Figure 49**) and remove the side panel.

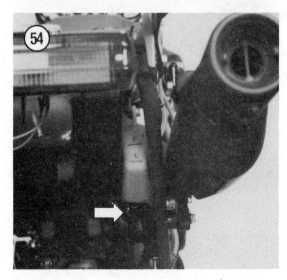

b. Unscrew the radiator cap (**Figure 50**). This will speed up the draining process.

2B. On 4-wheeled models perform the following.

a. Remove the front fender assembly as described in Chapter Twelve.

b. Remove the fuel tank as described in Chapter Six.

c. Unscrew the radiator cap (**Figure 51**). This will speed up the draining process.

3. Place a drain pan under the water pump cover on the right-hand side of the engine.

4. Remove the drain plug and gasket (**Figure 52**) on the water pump cover.

5. Place a drain pan under the drain plug on the left-hand side of the engine.

6. Remove the drain plug and gasket (**Figure 53**) on the cylinder.

7. Tip the ATV from side to side to drain all remaining coolant from the cooling system.

8. Inspect the gasket on both drain screws. Replace the gasket, if necessary. Install both drain screws and tighten securely.

9. Place a drain pan under the reserve tank.

10A. On 3-wheeled models, disconnect the hose (**Figure 54**) from the base of the reserve tank and drain out all coolant.

10B. On 4-wheeled models, disconnect the hose (**Figure 55**) from the base of the reserve tank and drain out all coolant.

11. Reconnect the hose and make sure the hose clamp is tight.

12. Place a funnel into the radiator filler neck and refill the radiator and engine. Slowly add the coolant mixture through the radiator filler neck. Use the recommended mixture of coolant and purified water as indicated in **Table 8**. Do not install the radiator cap at this time.

13. Tip the vehicle about 20° to the left and then to the right several times. This will help bleed off some of the air trapped in the cooling system. If necessary, add additional coolant mixture to the system.

14. Place a funnel into the reserve tank filler neck and refill the reserve tank to the "F" line. Refer to **Figure 56** for 3-wheeled models or **Figure 57** for 4-wheeled models. Install the reserve tank cap.

NOTE
On 4-wheeled models in the following step, if you use all of the fuel in the float bowl, temporarily install the fuel tank.

15. Start the engine and let it idle at a fast idle. Snap the throttle a couple of times to make sure the coolant is moving throughout the engine and

radiator. At a slow idle the water pump is not rotating fast enough to move the coolant sufficiently.

16. Check that there are no bubbles in the radiator filler neck and that the level stabilizes.

17. Turn off the engine and add coolant to the radiator if necessary.

18. Install the radiator cap and tighten securely.

> ### CAUTION
> *If the radiator cap is not installed correctly, coolant loss and engine damage will occur.*

19. Recheck the level in the reserve tank, add coolant if necessary to bring the level up to the "F" mark.

20. Install all items removed.

21. Start the engine and check for leaks. Test ride the ATV, shut the engine off and let the cooling system cool down. Recheck the coolant level. Add additional coolant mixture if necessary.

Spark Arrester Cleaning

The spark arrester should be cleaned at the interval indicated in **Table 1** or sooner if a considerable amount of slow riding is done.

> ### WARNING
> *To avoid burning your hands, do not perform this cleaning operation with the exhaust system hot. Work in a well-ventilated area (outside your garage) that is free of any fire hazards. Be sure to protect your eyes with safety glasses or goggles.*

1. Remove the bolts securing the muffler plate and remove the muffler plate and gasket (**Figure 58**).

2. Wear heavy gloves and use several shop cloths to block off the end of the muffler. This will direct the exhaust gases out through the muffler opening covered by the muffler plate.

3. Start the engine and rev it up about 20 times to blow out accumulated carbon in the tail section of the muffler. Continue until carbon stops coming out through the muffler opening.

4. Turn the engine off and let the muffler cool off. Remove the shop cloths.

5. Inspect the gasket on the muffler plate. If it is damaged or deteriorated, replace it before installing the muffler plate.

6. Install the muffler plate and gasket and tighten the bolts securely.

Wheel Bearings

There is no factory-recommended interval for cleaning and repacking the wheel bearings. They

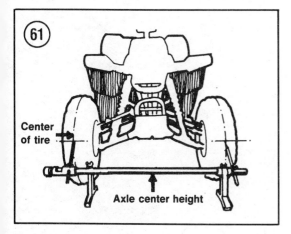

Center of tire

Axle center height

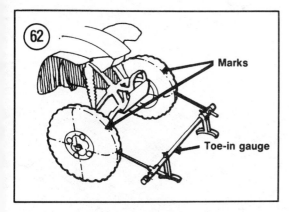

Marks

Toe-in gauge

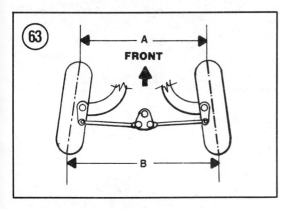

A

FRONT

B

1. Visually inspect all components of the steering system. Pay close attention to the tie-rods and steering shaft, especially after a hard spill or collision. If any signs of damage are apparent the steering components must be repaired as described in Chapter Nine.

2. Check the tightness of the handlebar holder bolts (**Figure 59**) securing the handlebar.

3. Make sure the front axle nut(s) are tight and on models so equipped, that the cotter pins are in place (**Figure 60**).

> *NOTE*
> *You may want to consider replacing the cotter pins with the reusable quick removal wire pins that slip in and out.*

> *CAUTION*
> *If any of the previously mentioned bolts and nuts are loose, refer to Chapter Nine for correct procedures and torque specifications.*

Front Wheel Toe-in Adjustment (4-Wheeled Models)

The front wheel toe-in alignment should be checked at the interval indicated in **Table 1**.

1. Inflate all 4 tires to the recommended tire pressure (**Table 3**).

2. Place the ATV on level ground and set the parking brake. Block the rear wheels so the vehicle will not roll in either direction.

3. Turn the handlebar so the wheels are at the straight-ahead position.

4. Hold a scribe (**Figure 61**), white crayon or white tire marker aginst the center of the front tire and spin the wheel slowly. Make sure the line is visible at both the front and rear of the tire. Repeat for the other tire.

5. Carefully measure the distance between the center line of both front tires at the front and rear as shown in **Figure 62**. The front dimension "A" should be less than the rear dimension "B" by 10 ± 10 mm (0.4 ± 0.4 in.) as shown in **Figure 63**. This amount of toe-in is necessary for proper steering. Too much toe-in can cause excessive tire wear and hard steering. Too little toe-in will allow the front end to wander.

6. If the toe-in is incorrect, refer to Chapter Nine for the adjustment service procedure.

should be serviced whenever the wheel or disc is removed or whenever there is the likelihood of water contamination, especially salt water. The correct service procedures are covered in Chapter Nine and Chapter Ten.

Steering System and Front Suspension Inspection

The steering system and front suspension should be checked at the interval indicated in **Table 1**.

Rear Suspension Check

1. Place wood block(s) under the frame to support the ATV securely with the rear wheels off the ground.

2. Push hard on the rear wheels (sideways) to check for side play in the rear swing arm bearings.

3. Make sure the swing arm pivot bolt and nut are tight (**Figure 64**).

4. Make sure the shock absorber upper (**Figure 65**) and lower (**Figure 66**) bolts are tight.

5. Make sure the rear axle nuts (**Figure 60**) are tight and that the cotter pin is in place on each side.

> *NOTE*
> *You may want to consider replacing the cotter pins with the reusable quick removal wire pins that slip in and out.*

> *CAUTION*
> *If any of the previously mentioned bolts and nuts are loose, refer to Chapter Ten for correct procedures and torque specifications.*

Nuts, Bolts and Other Fasteners

Constant vibration can loosen many of the fasteners on the ATV. Check the tightness of all fasteners, especially those on:

   a. Engine mounting hardware.
   b. Engine crankcase covers.
   c. Handlebar and front steering components.
   d. Gearshift lever.
   e. Kickstarter lever.
   f. Brake pedal and lever.
   g. Exhaust system.

ENGINE TUNE-UP

A complete tune-up should be performed at the interval indicated in **Table 1** with normal riding. More frequent tune-ups may be required if the ATV is ridden primarily in dusty areas.

The number of definitions of the term "tune-up" is probably equal to the number of people defining it. For the purposes of this book, a tune-up is general adjustment and maintenance to ensure peak engine performance.

Table 9 summarizes tune-up specifications.

The spark plug should be routinely replaced at every tune-up or if the electrodes show signs of erosion. Have new parts on hand before you begin.

The air filter element should be cleaned or replaced before doing other tune-up procedures as described in this chapter.

Because different systems in an engine interact, the procedures should be done in the following order.

   a. Clean or replace the air filter element.
   b. Check or replace the spark plug.
   c. Adjust the carburetor idle speed.

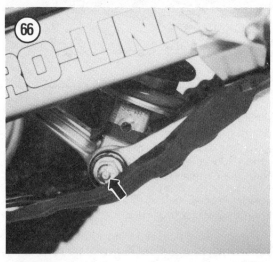

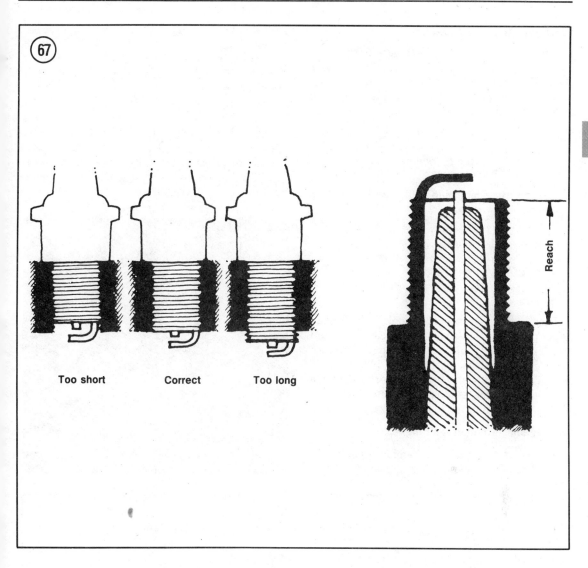

Too short   Correct   Too long

Reach

To perform a tune-up on your Honda, you will need the following tools and equipment.

a. 21 mm (13/16 in.) spark plug wrench.
b. Spark plug wire feeler gauge and gapper tool.
c. Portable tachometer.

Spark Plug Selection

Spark plugs are available in various heat ranges, hotter or colder than the plugs originally installed at the factory.

Select a plug of the heat range designed for the loads and conditions under which the ATV will be run. Use of incorrect heat ranges can cause a siezed piston, scored cylinder wall or damaged piston crown.

NOTE
For NGK and ND spark plugs, higher plug numbers designate colder plugs;

lower plug numbers designate hotter plugs. For example, an NGK BP9ES plug is colder than a BP8ES plug.

In general, use a hot plug for low speeds and low temperatures. Use a cold plug for high speeds, high engine loads and high temperatures. The plug should operate hot enough to burn off unwanted deposits, but not so hot that it is damaged or causes preignition. A spark plug of the correct heat range will show a light tan color on the portion of the insulator within the cylinder after the plug has been in service.

The reach (length) of a plug is also important. A longer than normal plug could interfere with the piston, causing permanent and severe damage; refer to **Figure 67**. Refer to **Table 9** for Honda factory recommended spark plug heat ranges.

Spark Plug Removal/Cleaning

1. Grasp the spark plug lead (**Figure 68**) as near the plug as possible and pull it off the plug. If it is stuck to the plug, twist it slightly to break it loose.
2. Wipe away any dirt that has accumulated on the cylinder head around the spark plug.

CAUTION
The dirt could fall into the cylinder when the plug is removed, causing serious engine damage.

3. Remove the spark plug with a 21 mm (13/16 in.) spark plug wrench.

NOTE
If the plug is difficult to remove, apply penetrating oil, such as WD-40 or Liquid Wrench around the base of the plug and let it soak in about 10-20 minutes.

4. Inspect the plug carefully. Look for a broken center porcelain, excessively eroded electrodes and excessive carbon or oil fouling. If present, replace the plug. If deposits are light, the plug may be cleaned in solvent with a wire brush or cleaned in a special spark plug sandblast cleaner. Regap the plug as explained in the following section.

Gapping and Installing the Plug

A spark plug should be carefully gapped to ensure a reliable, consistent spark. You must use a special spark plug gapping tool and a wire feeler gauge.

1. Remove the new spark plug from its box. If removed, screw on the small piece that is loose in the box (**Figure 69**).
2. Insert a wire feeler gauge between the center and side electrode of the plug (**Figure 70**). The correct gap is listed in **Table 9**. If the gap is correct, you will feel a slight drag as you pull the wire through. If there is no drag, or the gauge won't pass through, bend the side electrode with a gapping tool (**Figure 71**) to set the proper gap.

3. Put a small drop of oil on the threads of the spark plug.

4. Screw the spark plug in by hand until it seats. Very little effort is required. If force is necessary, you have the plug cross threaded. Unscrew it and try again.

5. Use a spark plug wrench and tighten the plug to the torque specification listed in **Table 5**.

> *CAUTION*
> *Do not overtighten. This will only squash the gasket and destroy its sealing ability.*

6. Install the spark plug lead. Rotate it slightly in both directions and make sure it is on tight.

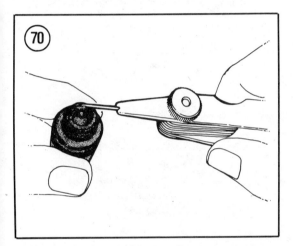

Reading Spark Plugs

Much information about engine and spark plug performance can be determined by careful examination of the spark plug. This information is more valid after performing the following steps.

1. Ride the ATV a short distance at full throttle in any gear.

2. Turn the engine kill switch to the OFF position before closing the throttle and simultaneously shift to NEUTRAL. Coast and brake to a stop.

3. Remove the spark plug and examine it. Compare it to **Figure 72**.

4. If the plug is defective, replace it. If its condition indicates other engine problems, the engine cannot be properly tuned until repairs are made.

Ignition Timing

The engine is equipped with a capacitor discharge ignition system (CDI). This system uses no breaker points, and there are no means of adjusting ignition timing.

Incorrect ignition timing can cause a drastic loss of engine performance and efficiency. It may also cause overheating.

Before starting this procedure, check all electrical connections related to the ignition system. Make sure all connections are tight and free of corrosion and that all ground connections are clean and tight.

1. Place the ATV on level ground and set the parking brake.

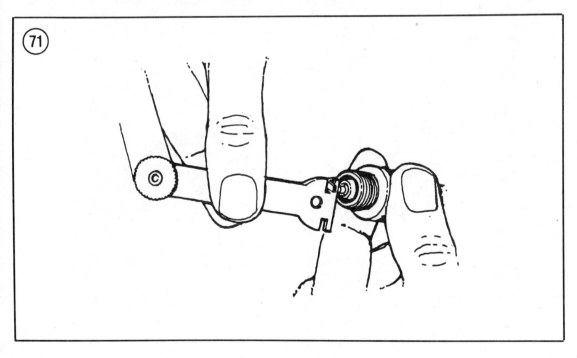

(72)

Normal plug appearance noted by the brown to grayish-tan deposits and slight electrode wear. This plug indicates the correct plug heat range and proper air fuel ratio.

Red, brown yellow and white coatings caused by fuel and oil additives. These deposits are not harmful if they remain in a powdery form.

Carbon fouling distinguished by dry, fluffy black carbon deposits which may be caused by an over-rich air/fuel mixture, excessive hand choking, clogged air filter or excessive idling.

Shiny yellow glaze on insulator cone is caused when the powdery deposits from fuel and oil additives melt. Melting occurs during hard acceleration after prolonged idling. This glaze conducts electricity and shorts out the plug.

Oil fouling indicated by wet, oily deposits caused by oil pumping past worn rings. A hotter plug temporarily reduces oil deposits, but a plug that is too hot leads to pre-ignition and possible engine damage.

Overheated plug indicated by burned or blistered insulator tip and badly worn electrodes. This condition may be caused by pre-ignition, cooling system defects, lean air/fuel ratios, low octane fuel or over advanced ignition timing.

Spark plug condition photos courtesy of AC Spark Plug Division, General Motors Corporation.

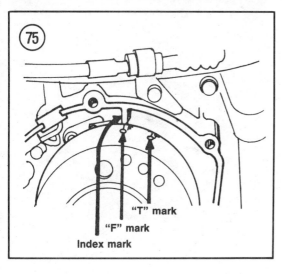

"T" mark
"F" mark
Index mark

2. Connect a portable tachometer following the manufacturer's instructions.

3. Start the engine and let it reach normal operating temperature. Turn the engine off.

4. Remove the clamping bolt and remove the gearshift lever (**Figure 73**).

5. Remove the bolts securing the alternator cover and remove the cover and gasket (**Figure 74**).

6. Connect a timing light following the manufacturer's instructions.

7. Start the engine and let it idle at the idle speed indicated in **Table 9**.

8. Adjust the idle speed if necessary as described in this chapter.

9. Aim the timing light at the top of the alternator rotor next to the fixed pointer and pull the trigger. The timing is correct if the "F" mark (**Figure 75**) aligns with the fixed pointer on the crankcase.

10. Gradually increase idle speed and check that the fixed pointer is between the "F" mark and the "T" mark.

11. If the timing is incorrect, inspect all ignition components in Chapter Seven.

12. Disconnect the timing light and portable tachometer.

13. Install the alternator cover and gasket. Tighten the bolts securely.

14. Install the gearshift lever and tighten the bolt securely.

Idle Speed Adjustment

Before making this adjustment, the air filter must be clean as described in this chapter.

1. Place the ATV on level ground and set the parking brake.

2. Connect a portable tachometer following the manufacturer's instructions.

3. Start the engine and let it reach normal operating temperature.

4. Adjust the throttle free play as described in this chapter.

5A. On 1985 3-wheeled models perform the following.

   a. Set the idle speed to the rpm listed in **Table 9** by turning the idle speed stop screw (**Figure 76**).

   b. Open and close the throttle a couple of times and check for variation in idle speed. Readjust if necessary.

5B. On 1986 3-wheeled models and all 4-wheeled models, perform the following.

   a. Set the idle speed to the rpm listed in **Table 9** by turning the choke/idle speed knob (**Figure 77**).

b. Open and close the throttle a couple of times. Check for variation in idle speed. Readjust if necessary.

> *WARNING*
> *With the engine idling, move the handlebar from side to side. If idle speed increases during this movement, the throttle cable needs adjusting or may be incorrectly routed through the frame. Correct this problem immediately. Do not ride the vehicle in this unsafe condition.*

6. Turn the engine off and disconnect the portable tachometer.

Carbon Removal

Carbon buildup should be removed from the engine and exhaust system at the intervals listed in **Table 1**.

On a 2-stroke engine, carbon builds up quickly in the combustion chamber, on the piston crown, in the cylinder's exhaust port and in the exhaust system. The carbon deposits will increase the compression ratio and decrease engine performance. Overheating and preignition from carbon deposits can cause engine damage.

If the carbon is removed at the specified intervals and a good grade of 2-stroke oil is used, the carbon buildup will rarely amount to more than a thick film which can be removed with a soft cloth soaked in solvent. If the deposits are left too long, they will have to be scraped off with a soft metal scraper.

1. Remove the exhaust system as described in Chapter Six.
2. Remove the cylinder head and cylinder as described in Chapter Four.
3. Gently scrape off the carbon deposits from the piston crown and cylinder head (**Figure 78**) with a dull screwdriver or the end of a hacksaw blade (**Figure 79**). Do not scratch the surface as this can cause hot spots.
4. Wipe the surfaces with a shop cloth dipped in solvent.

> *NOTE*
> *In the following step, the cylinder is shown removed from the engine for clarity. It is not necessary to remove it to perform this procedure.*

5. Wipe off the carbon deposits in the exhaust port (**Figure 80**) with a dull screwdriver or the end of a hacksaw blade (**Figure 79**). Do not scratch the surface.
6. Install the cylinder and cylinder head as described in Chapter Four.

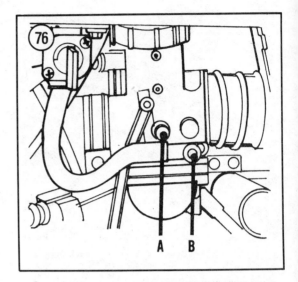

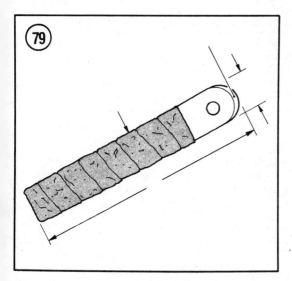

7. Gently scrape off the carbon deposits from the interior of the exhaust head pipe where it attaches to the cylinder.

8. Remove the muffler from the expansion chamber.

9. Clean out the expansion chamber as follows.

   a. Run a piece of used ATV or motorcycle drive chain around inside it.

   b. Another way is to chuck a length of wire cable, with the loose end frayed, in an electric drill.

   c. Run the drive chain or frayed cable around in the expansion chamber a couple of times.

   d. Shake out all loose carbon.

   e. Tap on the exterior of the expansion chamber with a soft-faced mallet to break loose any additional carbon.

   f. Blow out the interior with compressed air.

10. Clean out the interior of the muffler using the same methods described in Step 9.

11. Visually inspect the exterior of the entire exhaust system assembly, expecially in the areas of welds, for any cracks or damage. Repair or replace any faulty component.

12. Install the exhaust system.

Tables are on the following pages.

Table 1 MAINTENANCE SCHEDULE*

Every 30 operating days	• Inspect and lubricate drive chain
	• Inspect drive chain slider(s)
	• Clean air filter element
	• Remove the air filter air box drain tube
	  and clean out
	• Clean and inspect the spark plug
	• Check and adjust idle speed
	• Clean the spark arrester
	• Remove carbon build-up from engine and
	  exhaust system
	• Check and adjust throttle operation and free play
	• Check and adjust clutch operation and free play
	• Check clutch/transmission oil level
	• Check coolant level
	• Inspect all cooling system components
	• Inspect steering head bearings
	• Check brake fluid level in both master cylinders
	• Check all brake system components
	• Check skid plate(s) for damage
	• Check all suspension components for wear
	  or damage
	• Check and tighten wheel lug nuts and axle nuts
	• Lubricate control cables
	• Lubricate rear suspension linkage (Pro-link linkage)

Every 6 months	• Inspect the brake pads for wear • Change front fork oil

Every year	• Inspect the fuel line to the carburetor
	• Drain and replace enginecoolant
	  (liquid-cooled models)
	• Check steering head bearings (3-wheeled models)
	• Check steering shaft holder bearings
	  (4-wheeled models)

Every 2 years	• Drain and replace coolant • Drain and replace hydraulic brake fluid

*This Honda factory maintenance schedule should be considered as a guide to general maintenance and lubrication intervals. Harder than normal use and exposure to mud, water, sand, high humidity, etc. will naturally dictate more frequent attention to most maintenance items.

Table 2 PERIODIC PARTS REPLACEMENT
(VEHICLES USED IN COMPETITION*)

As necessary	• Replace drive chain • Front brake pads • Rear brake pads • Clutch discs • Exhaust chamber retaining spring • Skid plate(s) • Lubricate control cables
Every 20 hours	• Replace spark plug • Replace drive sprocket
Every 30 hours	• Replace piston • Replace piston pin • Replace piston rings • Replace connecting rod small end bearing (continued)

**Table 2 PERIODIC PARTS REPLACEMENT
(VEHICLES USED IN COMPETITION*)** (continued)

Every 30 hours (continued)	• Replace cylinder head gasket • Replace drive chain sliders • Replace drive chain master link • Drain and replace clutch/transmission oil
Every year	• Replace front hydraulic brake fluid • Replace rear hydraulic brake fluid
Every 2 years	• Replace master cylinder top cover diaphragm
Every 4 years	• Replace front flexible brake hose(s) • Replace rear flexible brake hose • Replace fuel hose

*This Honda factory competition maintenance schedule should be considered as a guide for machines that are used in competition (subject to harder than normal use) and are exposed to unusually dusty and/or muddy areas.

Table 3 TIRE INFLATION PRESSURE (COLD)*

	Tire pressure				Circumference	
	Minimum		Maximum			
Model	kPa	psi	kPa	psi	mm	in.
ATC250R						
Front	27	3.9	33	4.7	1,844	72.6
Rear	22	3.2	28	4.0	1,565	61.6
TRX250R/						
Fourtrax 250R						
1986-1987						
Front	24.5	3.6	30.5	4.4	—	—
Rear	17	2.5	23	3.3	—	—
1988-on						
Front	24.5	3.6	30.5	4.4	—	—
Rear	19.5	2.9	25.5	3.7	—	—

*Tire inflation pressure for factory equipped tires. Aftermarket tires may require different inflation pressure.

Table 4 FUEL AND OIL MIXTURE RATIO (20:1)

Gasoline quantity	Oil	
Liters/U.S. qt*	cc	U.S. oz
0.5	25	0.8
1.0	50	1.6
1.5	75	2.4
2.0	100	3.2
2.5	125	4.0
3.0	150	4.8
3.5	175	5.6
4.0	200	6.4
4.5	225	7.2
(continued)		

Table 4 FUEL AND OIL MIXTURE RATIO (20:1) (continued)

Gasoline quantity Liters/U.S. qt*	Oil cc	U.S. oz
5.0	250	8.0
5.5	275	8.8
6.0	300	9.6
6.5	325	10.4
7.0	350	11.2
7.5	375	12.0
8.0	400	12.8
8.5	425	13.6
9.0	450	14.4
9.5	475	15.2
10.0	500	16.0

* If gasoline is measured in liters, oil must be measured in cc. If gasoline is measured in U.S. quarts, oil must be measured in U.S. ounces.

Table 5 MAINTENANCE AND TUNE-UP TORQUE SPECIFICATIONS

Item	N•m	ft.-lb.
Oil drain plug	25-35	18-25
Rear axle bearing holder lockbolts	20-23	14-17
Parking brake adjuster bolt locknut	15-20	11-14
Spark plug	15-20	11-14

Table 6 FRONT FORK OIL CAPACITY AND DIMENSION (3-WHEELED MODELS)

Model	Capacity cc	oz.	Dimension mm	in.
ATC250R				
1985	400	13.56	186	7.3
1986	465	15.5	113	4.4

Table 7 DRIVE CHAIN REPLACEMENT NUMBERS

Model	Number Diado	Takasago
ATC250R	S20VS-96	RK520HMOX 96RJ
TRX250R/Fourtrax 250R		
1986	DID520V4 96L	RK520HMO 96L
1987	DID520V6 96L	RK520SMO 96L
1988-on	DID520V6 92RJ	RK520SMOZ 92RJ

Table 8 ANTIFREEZE PROTECTION

Temperature	Antifreeze-to-water ratio
Above -25° F (-32° C)	45:55
Above -34° F (-37° C)	50:50
Above -48° F (-44.5° C)	55:45

Table 9 TUNE-UP SPECIFICATIONS

Spark plug type	
ATC250R	
Standard heat range	Champion RN-2C, NGK BR9ES
Cold weather	Champion RN-3C, NGK BR8ES
TRX250R/Fourtrax 250R	
Standard heat range	
1986, 1989	Champion RN-3C, NGK BR8ES
1987-1988	Champion RN-2C, NGK BR9ES
Spark plug gap	0.7-0.8 mm (0.028-0.031 in.)
Ignition timing	"F" mark @ 1,500 ±100 rpm
Carburetor air screw initial screw setting*	
ATC250R	
1985	2 turns out
1986	2 1/4 turns out
TRX250R/Fourtrax 250R	
1986-1987	1 7/8 turns out
1988	1 3/4 turns out
1989	1 1/2 turns out
Idle speed	
ATC250R	
1985	1,400 ±150 rpm
1986	1,580 ±150 rpm
TRX250R/Fourtrax 250R	1,500 ±150 rpm

*Number of turns out from a lightly seated position.

3

CHAPTER FOUR

ENGINE

This chapter contains information for removal, inspection, service and reassembly for the liquid-cooled Honda 250R engine.

Although the clutch and transmission are located within the engine crankcase, they are covered in Chapter Five to simplify this material.

Before beginning any engine work, re-read the service hints in Chapter One. You will do a better job with this information fresh in your mind.

Refer to **Table 1** for engine specifications and **Table 2** for torque specifications. **Table 1** and **Table 2** are located at the end of this chapter.

ENGINE OPERATING PRINCIPLES

Figure 1 explains how the engine works. This will be helpful when troubleshooting or repairing the engine.

ENGINE LUBRICATION

Lubrication for the engine is provided by the fuel/oil mixture used to power the engine. There is no oil supply in the crankcase as it would be drawn into the cylinder and foul the spark plug. There is sufficient oil in the mixture to lubricate the crankshaft bearings, the piston and the cylinder. The clutch and transmission assemblies have their own separate oil supply.

Refer to Chapter Three for fuel/oil mixing procedure and recommended fuel-to-oil percentage.

SERVICING ENGINE IN FRAME

The following components can be serviced while the engine is mounted in the frame. The ATV's frame is a great holding fixture, especially when breaking loose stubborn bolts and nuts.

a. Cylinder head.
b. Cylinder.
c. Piston.
d. Carburetor.
e. Alternator.

ENGINE REMOVAL/INSTALLATION

NOTE
Removal of the seat/rear fender and the front fender on 4-wheeled models is not a required step but it does allow more working room.

1A. On 3-wheeled models, remove the seat/rear fender assembly as described in Chapter Twelve.
1B. On 4-wheeled models, remove the front fender and the seat/rear fender assembly as described in Chapter Twelve.

2-STROKE OPERATING PRINCIPLES

As the piston travels downward, it uncovers the exhaust port allowing the exhaust gases to leave the cylinder. A fresh fuel/air mixture, which has been compressed slightly, travels from the crankcase to the cylinder through the transfer port.

Exhaust

Air/fuel

As the crankshaft rotates, the piston moves upward covering the transfer and exhaust ports while compressing the new fuel/air mixture. It also creates a low pressure area in the crankcase allowing the new fuel/air mixture to enter the crankcase.

Carburetor

Air

Air/fuel

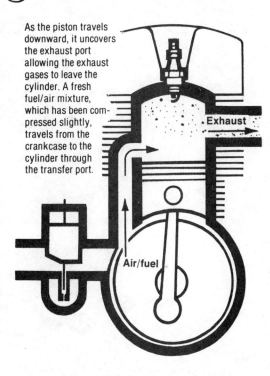

As the piston travels down, the exhaust gases leave the cylinder and the complete cycle starts all over again.

Exhaust

As the piston almost reaches the top of its travel, the spark plug fires, thus igniting the compressed fuel/air mixture. The piston continues to top dead center and is pushed downward by the expanding gases.

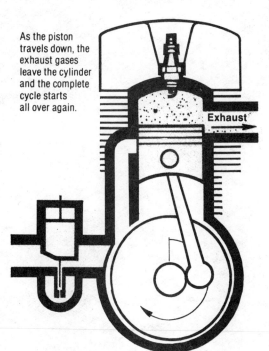

2. Remove the fuel tank as described in Chapter Six.

3. Thoroughly clean the exterior of the engine and frame. Be sure to remove all dirt and grease from tiny crevices on the outside of the engine. If water is used to flush away dirt and solvent, use compressed air and blow or wipe the engine dry.

4. Place the ATV on level ground and set the parking brake.

5. Drain the transmission/clutch oil as described in Chapter Three.

6. Disconnect the high tension lead from the spark plug (**Figure 2**).

7. Remove the exhaust system as described in Chapter Six.

8. Remove the carburetor assembly as described in Chapter Six.

9. On 4-wheeled models, remove the air filter case inlet pipes as described in Chapter Six.

10. Drain the coolant as described under *Coolant Change* in Chapter Three.

11. Disconnect the coolant hoses from the cylinder head and water pump cover as described in Chapter Eight.

12. Loosen the locknut (A, **Figure 3**) and disconnect the clutch cable from the clutch arm (B, **Figure 3**) and cable receptacle (C, **Figure 3**) on the right-hand side of the engine.

13. Disconnect the alternator electrical connector. Refer to **Figure 4** for 3-wheeled models or **Figure 5** for 4-wheeled models.

14. Remove the drive sprocket as described in this chapter.

15. Remove the bolt securing the gearshift pedal and remove the pedal.

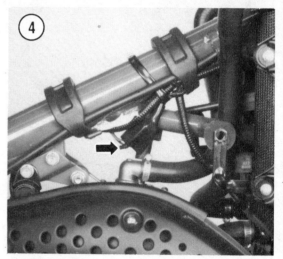

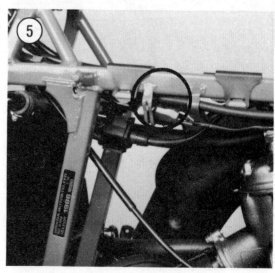

16. Remove the bolt securing the kickstarter pedal and remove the pedal.

17. If the engine is going to be totally disassembled, remove the following components as described in their respective chapters.

    a. Cylinder head (this chapter).

    b. Cylinder (this chapter).

    c. Piston assembly (this chapter).

    d. Alternator (this chapter).

18A. On 3-wheeled models, perform the following.

    a. Remove the bolts and nuts securing the engine upper mounting plates (**Figure 6**) and remove the upper mounting plates.

    b. Remove the mounting bolts and nuts securing the engine front mounting brackets. Remove the mounting brackets.

    c. Place wood blocks under the engine to hold the engine in place after the mounting bolts are removed.

    d. Remove the engine front mounting through-bolt and nut (**Figure 7**) from the left-hand side.

    e. Remove the engine rear mounting through-bolts and nuts (**Figure 8**) from the left-hand side.

18B. On 4-wheeled models, perform the following.

    a. Remove the bolts and nuts securing the engine upper mounting pipe (**Figure 9**) and remove the upper mounting pipe assembly.

    b. Remove the mounting bolts and nuts (A, **Figure 10**) securing the engine front mounting brackets. Remove the mounting brackets.

    c. Place wood blocks under the engine to hold the engine in place after the mounting bolts are removed.

    d. Remove the engine front mounting through-bolt and nut (B, **Figure 10**) from the left-hand side.

4

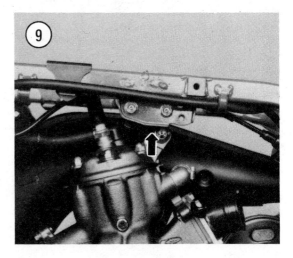

e. Remove the engine rear mounting through-bolts and nuts (C, **Figure 10**) from the left-hand side.

19. Remove the engine from the frame and take it to your workbench for further disassembly.

20. Install the engine by reversing these removal steps, noting the following.

21. Install all through-bolts from the left-hand side.

22. If the swing arm is removed while the engine is removed, install the engine rear hanger with the UP mark (**Figure 11**) facing up. If installed upside down, the bolt holes will not align with the bolt holes in the crankcase.

23. Tighten all bolts and nuts to the torque specification listed in **Table 2**.

24. Refill the cooling system as described under *Coolant Change* in Chapter Three.

25. Before starting the engine, be sure to refill or check the following items listed in Chapter Three.

   a. Transmission/clutch oil level.
   b. Clutch adjustment.
   c. Throttle cable adjustment.
   d. Drive chain adjustment.

CYLINDER HEAD

The cylinder head, cylinder and the piston may be removed without removing the engine from the frame. Allow the engine to cool to room temperature before removing the head to avoid possible distortion.

NOTE
The Honda factory has determined that some 1986 ATC250R's have experienced cylinder head gasket problems. The original cylinder head gasket, in some cases, allowed coolant to leak into the cylinder. If you have had this problem, a replacement metal gasket is available from Honda dealers and will be installed at no cost to the consumer (Honda Service Bulletin ATC250R No. 6, June 1986). If you have also experienced an engine pinging problem, refer to Chapter Six to change the jet needle clip position.

Removal/Installation

1. Place the ATV on level ground and set the parking brake. Place wood block(s) under the frame to hold the ATV securely in place.

NOTE
Removal of the seat/rear fender and the front fender on 4-wheeled models is not

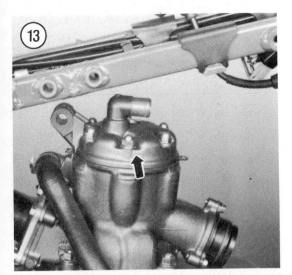

a required step but it does allow more working room.

2. Remove the seat/rear fender and the front fender on 4-wheeled models as described in Chapter Twelve.

3. Remove the fuel tank as described in Chapter six.

4. Drain the cooling system as described in Chapter Three.

5. Remove the carburetor assembly as described in Chapter Six.

6A. On 3-wheeled models, remove the bolts and nuts securing the engine upper mounting plates (**Figure 6**) and remove the upper mounting plates.

6B. On 4-wheeled models, remove the bolts and nuts securing the engine upper mounting pipe (**Figure 9**) and remove the upper mounting pipe assembly.

7. Disconnect the high tension lead from the spark plug (A, **Figure 12**).

8. Loosen the screw on the clamping band (B, **Figure 12**) securing the coolant hose to the cylinder head. Carefully remove the coolant hose from the cylinder head.

9. Remove the exhaust system as described in Chapter Six.

10. Loosen the cylinder head (**Figure 13**) nuts in a crisscross patttern. Loosen the nuts in 2-3 stages, turning each nut about 1/4-1/2 turn and repeating the sequence until all the nuts have been loosened 2 full turns. Remove each cylinder head nut.

11. Loosen the cylinder head by tapping around the perimeter with a rubber or soft faced mallet.

12. Remove the cylinder head by pulling it straight up and off the cylinder studs and cylinder.

13. Remove the cylinder head gasket and discard it.

14. Install by reversing these removal steps, noting the following.

15A. On 3-wheeled models, position the new cylinder head gasket with the tab facing toward the rear. Install the new cylinder head gasket.

15B. On 4-wheeled models, position the new cylinder head gasket with the UP mark facing up and with the tabs toward the front and rear. Install the new cylinder head gasket (**Figure 14**).

16. Install the cylinder head and cylinder head nuts.

17. Tighten the cylinder head nuts in a crisscross pattern in 2-3 steps to the torque specification listed in **Table 2**.

Inspection

1. Inspect the cylinder head (**Figure 15**) for warpage with a straight edge and flat feeler gauge.

Replace the cylinder head if warpage exceeds the service limit listed in **Table 1**.

2. Check for cracks around any of the cylinder stud holes or spark plug hole. A cracked cylinder head must be replaced.

3. Clean off all carbon deposits in the combustion chamber portion of the cylinder head (**Figure 16**). Use a broad-tipped dull screwdriver or the end of a hacksaw blade (**Figure 17**). Do not scratch the surface. Wipe off the cylinder head with a shop cloth and cleaning solvent.

CYLINDER

Removal/Installation

1. Remove the cylinder head as described in this chapter.

2. Loosen the screw on the upper (A, **Figure 18**) and lower (B, **Figure 18**) clamping band securing the coolant hose to the cylinder and to the water pump. Carefully remove the coolant hose from the cylinder and water pump.

3. Remove the flange nuts securing the cylinder to the crankcase. Refer to **Figure 19** and **Figure 20**.

4. Loosen the cylinder by tapping around the perimeter with a rubber or soft-faced mallet. If necessary, *gently* pry the cylinder loose with a broad-tipped screwdriver.

5. Pull the cylinder straight up and off of the crankcase studs. Don't lose the locating dowels on the left-hand crankcase studs.

6. Remove the base gasket and discard it. Stuff a clean shop cloth into the top of the crankcase around the piston to prevent the entry of dirt and foreign matter.

Inspection

The following procedure requires the use of highly specialized and expensive measuring instruments. If such equipment is not readily available, have the measurements performed by a dealer or qualified machine shop.

1. Soak with solvent any old cylinder base gasket material on the cylinder. Use a broad tipped *dull*

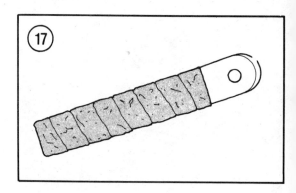

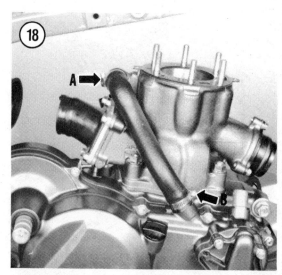

chisel and gently scrape off all gasket residue. Do not gouge the sealing surface as an air leak will result.

2. Measure the cylinder bore (**Figure 21**) with a cylinder gauge or inside micrometer. Measure first in a plane parallel to the piston pin, then in a plane

90° to the first (**Figure 22**). If the distortion (taper or out-of-round) exceeds the service limit listed in **Table 1** the cylinder must be rebored to the next oversize and a new oversize piston installed. Pistons are available in oversizes of 0.25 mm (0.01 in.) and 0.50 mm (0.02 in.).

> *NOTE*
> *The new piston should be obtained before the cylinder is rebored so that the piston can be measured. Slight manufacturing tolerances must be taken into account to determine the actual size and working clearance. Piston-to-cylinder wear limit is listed in* ***Table 1***.

3. If the cylinder requires reboring, remove the dowel pins from the cylinder before leaving the cylinder with the dealer or machine shop.

> *NOTE*
> *After having the cylinder rebored, wash it thoroughly in hot soapy water. This is the best way to clean the cylinder of all fine grit material left from the bore job. After washing the cylinder, run a clean white cloth through the bore. The cloth should show no traces of dirt or other debris. If the cloth is dirty, the cylinder is not clean and must be rewashed. After the cylinder is thoroughly cleaned, dry and then lubricate the cylinder walls with clean 2-stroke engine oil to prevent the cylinder from rusting.*

4. Inspect the transfer port in the cylinder. Refer to **Figure 23** and **Figure 24**. Clean off any carbon and check for any cracks. A cracked cylinder must be replaced.

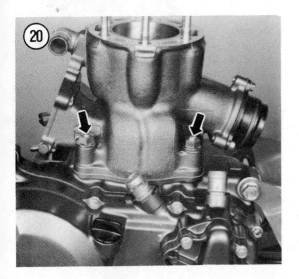

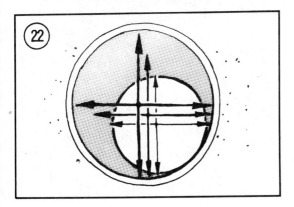

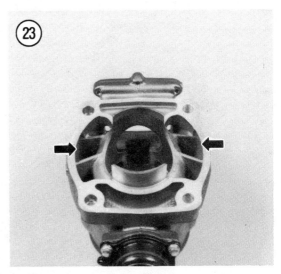

5. Clean off all carbon deposits in the exhaust port of the cylinder (**Figure 25**). Use a broad-tipped dull screwdriver or the end of a hacksaw blade (**Figure 17**). Do not scratch the surface. Wipe out the exhaust port with a shop cloth and cleaning solvent.

6. Inspect the seal ring (**Figure 26**) on the exhaust port outlet fitting for wear or damage. Replace the seal ring, if necessary.

Installation

1. Remove the shop cloth.

> *NOTE*
> *In the following step, the piston is removed for clarity only. It is not necessary to remove the piston for this procedure.*

2. If removed, install the locating dowels (**Figure 27**) onto the left-hand crankcase studs.

3. Install a new cylinder base gasket (**Figure 28**) on the crankcase.

4. Make sure the end gaps of the piston rings are lined up with the locating pins in the ring grooves.

5. Lightly oil the piston, piston rings and the cylinder bore with 2-stroke oil. Rotate the crankshaft to bring the piston to the bottom of its stroke.

6. Start the cylinder down over the piston.

7. Make sure the ring gap aligns with the pin in the piston groove. Compress the top ring and start the chamfered edge of the cylinder over the ring.

8. Compress the secondary ring and slide the cylinder down over the ring (**Figure 29**). Continue

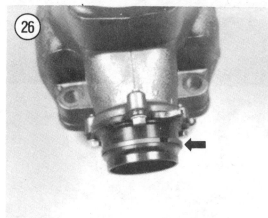

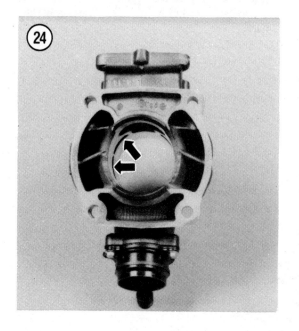

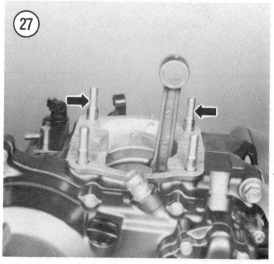

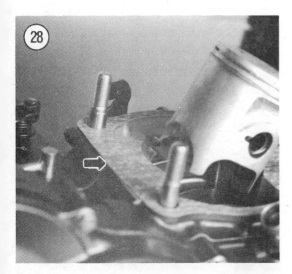

to slide the cylinder down until it completely covers the rings.

9. Install the flange nuts on the cylinder base and tighten them in a crisscross pattern in 2-3 steps to the torque specification listed in **Table 2**. Refer to **Figure 19** and **Figure 20**.

REED VALVE ASSEMBLY

The engine is equipped with a power reed valve assembly installed in the intake port of the cylinder head.

Particular care must be taken when handling the reed valve assembly. A malfunctioning reed valve will cause severe performance loss as well as contributing to early engine failure due to a too-lean fuel mixture.

The reed valve must be replaced as an assembly if faulty as replacement parts are not available.

Removal/Installation

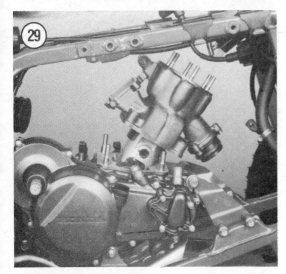

1. Remove the screws securing the carburetor insulator (**Figure 30**) and reed valve to the base of the cylinder and remove the assembly. If the reed valve assembly is difficult to remove, use a drift or broad-tipped screwdriver and gently tap the side of the assembly to help break it loose from the gasket and the cylinder.

2. Remove the carburetor insulator, gasket (on models so equipped), reed valve assembly and other gasket from the cylinder.

3. Clean all old gasket residue from the cylinder mating surface.

4. Install a new gasket (**Figure 31**) onto the carburetor insulator.

5. Install a new gasket (**Figure 32**) onto the cylinder and install the reed valve assembly and carburetor insulator (**Figure 30**).

6. Install the screws securing the assembly and tighten them securely.

7. Install the cylinder as described in this chapter.

Inspection

Stainless steel reed plates open and close the inlet port in response to crankcase pressure changes, allowing the fuel/air mixture to enter. They then close to allow the crankcase to pressurize. The reed stopper plates prevent the reeds from opening too far.

Carefully examine the reed valve assembly (**Figure 33**) for visible signs of wear, distortion or damage. Check for signs of cracks, metal fatigue, distortion or foreign matter damage. Replacement parts are not available from Honda dealers for the stock reed valve assembly.

Make sure the screws securing the reed stopper plates (**Figure 34**) are tight.

> *NOTE*
> *Make sure all parts are clean and free of any small dirt particles or lint from a shop cloth as they may cause a small amount of distortion in the reed plate.*

PISTON, PISTON PIN AND PISTON RINGS

The piston is made of an aluminum alloy. It is fitted with a Keystone type top ring. The Keystone cross section is designed to move in and out in the groove and prevent carbon buildup. Make sure that the ring identification marks face upward.

Removal

1. Remove the cylinder as described in this chapter.

> *WARNING*
> *The edges of all piston rings are sharp. Be careful when handling them to avoid cut fingers.*

2. Cover the crankcase opening with a clean shop cloth to prevent parts or foreign matter from entering.

3. Remove the piston pin clip (**Figure 35**) from each side of the piston with a small screwdriver or scribe. Hold your thumb over one edge of the clip during removal to prevent it from springing out.

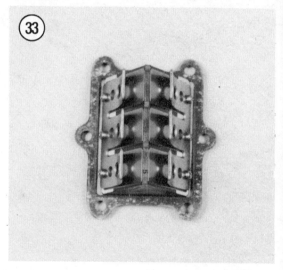

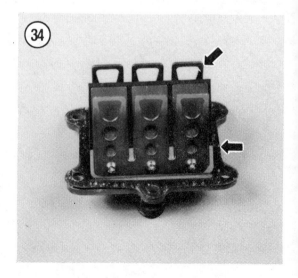

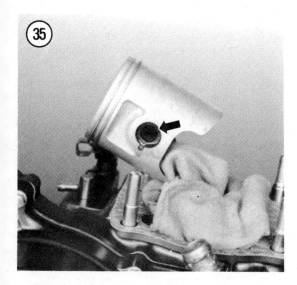

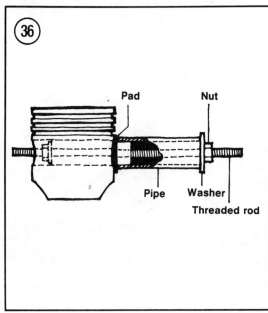

4. Hold the piston firmly in one hand and press the pin out with a drift or deep socket that is slightly smaller in diameter than the pin.

CAUTION
Be careful when removing the piston pin to avoid damaging the connecting rod. If it is necessary to gently tap the pin to remove it, be sure that the piston is properly supported so that the lateral shock is not transmitted to the lower connecting rod bearing.

5. If the piston pin is difficult to remove, heat the piston with a butane torch. The pin will probably push right out. Heat the piston to only about 140° F (60° C), i.e., until it is too warm to touch, but not excessively hot. If the pin is still difficult to push out, use a homemade tool as shown in **Figure 36**.

6. When the pin has been pushed clear of the opposite side of the bearing, remove the piston from the connecting rod.

7. Remove the piston pin needle bearing from the connecting rod.

8. Thoroughly clean all parts in solvent and dry with compressed air.

WARNING
The edges of all piston rings are very sharp. Be careful when handling them to avoid cut fingers.

9. Remove the top ring from the piston by spreading the ends with your thumbs just enough to slide the ring up over the piston (**Figure 37**). Repeat for the lower ring.

10. If the piston is going to be left off for some time, place a piece of foam insulation tube over the end of the connecting rod to protect it.

Inspection

1. Examine the bearing cage for cracks at the corners of the needle slots (**Figure 38**) and inspect

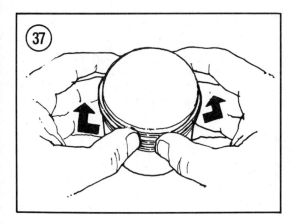

the needles themselves for cracking. If any cracks are found, the bearing must be replaced.

2. Wipe the bore in the connecting rod (**Figure 39**) with a clean rag and check it for galling, scratches or any other signs of damage. If any of these conditions exist, replace the connecting rod as described in this chapter.

3. Install the needle bearing assembly into the connecting rod (**Figure 40**). Oil the piston pin and install it in the connecting rod bearing. Slowly rotate the piston pin and check for radial play (**Figure 41**). If there is play, the piston pin and bearing should be replaced, providing the rod bore is in good condition.

4. Measure the inside diameter of the piston pin bore of the connecting rod (**Figure 42**) with a snap gauge. Compare with dimensions given in **Table 1**. Replace the connecting rod, if necessary.

5. Measure the inside diameter of the piston pin bore with a snap gauge (**Figure 43**) and measure the outside diameter of the piston pin with a micrometer (**Figure 44**) or vernier caliper. Compare with dimensions given in **Table 1**. Replace the piston and piston pin as a set if either or both are worn.

6. Carefully check the piston for cracks at the top edges of the transfer cutaways (**Figure 45**) and replace it if any are found. Check the piston skirt for brown varnish buildup. More than a very slight amount is an indication of worn or sticking rings. The piston rings should be replaced.

7. Measure each of the rings for wear as shown in **Figure 46**. Place each ring, one at a time, into the cylinder and push it in past the transfer cutaway. Use the crown of the piston to ensure that the ring is square in the cylinder. Measure the gap with a flat feeler gauge. Refer to dimensions given in **Table 1**. If gap is greater than the wear limit, the rings should be replaced.

8. Measure the end gap of each piston ring with a vernier caliper. Refer to dimensions given in **Table 1**. If gap is greater than the wear limit, the rings should be replaced.

9. When installing new rings, measure their end gap in the same manner as for the old ones. If the gap is less than the minimum specified, carefully file the ends of the rings with a fine file until the gap is correct.

10. Measure the side clearance of each ring as shown in **Figure 47** and compare to dimensions given in **Table 1**. If clearance is greater than the wear limit, the rings should be replaced. If the clearance is still excessive with new rings, the piston must also be replaced.

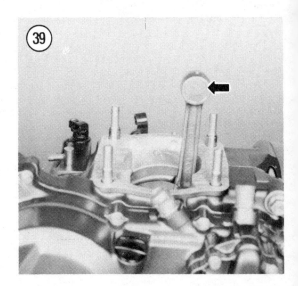

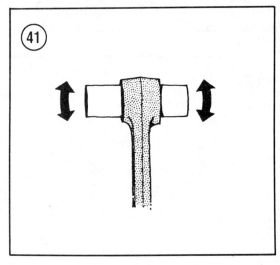

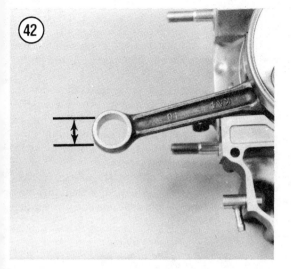

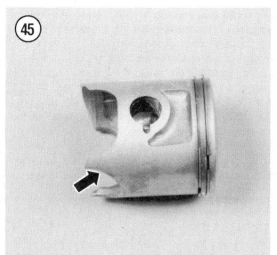

4

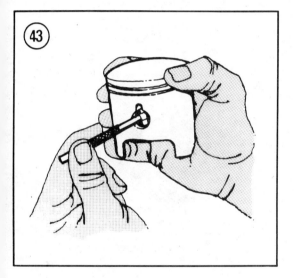

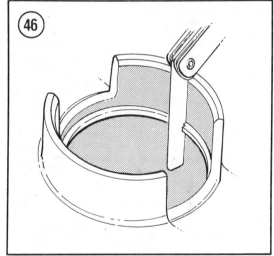

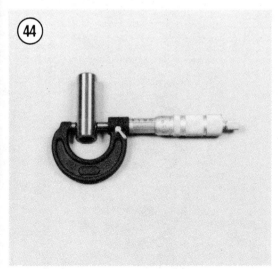

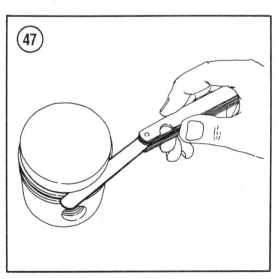

11. Clean the ring groove with a piece of a broken Keystone type ring (**Figure 48**). Inspect the groove for carbon buildup or burrs and correct the condition before installing the rings.

12. Measure the diameter of the piston across the skirt at a right angle to the wrist pin bore and 25 mm (1.0 in.) up from the bottom of the skirt (**Figure 49**). Replace the piston if it is worn to the service limit shown in **Table 1**.

13. Inspect the boss (**Figure 50**) on the underside of the piston where the connecting rod rides for wear or damage. Replace the piston, if necessary.

Installation

> *WARNING*
> *The edges of all piston rings are very sharp. Be careful when handling them to avoid cut fingers.*

1. Position the top piston ring with the angled face and the marks toward the top of the piston (**Figure 51**).

2. Install the piston rings, first the bottom one and then the top one, by carefully spreading the ends with your thumbs just enough to slip the ring over the piston (**Figure 37**). Repeat for the top ring.

3. Make sure that the rings are seated completely in their grooves all the way around the piston. Press the piston ring in until it bottoms out in the piston ring groove. When it bottoms out it must be flush with the piston surface. If the ring is not flush with the piston surface, there are some carbon deposits in the ring groove. Remove the ring and clean out the ring groove as described in this chapter.

4. Make sure the end gaps of the piston rings are lined up with the locating pins in the ring groove.

5. Lightly oil the needle bearing assembly and install it in the connecting rod (**Figure 40**).

6. Oil the pin and install it in the piston until the end of it extends slightly beyond the inside of the boss.

7. Place the piston over the connecting rod with the IN mark on the piston crown (**Figure 52**) toward the rear of the engine (intake side). Line up the pin with the bearing and push the pin into the piston until it is even with the piston pin clip grooves.

8. Install a new piston pin clip (**Figure 35**) in each end of the pin bosses. Make sure that they are seated in the grooves and that one end crosses the removal notch.

> *CAUTION*
> *Never reuse an old piston pin clip, as it can lead to serious engine damage.*

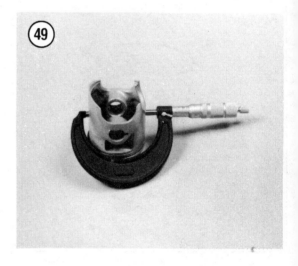

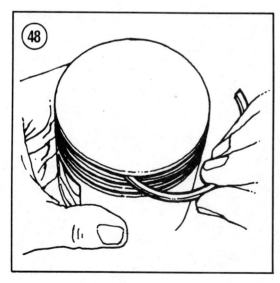

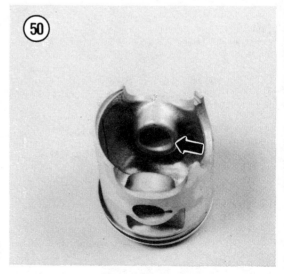

9. Apply a light coat of 2-stroke oil to the side walls of the piston and to the ring grooves.

10. Install the cylinder and cylinder head as described in this chapter.

PRIMARY DRIVE GEAR AND BALANCER SYSTEM

CAUTION
*Do **not** disconnect or remove the balancer system from the engine. The engine is designed to operate with it to reduce engine vibration. If the balancer is removed or disconnected, an excessive amount of engine vibration could result in cracks or damage to the frame or engine. Also any applicable manufacturer's warranty will be voided.*

Removal

1. Remove the clutch as described in Chapter Five.

2. Place a copper washer (or copper penny) between the balancer drive gear and the balancer gear (A, **Figure 53**). Then loosen the bolt (B, **Figure 53**) securing the primary drive gear. Remove the copper washer.

3. Remove the bolt and lockwasher (**Figure 54**).

4. Slide off the primary drive gear and the balancer drive gear from the crankshaft.

5. Remove the bolts (**Figure 55**) securing the balancer bearing holder plate and remove the holder plate.

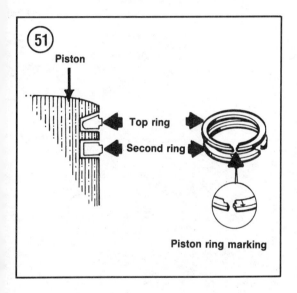

Piston

Top ring

Second ring

Piston ring marking

6. Rotate the balancer until the hole (A, **Figure 56**) on the balancer gear is pointing at the 9 o'clock position. This is necessary to align the balancer weight with the crankshaft for removal.

7. Withdraw the balancer shaft assembly from the crankcase (B, **Figure 56**).

8. Inspect the balancer gears and balancer shaft assembly as described in this chapter.

Installation

1. Position the balancer with the hole (A, **Figure 57**) on the balancer gear pointing at the 9 o'clock position and insert the assembly into the crankcase. This is necessary so the flat on the balancer shaft (B, **Figure 57**) will clear the crankcase and crankshaft for installation.

2. Install the balancer holder plate and bolts (**Figure 55**). Tighten the bolts securely.

> *CAUTION*
> *The alignment index marks in Steps 3-5 must be correct. Each index mark must be accurately placed or extreme engine vibration will occur.*

3. Position the balancer drive gear with the OUT mark facing out (A, **Figure 58**).

4. Align the inner index mark on the balancer drive gear with the index mark on the crankshaft (B, **Figure 58**).

5. Also align the outer index mark on the balancer drive gear with the index mark on the balancer gear (**Figure 59**) and slide on the balancer drive gear.

6. Slide on the primary drive gear (**Figure 60**).

7. Position the lockwasher with the OUT mark (**Figure 61**) facing out and install the lockwasher and bolt (**Figure 54**).

8. Place a copper washer (or copper penny) between the balancer drive gear and the balancer gear (C, **Figure 53**). Then tighten the bolt (B, **Figure 53**) securing the primary drive gear to the torque specification listed in **Table 2**. Remove the copper washer.

9. Install the clutch assembly as described in Chapter Five.

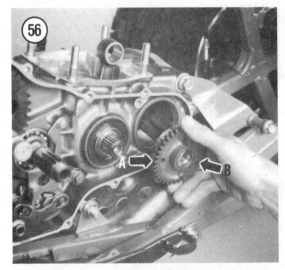

Inspection

1. Inspect the teeth on the balancer driven gear, primary drive gear (**Figure 62**) and balancer gear (**Figure 63**). Remove any small nicks on the teeth with an oilstone. If damage is severe, the gears should be replaced as a set.

2. Inspect the balancer shaft assembly bearing (**Figure 64**). It must rotate smoothly with no signs of wear. If the bearing is worn or damaged, replace

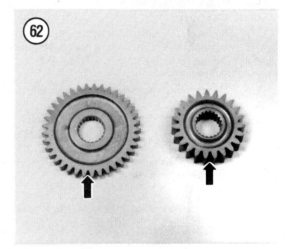

the balancer shaft assembly. The bearing cannot be replaced separately.

3. Inspect the balancer shaft bearing surface (**Figure 65**) where it rides in the bearing holder. It should be smooth with no signs of wear. If damaged or worn, replace the balancer shaft assembly.

Balancer Shaft Assembly Bearing Holder Removal/Installation

This procedure is shown with the engine removed from the frame for clarity. It is not necessary to remove the engine for this procedure.

1. Remove the alternator rotor and stator as described in this chapter.
2. Remove the bolts (**Figure 66**) securing the bearing holder.
3. From the balancer opening in the right-hand side of the crankcase (**Figure 67**), insert a long 1/2 in. drive socket extension or large drift into the opening (A, **Figure 68**) of the bearing inner race (where the balancer rides). Use a hammer and carefully tap the bearing holder (**Figure 69**) out from the crankcase.
4. Install by reversing these removal steps, noting the following.
5. Inspect the bearing as described in this chapter.
6. Install a new O-ring seal (**Figure 70**) on the bearing holder and apply a light coat of oil to it.
7. Tighten the bearing holder bolts securely.

Inspection

Inspect the balancer holder bearing (B, **Figure 68**). It must rotate smoothly with no signs of wear.

If the bearing is worn or damaged, have it replaced by a Honda dealer as special tools are required for removal and installation. These special tools would cost more than the cost of bearing replacement.

ALTERNATOR

Refer to **Figure 71** for this procedure.

Rotor Removal/Installation

1. Place the ATV on level ground and set the parking brake.
2. Place wood block(s) under the frame to hold the ATV securely in place.
3. Shift the transmission into 5th gear.

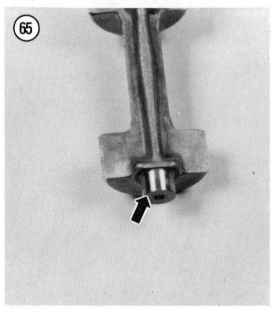

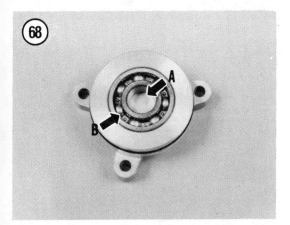

4

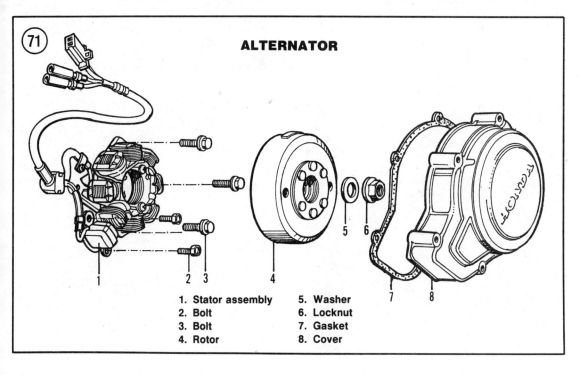

ALTERNATOR

1. Stator assembly
2. Bolt
3. Bolt
4. Rotor
5. Washer
6. Locknut
7. Gasket
8. Cover

4. Remove the clamping bolt on the gearshift lever and remove the gearshift lever (**Figure 72**).

5. Remove the screws securing the alternator cover and remove the cover and gasket (**Figure 73**).

6. Have an assistant apply the rear brake. Loosen then remove the nut and washer (**Figure 74**) securing the rotor in place.

NOTE
The rear brake still has to be applied even though the parking brake is set.

7. Screw a flywheel puller (**Figure 75**) into the rotor until it stops. Use the Honda flywheel puller (part No. 07733-001000 or 07933-0010000), K & N (part No. 82-0150), or equivalent (**Figure 76**).

CAUTION
Do not try to remove the rotor without a puller. Any attempt to do so will damage the engine or rotor. Many aftermarket pullers are available from motorcycle dealers or mail order houses. The cost of a puller is about $10 and it makes an excellent addition to any mechanic's tool box. If you can't borrow one, have a dealer remove it for you.

8. Tap the end of the rotor puller with a hammer. This will usually disengage the rotor from the crankshaft. If the rotor will not break free, turn the puller until the rotor disengages from the crankshaft.

9. Remove the rotor and puller. Don't lose the Woodruff key on the crankshaft.

CAUTION
Carefully inspect the inside of the rotor (Figure 77) for small bolts, washers, or other metal "trash" that may have been picked up by the magnets. These small metal bits can cause severe damage to the stator assembly components.

10. Install by reversing these removal steps, noting the following.

11. Make sure the Woodruff key is in place in the slot in the crankshaft (**Figure 78**). Align the keyway in the rotor with the key when installing the rotor.

12. Be sure to install the washer (**Figure 79**) before installing the rotor nut, then install the rotor nut (**Figure 74**).

13. Tighten the rotor nut to the torque specification listed in **Table 2**.

14. Install a new alternator cover gasket.

15. Install the gearshift pedal and tighten the clamping bolt securely.

Stator Assembly
Removal/Installation

Test procedures for the alternator rotor and stator assembly are covered in Chapter Seven.

1. Disconnect the alternator electrical connector (A, **Figure 80**) from the chassis wiring harness.

2. Carefully remove the electrical wire harness from the retaining clips (B, **Figure 80**) on the frame and engine.

3. Remove the alternator rotor (C, **Figure 80**) as described in this chapter.

4. Remove the bolts securing the stator assembly (A, **Figure 81**) and the pulse generator (B, **Figure 81**) to the left-hand crankcase housing. Pull the

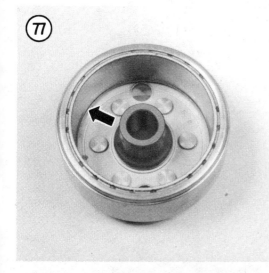

grommet and electrical harness (C, **Figure 81**) out of the left-hand crankcase and remove the stator assembly and pulse generator.

5. Inspect the stator assembly (**Figure 82**) for damage or frayed electrical wires; replace if necessary.

6. Install by reversing these removal steps, noting the following.

7. Install all bolts and tighten them securely.

8. Make sure the electrical connection is tight.

Flywheel nut, 40 ft.

DRIVE SPROCKET

Removal/Installation

1. Place the ATV on level ground and set the parking brake.

2. Remove the clamping bolt (**Figure 72**) securing the gearshift lever and remove the lever.

3. Remove the bolts securing the sprocket cover (**Figure 83**). Remove the sprocket cover and the guide plate.

4. Have an assistant apply the rear brake. Loosen the bolt securing the drive sprocket (**Figure 84**).

5. Remove the nut and the lockwasher.

6. Loosen the drive chain as described under *Drive Chain Adjustment* in Chapter Three.

7. On 4-wheeled models, remove the bolt (A, **Figure 85**) securing the drive chain slider on the frame and remove the slider.

8. Slide the drive sprocket and drive chain (B, **Figure 85**) off the transmission mainshaft.

9. If the engine is going to be disassembled, remove the spacer and O-ring seal from the transmission shaft.

10. Inspect the drive sprocket teeth for wear or damage. If the teeth are visibly worn (**Figure 86**), replace the sprocket.

NOTE
If the drive sprocket is worn or damaged and must be replaced, also inspect the drive chain and the driven sprocket for damage. Never replace just one of the 3 components without a thorough inspection of all the rest. If one is replaced, the other 2 should also be replaced or the new component will wear out prematurely.

11. Install by reversing these removal steps, noting the following.

NOTE
The following step is not necessary if the engine has not been disassembled.

12. If the engine has been disassembled, install a new O-ring seal (**Figure 87**) on the transmission shaft, then install the spacer (**Figure 88**).

13. Position the drive sprocket with the shoulder side (**Figure 89**) going on first.
14. Tighten the sprocket nut to the torque specification listed in **Table 2**.

KICKSTARTER

Refer to **Figure 90** for this procedure.

Removal

1. Remove the clutch as described in Chapter Five.
2A. On 1985 3-wheeled models, slide the washer, collar and second washer from the kickstarter shaft.
2B. On 1988-on 4-wheeled models, slide the washer and collar from the kickstarter shaft.
2C. On all other models, slide the collar (**Figure 91**) from the kickstarter shaft.

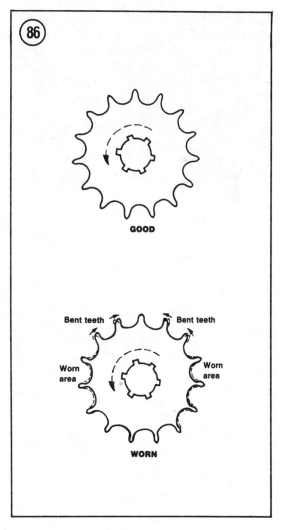

3. Remove the kickstarter drive gear (**Figure 92**) from the kickstarter shaft.

4. Remove the bolts (**Figure 93**) securing the ratchet guide plate.

5. Using Vise Grip pliers, unhook the return spring (A, **Figure 94**) from the post on the crankcase.

6. Withdraw the kickstarter shaft assembly (B, **Figure 94**) from the crankcase.

Disassembly/Inspection/Assembly

1. Slide off the spring guide (**Figure 95**).

2. Unhook the return spring from the hole in the kickstarter shaft and remove the return spring (**Figure 96**).

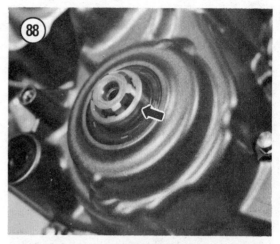

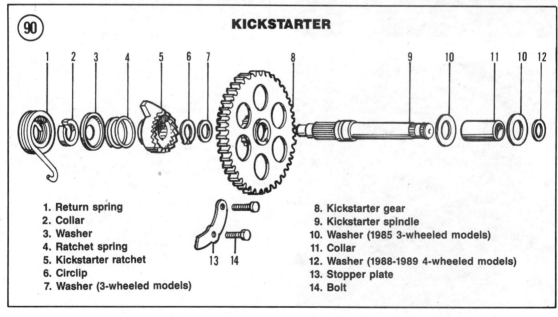

KICKSTARTER

1. Return spring
2. Collar
3. Washer
4. Ratchet spring
5. Kickstarter ratchet
6. Circlip
7. Washer (3-wheeled models)

8. Kickstarter gear
9. Kickstarter spindle
10. Washer (1985 3-wheeled models)
11. Collar
12. Washer (1988-1989 4-wheeled models)
13. Stopper plate
14. Bolt

4

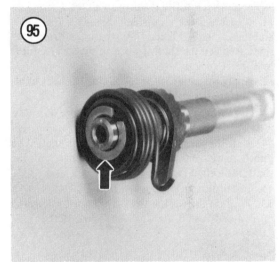

3. Slide off the spring retainer, ratchet spring and kickstarter ratchet from the shaft.

4. Clean all parts and the assembled shaft in solvent and dry with compressed air.

5. Remove the circlip and washer (**Figure 97**) from the shaft.

6. Check for chipped, broken or missing teeth on the gear (A, **Figure 98**); replace as necessary.

7. Inspect the ratchet surfaces (**Figure 99**) on both the kickstarter ratchet and the kickstarter drive gears. If either is worn or damaged, replace both as a set.

8. Make sure the kickstarter ratchet operates smoothly on the shaft.

9. Check all parts for uneven wear. Replace any that are questionable.

10. Measure the inside diameter of the kickstarter drive gear (B, **Figure 98**). Replace the gear if worn to the service limit in **Table 1** or more.

11. Measure the outside diameter of the kickstarter shaft (**Figure 100**) where the drive gear rides. Replace the shaft if worn to the service limit in **Table 1** or less.

12. Apply assembly oil to all sliding surfaces of all parts before assembly.

13. Install the washer and circlip (**Figure 97**) onto the shaft.

14. Slide the kickstarter ratchet onto the shaft. The punch marks on the kickstarter ratchet and the shaft must align (**Figure 101**).

15. Install the spring (**Figure 102**).

16. Position the washer with the cupped side going on first and install the washer (**Figure 103**).

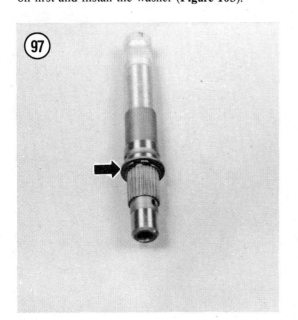

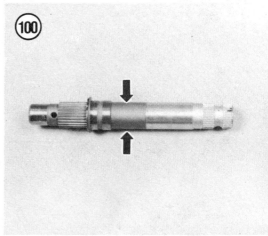

17. Install the return spring onto the kickstarter shaft and hook the inner end of the spring into the hole in the kickstarter shaft (**Figure 104**).

18. Slide the spring guide (**Figure 95**) onto the kickstarter shaft and into the return spring. Make sure the notch in the spring guide fits around the inner end of the return spring.

Installation

1. Install the kickstarter shaft assembly into the crankcase and hook the end of the spring onto the post on the crankcase (**Figure 105**).

2. Temporarily install the kickstarter lever (**Figure 106**) and rotate the lever about 180° *clockwise* or until the kickstarter pawl engages the post on the

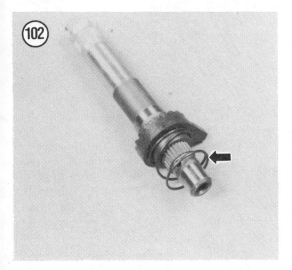

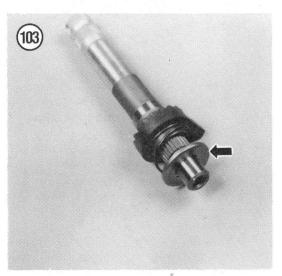

crankcase (**Figure 107**). Push the kickstarter shaft in all the way until it bottoms out.

3. Remove the kickstarter lever.

4. Install the guide plate and screws. Tighten the screws securely.

5. Position the kickstarter drive gear with the ratchet gear side going on first and install the drive gear (**Figure 92**) onto the kickstarter shaft.

6A. On 1985 3-wheeled models, slide the washer, collar and second washer onto the kickstarter shaft.

6B. On 1988-on 4-wheeled models, slide the collar and washer onto the kickstarter shaft.

6C. On all other models, slide the collar (**Figure 91**) onto the kickstarter shaft.

7. Install the clutch as described in Chapter Five.

CRANKCASE AND CRANKSHAFT

Disassembly of the crankcase—splitting the cases—and removal of the crankshaft assembly require that the engine be removed from the frame.

The crankcase is made in 2 halves of precision diecast aluminum alloy and is of the "thin-walled" type. To avoid damage do not hammer or pry on any of the interior or exterior projected walls. These areas are easily damaged. They are assembled with a gasket between the 2 halves and 2 dowel pins align the crankcase halves when they are bolted together.

The crankshaft assembly is made up of 2 full-circle flywheels pressed together on a hollow crankpin. The connecting rod big end bearing on the crankpin is a needle bearing assembly. The crankshaft assembly is supported in 2 ball bearings in the crankcase. Service to the crankshaft assembly is limited to removal and replacement.

The procedure which follows is presented as a complete, step-by-step, major lower end rebuild

that should be followed if an engine is to be completely reconditioned. However, if you're replacing a part that you know is defective, the disassembly should be carried out only until the failed part is accessible. There is no need to disassemble the engine beyond that point so long as you know the remaining components are in good condition and that they were not affected by the failed part.

Crankcase Disassembly

1. Remove the engine as described in this chapter.
2. If not already removed, remove all exterior engine assemblies as described in this chapter and other related chapters.
   a. Cylinder head.
   b. Cylinder.

c. Piston.

d. Alternator rotor and stator assembly.

e. Clutch assembly.

f. Balancer assembly (including the bearing holder).

g. External shift mechanism.

h. Drive sprocket.

3. On the left-hand crankcase side, remove the bolts securing the crankcase halves together (**Figure 108**). To prevent warpage, loosen them in a crisscross pattern. Don't lose the electrical wire harness clip (A, **Figure 108**) under one of the bolts. Be sure to install the clip in the same position during assembly.

NOTE
*Set the engine on wood blocks or fabricate a holding fixture of 2×4 inch wood as shown in **Figure 109**.*

CAUTION
*Perform the next step directly over and close to the workbench as the crankcase halves may easily separate. Do **not** hammer on the crankcase halves or they will be damaged.*

4. Hold onto the right-hand crankcase and studs and tap on the left-hand end of the crankshaft and transmission shaft with a plastic or soft-faced mallet until the crankshaft and crankcase separate.

CAUTION
Never pry between case halves. Doing so may result in oil leaks, requiring replacement of the case halves.

5. If the crankcase and crankshaft will not separate using this method, check to make sure that all screws are removed. If all screws are removed, install a crankcase separating tool onto the right-hand crankcase half (**Figure 110**). Use Honda part No. 07937-4300000 or equivalent.

CAUTION
*While tightening the center bolt make sure the disassembler body is kept parallel to the crankcase surface (**Figure 111**). Otherwise, it will put an uneven stress on the case halves and damage them.*

6. Don't lose the 2 locating dowels if they came out of the case. They do not have to be removed from the case if they are secure.

7. Lift up and carefully remove the transmission, shift drum, shift fork shaft assemblies and cam stopper and spring as described in Chapter Five.

8. Removal and installation of the crankshaft assembly should be entrusted to a Honda dealer as special tools and a hydraulic press are required for both removal and installation.

9. Inspect the crankcase halves and crankshaft as described in this chapter.

Crankcase Assembly

1. Make sure all old sealant material is removed from both crankcase halves. Clean the mating surfaces of both crankcase halves with contact cleaner. Make sure you get an air-tight, leak-free seal.

2. Apply assembly oil to the inner race of all bearings in both crankcase halves.

> *NOTE*
> *Set the left-hand crankcase half assembly on wood blocks or the wood holding fixture shown in the disassembly procedure.*

3. If the crankshaft was removed, have it installed by a Honda dealer as special tools are required to pull the crankshaft into the crankshaft main bearing in the left-hand crankcase half (**Figure 112**).

> *CAUTION*
> *Do not attempt to drive the crankshaft into the left-hand main bearing with a hammer or mallet or the crankshaft alignment will be disturbed.*

4. Install the transmission assemblies, shift shafts and shift drum in the left-hand crankcase half and lightly oil all shaft ends. Refer to Chapter Five for the correct procedure.

5. Make sure the crankshaft spacer (**Figure 113**) is in place on the right-hand end of the crankshaft.

6. Install a new gasket (A, **Figure 114**).

7. Install the 2 locating dowels (B, **Figure 114**) if they were removed.

8. Set the right-hand crankcase half over the left-hand case on the blocks. Push the case half down squarely into place until it reaches the crankshaft bearing. There is usually about 1/2 inch left to go (**Figure 115**).

9. Lightly tap the case halves together with a plastic or soft-faced mallet until they seat.

> *CAUTION*
> *Crankcase halves should fit together without force. If the crankcase halves do not fit together completely, do not attempt to pull them together with the crankcase screws. Separate the crankcase halves and investigate the cause of the interference. If the transmission shafts were disassembled, recheck to make sure that a gear is not installed backwards. Do not risk damage by trying to force the cases together.*

10. Into the left-hand crankcase, install all of the crankcase screws only finger-tight.

11. Securely tighten the screws in 2 stages in a crisscross pattern until they are firmly hand tight.

12. After the crankcase halves are completely assembled, rotate the crankshaft and transmission shafts to make sure there is no binding. If any is present, disassemble the crankcase and correct the problem.

13. Trim off the excess gasket material (**Figure 116**) flush with the top surface of the crankcase. If not trimmed off, the cylinder base gasket will not seal properly.

14. Install the collar (**Figure 117**) onto the right-hand end of the crankshaft.

15. Install all exterior engine assemblies as described in this chapter and other related chapters.

   a. Cylinder head.
   b. Cylinder.
   c. Piston.
   d. Alternator stator and rotor.
   e. Clutch assembly.
   f. Balancer assembly (including bearing holder).
   g. External shift mechanism.
   h. Drive sprocket.

**Crankcase and
Crankshaft Inspection**

1. Clean both crankcase halves inside and out with cleaning solvent. Thoroughly dry with compressed air and wipe off with a clean shop cloth. Be sure to remove all traces of old gasket material from all mating surfaces.

2. Check the crankshaft, balancer, transmission and shift drum bearings for roughness, pitting, galling and play by rotating them slowly by hand. Refer to **Figure 118** and **Figure 119**. If any

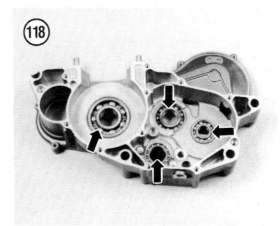

roughness or play can be felt in the bearing, it must be replaced.

3. Carefully inspect the cases for cracks and fractures, especially in the lower areas; they are vulnerable to rock damage. Also check the areas around the stiffening ribs, around bearing bosses and threaded holes. If any are found, have them repaired by a shop specializing in the repair of precision aluminum castings or replace them.

4. Make sure the crankcase studs (**Figure 120**) are tight in each case half. Retighten the studs if necessary.

5. Check the connecting rod big end bearing by grasping the rod (**Figure 121**) in one hand and lifting up on it. With the heel of your other hand, rap sharply on the top of the rod. A sharp metallic sound, such as a click, is an indication that the bearing or crankpin or both are worn and the crankshaft assembly should be replaced.

> *NOTE*
> *Other inspections of the crankshaft assembly involve accurate measuring equipment and should be entrusted to a dealer or competent machine shop. The crankshaft assembly operates under severe stress and dimensional tolerances are critical. These dimensions are given in **Table 1**. If any are off by the slightest amount, it may cause a considerable amount of damage or destruction of the engine. The crankshaft assembly must be replaced as a unit as it cannot be serviced without the aid of a 10-12 ton (9,000-11,000 kilogram) capacity press, holding fixtures and crankshaft jig.*

6. Inspect the oil seals (**Figure 122**). They should be replaced every time the crankcase is disassembled. Refer to *Bearing and Oil Seal Replacement* in this chapter.

Bearing and Oil Seal Replacement

1. Pry out the oil seals (**Figure 122**) with a small screwdriver, taking care not to damage the crankcase bore. If the seals are old and difficult to remove, heat the cases as described in Step 2 and use an awl to punch a small hole in the steel backing of the seal. Install a small sheet metal screw part way into the seal and pull the seal out with a pair of pliers.

> *CAUTION*
>
> *Do not install the screw too deep or it may contact and damage the bearing behind it.*

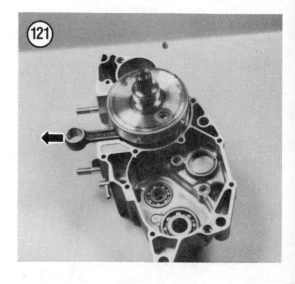

2. On bearings so equipped, remove the bearing retainer screws and retainers (**Figure 123**).

> *CAUTION*
> *There **may** be a residual oil or solvent odor left in the oven after heating the crankcases. If you use a household oven, first check with the person who uses the oven for food preparation to avoid getting into trouble.*

3. The bearings are installed with a slight interference fit. The crankcase must be heated in an oven to a temperature of about 100° C (212° F). An easy way to check the proper temperature is to drop tiny drops of water on the case. If they sizzle and evaporate immediately, the temperature is correct. Heat only one case at a time.

> *CAUTION*
> *Do not heat the cases with a torch (propane or acetylene). Never bring a flame into contact with the bearing or case. The direct heat will destroy the case hardening of the bearing and will likely cause warpage of the case.*

4. Remove the case from the oven and hold onto the 2 crankcase studs with a kitchen pot holder, heavy gloves or heavy shop cloths—it is *hot*.

5. Remove the oil seals if not already removed (see Step 1).

6. Hold the crankcase with the bearing side down and tap it squarely on a piece of soft wood. Continue to tap until the bearing(s) fall out. Repeat for the other half.

> *CAUTION*
> *Be sure to tap the crankcase squarely on the piece of wood. Avoid damaging the sealing surface of the crankcase.*

7. If the bearings are difficult to remove, they can be gently tapped out with a socket or piece of pipe the same size as the bearing outer race.

> *CAUTION*
> *If the bearings or seals are difficult to remove or install, don't take a chance on expensive damage. Have the work performed by a dealer or competent machine shop.*

8. While heating up the crankcase halves, place the new bearings in a freezer if possible. Chilling them will slightly reduce their overall diameter while the hot crankcase is slightly larger due to heat expansion. This will make bearing installation much easier.

9. While the crankcase is still hot, press each new bearing(s) into place in the crankcase by hand until it seats completely. Do not hammer it in. If the bearing will not seat, remove it and cool it again. Reheat the crankcase and install the bearing again.

10. Oil seals are best installed with a special tool available at a dealer or motorcycle supply store. However, a proper size socket or piece of pipe can be substituted. Make sure that the bearings and seals are not cocked in the crankcase hole and that they are seated properly.

11. On bearings so equipped, install the retainers and screws. Tighten the screws securely.

BREAK-IN PROCEDURE

If the rings were replaced, new piston installed, the cylinder rebored or honed or major lower end work performed, the engine should be broken in just as though it were new. The performance and service life of the engine depends greatly on a careful and sensible break-in.

CAUTION
Do not allow the engine to idle for any length of time. Run the throttle up a few times to speed up the water pump impeller. At idle speed the water pump impeller is not rotating fast enough to circulate the coolant and keep the cylinder cool.

For the first 5-10 hours of operation, no more than one-third throttle should be used and speed should be varied as much as possible within the one-third throttle limit. Prolonged steady running at one speed, no matter how moderate, is to be avoided as well as hard acceleration.

Following the first 5-10 hours, more throttle should not be used until the ATV has run for 100 hours and then it should be limited to short bursts of speed until 150 hours have been logged.

Table 1 ENGINE SPECIFICATIONS

Item	Specifications	Wear limit
General		
Engine type	Water-cooled, 2-stroke, single cylinder	
Bore and stroke	66×72 mm (2.60×2.83 in.)	
Displacement	246 cc (15.0 cu. in.)	
Compression ratio		
ATC250R	8.0 to 1	
TRX250R/Fourtrax 250R		
1986	7.5 to 1	
1987-on	7.7 to 1	
Lubrication	Fuel:oil mixture	
Air filtration	Foam element type	
Cylinder		
Bore	66.020-66.040 mm (2.599-2.600 in.)	66.07 mm (2.601 in.)
Taper	—	0.03 mm (0.001 in.)
Out-of-round	—	0.03 mm (0.001 in.)
Piston/cylinder clearance	0.060-0.080 mm (0.0024-0.0031 in.)	0.14 mm (0.006 in.)
Piston		
Diameter	65.94-65.96 mm (2.596-2.597 in.)	65.88 mm (2.594 in.)
Piston pin bore	18.007-18.013 mm (0.7089-0.7092 in.)	18.03 mm (0.409 in.)
Piston pin outer diameter	17.994-18.000 mm (0.7084-0.7087 in.)	17.98 mm (0.708 in.)
Piston-to-piston pin clearance	0.007-0.019 mm (0.0002-0.00075 in.)	0.03 mm (0.0012 in.)
Piston rings		
Number per piston		
Compression	2	
Ring end gap	0.20-0.40 mm (0.01-0.02 in.)	0.5 mm (0.02 in.)
Ring side clearance	0.045-0.075 mm (0.0018-0.0030 in.)	0.095 mm (0.0037 in.)
Connecting rod		
Small end inner diameter	21.997-22.009 mm (0.8860-0.8665 in.)	22.022 mm (0.8670 in.)
Crankshaft		
Journal runout	—	0.05 mm (0.002 in.)
Big end radial runout	0.010-0.022 mm (0.0004-0.0009 in.)	0.040 mm (0.002 in.)
		(continued)

Table 1 ENGINE SPECIFICATIONS (continued)

Item	Specifications	Wear limit
Connecting rod big end side clearance	0.20-0.60 mm (0.010-0.020 in.)	1.0 mm (0.040 in.)
Cylinder head warpage	0.05 mm (0.002 in.)	0.07 mm (0.003 in.)
Kickstarter shaft OD	21.959-21.980 mm (0.8645-0.8654 in.)	21.94 mm (0.864 in.)
Kickstarter gear ID	20.020-20.041 mm (0.7882-0.7890 in.)	20.060 mm (0.869 in.)

Table 2 ENGINE TORQUE SPECIFICATIONS

Item	N•m	ft.-lb.
Engine mounting brackets		
8 mm bolts	25-35	18-25
10 mm bolts	50-60	36-43
Cylinder head nuts	24-29	17-21
Cylinder base nuts	38-48	27-35
Alternator rotor	65-75	47-54
Primary drive gear bolt	40-50	29-36
Drive sprocket nut	30-34	22-25

CHAPTER FIVE

CLUTCH AND TRANSMISSION

This chapter contains service procedures for the clutch assembly, shift mechanism and the transmissions. **Tables 1-4** are at the end of this chapter.

CLUTCH OPERATION

The clutch is a wet multiplate type that is mounted on the right-hand end of the transmission countershaft. The inner clutch hub is splined to the countershaft and the outer clutch housing can rotate freely on the countershaft. The outer clutch housing is geared to the crankshaft via the primary drive gear.

The clutch release mechanism is mounted within the crankcase on the left-hand side and is operated by the clutch cable and hand lever mounted on the handlebar.

CLUTCH

Removal/Disassembly

Refer to **Figure 1** for this procedure.

1. Place the ATV on level ground and set the parking brake.
2. Remove the seat/rear fender assembly as described in Chapter Twelve.
3. Remove the clamping bolt (**Figure 2**) on the kickstarter lever and remove the lever.
4. On 3-wheeled models remove the rear brake pedal assembly as described in Chapter Eleven.

5. Drain the cooling system as described in Chapter Three.
6. Drain the transmission/clutch oil as described in Chapter Three.
7. Loosen the clamping bolts (**Figure 3**) on the water pump coolant hoses and carefully remove both hoses from the water pump.
8. Remove the bolts securing the water pump cover (**Figure 4**) and remove the cover and gasket. Don't lose the locating dowels. The water pump cover is removed to gain access to the water pump impeller during the installation procedure. There are *no* hidden clutch cover bolts under this cover.
9. Remove the bolts securing the clutch cover (**Figure 5**) and remove the clutch cover and gasket. Don't lose the locating dowels.
10. Using a crisscross pattern, remove the clutch bolts (**Figure 6**) securing the clutch pressure plate and remove the springs (**Figure 7**) and the pressure plate (**Figure 8**).
11. Slide off the clutch plates and friction discs.

12A. On 3-wheeled models and 1986 4-wheeled models, remove the clutch lifter (**Figure 9**), steel ball (**Figure 10**) and lifter rod (**Figure 11**).

12B. On 1987-1988 models, remove the clutch lifter and lifter rod.

12C. On 1989 models, remove the washer (C, **Figure 12**), needle bearing (B, **Figure 12**) and the clutch lifter (A, **Figure 12**).

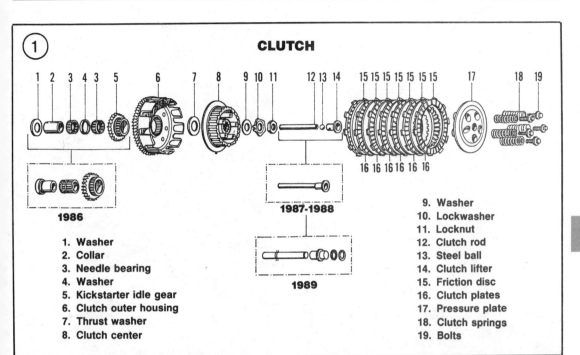

CLUTCH

1986

1987-1988

1989

1. Washer
2. Collar
3. Needle bearing
4. Washer
5. Kickstarter idle gear
6. Clutch outer housing
7. Thrust washer
8. Clutch center

9. Washer
10. Lockwasher
11. Locknut
12. Clutch rod
13. Steel ball
14. Clutch lifter
15. Friction disc
16. Clutch plates
17. Pressure plate
18. Clutch springs
19. Bolts

5

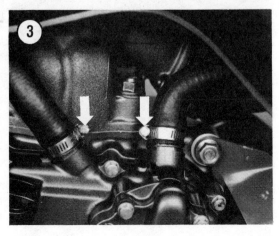

13. Straighten the tab on the lockwasher.

NOTE
The special tool used in the next step is the Grabbit, available from Joe Bolger Products Inc., Summer Street, Barre MA 01005.

14. Install the Grabbit special tool onto the clutch center (**Figure 13**). Do *not* install the Grabbit too tightly or the jaws will gouge the inner splines in the clutch center. This special tool will keep the clutch center from turning during the next step.

15. Remove the locknut, lockwasher and washer (**Figure 14**) securing the clutch center. Discard the lockwasher as a new one must be installed.

16. Remove the Grabbit special tool.

17. Remove the clutch center (**Figure 15**).

18. Remove the thrust washer (**Figure 16**).

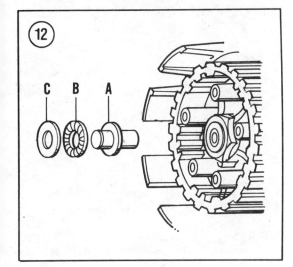

19. Remove the clutch outer housing (**Figure 17**).

20. Remove the kickstarter idle gear (**Figure 18**).

21A. On 1985 3-wheeled models, remove the needle bearing, washer, needle bearing, clutch outer guide and thrust washer.

21B. On all other models remove the needle bearings (**Figure 19**) and clutch outer guide (**Figure 20**).

22. Inspect all components as described in this chapter.

Assembly/Installation

Refer to **Figure 1** for this procedure.

NOTE
If new friction discs and clutch plates are being installed, apply new engine oil to all surfaces to avoid having the clutch lock up when used for the first time.

1A. On 1985 3-wheeled models, install the thrust washer, clutch outer guide, needle bearing, washer and needle bearing.

1B. On all other models, install the clutch outer
guide (**Figure 20**) with the flange side on first, then
install the needle bearings (**Figure 19**).

2. Position the kickstarter idle gear with the larger
diameter gear going on first and install the
kickstarter idle gear (**Figure 18**). Make sure the
kickstarter idle gear is meshed properly with the
kickstarter driven gear.

3. Install the clutch outer housing (**Figure 17**).

4. Install the thrust washer (**Figure 16**).

5. Install the clutch center (**Figure 15**) and washer
(**Figure 21**).

6. Align the tab of the lockwasher with the groove
in the clutch center (**Figure 22**) and install a new
lockwasher.

7. Use the same tool set-up as used in *Removal*
Step 10.

8. Install the locknut (**Figure 14**) and tighten to the
torque specification listed in **Table 1**. Remove the
Grabbit special tool.

9. Bend down the tabs on the new lockwasher onto
the flats on the locknut.

10A. On 3-wheeled models and 1986 4-wheeled
models, install the lifter rod (**Figure 11**), steel ball
(**Figure 10**) and the clutch lifter (**Figure 9**).

10B. On 1987-1988 models, install the clutch lifter
rod and lifter.

10C. On 1989 models, install the clutch lifter (A,
Figure 12), the needle bearing (B, **Figure 12**) and
the washer (C, **Figure 12**).

11. Install a friction disc (**Figure 23**) and then a
clutch plate (**Figure 24**) onto the clutch center.
Continue to install a friction disc, then a clutch
plate and alternate them until all are installed. The
last item installed is a friction disc (**Figure 25**).

12. Install the pressure plate (**Figure 8**).

13. Place a copper washer (**Figure 26**), or copper penny, between the clutch outer housing and the balancer drive gear. This will prevent the clutch outer housing from rotating during the following steps.

14. Install the clutch springs (**Figure 7**) and bolts (**Figure 6**). Tighten the bolts securely in a crisscross pattern in 2-3 steps.

15. Install a new clutch cover gasket (A, **Figure 27**) and locating dowels (B, **Figure 27**) onto the crankcase.

16. Align the groove in the water pump drive shaft (**Figure 28**) with the raised tab on the water pump drive (part of the balancer gear) (**Figure 29**).

> *CAUTION*
> *The clutch cover should fit snugly against the crankcase without force. In the Step 16, if the water pump drive shaft and water pump drive are **not** properly meshed, the front portion of the clutch cover will not fit snugly against the crankcase. Remove the clutch cover and realign the 2 parts, then reinstall the clutch cover. Do not try to force the cover against the crankcase with the cover bolts as the cover will be damaged.*

17. Install the clutch cover and make sure the water pump drive shaft is properly meshed with the water pump drive. If alignment is not correct, slightly wiggle the water pump impeller until the 2 parts mesh properly. When the clutch cover fits properly against the crankcase then install the cover bolts and tighten all bolts securely.

18. Install a new water pump cover gasket (A, **Figure 30**) and if removed, install the locating dowels (B, **Figure 30**).

19. Install the cover (**Figure 4**) and tighten the screws securely.

20. Install the coolant hoses to the water pump and tighten the clamping bolts securely.

21. Install the kickstarter lever and pinch bolt. Tighten the bolt to the torque specification listed in **Table 1**.

22. On 3-wheeled models, install the rear brake pedal assembly as described in Chapter Eleven.

23. Refill the cooling system as described in Chapter Three.

24. Refill the tranmission/clutch with the recommended type and quantity of engine oil as described in Chapter Three.

25. Adjust the clutch as described in Chapter Three.

Clutch Inspection

1. Clean all parts in a petroleum based solvent such as kerosene and thoroughly dry with compressed air.

2. Measure the free length of each clutch spring as shown in **Figure 31**. If any of the springs are worn to service limit listed in **Table 2** or less, replace all springs as a set.

3. Measure the thickness of each friction disc at several places around the disc as shown in **Figure 32**. Replace any disc that is worn to the service limit listed in **Table 2** or less. For optimum performance, replace all discs as a set even if only a few need replacement.

4. Check the clutch plates for warpage on a surface plate such as a piece of plate glass (**Figure 33**). Replace any that are warped to the service limit listed in **Table 2** or more. For optimum performance, replace all plates as a set even if only a few need replacement.

5. Inspect the grooves and studs in the pressure plate. Refer to **Figure 34**. If either show signs of wear or galling the plate should be replaced.

5

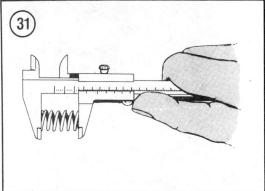

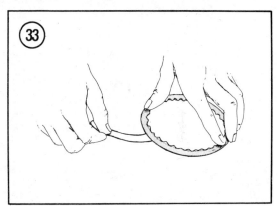

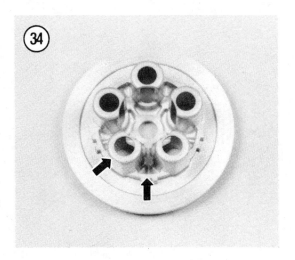

6. Inspect the inner splines and outer grooves in the clutch center. Refer to **Figure 35** or **Figure 36**. If damaged, the clutch center should be replaced.

7. Inspect the teeth on the clutch outer housing and the kickstarter idle gear (**Figure 37**). Remove any small nicks on the gear teeth with an oilstone. If damage is severe, the clutch housing and/or kickstarter idle gear should be replaced.

8. Inspect the splines of the clutch outer housing (**Figure 38**) and the kickstarter idle gear (**Figure 39**) for wear or damage. If damage is severe, the clutch housing and/or kickstarter idle gear should be replaced.

9. Inspect the slots in the clutch outer housing for cracks, nicks or galling where they come in contact with the friction disc tabs (**Figure 40**). If any severe damage is evident, the clutch housing must be replaced.

10. Examine the bearing cages for cracks at the corner of the needle slots (**Figure 41**) and inspect the needles themselves for damage. If any damage is evident, the bearing(s) must be replaced.

11. Measure the inside diameter of the kickstarter idle gear (A, **Figure 39**). If worn to the service limit dimension listed in **Table 2** or more, replace the kickstarter idle gear.

12. Measure the inside diameter of the clutch outer housing guide (**Figure 42**). If worn to the service limit dimension listed in **Table 2** or more, replace the kickstarter idle gear.

CLUTCH RELEASE MECHANISM

The clutch release mechanism is mounted within the left-hand crankcase half. When the clutch lever

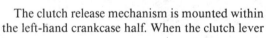

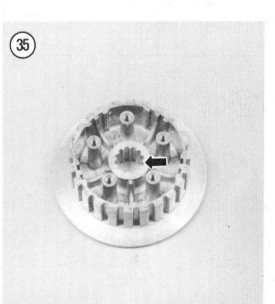

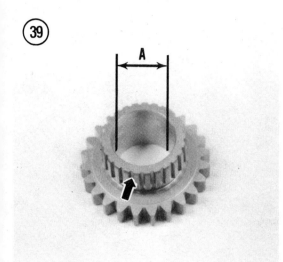

is pulled, the cable moves the clutch release arm. The release arm rotates and pushes in on the clutch lifter rod, thus actuating the clutch.

Removal/Installation

1. Slide back the rubber boot (**Figure 43**). Loosen the clutch cable locknut (A, **Figure 44**) and adjuster (B, **Figure 44**) at the clutch lever on the handlebar to allow slack in the clutch cable.

2. Loosen the locknut (A, **Figure 45**) and the cable adjuster (B, **Figure 45**). Then disconnect the clutch cable from the clutch release lever on the crankcase.

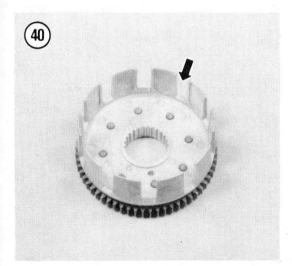

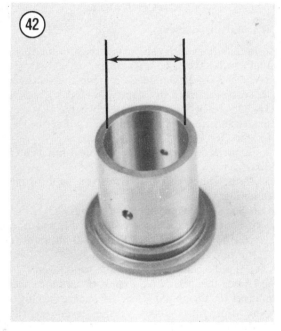

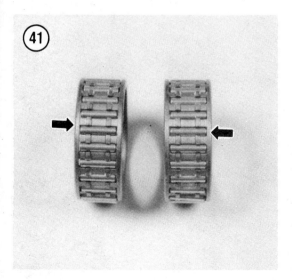

3. Perform Steps 1-13 of *Clutch Removal/Disassembly* as described in this chapter.

4. Withdraw the clutch release arm and return spring from the crankcase (**Figure 46**).

5. Inspect the oil seal in the recess in the top of the crankcase; replace if necessary.

6. Inspect all moving parts and the spring (**Figure 47**); replace if necessary.

7. Install by reversing these removal steps, noting the following.

8. Hook the return spring onto the boss on the top of the crankcase.

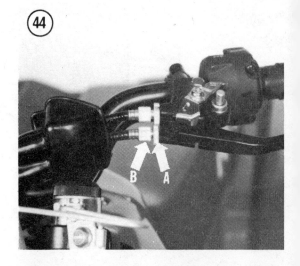

CLUTCH CABLE

Removal/Installation

In time the clutch cable will stretch to the point that it will have to be replaced.

1A. On 3-wheeled models, remove the seat/rear fender as described in Chapter Twelve.

1B. On 4-wheeled models, remove the seat/rear fender and front fender assembly as described in Chapter Twelve.

2. Remove the fuel tank as described in Chapter Six.

3. At the clutch/parking brake lever, perform the following.

    a. Slide back the rubber boot (**Figure 43**).

    b. Loosen the locknut (A, **Figure 44**) and turn the adjuster barrel (B, **Figure 44**) all the way toward the cable sheath.

    c. Slip the cable end out of the hand lever.

4. Loosen the locknut (A, **Figure 45**) and the cable adjuster (B, **Figure 45**). Then disconnect the clutch cable from the clutch release lever on the crankcase.

5. Remove the retaining straps securing the clutch cable to the frame.

NOTE
The piece of string attached in the next step will be used to pull the new clutch cable back through the frame so it will be routed in the exact same position.

6. Tie a piece of heavy string or cord (approximately 7 ft./2.0 m long) to the clutch mechanism end of the cable. Wrap this end with masking or duct tape. Do not use an excessive amount of tape. Tie the other end of the string to the foot peg or frame.

7. At the handlebar end of the cable, carefully pull the cable and attached string out through the frame. Make sure the attached string follows the

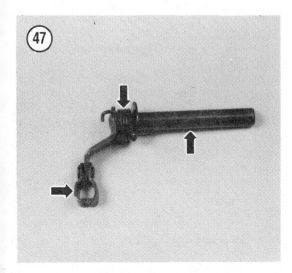

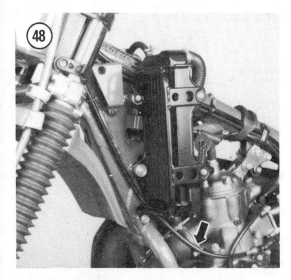

same path of the cable through the frame. Refer to **Figure 48** for 3-wheeled models or **Figure 49** for 4-wheeled models.

8. Remove the tape and untie the string from the old cable.

9. Lubricate the new cable as described under *Control Cables* in Chapter Three.

10. Tie the string to the clutch release mechanism end of the new clutch cable and wrap it with tape.

11. Carefully pull the string back through the frame, routing the new cable through the same path as the old cable.

12. Remove the tape and untie the string from the cable and the footpeg or frame. Attach the new cable to the clutch release arm and the clutch cover bracket.

13. Install all clutch cable retaining straps onto the frame.

14. Install the fuel tank as described in Chapter Six.

15A. On 3-wheeled models, install the seat/rear fender as described in Chapter Twelve.

15B. On 4-wheeled models, install the seat/rear fender and front fender assembly as described in Chapter Twelve.

16. Adjust the clutch cable as described in Chapter Three.

EXTERNAL SHIFT MECHANISM

The external shift mechanism is located on the same side of the crankcase as the clutch assembly and can be removed with the engine in the frame. This procedure is shown with the engine removed from the frame for clarity. To remove the shift drum and shift forks it is necessary to remove the engine and split the crankcase. This procedure is covered under *Internal Shift Mechanism* in this chapter.

NOTE
The gearshift lever is subject to a lot of abuse. If the ATV has been in a hard spill, the gearshift lever may have been hit and the shift shaft bent. It is very hard to straighten the shaft without subjecting the crankcase to abnormal stress where the shaft enters the case. If the shaft is bent enough to prevent it from being withdrawn from the crankcase, there is little recourse but to cut the shaft off with a hacksaw very close to the crankcase. It is much cheaper in the long run to replace the shaft than risk damaging a very expensive crankcase assembly.

5

Removal

Refer to **Figure 50** for this procedure.
1. Place the ATV on level ground and set the parking brake.
2. Shift the transmission into NEUTRAL.
3. Remove the clutch as described in this chapter.
4. On 4-wheeled models, remove the right-hand footpeg and rear brake pedal assembly as described in Chapter Eleven.
5. Remove the clamping bolt on the gearshift lever (**Figure 51**). Remove the gearshift lever.

> *NOTE*
> *See the NOTE in the introduction to this procedure regarding a bent shaft if the assembly is difficult to remove.*

6. Withdraw the gearshift spindle assembly (**Figure 52**) from the crankcase.
7. Remove the collar (**Figure 53**) from the drum shifter.
8. Remove the bolts (A, **Figure 54**) securing the guide plate and remove the guide plate and drum shifter assembly (B, **Figure 54**). Remove the shift drum shifter from the guide plate and store in a spray paint can top to keep all components together.
9. Loosen the bolt (**Figure 55**) securing the stopper arm and remove the stopper arm, spring and washer.
10. Remove the bolt (A, **Figure 56**) securing the shift drum center (B, **Figure 56**). Remove the shift drum center and dowel pin.

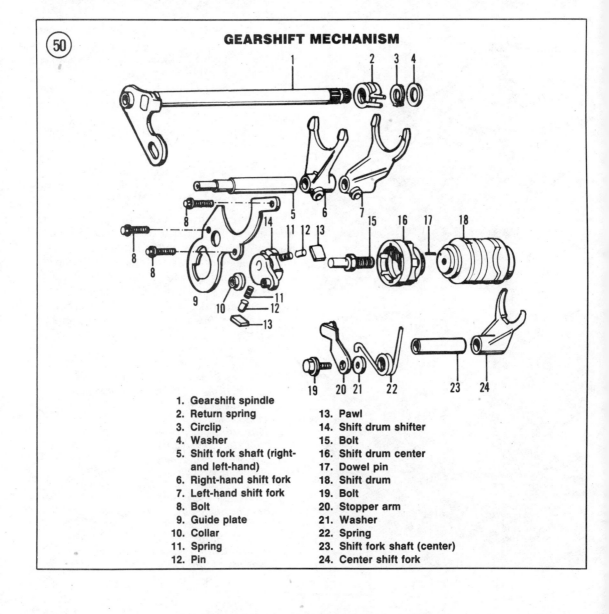

GEARSHIFT MECHANISM

1. Gearshift spindle
2. Return spring
3. Circlip
4. Washer
5. Shift fork shaft (right- and left-hand)
6. Right-hand shift fork
7. Left-hand shift fork
8. Bolt
9. Guide plate
10. Collar
11. Spring
12. Pin
13. Pawl
14. Shift drum shifter
15. Bolt
16. Shift drum center
17. Dowel pin
18. Shift drum
19. Bolt
20. Stopper arm
21. Washer
22. Spring
23. Shift fork shaft (center)
24. Center shift fork

5

Inspection

1. Inspect the return spring (**Figure 57**) on the gearshift spindle assembly. If broken or weak it must be replaced.

2. Inspect the gearshift lever assembly shaft (**Figure 58**) for bending, wear or other damage; replace, if necessary.

3. Disassemble the shift drum shifter (**Figure 59**) and inspect the pins, springs and pawls for wear or damage.

4. Assemble the shift drum shifter as follows.

    a. Install the springs and plungers into the shifter body (**Figure 60**).

    b. Install the pawls onto the pins and into the shifter body (**Figure 61**).

    c. Hold the pawls in place and place the assembly into the guide plate (**Figure 62**).

5. Inspect the parts of the stopper arm (**Figure 63**) for wear or damage. Replace any worn parts.

Installation

1. Install the dowel pin (**Figure 64**) into the shift drum.

2. Align the dowel pin hole in the shift drum center with the dowel pin and install the shift drum center (**Figure 65**).

3. Install the shift drum center bolt and tighten to the torque specification listed in **Table 1**.

4. Install the spring, washer and bolt onto the stopper arm. Install this assembly and partially screw the bolt into the crankcase (**Figure 66**) at this time. Correctly position the stopper arm onto the shift drum center (**Figure 67**), then tighten the bolt to the torque specification listed in **Table 2**.

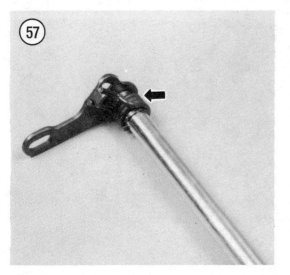

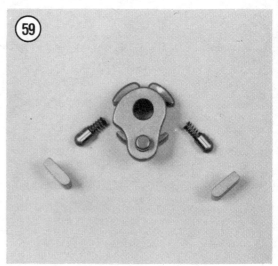

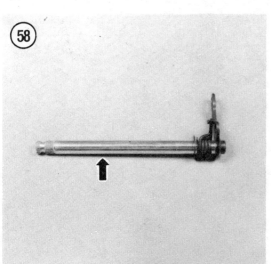

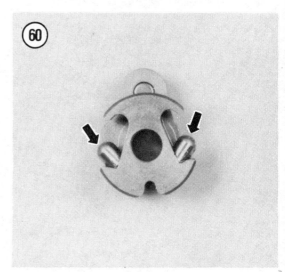

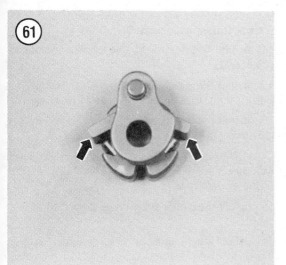

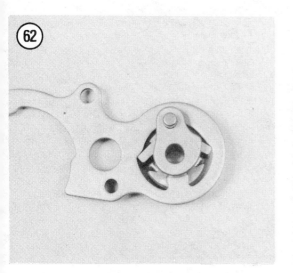

5

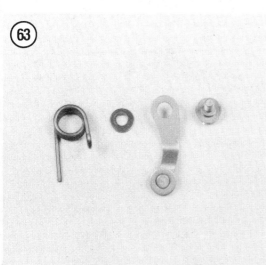

5. Partially install the drum shifter and the guide plate onto the shift drum (**Figure 68**).

6. Using 2 small flat-bladed screwdrivers, compress the spring-loaded shifting pawls into the drum shifter as shown in **Figure 69**.

7. Push the cam guide plate and shift drum shifter assembly down into position (B, **Figure 54**). Apply a light coat of blue Loctite (Lock N' Seal No. 2114) to the screws and install the screws (A, **Figure 54**). Tighten the screws securely.

8. Install the collar (**Figure 53**) onto the drum shifter.

9. Make sure the thrust washer (**Figure 70**) is in place on the gearshift spindle assembly.

10. Install the gearshift spindle assembly into the crankcase. Align the hole in the spindle arm with

the collar (**Figure 71**) on the drum shifter and push the gearshift spindle assembly all the way in.

11. Apply engine oil to the shift mechanism (**Figure 72**).

12. Install the gearshift lever and bolt. Tighten the bolt to the torque specification listed in **Table 1**.

13. Install the clutch assembly as described in this chapter.

14. On 4-wheeled models, install the right-hand foot peg and rear brake pedal assembly to the frame as described in Chapter Eleven.

15. Install the clutch assembly as described in this chapter.

16. Adjust the clutch as described in Chapter Three.

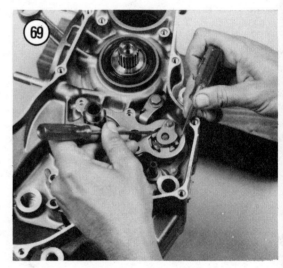

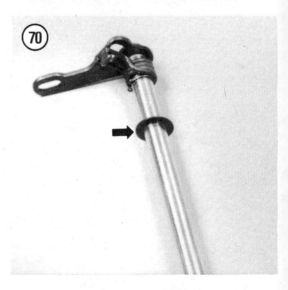

TRANSMISSION AND INTERNAL SHIFT MECHANISM

To gain access to the transmission and internal shift mechanism it is necessary to remove the engine and split the crankcase.

Refer to **Table 3** for specifications on the internal shift mechanism and **Table 4** for transmission specifications.

Refer to **Figure 73** for the transmission assemblies and **Figure 50** for the internal shift mechanism.

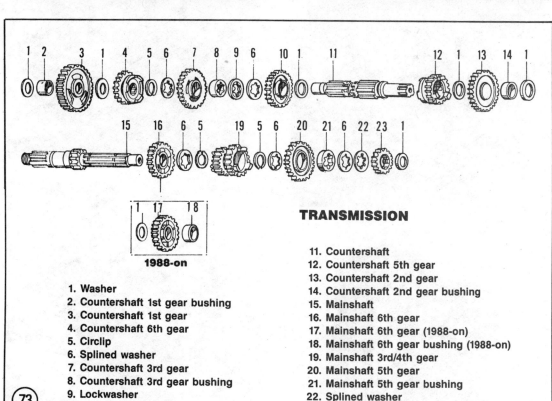

TRANSMISSION

1. Washer
2. Countershaft 1st gear bushing
3. Countershaft 1st gear
4. Countershaft 6th gear
5. Circlip
6. Splined washer
7. Countershaft 3rd gear
8. Countershaft 3rd gear bushing
9. Lockwasher
10. Countershaft 4th gear

11. Countershaft
12. Countershaft 5th gear
13. Countershaft 2nd gear
14. Countershaft 2nd gear bushing
15. Mainshaft
16. Mainshaft 6th gear
17. Mainshaft 6th gear (1988-on)
18. Mainshaft 6th gear bushing (1988-on)
19. Mainshaft 3rd/4th gear
20. Mainshaft 5th gear
21. Mainshaft 5th gear bushing
22. Splined washer
23. Mainshaft 2nd gear

1988-on

Removal

1. Remove the engine and split the crankcase as described in Chapter Four.
2. Withdraw the long and short shift fork shafts (A, **Figure 74**).
3. Swing the shift forks out of mesh with the shift drum.
4. Remove the shift drum (B, **Figure 74**). If not already removed, don't lose the pin on the end of the shift drum.
5. Remove the shift forks.
6. Remove both transmission assemblies (**Figure 75**).

Installation

1. Apply a liberal amount of molybdenum disulfide grease to the thrust washers to hold them in place on the end of both transmission assemblies (**Figure 76**).
2. Install the 2 transmission assemblies by meshing them together in their proper relationship to each other.

3. Hold onto the thrust washer on the end of the shaft assemblies and install both transmission assemblies into the left-hand crankcase.
4. After both assemblies are installed, tap on the end of both shafts (**Figure 77**) with a plastic or soft-faced mallet to make sure they are completely seated.
5. Coat all bearing and sliding surfaces of the shift drum with assembly oil.
6. Make sure that the thrust washer (**Figure 78**) is installed on the countershaft.
7. Install the center shift fork into position in its gear (**Figure 79**).
8. Install the shift drum (**Figure 80**).
9. Mesh the center shift fork with the shift drum (**Figure 81**) and install the *short* shift fork shaft (**Figure 82**).
10. Install the left shift fork (**Figure 83**) and the right shift fork (**Figure 84**) into their respective gears and into mesh with the shift drum.

5

11. Install the *long* shift fork shaft through the left and right shift forks (**Figure 85**).

12. Make sure all 3 cam pin followers are in mesh with the shift drum grooves.

> *NOTE*
> *The next procedure is best done with the aid of a helper as the assemblies are loose and won't spin very easily. Have the helper hold the crankcase and spin the transmission shaft while you turn the shift drum through all the gears.*

13. Turn the crankcase to a near vertical position. Do not try this step with the crankcase horizontal as the gears are loaded, by their own weight, in an abnormal way and will not shift easily, or in some cases will not shift at all. This may give a false impression that something is installed incorrectly.

14. Spin the transmission shafts and shift through the gears using the shift drum. Make sure you can shift into all gears. This is the time to find that something may be installed incorrectly—not after the crankcase is completely assembled.

15. Assemble the crankcase as described in Chapter Four.

Transmission
Preliminary Inspection

After the transmission shaft assemblies have been removed from the crankcase, clean and inspect the assemblies before disassembling them. Place the assembled shaft into a large can or plastic bucket and thoroughly clean with a petroleum based solvent such as kerosene and a stiff brush. Dry with compressed air or let it sit on rags to drip dry. Repeat for the other shaft assembly.

1. After they have been cleaned, visually inspect the components of the assemblies for excessive wear. Any burrs, pitting or roughness on the teeth of a gear will cause wear on the mating gear. Minor roughness can be cleaned up with an oilstone but there's little point in attempting to remove deep scars.

> *NOTE*
> *Defective gears should be replaced. It's a good idea to replace the mating gear on the other shaft even though it may not show as much wear or damage.*

2. Carefully check the engagement dogs. If any are chipped, worn, rounded or missing, the affected gear must be replaced.

3. Rotate the transmission bearings in both crankcases by hand. Check for roughness, noise and radial play. Any bearing that is suspect should be replaced as described in Chapter Four.

4. If the transmission shafts are satisfactory and are not going to be disassembled, apply assembly oil or engine oil to all components and reinstall them in the crankcase as described in this chapter.

> *NOTE*
> *If disassembling a used, well run-in (high mileage) transmission for the first time by yourself, pay particular attention to any additional shims that may have been added by a previous owner. These may have been added to take up the tolerance of worn components and must be reinstalled in the same position since the shims have developed a wear pattern. If new parts are going to be installed these shims may be eliminated. This is something you will have to determine upon reassembly.*

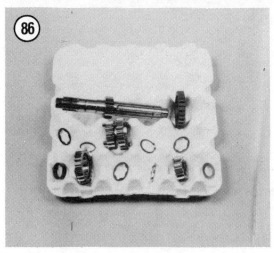

Mainshaft
Disassembly/Inspection

Refer to **Figure 73** for this procedure.

NOTE
*A helpful "tool" that should be used for transmission disassembly is a large egg flat (the type that restaurants get their eggs in) (**Figure 86**). As you remove a part from the shaft, set it in one of the depressions in the same position from which it was removed. This is an easy way to remember the correct relationship of all parts.*

NOTE
*On 4-wheeled models the mainshaft 5th and 6th gears are **not** interchangeable between 1986 and 1987 models. The 1987 model has one less tooth on each gear.*

1. Clean the assembled shaft as described under *Preliminary Inspection* in this chapter.
2. Slide off the thrust washer.

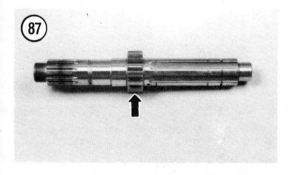

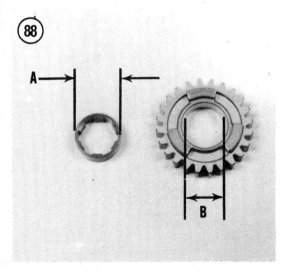

3. Slide off the 2nd gear.
4. Slide off the splined lockwasher. Rotate the splined washer in either direction to disengage the tangs from the grooves on the transmission shaft. Slide off the splined washer.
5. Slide off the 5th gear and 5th gear bushing.
6. Slide off splined washer.
7. Remove the circlip.
8. Slide off the 3rd/4th combination gear.
9. Remove the circlip and slide off the splined washer.
10A. On 1985-1987 models, slide off the 6th gear.
10B. On 1988-on models, slide off the 6th gear, the 6th gear bushing and the washer.
11. Check each gear for excessive wear, burrs, pitting or chipped or missing teeth. Make sure the lugs on the gears are in good condition.

NOTE
Defective gears should be replaced. It is a good idea to replace the mating gear on the countershaft even though it may not show as much wear or damage.

NOTE
*The first gear (**Figure 87**) is part of the mainshaft. If the gear is defective, the shaft must be replaced.*

12. Make sure all gears slide smoothly on the mainshaft splines.
13A. On 1985-1987 models, measure the outside diameter of the 5th gear bushing (A, **Figure 88**). Compare to dimensions listed in **Table 4**. If the bushing is worn to the service limit or less, replace the bushing.
13B. On 1988-on models, perform the following:
  a. Measure the outside diameter of the 5th and 6th gear bushings (A, **Figure 88**). Compare to dimensions listed in **Table 4**. If the bushing is worn to the service limit or less, replace the bushing.
  b. Measure the inside diameter of the 6th gear bushing. Compare to dimensions listed in **Table 4**. If the bushing is worn to the service limit or more, replace the bushing.
14. Measure the inside diameter of the 5th and 6th gears (B, **Figure 88**). Compare to dimensions listed in **Table 4**. If the gear is worn to the service limit or more, replace the gear.
15. Measure the outside diameter of the shaft at the location of the clutch outer guide (A, **Figure 89**) and the 6th gear (1985-1987 models) or 6th gear bushing (1988-on models) (B, **Figure 89**). Compare to dimensions listed in **Table 4**. If the shaft is worn to the service limit or less, replace the shaft.

NOTE
Honda suggests that all circlips be replaced every time the transmission is disassembled to ensure proper gear alignment. Do not expand a circlip more than necessary to slide it over the shaft.

Mainshaft Assembly

1A. On 1985-1987 models, slide on the 6th gear (A, **Figure 90**) and splined washer (B, **Figure 90**).
1B. On 1988-on models, slide on the washer, the 6th gear bushing, the 6th gear and the splined washer.

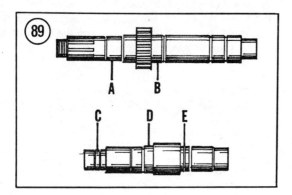

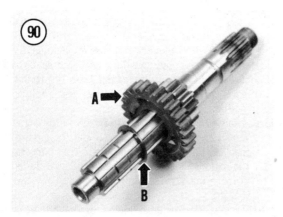

2. Install the circlip (**Figure 91**).
3. Slide on the 3rd/4th combination gear (**Figure 92**) with the smaller diameter gear going on first (**Figure 93**).
4. Install the circlip and thrust washer (**Figure 94**).

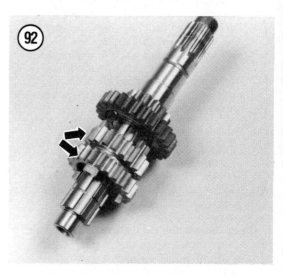

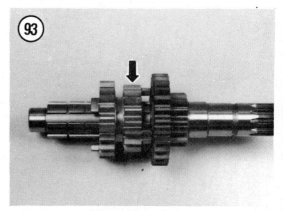

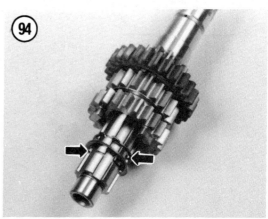

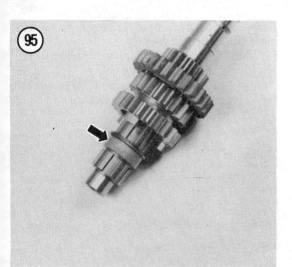

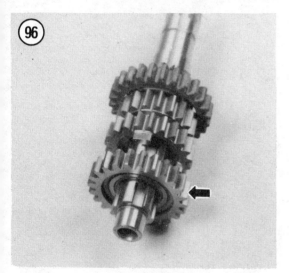

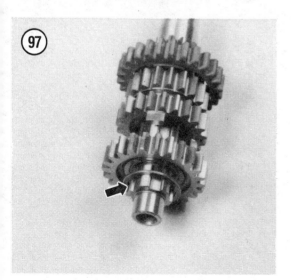

5. Slide on the 5th gear bushing (**Figure 95**) and the 5th gear (**Figure 96**).

6. Slide on the splined washer (**Figure 97**) and rotate it in either direction so its tangs are engaged in the groove in the transmission shaft (**Figure 98**).

7. Slide on the splined lockwasher (**Figure 99**) so that the tangs go into the open areas of the splined washer and lock the splined washer in place (**Figure 100**).

8. Position the 2nd gear with the flush side going on last and slide on the 2nd gear (**Figure 101**) and the thrust washer (**Figure 102**).

9. After assembly is complete check for correct placement of all gears (**Figure 103**).

10. Make sure all circlips are seated correctly in the mainshaft grooves.

Countershaft
Disassembly/Inspection

Refer to **Figure 73** for this procedure.

NOTE
A helpful "tool" that should be used for transmission disassembly is a large egg flat (the type that restaurants get their eggs in) as used in the mainshaft procedure.

NOTE
*On 4-wheeled models the countershaft 5th and 6th gears are **not** interchangeable between 1986 and 1987 models. The 1987 model has one less tooth on each gear.*

1. Clean the assembled shaft as described under *Preliminary Inspection* in this chapter.

2. Slide off the thrust washer, the 2nd gear and the 2nd bushing.

3. Slide off the thrust washer and the 5th gear.

4. From the other end of the shaft, remove the thrust washer.

5. Slide off the 1st gear and the 1st gear bushing.

6. Slide off the thrust washer and the 6th gear.

7. Remove the circlip and slide off the splined washer.

8. Slide off the 3rd gear and 3rd gear bushing.

9. Slide off the splined lockwasher. Rotate the splined washer in either direction to disengage the

tangs from the grooves on the transmission shaft. Slide off the splined washer.

10. Slide off the 4th gear and the thrust washer.

11. Check each gear for excessive wear, burrs, pitting, or chipped or missing teeth. Make sure the lugs on the gears are in good condition.

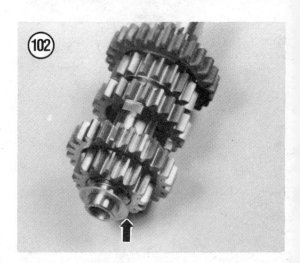

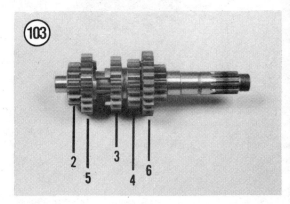

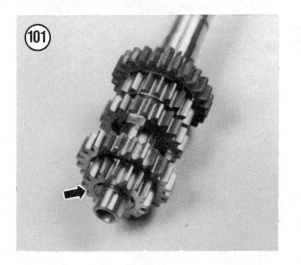

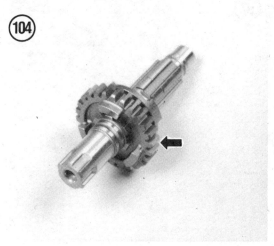

NOTE
Defective gears should be replaced. It is a good idea to replace the mating gear on the mainshaft even though it may not show as much wear or damage.

12. Make sure that all gears slide smoothly on the countershaft splines.

13. Measure the inside diameter of the 1st and 2nd gear bushings (A, **Figure 88**). Compare to dimensions listed in **Table 4**. If the bushing(s) are worn to the service limit or more, replace the bushing(s).

14. Measure the inside diameter of the 1st, 2nd, 3rd and 4th gears (B, **Figure 88**). Compare to dimensions listed in **Table 4**. If the gear(s) are worn to the service limit or more, replace the gear(s).

15. Measure the outside diameter of the 1st, 2nd and 3rd gear bushings. Compare to dimensions listed in **Table 4**. If the bushing(s) are worn to the service limit or less, replace the bushing(s).

16. Measure the outside diameter of the shaft at the location of the 1st gear (C, **Figure 89**), the 4th gear (D, **Figure 89**) and the 2nd gear (E, **Figure 89**). Compare to dimensions listed in **Table 4**. If the shaft is worn to the service limit or less, replace the shaft.

NOTE
Honda suggests that all circlips be replaced every time the transmission is disassembled to ensure proper gear alignment. Do not expand a circlip more than necessary to slide it over the shaft.

Countershaft Assembly

1. Install the 5th gear (**Figure 104**) and thrust washer (**Figure 105**).

2. Slide on the 2nd gear bushing (**Figure 106**) and the 2nd gear (**Figure 107**).

3. Slide on the thrust washer (**Figure 108**).

4. Onto the other end of the shaft, slide on the thrust washer (**Figure 109**).

5. Position the 4th gear with the flush side going on last and slide on the 4th gear (**Figure 110**).

6. Slide on the splined washer (**Figure 111**) and rotate it in either direction so its tangs are engaged in the groove in the transmission shaft.

7. Slide on the splined lockwasher (**Figure 112**) so that the tangs go into the open areas of the splined washer and lock the splined washer in place.

8. Slide on the 3rd gear bushing (**Figure 113**).

9. Position the 3rd gear with the flush side going on first and slide on the 3rd gear (**Figure 114**).

10. Slide on the splined washer (**Figure 115**) and install the circlip (**Figure 116**).

11. Slide on the 6th gear (**Figure 117**) and the thrust washer (**Figure 118**).

12. Slide on the 1st gear bushing (**Figure 119**) and the 1st gear (**Figure 120**).

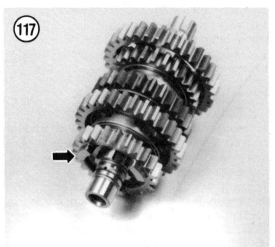

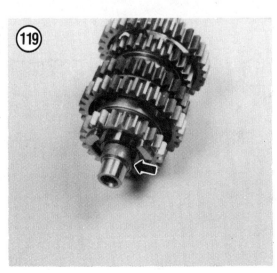

5

13. Slide on the thrust washer (**Figure 121**).

14. After assembly is complete, check for correct placement of all gears (**Figure 122**).

15. Make sure all circlips are seated correctly in the mainshaft grooves.

Internal Shift Mechanism Inspection

Refer to **Figure 50** for this procedure.

1. Inspect each shift fork for signs of wear or cracking. Check for bending and make sure each fork slides smoothly on its respective shaft. Replace any worn or damaged forks.

2. Check for any arc-shaped wear or burn marks on the shift forks (**Figure 123**). This indicates that the shift fork has come in contact with the gear. The fork fingers have become excessively worn and the fork must be replaced.

3. Check the shift fork dowel pins (**Figure 124**) for wear or damage; replace, as necessary.

4. Roll each shift fork shaft on a flat surface such as a piece of plate glass and check for any bends. If the shaft is bent, it must be replaced.

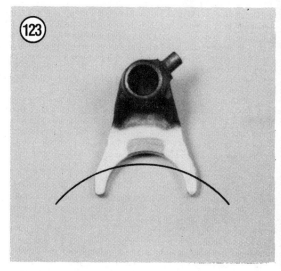

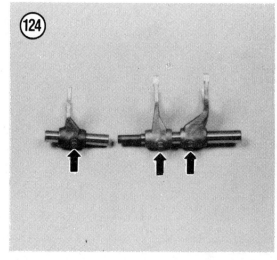

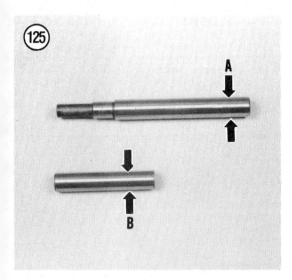

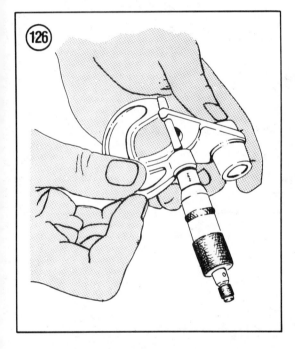

5. Measure the outside diameter of shift fork shafts with a micrometer. The mainshaft forkshaft is the long shaft (A, **Figure 125**) and the countershaft forkshaft is the short shaft (B, **Figure 125**) and is slightly bigger in diameter. Replace if worn to the service limit listed in **Table 3** or less.

6. Measure the thickness of the gearshift fork fingers with a micrometer (**Figure 126**). Replace the ones worn to the service limit listed in **Table 3** or less.

CAUTION
It is recommended that marginal shift forks be replaced. Worn forks can cause the transmission to slip out of gear, leading to more serious and expensive damage.

7. Check the grooves in the shift drum (**Figure 127**) for wear or roughness. If any of the groove profiles have excessive wear or damage, replace the shift drum.

8. Inspect the drum shifter recess (**Figure 128**) and the detents (**Figure 129**) for wear or damage. Replace the drum shifter if wear is evident.

9. Apply a light coat of oil to the shift fork shafts and the inside bores of the shift forks before installation.

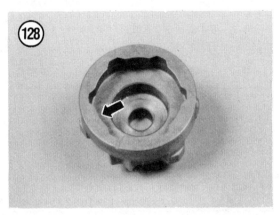

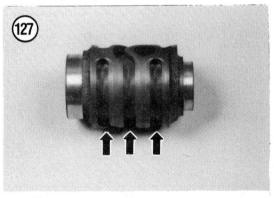

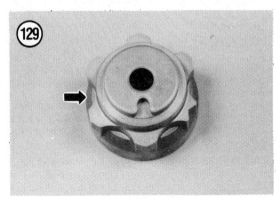

Table 1 CLUTCH AND EXTERNAL SHIFT MECHANISM TORQUE SPECIFICATIONS

Item	N•m	ft.-lb.
Clutch locknut	55-65	40-47
Kickstarter lever bolt	20-35	14-25
Shift drum center bolt	20-24	14-17
Stopper arm bolt	10-14	7-10
Gearshift lever bolt	10-14	7-10

Table 2 CLUTCH SPECIFICATIONS

Item	Standard	Wear limit
Friction disc thickness	2.92-3.08 mm (0.115-0.121 in.)	2.85 mm (0.112 in.)
Clutch plate warpage	—	0.15 mm (0.006 in.)
Clutch spring free length		
1985-1987	47 mm (1.85 in.)	45 mm (1.77 in.)
1988-on	48 mm (1.90 in.)	46 mm (1.81 in.)
Clutch outer housing guide outside diameter		
ATC250R	27.987-28.00 mm (1.1018-1.1023 in.)	27.97 mm (1.101 in.)
Clutch outer housing guide inside diameter		
TRX250R/Fourtrax 250R	23.000-23.021 mm (0.9055-0.9063 in.)	23.04 mm (0.907 in.)

Table 3 INTERNAL SHIFT MECHANISM SPECIFICATIONS

Item	Specifications	Wear limit
Shift fork ID		
Right- and left-hand	12.041-12.056 mm (0.4741-0.4746 in.)	12.09 mm (0.476 in.)
Center	11.041-11.056 mm (0.4347-0.4353 in.)	11.09 mm (0.436 in.)
Shift fork shaft OD		
Mainshaft fork shaft	10.983-10.994 mm (0.4324-0.4328 in.)	10.97 mm (0.432 in.)
Countershaft fork shaft	11.983-11.994 mm (0.4718-0.4722 in.)	11.97 mm (0.471 in.)
Shift fork fingers	4.93-5.00 mm (0.194-0.197 in.)	4.88 mm (0.192 in.)

Table 4 TRANSMISSION SPECIFICATIONS

Item	Specification	Wear limit
Gear ID mainshaft		
5th gear	28.007-28.028 mm	28.05 mm
	(1.1026-1.1035 in.)	(1.104 in.)
6th gear		
1985-1987	25.020-25.041 mm	25.06 mm
	(0.9850-0.9859 in.)	(0.987 in.)
1988-on	28.020-28.041 mm	28.06 mm
	(1.1031-1.1040 in.)	(1.105 in.)
Gear ID countershaft		
1st gear	22.020-22.041 mm	22.06 mm
	(0.8669-0.8678 in.)	(0.869 in.)
2nd gear	27.020-27.041 mm	27.06 mm
	(1.0638-1.0646 in.)	(1.065 in.)
3rd gear	28.020-28.041 mm	28.06 mm
	(1.1031-1.1040 in.)	(1.105 in.)
4th gear	25.020-25.041 mm	25.06 mm
	(0.9850-0.9859 in.)	(0.987 in.)
Gear bushing OD mainshaft		
5th gear	27.959-27.979 mm	27.94 mm
	(1.1007-1.1015 in.)	(1.100 in.)
6th gear (1988-on)	27.969-27.990 mm	27.95 mm
	(1.1011-1.1020 in.)	(1.100 in.)
Gear bushing ID countershaft		
1st gear	19.000-19.021 mm	19.04 mm
	(0.7480-0.7489 in.)	(0.750 in.)
2nd gear	24.000-24.021 mm	24.04 mm
	(0.9449-0.9457 in.)	(0.947 in.)
Gear bushing OD countershaft		
1st gear	21.979-22.000 mm	21.96 mm
	(0.8653-0.8661 in.)	(0.865 in.)
2nd gear	26.979-27.000 mm	26.96 mm
	(1.0622-1.0630 in.)	(1.061 in.)
3rd gear	27.959-27.979 mm	27.94 mm
	(1.1007-1.1015 in.)	(1.100 in.)
Mainshaft OD		
At location A		
(TRX250R/Fourtrax 250R		
only)	22.959-22.980 mm	22.94 mm
	(0.9039-0.9047 in.)	(0.903 in.)
At location B	24.959-24.980 mm	24.94 mm
	(0.9826-0.9835 in.)	(0.982 in.)
Countershaft OD		
At location C	18.959-18.980 mm	18.94 mm
	(0.7464-0.7472 in.)	(0.746 in.)
At location D	24.959-24.980 mm	24.94 mm
	(0.9826-0.9835 in.)	(0.982 in.)
At location E	23.959-23.980 mm	23.94 mm
	(0.9433-0.9441 in.)	(0.943 in.)

5

FUEL AND EXHAUST SYSTEMS

The fuel system consists of the fuel tank, the shutoff valve, a single carburetor and an air filter. There are 2 different carburetors used among the various models.

The exhaust system consists of an exhaust chamber, a muffler and a spark arrester.

This chapter includes service procedures for all parts of the fuel system and exhaust system. Air filter service is covered in Chapter Three.

Carburetor specifications are covered in **Table 1**. **Tables 1-7** are located at the end of this chapter.

CARBURETOR OPERATION

For proper operation a gasoline engine must be supplied with fuel and air mixed in proper proportions by weight. A mixture in which there is an excess of fuel is said to be rich. A lean mixture is one which contains insufficient fuel. A properly adjusted carburetor supplies the proper mixture to the engine under all operating conditions.

The carburetor consists of several major systems. A float and float valve mechanism maintain a constant fuel level in the float bowl. The pilot system supplies fuel at low speeds. The main fuel system supplies fuel at medium and high speeds. A starter (choke) system supplies the very rich mixture needed to start a cold engine.

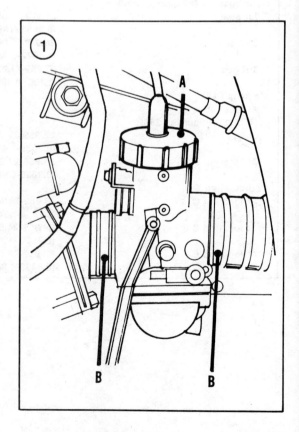

CARBURETOR SERVICE

Major carburetor service, such as removal and cleaning, should be performed at the intervals indicated in **Table 1** in Chapter Three or when poor engine performance, hesitation and little or no response to mixture adjustment is observed. Alterations in jet size, throttle slide cutaway and changes in jet needle position, etc., should be attempted only if you're experienced in this type of "tuning" work. A bad guess could result in costly engine damage or, at best, poor performance. If, after servicing the carburetor and making the adjustments described in this chapter, the ATV

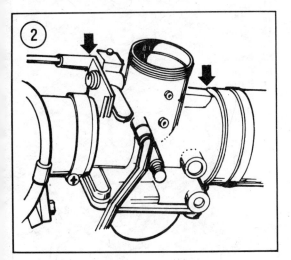

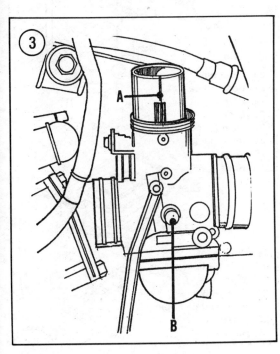

does not perform correctly and, assuming that other factors affecting performance are correct (e.g. ignition timing and condition, etc.), the vehicle should be checked by a dealer or a qualified performance tuning specialist.

CARBURETOR
(1985 3-WHEELED MODELS)

Removal/Installation

1. Place the ATV on level ground and set the parking brake or block the wheels so the vehicle will not roll in either direction.
2. Remove the seat/rear fender assembly as described in Chapter Twelve.
3. Remove the fuel tank as described in this chapter.

> *NOTE*
> *Before removing the top cap, thoroughly clean the area around it so no dirt will fall into the carburetor.*

4. Unscrew the carburetor top cap (A, **Figure 1**) and pull the throttle valve assembly up and out of the carburetor.

> *NOTE*
> *If the top cap and throttle valve assembly are not going to be removed from the throttle cable for cleaning, wrap them in a clean shop cloth or place them in a plastic bag to help keep them clean.*

5. Loosen the screws on the clamping band on the carburetor inlet and outlet (B, **Figure 1**).
6. Slide the clamping bands away from the carburetor.
7. Note the routing of the carburetor drain tube through the frame. Carefully pull the tube free from the frame and leave it attached to the carburetor.
8. Carefully remove the carburetor from the engine and frame and take it a workbench for disassembly and cleaning.
9. Install by reversing these removal steps, noting the following.
10. Align the lug on the carburetor with the notch (**Figure 2**) in the rubber insulator.
11. Align the groove (A, **Figure 3**) in the throttle slide with the pin in the carburetor body (B, **Figure 3**).
12. Make sure the clamping band screws are tight to avoid a vacuum loss.

Disassembly/Assembly

Refer to **Figure 4** for this procedure and to **Table 1** for carburetor specifications.

1. Remove the screws (**Figure 5**) securing the float bowl and remove the float bowl.

2. Remove the float pivot pin (A, **Figure 6**) and remove the float and float valve assembly (B, **Figure 6**).

3. Remove the main jet (A, **Figure 7**).

4. Remove the main jet holder (B, **Figure 7**).

5. Remove the needle jet and the baffle (C, **Figure 7**).

6. Remove the slow jet (D, **Figure 7**).

NOTE
*Before removing the idle adjust screw and the air screw, carefully screw each in until it **lightly** seats. Count and record the number of turns so they can be installed in their same position.*

7. Unscrew the idle adjust screw (A, **Figure 8**) and the air screw (B, **Figure 8**) and their springs.

8. Remove the screw (A, **Figure 9**), collar, washer and choke lever from the carburetor body.

9. Unscrew the locknut and remove the choke assembly (B, **Figure 9**).

10. Remove the float bowl gasket from the float bowl.

11. To remove the throttle valve from the throttle cable, perform the following.
   a. Depress the throttle spring away from the throttle valve.
   b. Remove the retaining plate clip (**Figure 10**).
   c. Push the throttle cable end (A, **Figure 11**) down and out along the groove in the side of the throttle valve (B, **Figure 11**) and remove the throttle valve and needle jet assembly.
   d. Remove the jet needle from the throttle valve (**Figure 12**).

NOTE
If the needle clip is going to be removed, record the clip position before removal.

NOTE
Further disassembly is neither necessary nor recommended. If throttle shaft or butterfly are damaged, take the carburetor body to a dealer for replacement.

12. Clean and inspect all parts as described in this chapter.

13. Assembly is the reverse of these disassembly steps, noting the following.

14. Install the needle jet clip in the correct groove. Refer to **Table 1** at the end of this chapter.

CARBURETOR
(1985 3-WHEELED MODELS)

1. Top cover set
2. Spring
3. Set plate
4. Jet needle and clip
5. Throttle valve
6. Starter choke
7. Hose
8. Hose clip
9. Air screw and spring
10. Throttle adjust screw and spring
11. Screw
12. Collar
13. Washer
14. Starter choke lever
15. Screw
16. Clamp
17. Baffle
18. Slow jet
19. Gasket
20. Float bowl
21. Hose guide
22. Screw
23. O-ring
24. Main jet cover
25. Hose guide
26. Screw
27. Hose
28. Needle jet
29. Main jet holder
30. Mainjet
31. Float valve
32. Float and pivot pin
33. Screw
34. Hose

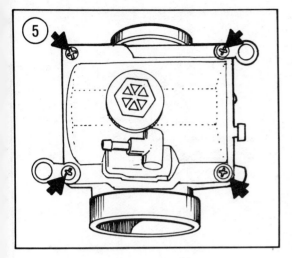

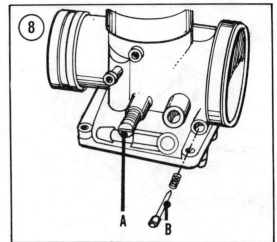

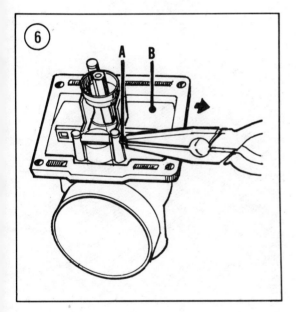

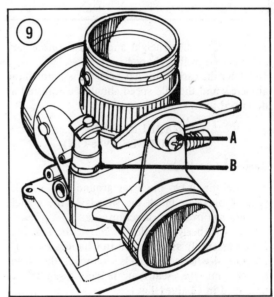

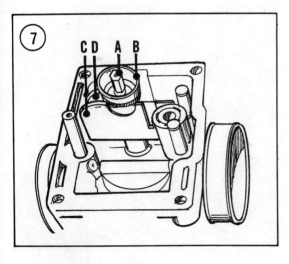

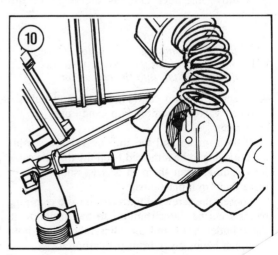

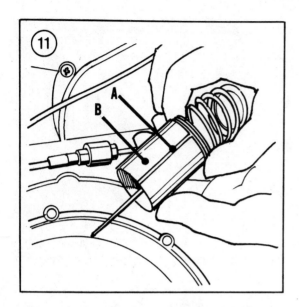

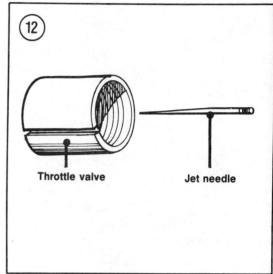

Throttle valve   Jet needle

15. Check the float height and adjust if necessary as described in this chapter.

16. After the carburetor has been disassembled the air screw and the idle speed should be adjusted as described in this chapter.

CARBURETOR
(ALL MODELS 1986-ON)

Removal/Installation

1. Place the ATV on level ground and set the parking brake or block the wheels so the vehicle will not roll in either direction.

2A. On 3-wheeled models, remove the seat/rear fender assembly as described in Chapter Twelve.

2B. On 4-wheeled models, remove the front fender and the seat/rear fender assembly as described in Chapter Twelve.

3. Remove the fuel tank as described in this chapter.

NOTE
Before removing the top cap, thoroughly clean the area around it so no dirt will fall into the carburetor.

4. Unscrew the top cap (**Figure 13**) and pull the throttle valve assembly up and out of the carburetor.

5. If the top cap and the throttle valve assembly are not going to be removed from the throttle cable for cleaning, wrap them in a clean shop cloth or place them in a plastic bag.

6. Loosen the screws (**Figure 14**) on the clamping bands securing the carburetor to the insulator on the cylinder head and air filter tube. Slide both clamping bands away from the carburetor.

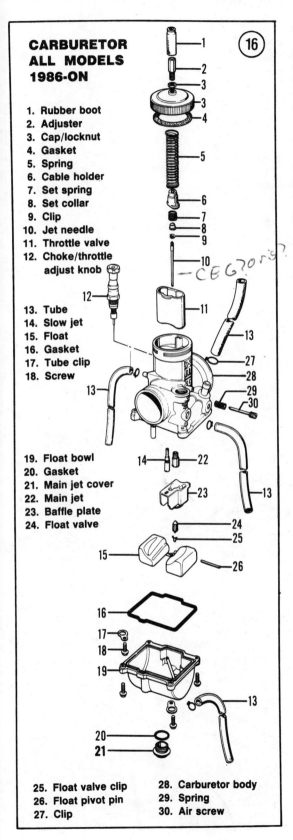

CARBURETOR ALL MODELS 1986-ON

1. Rubber boot
2. Adjuster
3. Cap/locknut
4. Gasket
5. Spring
6. Cable holder
7. Set spring
8. Set collar
9. Clip
10. Jet needle
11. Throttle valve
12. Choke/throttle adjust knob
13. Tube
14. Slow jet
15. Float
16. Gasket
17. Tube clip
18. Screw
19. Float bowl
20. Gasket
21. Main jet cover
22. Main jet
23. Baffle plate
24. Float valve

25. Float valve clip
26. Float pivot pin
27. Clip
28. Carburetor body
29. Spring
30. Air screw

7. Note the routing of the carburetor air vent and overflow tubes through the frame. Carefully pull the tubes free from the frame and leave them attached to the carburetor.

8. Carefully work the carburetor free from the rubber boots and remove the carburetor from the engine insulator and air filter air box.

9. Install by reversing these removal steps, noting the following.

10. Position the cutaway in the throttle valve (**Figure 15**) toward the air filter air box and install the throttle valve into the carburetor.

11. Make sure the screws on the clamping bands are tight to avoid a vacuum loss.

12. Adjust the throttle as described in Chapter Three.

Disassembly/Assembly

Refer to **Figure 16** for this procedure and to **Table 1** for carburetor specifications.

> *NOTE*
> *The Honda factory has determined that some 1986 ATC250R's have experienced pinging problems as well as cylinder head gasket leakage. If you have had a pinging problem, the clip on the jet needle must be repositioned to the 4th groove instead of the 3rd groove. This adjustment will be performed for no cost to the owner (Honda Service Bulletin ATC250R No. 6, June 1986). At the same time the Honda dealer will install a new cylinder head gasket, also at no cost to the owner.*

1. Remove the overflow tube (A, **Figure 17**).
2. Remove the screws (B, **Figure 17**) securing the float bowl and remove the float bowl.

3. Remove the float pivot pin (A, **Figure 18**) and remove the float valve assembly (B, **Figure 18**).
4. Remove the baffle plate (**Figure 19**).
5. Remove the main jet (**Figure 20**).
6. Remove the slow jet (**Figure 21**).

> *NOTE*
> *Before removing the air screw, carefully screw it in until it **lightly** seats. Count and record the number of turns so it can be installed in the same position.*

7. Unscrew the air screw (**Figure 22**) and remove the screw and spring.

> *CAUTION*
> *Do not try to remove the jet block (A, **Figure 23**) from the carburetor body.*

8. Unscrew the locknut and remove the choke/idle speed knob assembly (**Figure 24**).
9. Remove the float bowl gasket (**Figure 25**) from the float bowl.
10. Unscrew the main jet cover and O-ring from the float bowl.
11. To remove the throttle valve from the throttle cable, compress the throttle valve spring (A, **Figure 26**) into the top cap (B, **Figure 26**) and remove the throttle cable from the cable holder in the throttle valve (C, **Figure 26**). Remove the throttle valve spring (**Figure 27**).

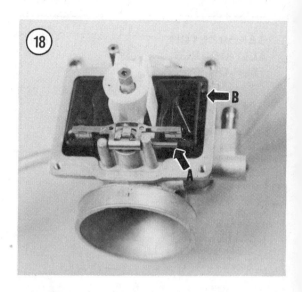

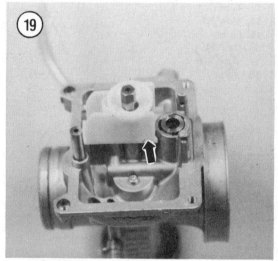

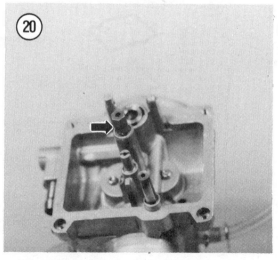

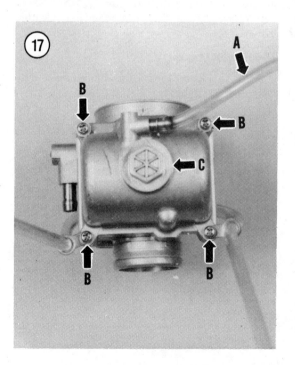

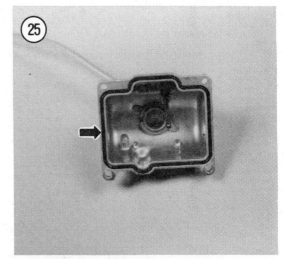

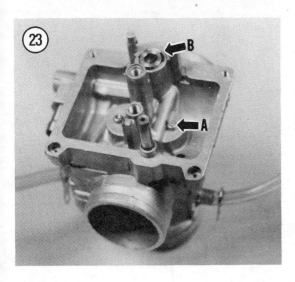

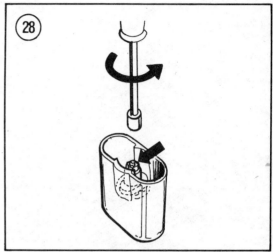

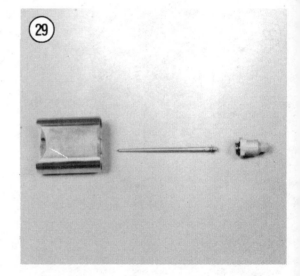

NOTE
If the needle clip is going to be removed, record the clip position before removal.

12. To disassemble the throttle valve, perform the following.

   a. Use a 6 mm socket or Phillips screwdriver and rotate the cable adjuster 90° *counterclockwise* (**Figure 28**).

   b. Remove the cable holder, set spring, set collar and jet needle from the throttle valve (**Figure 29**).

NOTE
Further disassembly is neither necessary nor recommended. If throttle shaft or butterfly are damaged, take the carburetor body to a dealer for replacement.

13. Clean and inspect all parts as described in this chapter.

14. Assembly is the reverse of these disassembly steps, noting the following.

15. Install the needle jet clip in the correct groove. Refer to **Table 1** at the end of this chapter.

16. If disassembled, assemble the throttle valve as follows.

   a. Install the jet needle into the throttle valve.

   b. Install the set collar onto the jet needle and clip.

   c. Install the set spring and the cable holder.

   d. Use a 6 mm socket or Phillips screwdriver and rotate the cable adjuster 90° *clockwise* to lock it in place.

17. Be sure to install the float valve (**Figure 30**) onto the float before installation.

18. Screw the air screw in the same number of turns as noted during disassembly.

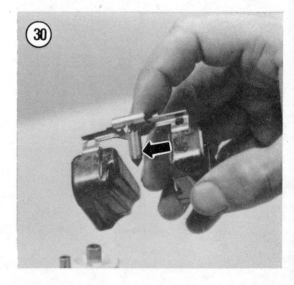

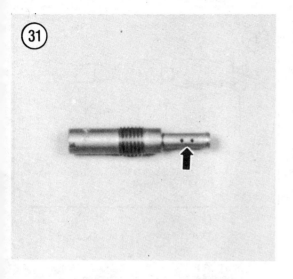

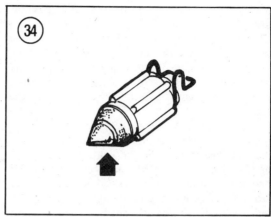

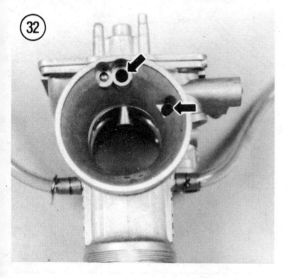

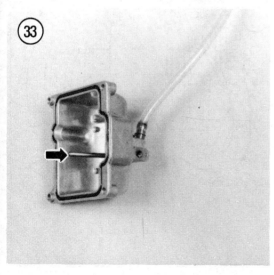

19. Check the float height and adjust if necessary as described in this chapter.

20. After the carburetor has been disassembled, the air screw and the idle speed should be adjusted as described in this chapter.

CLEANING/INSPECTION (ALL MODELS)

1. Clean all parts, except rubber or plastic parts, in a good grade of carburetor cleaner. This solution is available at most automotive or motorcycle supply stores in a small, resealable tank with a dip basket for just a few dollars. If it is tightly sealed when not in use, the solution will last for several cleanings. Follow the manufacturer's instructions for correct soak time—usually about 1/2 hour.

2. Remove all parts from the cleaner and blow dry with compressed air. Blow out the jets and needle jet holder (**Figure 31**) with compressed air.

3. Use compressed air and blow out the air passages (**Figure 32**) in the carburetor body.

> *CAUTION*
> *If compressed air is not available, allow the parts to air dry or use a clean lint-free cloth. Do **not** use a paper towel to dry carburetor parts, as small paper particles may plug openings in the carburetor body or jets.*

> *CAUTION*
> *Do **not** use a piece of wire to clean air passages, as minor gouges can alter flow rate and upset the fuel/air mixture.*

4. Be sure to clean out the overflow tube in the float bowl from both ends (**Figure 33**).

5. Inspect the end of the float valve needle (**Figure 34**) for wear or damage. Also check the inside of the needle valve body. If either part is damaged, replace as a set. A damaged needle valve or a particle of dirt or grit in the needle valve assembly

will cause the carburetor to flood and overflow fuel.

6. Unscrew the locknut (2, **Figure 35**) and remove the choke/idle adjust knob (1, **Figure 35**). Check the valve (3, **Figure 35**) for wear or damage. If any parts are worn the entire assembly must be replaced. If okay, reassemble and tighten the locknut.

7. Inspect all O-ring seals. O-ring seals tend to become hardened after prolonged use and heat and therefore lose their ability to seal properly.

8. Examine the end of the air screw (**Figure 36**) and the throttle adjust screw (**Figure 37**). If any grooves or roughness are present on either screw, replace if defective. A damaged end will prevent smooth low-speed engine operation.

9. Inspect the float valve seat (B, **Figure 23**) for wear or damage; replace as necessary.

CARBURETOR ADJUSTMENTS

Idle speed adjustment is covered in Chapter Three.

Air Screw Adjustment

1. Warm the engine to normal operating temperature. Usually 10-15 minutes of riding is sufficient. Shut the engine off.

2. Place the ATV on level ground and set the parking brake or block the wheels so the vehicle will not roll in either direction.

3. Turn the air screw *clockwise* until it *lightly* seats, then back it out the number of turns indicated in **Table 1**. Refer to A, **Figure 38** for 1985 3-wheeled models or A, **Figure 39** for all other models.

4. Connect a portable tachometer following the manufacturer's instructions.

5. Start the engine and turn the idle adjust screw or knob to the idle speed indicated in **Table 1**. Refer to B, **Figure 38** for 1985 3-wheeled models or B, **Figure 39** for all other models.

6. Turn the air screw in either direction to achieve the highest idle speed. Make sure the engine does not run or idle erratically or miss. If this happens, readjust as necessary.

7. Turn the idle adjust screw or knob to the idle speed indicated in **Table 2**.

8. Disconnect the portable tachometer.

Float Adjustment

The carburetor assembly has to be removed and partially disassembled for this adjustment.

1. Remove the carburetor as described in this chapter.

2. Remove the screws (B, **Figure 17**) securing the float bowl and remove float bowl.

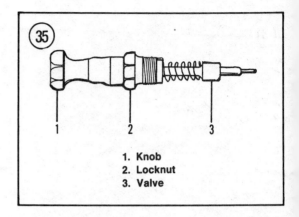

1. Knob
2. Locknut
3. Valve

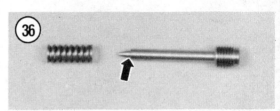

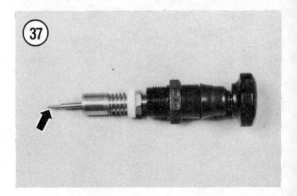

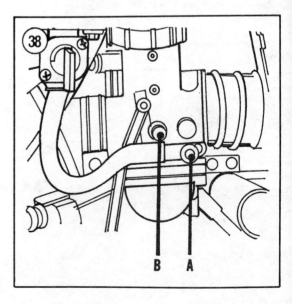

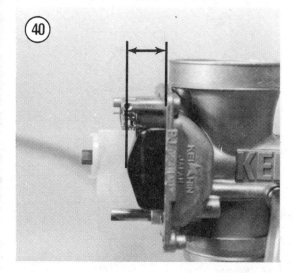

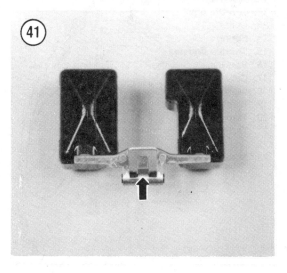

3. Hold the carburetor so the float arm is just touching the float needle; *not* pushing it down. Use a float level gauge, vernier caliper or small ruler and measure the distance from the carburetor body to the float (**Figure 40**). The correct height is listed in **Table 1**.

4. Adjust by carefully bending the tang on the float arm (**Figure 41**). If the float level is set too high, fuel will run from the float bowl overflow tube and cause the engine to flood. Also, the result will be a rich fuel/air mixture. If it is set too low, the mixture will be too lean and the engine will stumble on acceleration and run too lean to develop peak efficiency and power.

5. Reassemble and install the carburetor.

High-elevation and
Temperature Adjustment

High-elevation and ambient temperature adjustment consists of 3 different changes to the carburetor; main jet size change, a different location of the clip on the jet needle and a different air screw setting. Refer to **Tables 2-7** for the various adjustment combinations for different riding conditions for all models.

If the ATV is going to be ridden for any sustained period of time at high altitudes (above 1,500 m/5,000 ft.) the carburetor must be readjusted to improve performance.

The carburetor is set with a standard main jet for normal sea level conditions. If the vehicle is run at higher altitudes or under heavy load, deep sand or mud, the main jet should be replaced with a one-step smaller size. Never change the main jet by more than one size at a time without test riding the bike and running a spark plug test. Refer to *Reading Spark Plugs* in Chapter Three.

> *CAUTION*
> *If the carburetor has been adjusted for high-elevation operation (smaller jet, jet needle clip location and air screw setting), it must be changed back to standard settings when ridden at elevations below 1,500 m (5,000 ft.). Engine overheating and piston seizure will occur if the engine runs too lean with the smaller jet, changed jet needle clip position and different air screw setting.*

1. Place the ATV on level ground and set the parking brake or block the wheel so the vehicle will not roll in either direction.

2. Remove the carburetor as described in this chapter.

3. Disassemble the carburetor top cap to gain access to the jet needle as described in this chapter.

4. Remove the jet needle from the throttle valve. Remove the jet needle clip and reposition it (**Figure 42**) according to your specific needs. Refer to **Tables 2-5**.

5. Reinstall the jet needle into the throttle valve and reassemble the carburetor top cap as described in this chapter.

6. Unscrew the main jet access plug (C, **Figure 17**) from the float bowl.

7. Remove the main jet (**Figure 20**) and replace it with the factory recommended size according to your specific needs. Refer to **Tables 2-5**.

8. Install the main jet access plug into the float bowl and tighten securely.

9. Install the carburetor as described in this chapter and check for fuel leaks.

10. Adjust the air screw as described in this chapter using the correct setting listed in **Tables 2-5**.

11. Start the engine and adjust the idle speed as described in Chapter Three.

12. Test ride the bike and perform a spark plug test; refer to *Reading Spark Plugs* in Chapter Three.

13. When the ATV is returned to lower altitudes (near sea level), the carburetor must be returned to its original condition and the idle speed readjusted as listed in **Table 1**.

THROTTLE CABLE

Removal

1. Place the ATV on level ground and set the parking brake or block the wheels so the vehicle will not roll in either direction.

2A. On 3-wheeled models, remove the seat/rear fender assembly as described in Chapter Twelve.

2B. On 4-wheeled models, remove the front fenders and the seat/rear fender assembly as described in Chapter Twelve.

3. Remove the fuel tank as described in this chapter.

NOTE
Before removing the top cap, thoroughly clean the area around it so no dirt will fall into the carburetor.

4. Disassemble the carburetor top cap and disconnect the throttle cable as described in this chapter.

NOTE
Place a clean shop rag over the top of the carburetor to keep any foreign

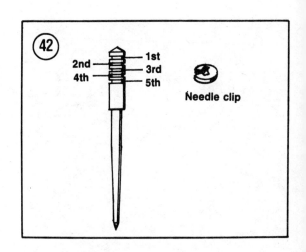

Needle clip

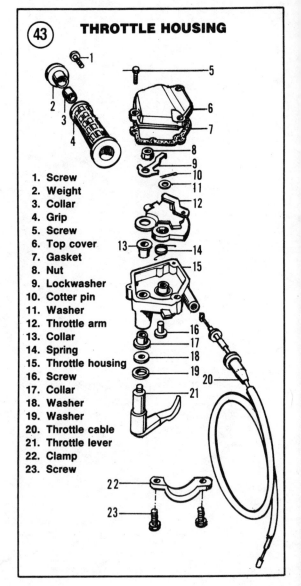

THROTTLE HOUSING

1. Screw
2. Weight
3. Collar
4. Grip
5. Screw
6. Top cover
7. Gasket
8. Nut
9. Lockwasher
10. Cotter pin
11. Washer
12. Throttle arm
13. Collar
14. Spring
15. Throttle housing
16. Screw
17. Collar
18. Washer
19. Washer
20. Throttle cable
21. Throttle lever
22. Clamp
23. Screw

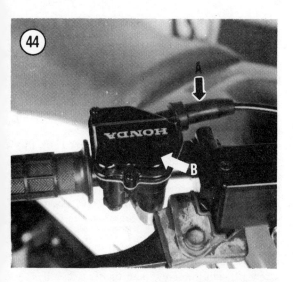

matter from falling into the throttle slide area.

5. Disassemble the throttle housing as described in this chapter to gain access to the throttle cable end.
6. Withdraw the throttle cable from the throttle housing.
7. Disconnect the throttle cable from any clips holding the cable to the frame.

NOTE
The piece of string attached in the next step will be used to pull the new throttle cable back through the frame so it will be routed in the exact same position as the old one.

8. Tie a piece of heavy string or cord, approximately 2 m (7 ft.), to the carburetor end of the throttle cable. Wrap this end with masking or

duct tape. Do not use an excessive amount of tape as it will be pulled through the frame. Tie the other end of the string to the frame.
9. At the throttle lever end of the cable, carefully pull the cable and attached string out through the frame. Make sure the attached string follows the same path of the cable through the frame.
10. Remove the tape and untie the string from the old cable.

Installation

1. Lubricate the new cable as described in Chapter Three.
2. Tie the string used during removal to the new throttle cable and wrap it with tape.
3. Carefully pull the string back through the frame, routing the new cable through the same path as the old cable.
4. Remove the tape and untie the string from the cable and the frame.
5. Reverse Steps 2-7 of *Removal,* noting the following.
6. Apply grease to the pivot bushing in the throttle lever cover and to the throttle lever.
7. Operate the throttle lever and make sure the carburetor throttle linkage is operating correctly and with no binding. If operation is incorrect or there is binding, carefully check that the cable is attached correctly and there are no tight bends in the cable.
8. Adjust the throttle cable as described in Chapter Three.
9. Test ride the ATV and make sure the throttle is operating correctly.

THROTTLE HOUSING

Disassembly

Refer to **Figure 43** for this procedure.
1. Slide back the rubber boot (A, **Figure 44**).
2. Remove the screws securing the throttle cover (B, **Figure 44**) and remove the cover and gasket.
3. Loosen the throttle cable locknut and adjuster (A, **Figure 45**).
4. Bend down the tab on the lockwasher and remove the nut and lockwasher (B, **Figure 45**).
5. Withdraw the throttle lever (C, **Figure 45**).
6. Swing the metal portion of the throttle arm (**Figure 46**) over to the side.
7. Remove the cotter pin and washer (A, **Figure 47**).
8. Unhook the spring from the pin (B, **Figure 47**) on the throttle housing.
9. Disconnect the throttle cable end from the throttle arm (C, **Figure 47**).

10. Withdraw the throttle cable from the throttle housing.

Assembly

1. Insert the throttle cable into the throttle housing.
2. Connect the throttle cable to the throttle arm (C, **Figure 47**).
3. Install the throttle arm and hook the spring end into the groove of the throttle arm. Hook the other end of the spring onto the pin on the throttle housing.
4. Install the washer and new cotter pin. Bend the ends of the cotter pin over completely.
5. Apply a light coat of grease to the throttle lever shaft and insert the shaft into the throttle housing.
6. Align the flat of the throttle lever shaft and the flat on the metal portion of the throttle arm, then install the throttle arm onto the shaft.
7. Install a new lockwasher and nut. Tighten the nut securely. Bend the tab of the lockwasher up against a flat on the nut.
8. Install a new gasket (D, **Figure 45**), the cover and the screws. Tighten the screws securely.
9. Adjust the throttle as described in Chapter Three.

FUEL SHUTOFF VALVE AND FUEL STRAINER

Removal/Installation (3-Wheeled Models)

1. Place the ATV on level ground and set the parking brake or block the wheel so the vehicle will not roll in either direction.
2. Remove the fuel tank as described in this chapter.
3. Remove the screws and collars (**Figure 48**) securing the fuel shutoff valve to the base of the fuel tank and remove the shutoff valve assembly.
4. Install by reversing these removal steps, noting the following.
5. Install an O-ring seal between the shutoff valve and the fuel tank. Be sure to use the collars on the screws. Install the screws and tighten securely.
6. Check for fuel leakage after installation is completed.

Removal/Installation (4-Wheeled Models)

1. Place the ATV on level ground and set the parking brake or block the wheels so the vehicle will not roll in either direction.
2. Remove the fuel tank as described in this chapter.

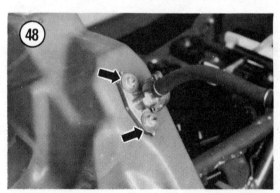

3. Remove the bolts (A, **Figure 49**) securing the fuel hose bracket and remove the bracket.

4. Remove the screws and collars (B, **Figure 49**) securing the fitting to the fuel tank and remove the fitting, gasket, fuel lines and shutoff valve.

5. Install by reversing these removal steps, noting the following.

6. Install an O-ring seal between the fitting and the fuel tank. Be sure to use the collars on the screws. Install the screws and tighten securely.

7. If the shutoff valve was disconnected from the fuel lines going to the fitting on the fuel tank, route the fuel hoses as shown in **Figure 50**.

8. Check for fuel leakage after installation is completed.

FUEL TANK

Removal/Installation
(3-wheeled Models)

Refer to **Figure 51** for this procedure.

1. Place the ATV on level ground and set the parking brake or block the wheel so the vehicle will not roll in either direction.

6

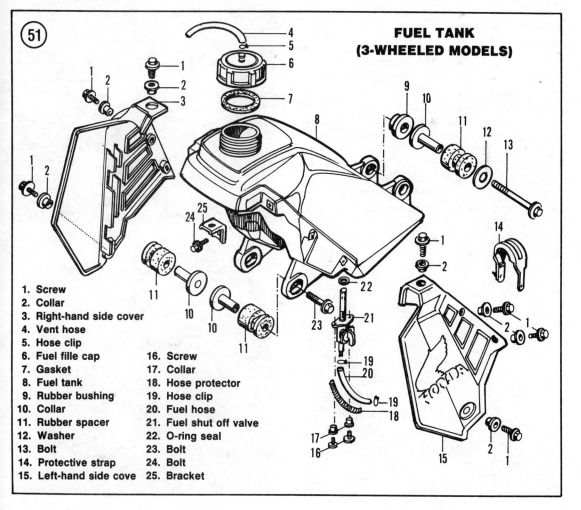

**FUEL TANK
(3-WHEELED MODELS)**

1. Screw
2. Collar
3. Right-hand side cover
4. Vent hose
5. Hose clip
6. Fuel fille cap
7. Gasket
8. Fuel tank
9. Rubber bushing
10. Collar
11. Rubber spacer
12. Washer
13. Bolt
14. Protective strap
15. Left-hand side cove

16. Screw
17. Collar
18. Hose protector
19. Hose clip
20. Fuel hose
21. Fuel shut off valve
22. O-ring seal
23. Bolt
24. Bolt
25. Bracket

2. Remove the seat/rear fender assembly as described in Chapter Twelve.

3. Turn the fuel shutoff valve to the OFF position.

4. Disconnect the fuel line going from the fuel tank to the carburetor. Plug the end with a golf tee to prevent any fuel leakage.

5. Remove the bolts and collars securing the radiator shroud on each side and remove both shrouds. Refer to **Figure 52** and **Figure 53**.

6. Remove the bolt (A, **Figure 54**) on each side securing the fuel tank at the front.

7. Remove the bolt and washer (B, **Figure 54**) on each side securing the fuel tank at the rear.

8. Pull the fuel tank to the rear and remove it.

9. Inspect the rubber cushions (**Figure 55**) on the frame where the fuel tank is held in place. Replace as a set if either are damaged or starting to deteriorate.

10. Install by reversing these removal steps, noting the following.

11. Check for fuel leakage after installation is completed.

Removal/Installation
(4-wheeled Models)

Refer to **Figure 56** for this procedure.

1. Place the ATV on level ground and set the parking brake or block the wheels so the vehicle will not roll in either direction.

2. Remove the front fenders and the seat/rear fender assembly as described in Chapter Twelve.

3. Turn the fuel shutoff valve to the OFF position (A, **Figure 57**) and disconnect the fuel line (B, **Figure 57**) going to the carburetor. Plug the fuel line with a golf tee to prevent fuel leakage.

4. Remove the screw (C, **Figure 57**) securing the fuel shutoff valve to the frame.

5. Remove the bolt and collar (A, **Figure 58**) securing the fuel tank at the center front.

6. Remove the bolts (B, **Figure 58**) on each side securing the fuel tank at the rear.

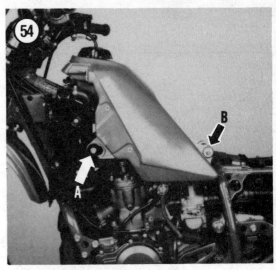

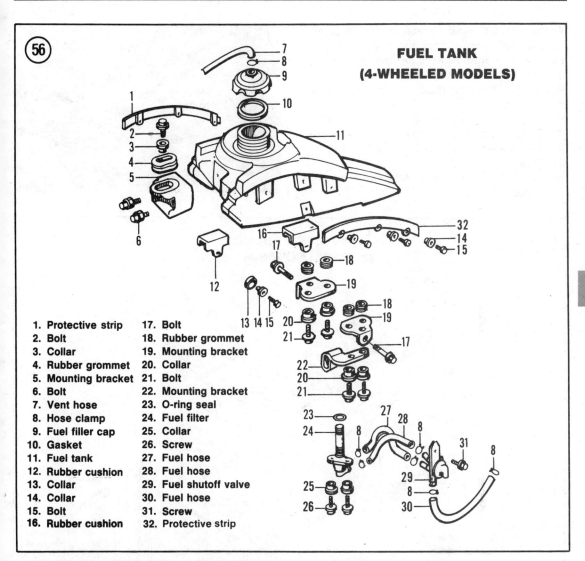

56 FUEL TANK
(4-WHEELED MODELS)

1. Protective strip
2. Bolt
3. Collar
4. Rubber grommet
5. Mounting bracket
6. Bolt
7. Vent hose
8. Hose clamp
9. Fuel filler cap
10. Gasket
11. Fuel tank
12. Rubber cushion
13. Collar
14. Collar
15. Bolt
16. Rubber cushion
17. Bolt
18. Rubber grommet
19. Mounting bracket
20. Collar
21. Bolt
22. Mounting bracket
23. O-ring seal
24. Fuel filter
25. Collar
26. Screw
27. Fuel hose
28. Fuel hose
29. Fuel shutoff valve
30. Fuel hose
31. Screw
32. Protective strip

6

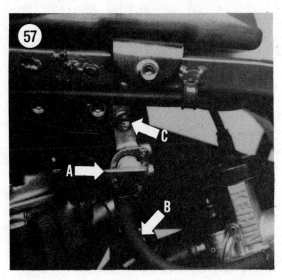

57

58

7. Pull the fuel tank up and to the front and carefully pull the fuel lines and shutoff valve (A, **Figure 59**) out from between the frame rail and the air inlet pipe. Remove the fuel tank.

8. Install by reversing these removal steps, noting the following.

9. Inspect the rubber cushions (B, **Figure 59**) on the frame where the fuel tank is held in place. Replace as a set if either is damaged or starting to deteriorate.

10. Check for fuel leakage after installation is completed.

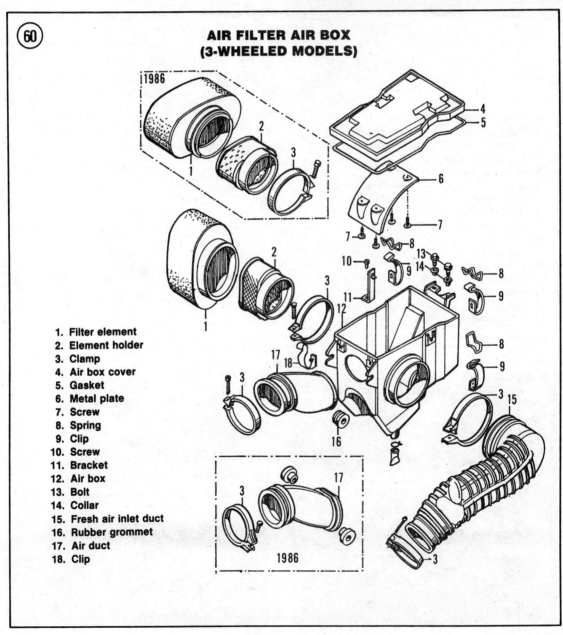

60

AIR FILTER AIR BOX
(3-WHEELED MODELS)

1986

1. Filter element
2. Element holder
3. Clamp
4. Air box cover
5. Gasket
6. Metal plate
7. Screw
8. Spring
9. Clip
10. Screw
11. Bracket
12. Air box
13. Bolt
14. Collar
15. Fresh air inlet duct
16. Rubber grommet
17. Air duct
18. Clip

1986

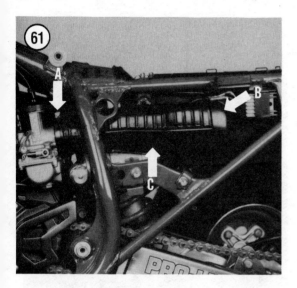

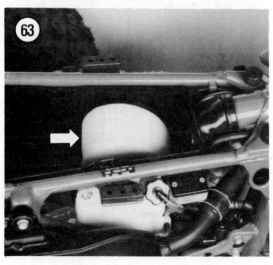

AIR FILTER AIR BOX
(3-WHEELED MODELS)

Removal/Installation

Refer to **Figure 60** for this procedure.

1. Remove the fuel tank as described in this chapter.

2. Remove the seat/rear fender assembly as described in Chapter Twelve.

3. Loosen the screws on the clamping bands on the carburetor-to-connecting tube (A, **Figure 61**) and the air box-to-connecting tube (B, **Figure 61**).

4. Disconnect the connecting tube (C, **Figure 61**) from the air box and carburetor and remove the connecting tube.

5. Unhook the hooks securing the air box cover (**Figure 62**) and remove the cover.

6. Loosen the screw on the clamping band securing the air filter element (**Figure 63**) and remove the element.

7. Loosen the screw on the clamping band (A, **Figure 64**) where the air box attaches to the frame.

8. Remove the bolts (B, **Figure 64**) securing the air box to the frame.

9. Withdraw the air box (C, **Figure 64**) up and out of the frame.

10. Install by reversing these removal steps, noting the following.

11. Make sure the clamping bands are seated correctly and that the screws are tight.

AIR FILTER AIR BOX AND
AIR INLET PIPE
(4-WHEELED MODELS)

Removal/Installation

Refer to **Figure 65** for this procedure.

1. Remove the seat/rear fender assembly as described in Chapter Twelve.

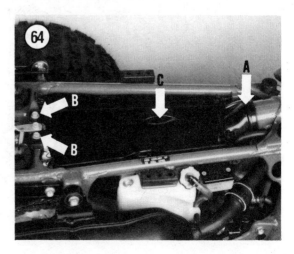

2. Remove the fuel tank as described in this chapter.

3. Remove the screw (A, **Figure 66**) securing the rear master cylinder to the air box. It is not necessary to disconnect the hydraulic brake line from the master cylinder.

4. Loosen the screw on the clamping bands on the carburetor-to-connecting tube (**Figure 67**) and the air box-to-connecting tube (B, **Figure 66**).

5. Disconnect the connecting tube from the air box and carburetor and remove the connecting tube.

6. Unhook the hooks securing the air box cover (**Figure 68**) and remove the cover.

7. Loosen the screw on the clamping band securing the air filter element and remove the element.

8. On 1987 models, perform the following.

   a. Remove the nut and washer securing the resonator to the frame.

   b. Loosen the screw on the clamping band securing the resonator to the connecting tube and remove the resonator.

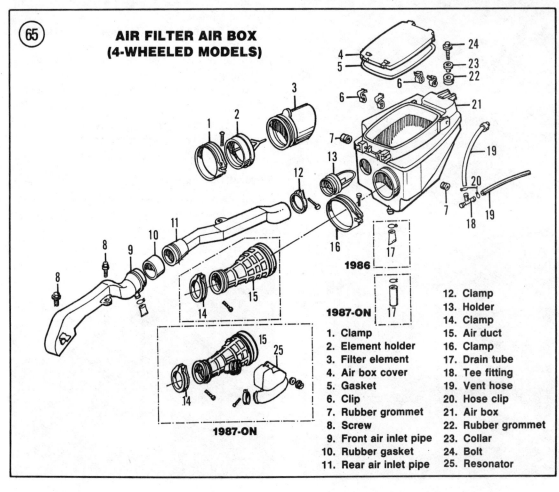

AIR FILTER AIR BOX (4-WHEELED MODELS)

1986

1987-ON

1987-ON

1. Clamp
2. Element holder
3. Filter element
4. Air box cover
5. Gasket
6. Clip
7. Rubber grommet
8. Screw
9. Front air inlet pipe
10. Rubber gasket
11. Rear air inlet pipe
12. Clamp
13. Holder
14. Clamp
15. Air duct
16. Clamp
17. Drain tube
18. Tee fitting
19. Vent hose
20. Hose clip
21. Air box
22. Rubber grommet
23. Collar
24. Bolt
25. Resonator

9. Loosen the screw on the clamping band (**Figure 69**) where the air box attaches to the rear air inlet pipe.

10. Remove the bolts securing the air box to the frame.

11. Withdraw the air box up and out of the frame.

12. To remove the air inlet pipes perform the following.

    a. Unhook the AC regulator and rubber mount (**Figure 70**) from the front air inlet pipe.

    b. Remove the bolts securing the front air inlet pipe (**Figure 71**).

    c. Pull the front air inlet pipe forward and remove it from the frame.

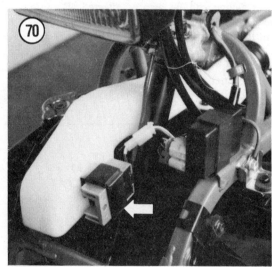

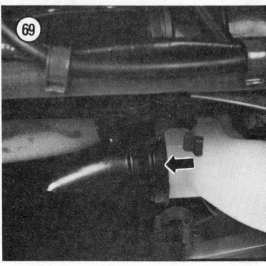

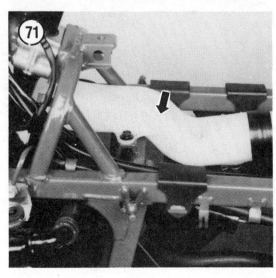

d. Remove the bolts securing the rear air inlet pipe (**Figure 72**).

e. Pull the rear air inlet pipe forward and up, then remove it from the frame.

13. Install by reversing these removal steps, noting the following.

14. Make sure the clamping bands are seated correctly and that the screws are tight.

15. If the air inlet pipes were removed, make sure the rubber gasket (**Figure 73**) is in place where the 2 pipes join.

EXHAUST SYSTEM

The exhaust system is a vital performance component and frequently, because of its design, it is a vulnerable piece of equipment.

If the exhaust system is damaged or if the muffler becomes clogged with carbon, the performance of the engine can be greatly affected. Because the exhaust system, especially the exhaust pipe, is out in the open, it can easily be damaged.

Check the exhaust system for deep dents and fractures and repair them or replace parts immediately. Check the muffler frame mounting flanges for fractures and loose bolts or nuts. Check

the cylinder mounting flange for tightness. A loose exhaust pipe connection will cause excessive exhaust noise and rob the engine of power.

The exhaust system consists of an exhaust chamber, a connector and a muffler. Refer to

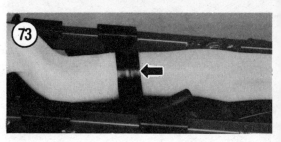

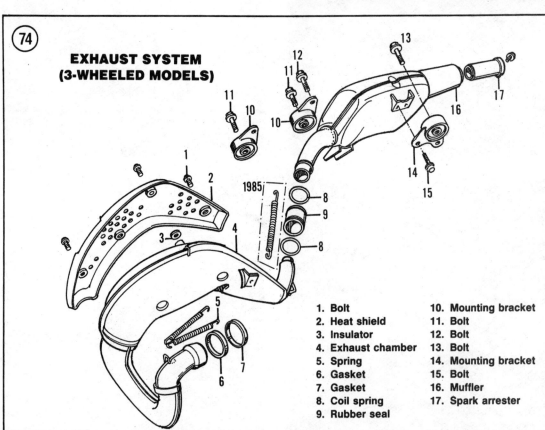

EXHAUST SYSTEM (3-WHEELED MODELS)

1. Bolt	10. Mounting bracket
2. Heat shield	11. Bolt
3. Insulator	12. Bolt
4. Exhaust chamber	13. Bolt
5. Spring	14. Mounting bracket
6. Gasket	15. Bolt
7. Gasket	16. Muffler
8. Coil spring	17. Spark arrester
9. Rubber seal	

Figure 74 for 3-wheeled models or Figure 75 for 4-wheeled models.

Removal/Installation
(3-Wheeled Models)

1. Place the ATV on level ground and set the parking brake or block the wheels so the vehicle will not roll in either direction.

2. Remove the seat/rear fender assembly as described in Chapter Twelve.

3. Remove the fuel tank as described in this chapter.

4A. On 1985 models, remove the exhaust chamber mounting bolt and spring.

4B. On 1986 models remove the bolt (Figure 76) securing the exhaust chamber to the frame.

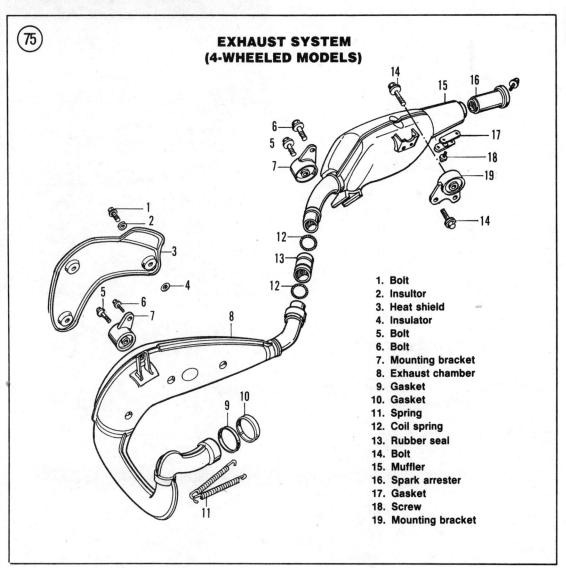

EXHAUST SYSTEM
(4-WHEELED MODELS)

1. Bolt
2. Insultor
3. Heat shield
4. Insulator
5. Bolt
6. Bolt
7. Mounting bracket
8. Exhaust chamber
9. Gasket
10. Gasket
11. Spring
12. Coil spring
13. Rubber seal
14. Bolt
15. Muffler
16. Spark arrester
17. Gasket
18. Screw
19. Mounting bracket

5. Use Vise Grips and remove both springs (**Figure 77**) securing the exhaust chamber to the exhaust joint on the cylinder.

> *NOTE*
> *If the exhaust chamber is difficult to remove, remove the muffler and connector first.*

6. Slide the rubber seal and springs (**Figure 78**) back and off the exhaust chamber where it joins the muffler.

7. Move the exhaust chamber toward the front of the ATV and disconnect it from the rubber seal at the front of the muffler. Don't lose the gasket in the fitting at the front of the exhaust chamber.

8. Remove the bolts (**Figure 79**) securing the muffler to the frame.

9. Remove the muffler from the frame.

10. Install by reversing these removal steps, noting the following.

11. Make sure the cylinder exhaust port gasket is in place.

> *NOTE*
> *In the following step, the cylinder is shown removed for clarity.*

12. Compress the seal ring (**Figure 80**) into the groove of the exhaust joint and connect the exhaust chamber onto the exhaust joint of the cylinder.

13. Install the retaining springs onto the cylinder head, then tighten the bolt securing the exhaust chamber to the frame. This will minimize the chances of an exhaust leak at the cylinder.

14. Tighten all bolts securely.

15. Make sure the rubber seal and springs (**Figure 78**) are correctly in place between the exhaust chamber and the muffler.

16. After installation is complete, start the engine and make sure there are no exhaust leaks.

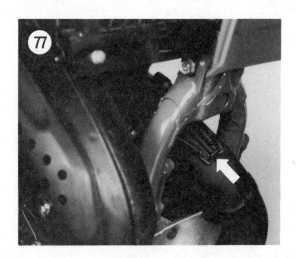

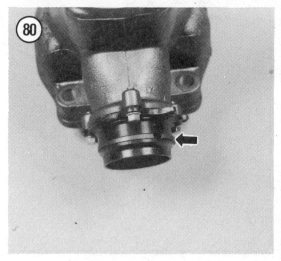

**Removal/Installation
(4-Wheeled Models)**

1. Place the ATV on level ground and set the parking brake or block the wheels so the vehicle will not roll in either direction.
2. Remove the front fenders and the seat/rear fender assembly as described in Chapter Twelve.
3. Slide the rubber seal and springs (**Figure 81**) back and off the exhaust chamber where it joins the muffler.
4. Use Vise Grips and remove both springs (**Figure 82**) securing the exhaust chamber to the exhaust joint on the cylinder.
5. Remove the bolt (**Figure 83**) securing the exhaust chamber to the frame.
6. Move the exhaust chamber slightly toward the front of the ATV and disconnect it from the muffler. Remove the exhaust chamber from the right-hand side of the frame. Don't lose the gasket in the fitting at the front of the exhaust chamber.
7. Remove the bolts (**Figure 84**) securing the muffler to the frame and remove the muffler from the frame.
8. Install by reversing these removal steps, noting the following.
9. Make sure the cylinder exhaust port gasket is in place.

NOTE
In the following step the cylinder is shown removed for clarity.

10. Compress the seal ring (**Figure 80**) into the groove of the exhaust joint and connect the exhaust chamber onto the exhaust joint of the cylinder.

11. Install the retaining springs onto the cylinder head, then tighten the bolt securing the exhaust chamber to the frame. This will minimize the chances of an exhaust leak at the cylinder.

12. Tighten all bolts securely.

13. Make sure the rubber seal and springs (**Figure 81**) are correctly in place between the exhaust chamber and the muffler.

14. After installation is complete, start the engine and make sure there are no exhaust leaks.

Exhaust System Repair

A dent in the exhaust chamber of a 2-stroke exhaust system will alter the system's flow characteristics and degrade performance. Minor damage can be easily repaired if you have welding equipment, some simple auto body repair tools and a bodyshop slide hammer. If damage is severe, the damaged portion of the system should be replaced.

Small Dents

1. Remove the exhaust chamber as described in this chapter.

2. Drill a small hole in the center of the dent.

3. Screw the end of the slide hammer into the hole.

4. Heat the area around the dent with an acetylene torch. While the dent is heated to a uniform orange-red color, operate the slide hammer to raise the dent.

5. When the dent is removed, unscrew the slide hammer and weld or braze the drilled hole closed.

6. After the welding is completed, wire brush the area and clean up all welds. Paint the entire area of the exhaust chamber with a high-temperature paint to prevent it from rusting.

Large Dents

Large dents that are not crimped can be removed with heat and a slide hammer as described under *Small Dents* in this chapter. However, several holes must be drilled along the center of the large dent so that it can be pulled out evenly.

If the dent is sharply crimped along the edges, the damaged section must be removed and repaired.

1. Before cutting out the damaged section, scribe several alignment marks over the area where the cuts will be made. This will aid in reassembling the section back into the main body.

2. Use a hacksaw and cut out the damaged section.

3. Straighten the section with an auto body dolly and hammer.

4. Weld the section back into place.

5. After the welding is completed, wire brush the area and clean up all welds. Paint the entire area of the exhaust chamber with a high-temperature paint to prevent it from rusting.

Table 1 CARBURETOR SPECIFICATIONS

Item	1985 ATC250R	1986 ATC250R
Carburetor model No.	PE37A	PJ03A
Venturi diameter	34 mm (1.3 in.)	34 mm (1.3 in.)
Float level	16 mm (0.63 in.)	16 mm (0.63 in.)
Air screw opening	2 turns out	2 1/4 turns out
Needle clip position	2nd groove	3rd groove*
Standard main jet No.	142**	145**
Slow jet No.	52	42
Idle speed	1500 ±150 rpm	1500 ±150 rpm

*Needle clip position changed to 4th groove if pinging problem occurs. See Service Bulletin Information in text.
**Optional main jets:
  1985: No. 138, 140, 145 and 148
  1986: No. 140, 142, 148 and 150

Item	1986 TRX250R/ Fourtrax 250R	1987 TRX250R/ Fourtrax 250R
Carburetor model No.	PJ05A	PJ07A
Venturi diameter	34 mm (1.3 in.)	34 mm (1.3 in.)
Float level	16 mm (0.63 in.)	16 mm (0.63 in.)
Air screw opening	1 7/8 turns out	1 7/8 turns out
Needle clip position	4th groove	3rd groove
Standard main jet No.	150*	152*
Slow jet No.	48	48
Idle speed	1500 ±150 rpm	1500 ±150 rpm

*Optional main jets:
  1986: No. 145, 148, 152 and 155
  1987: No. 148, 150, 155 and 158

Item	1988 TRX250R/ Fourtrax 250R	1989 TRX250R/ Fourtrax 250R
Carburetor model No.	PJ07B	PJ07C
Venturi diameter	34 mm (1.3 in.)	34 mm (1.3 in.)
Float level	16 mm (0.63 in.)	16 mm (0.63 in.)
Air screw opening	1 3/4 turns out	1 1/2 turns out
Needle clip position	3rd groove	4th groove
Standard main jet No.	158*	155*
Slow jet No.	45	42
Idle speed	1500 ±150 rpm	1500 ±150 rpm

*Optional main jets:
  1988: No. 152, 155 and 160
  1989: No. 150, 152 and 158

6

Table 2 HIGH ALTITUDE AND TEMPERATURE ADJUSTMENT—1985 ATC250R

	Temperature		
	−25° C to −17.5° C (−13° F to 0° F)	−17.5° C to −5° C (0° F to 22° F)	−5° C to 40° C (22° F to 104° F)
Altitude 0-1,500 m (0-5,000 ft.)			
Main jet	148	145	142
Jet needle position	4th groove	3rd groove	2nd groove
Air screw opening	1 1/2 turns out	2 turns out	2 turns out
Altitude 1,500 m (5,000 ft.)			
Main jet	142	140	138
Jet needle position	3rd groove	2nd groove	1st groove
Air screw opening	2 turns out	2 1/2 turns out	2 1/2 turns out
Altitude 1,000-2,000 m (3,300-6,600 ft.)			
Main jet	145	142	140
Jet needle position	4th groove	3rd groove	2nd groove
Air screw opening	1 1/2 turns out	2 turns out	2 turns out

Table 3 HIGH ALTITUDE AND TEMPERATURE ADJUSTMENT—1986 ATC250R

	Temperature		
	−25° C to −17.5° C (−13° F to 0° F)	−17.5° C to −5° C (0° F to 22° F)	−5° C to 40° C (22° F to 104° F)
Altitude 0-1,500 m (0-5,000 ft.)			
Main jet	150	148	145
Jet needle position	5th groove	4th groove	3rd groove
Air screw opening	1 3/4 turns out	2 1/4 turns out	2 1/4 turns out
Altitude 1,500 m (5,000 ft.)			
Main jet	145	142	140
Jet needle position	3rd groove	2nd groove	1st groove
Air screw opening	2 1/4 turns out	2 3/4 turns out	2 3/4 turns out
Altitude 1,000-2,000 m (3,300-6,600 ft.)			
Main jet	148	145	142
Jet needle position	4th groove	3rd groove	2nd groove
Air screw opening	1 3/4 turns out	2 1/4 turns out	2 1/4 turns out

Table 4 HIGH ALTITUDE AND TEMPERATURE ADJUSTMENT 1986 TRX250R/FOURTRAX 250R

	Temperature		
	−25° C to −17.5° C (−13° F to 0° F)	−17.5° C to −5° C (0° F to 22° F)	−5° C to 40° C (22° F to 104° F)
Altitude 0-1,500 m (0-5,000 ft.)			
Main jet	155	152	150
Jet needle position	5th groove	4th groove	4th groove
Air screw opening	1 1/2 turns out	2 turns out	1 7/8 turns out
Altitude 1,500 m (5,000 ft.)			
Main jet	150	148	145
Jet needle position	4th groove	3rd groove	2nd groove
Air screw opening	2 turns out	2 1/2 turns out	2 1/2 turns out

(continued)

Table 4 HIGH ALTITUDE AND TEMPERATURE ADJUSTMENT
1986 TRX250R/FOURTRAX 250R (continued)

	Temperature		
	−30° C to −17.5° C (−22° F to 0° F)	−17.5° C to −5° C (0° F to 22° F)	−5° C to 40° C (22° F to 104° F)
Altitude 1,000-2,000 m (3,300-6,600 ft.)			
Main jet	152	150	148
Jet needle position	5th groove	4th groove	3rd groove
Air screw opening	1 1/2 turns out	2 turns out	2 turns out

Table 5 HIGH ALTITUDE AND TEMPERATURE ADJUSTMENT
1987 TRX250R/FOURTRAX 250R

	Temperature		
	−25° C to −17.5° C (−13° F to 0° F)	−17.5° C to −5° C (0° F to 22° F)	−5° C to 40° C (22° F to 104° F)
Altitude 0-1,500 m (0-5,000 ft.)			
Main jet	155	155	152
Jet needle position	5th groove	4th groove	4th groove
Air screw opening	1 1/2 turns out	2 turns out	1 7/8 turns out
Altitude 1,500 m (5,000 ft.)			
Main jet	152	150	148
Jet needle position	4th groove	3rd groove	2nd groove
Air screw opening	2 turns out	2 1/2 turns out	2 1/2 turns out
Altitude 1,000-2,000 m (3,300-6,600 ft.)			
Main jet	155	152	150
Jet needle position	5th groove	4th groove	3rd groove
Air screw opening	1 1/2 turns out	2 turns out	2 turns out

6

Table 6 HIGH ALTITUDE AND TEMPERATURE ADJUSTMENT
1988 TRX250R/FOURTRAX 250R

	Temperature		
	−30° C to −17.5° C (−22° F to 0° F)	−17.5° C to −5° C (0° F to 22° F)	−5° C to 40° C (22° F to 104° F)
Altitude 0−1,500 m (0-5,000 ft.)			
Main jet	160	160	158
Jet needle position	5th groove	4th groove	3rd groove
Air screw opening	1 1/4 turns out	1 1/2 turns out	2 3/4 turns out
Altitude 1,500 m (5,000 ft.)			
Main jet	158	155	152
Jet needle position	4th groove	3rd groove	2nd groove
Air screw opening	1 3/4 turns out	2 turns out	2 1/4 turns out
Altitude 1,000-2,000 m (3,300-6,600 ft.)			
Main jet	160	158	155
Jet needle position	5th groove	4th groove	3rd groove
Air screw opening	1 1/2 turns out	1 3/4 turns out	2 turns out

Table 7 HIGH ALTITUDE AND TEMPERATURE ADJUSTMENT
1989 TRX250R/FOURTRAX 250R

	Temperature		
	−30° C to −17.5° C (−22° F to 0° F)	−17.5° C to −5° C (0° F to 22° F)	−5° C to 40° C (22° F to 104° F)
Altitude 0-1,500 m (0-5,000 ft.)			
Main jet	158	158	155
Jet needle position	5th groove	4th groove	4th groove
Air screw opening	1 turns out	1 1/4 turns out	1 1/2 turns out
Altitude 1,500 m (5,000 ft.)			
Main jet	155	152	150
Jet needle position	4th groove	3rd groove	2nd groove
Air screw opening	1 1/2 turns out	1 3/4 turns out	2 turns out
Altitude 1,000-2,000 m (3,300-6,600 ft.)			
Main jet	158	155	152
Jet needle position	5th groove	4th groove	3rd groove
Air screw opening	1 1/4 turns out	1 1/2 turns out	1 3/4 turns out

CHAPTER SEVEN

ELECTRICAL SYSTEM

This chapter contains operating principles, service and test procedures for the ignition and lighting components. Information regarding the spark plugs is covered in Chapter Three and alternator removal and installation is covered in Chapter Four.

The electrical system includes the following.

a. Ignition system.

b. Lighting system.

Tables 1-4 are at the end of this chapter.

CAPACITOR DISCHARGE IGNITION

The ATV is equipped with a capacitor discharge ignition (CDI) system, a solid-state system that uses no breaker points. The ignition circuit is shown in **Figure 1** for 3-wheeled models or **Figure 2** for 4-wheeled models.

As the rotor is turned by the crankshaft, the permanent magnets within the rotor cause an electronic pulse to develop in the primary coil of the stator assembly. This pulse is then routed to the CDI unit where it is amplified. A pulse from the pickup coil in the stator assembly is used to trigger the output of the CDI unit which in turn triggers the output of the ignition coil and fires the spark plug.

CDI Precautions

Certain measures must be taken to protect the capacitor discharge system. Damage to the semiconductors in the system will occur if the following precautions are not observed.

1. Never disconnect any of the electrical connections while the engine is running.

2. Keep all connections between the various units clean and tight. Be sure that the wiring connectors are pushed together firmly to help keep out moisture.

3. Do not substitute another type of ignition coil.

4. The CDI unit is mounted to the frame in a rubber mount. Always be sure that the CDI unit is mounted by this means as it is designed to help isolate vibrations.

CDI Troubleshooting

Problems with the capacitor discharge system fall into one of the following categories. See **Table 1**.

a. Weak spark.

b. No spark.

CDI Testing

Honda does not recommend the CDI test procedures previously used by the factory. This test procedure was to measure the resistance values between the various connector pins on the CDI unit. This inspection method has been determined to be unreliable because of the following.

a. The wrong type of multimeter will give incorrect resistance value readings.

b. Low multimeter battery voltage will result in an incorrect resistance value reading.

c. Human error in performing the test and/or misreading the specifications in the resistance value reading table.

d. Varying manufacturing tolerances among individual CDI units of the same type for the same model.

1. Test the CDI's unit ability to produce a spark. Perform the following.

a. Disconnect the high voltage lead from the spark plug. Remove the spark plug from the cylinder head.

b. Connect a new or known good spark plug to the high voltage lead and place the spark plug base on a good ground like the engine cylinder

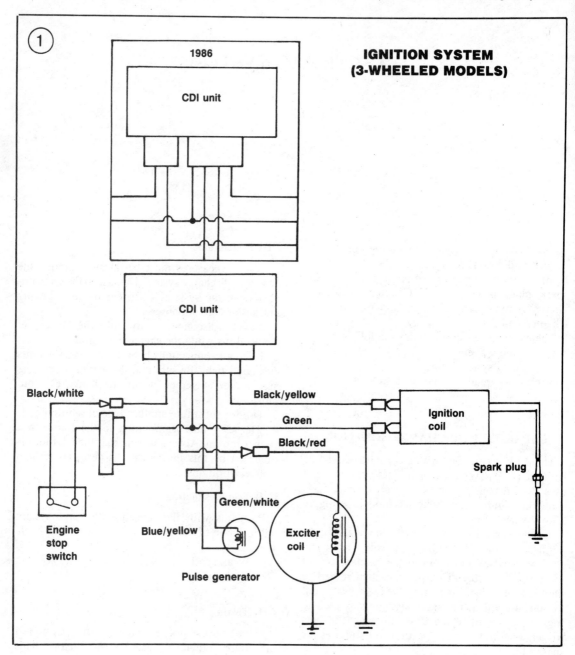

head (**Figure 3**). Position the spark plug so you can see the electrodes.

> *WARNING*
> *If it is necessary to hold the high voltage lead, do so with an insulated pair of pliers. The high voltage generated by the CDI could produce serious or fatal shocks.*

> *NOTE*
> *The engine must be kicked over **rapidly** since the ignition system does not produce a spark at a low rpm.*

c. Kick the engine over rapidly with the kickstarter and check for a spark. If there is a fat blue spark, replace the spark plug.

d. If a weak spark or no spark is obtained, continue with this procedure.

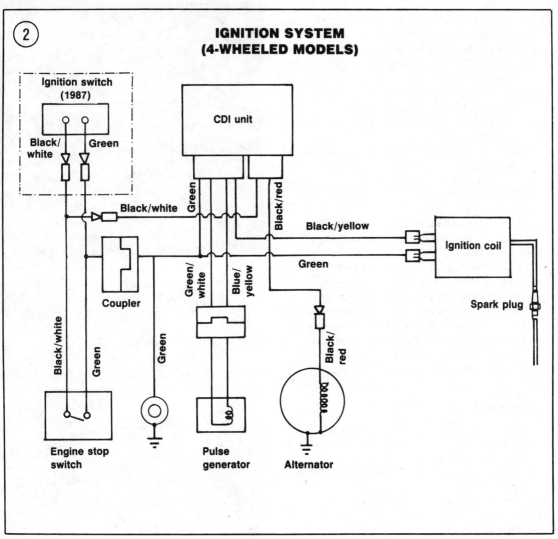

IGNITION SYSTEM
(4-WHEELED MODELS)

e. Reinstall the spark plug and connect the high voltage lead onto the spark plug.

2A. On 3-wheeled models, remove the seat/rear fender assembly as described in Chapter Twelve.

2B. On 4-wheeled models, remove the front fenders and the seat/rear fender assembly as described in Chapter Twelve.

3. Remove the spark plug and inspect it as described in Chapter Three.

4. Disconnect the electrical connector(s) from the CDI unit. See **Figure 4** (3-wheeled models) or **Figure 5** (4-wheeled models).

> *NOTE*
> *For best results, in the following step, use a quality digital multimeter (Honda part No. KS-AHM-32-003) or equivalent. Install a fresh battery in the multimeter before performing these tests.*

5. Refer to **Table 2** and measure the resistance values between each of the electrical connector(s) terminals on the wire harness side of the electrical connector(s). Do *not* perform these tests on the terminals of the CDI unit.

6. If any of the test results do not meet the specifications, then test and inspect the the following ignition system components as described in this chapter.

   a. Ignition coil: primary and secondary resistance.

   b. Alternator exciter coil.

   c. Pulse generator.

   d. Engine stop switch.

   e. Ignition switch on models so equipped.

7. If all of the ignition components are okay, then check the following.

   a. Check for an open or short in the wire harness between each component.

   b. Make sure all connections between the various components are clean and tight. Be sure that the wiring connectors are pushed together firmly to help keep out moisture.

8. If Steps 1-7 meet all specifications, then the CDI unit is faulty and must be replaced as described in this chapter.

Replacement

1A. On 3-wheeled models, perform the following.

   a. Remove the seat/rear fender assembly as described in Chapter Twelve.

   b. Remove the fuel tank as described in Chapter Six.

1B. On 4-wheeled models, remove the front fenders and the seat/rear fender assembly as described in Chapter Twelve.

2. Disconnect the electrical connector(s) to the CDI unit. Refer to **Figure 4** for 3-wheeled models or **Figure 5** for 4-wheeled models.

3. Withdraw the CDI unit from the rubber mount on the frame.

4. Install a new CDI unit into the rubber mount and attach the electrical connector(s) to it. Make sure the connector(s) are pushed all the way on to make a good electrical connection.

5. Install all parts removed.

IGNITION COIL

Testing

The ignition coil is a kind of transformer which develops the high voltage required to jump the spark plug gap. The only maintenance required is

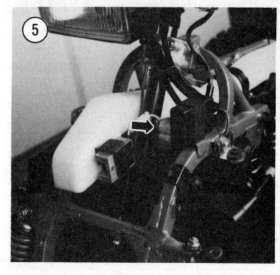

that of keeping the electrical connections clean and tight and occasionally checking to see that the coil is mounted securely.

If the condition of the coil is doubtful, there are several checks which can be made.

First as a quick check of coil condition, disconnect the high voltage lead from the spark plug. Remove the spark plug from the cylinder head. Connect a new or known good spark plug to the high voltage lead and place the spark plug base on a good ground like the engine cylinder head (**Figure 3**). Position the spark plug so you can see the electrodes.

WARNING
If it is necessary to hold the high voltage lead, do so with an insulated pair of pliers. The high voltage generated by the CDI could produce serious or fatal shocks.

NOTE
*The engine must be kicked over **rapidly** since the ignition system does not produce a spark below 600 rpm.*

Kick the engine over rapidly with the kickstarter and check for a spark. If a fat blue spark occurs the coil is in good condition; if not, proceed as follows. Make sure that you are using a known good spark

plug for this test. If the spark plug used is defective, the test results will be incorrect.

Reinstall the spark plug in the cylinder head and connect the spark plug lead.

Refer to **Figure 6** for this procedure.

Disconnect all ignition coil wires, including the spark plug lead, before testing.

NOTE
In order to get accurate resistance measurements the coil must be at approximately 68° F (20° C).

1. Measure the primary coil resistance between the black and green terminals of the ignition coil. The resistance value should be approximately 0.1-0.3 ohms.
2. Measure the secondary coil resistance between the positive primary terminal on the ignition coil and spark plug lead with the spark plug cap attached. The resistance value should be approximately 7,400-11,000 ohms.
3. Remove the spark plug cap, then measure the secondary coil resistance between the positive primary terminal on the ignition coil and spark plug lead. The resistance value should be approximately 3,700-4,500 ohms.
4. If the coil resistance does not meet any of these specifications, the coil must be replaced. If the coil is visibly damaged, it should be replaced.
5. Reconnect all ignition coil wires to the ignition coil.

Removal/Installation

1. Place the ATV on level ground and set the parking brake.
2A. On 3-wheeled models, remove the seat/rear fender assembly as described in Chapter Twelve.
2B. On 4-wheeled models, remove the front fenders and the seat/rear fender assembly as described in Chapter Twelve.
3. Remove the fuel tank as described in Chapter Six.
4. Disconnect the high voltage lead (A, **Figure 7**) from the spark plug.
5. Disconnect the electrical wires from the ignition coil.
6. Withdraw the ignition coil (B, **Figure 7**) from the mounting tab on the frame and remove the coil.
7. Install by reversing these removal steps, noting the following.

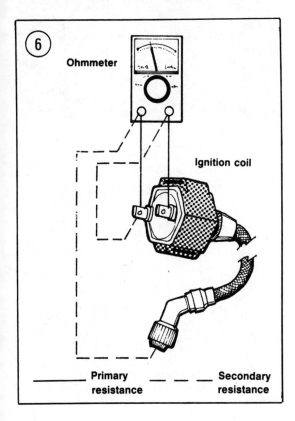

6

Ohmmeter

Ignition coil

————— **Primary resistance**   — — — **Secondary resistance**

7

8. Make sure all electrical connections are free of corrosion and are tight.

ALTERNATOR TESTING

Rotor Testing

The rotor is permanently magnetized and cannot be tested except by replacement with a rotor known to be good. A rotor can lose magnetism from old age or a sharp blow. If defective, the rotor must be replaced, as it cannot be remagnetized.

Stator Testing

It is not necessary to remove the stator plate to perform the following tests.

In order to get accurate resistance measurements, the stator assembly and coil must be warm with a minimum temperature of 68° F (20° C). If necessary, start the engine and let it warm up to normal operating temperature. If the engine won't run, warm the parts with a blow drier.

Ignition exciter coil test

1. Place the ATV on level ground and set the parking brake.
2A. On 3-wheeled models, remove the seat/rear fender assembly as described in Chapter Twelve.
2B. On 4-wheeled models, remove the front fender and the seat/rear fender assembly as described in Chapter Twelve.
3. Remove the fuel tank as described in Chapter Six.
4A. On 1985-1987 models, disconnect the black/red electrical wire connector (**Figure 8**) going to the exciter coil.
4B. On 1988-on models, disconnect the 2-pin electrical connector (containing a black/red wire and a white/yellow wire) going to the exciter coil.
5. Connect an ohmmeter to the stator assembly side of the black/red electrical wire connector and ground (**Figure 9**). The resistance value should be approximately 50-250 ohms.
6. If the exciter coil does not meet the resistance specification, the alternator stator and CDI pulse generator assembly must be replaced as a unit. Refer to Chapter Four.
7. Connect the electrical connector and make sure all connectors are free of corrosion and are tight.
8. Install all items removed.

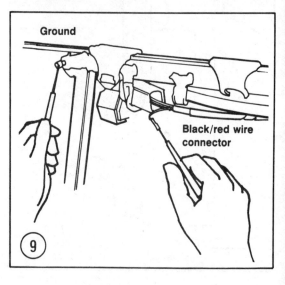

Ground

Black/red wire connector

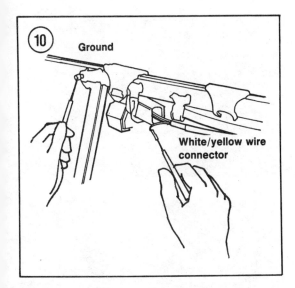

Ground

White/yellow wire connector

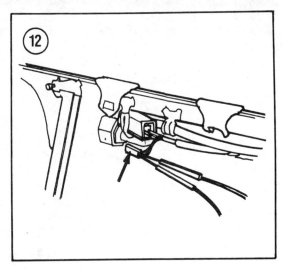

Lighting coil test

1. Place the ATV on level ground and set the parking brake.

2A. On 3-wheeled models, remove the seat/rear fender assembly as described in Chapter Twelve.

2B. On 4-wheeled models, remove the front fender and the seat/rear fender assembly as described in Chapter Twelve.

3. Remove the fuel tank as described in Chapter Six.

4A. On 1985-1987 models, disconnect the white/yellow electrical wire connector (**Figure 8**) going to the exciter coil.

4B. On 1988-on models, disconnect the 2-pin electrical connector (containing a black/red wire and a white/yellow wire) going to the exciter coil.

5. Connect an ohmmeter to the stator assembly side of the white/yellow electrical wire connector and ground (**Figure 10**). The resistance value should be approximately 0.1-1.0 ohm.

6. If the lighting coil does not meet the resistance specification, the alternator stator and CDI pulse generator assembly must be replaced as a unit. Refer to Chapter Four.

7. Connect the electrical connector and make sure all connectors are free of corrosion and are tight.

8. Install all items removed.

PULSE GENERATOR

Testing

1. Place the ATV on level ground and set the parking brake.

2A. On 3-wheeled models, remove the seat/rear fender assembly as described in Chapter Twelve.

2B. On 4-wheeled models, remove the front fenders and the seat/rear fender assembly as described in Chapter Twelve.

3. Remove the fuel tank as described in Chapter Six.

4. Disconnect the electrical connector (**Figure 11**) going to the pulse generator portion of the alternator stator assembly.

5. Connect an ohmmeter to the pulse generator side of the electrical connector's blue/yellow and green/white wires in the electrical connector (**Figure 12**). The resistance value should be approximately 50-200 ohms.

6. If the pulse generator does not meet the resistance specification, the alternator stator and CDI pulse generator assembly must be replaced as a unit.

7. Connect the electrical connectors and make sure all connectors are free of corrosion and are tight.

8. Install all items removed.

Removal/Installation

The CDI pulse generator is part of the alternator stator assembly. Removal and installation procedures are covered in Chapter Four.

LIGHTING SYSTEM

The lighting system consists of a headlight and taillight. **Table 3** lists replacement bulbs for these components.

Always use the correct wattage bulb as indicated in this section. The use of a larger wattage bulb will give a dim light and a smaller wattage bulb will burn out prematurely.

Headlight Bulb Replacement (3-wheeled Models)

Refer to **Figure 13** for this procedure.

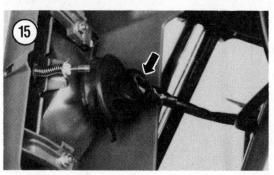

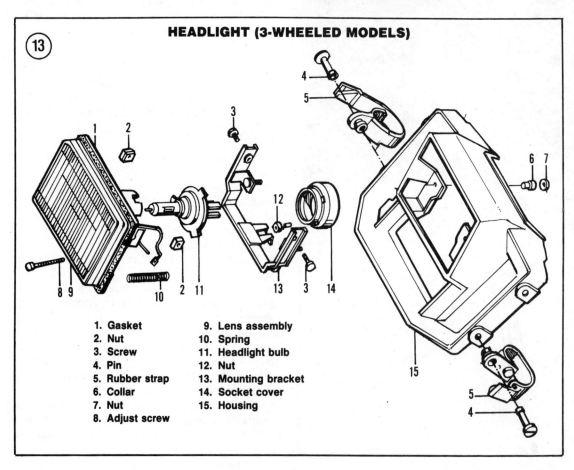

HEADLIGHT (3-WHEELED MODELS)

1. Gasket	9. Lens assembly
2. Nut	10. Spring
3. Screw	11. Headlight bulb
4. Pin	12. Nut
5. Rubber strap	13. Mounting bracket
6. Collar	14. Socket cover
7. Nut	15. Housing
8. Adjust screw	

1. Unhook the 4 rubber retaining straps (**Figure 14**) securing the headlight assembly onto the front forks.

2. Pull the headlight assembly unit away from the forks and rest it on the front fender.

3. Disconnect the electrical connector (**Figure 15**) from the headlight.

4. Remove the socket cover (**Figure 16**).

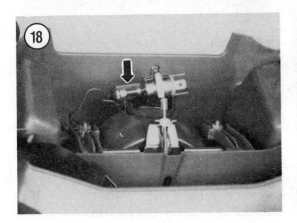

CAUTION
On 1986 models, carefully read all instructions shipped with the replacement quartz bulb. Do not touch the bulb glass with your fingers. Wear cottom gloves. Any traces of skin oil on the quartz halogen bulb will drastically reduce bulb life. Clean any traces of oil from the bulb with a cloth moistened in alcohol or lacquer thinner.

5. Unhook the bulb wire retaining clip (**Figure 17**) and remove the bulb (**Figure 18**) from the lens unit. Replace with a new bulb.

6. Install by reversing these removal steps, noting the following.

7. Make sure the socket cover is securely in place.

8. Make sure all electrical connections are free of corrosion and are tight.

Headlight Housing and Lens Removal/Installaton (3-wheeled Models)

7

Refer to **Figure 13** for this procedure.

1. Unhook the 4 rubber retaining straps (**Figure 14**) securing the headlight assembly onto the front forks.

2. Pull the headlight assembly unit away from the forks and rest it on the front fender.

3. Disconnect the electrical connector (**Figure 15**) from the headlight.

4. Remove the headlight case assembly.

5. To remove the lens assembly, perform the following.

   a. Remove adjust screw and spring (A, **Figure 19**).

   b. Remove the nuts (B, **Figure 19**) securing the lens assembly.

   c. Remove the lens assembly.

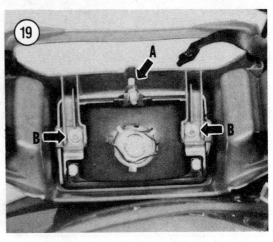

6. Install by reversing these removal steps. Make sure all electrical connections are free of corrosion and are tight.

Headlight Bulb Replacement
(4-wheeled Models)

Refer to **Figure 20** for this procedure.

1. On models equipped with the optional headlight guard, remove the guard.

2. Remove the screw (**Figure 21**) on top of the headlight housing.

3. Remove the screws (**Figure 22**) on the bottom of the headlight housing securing the headlight assembly into the housing.

4. Carefully pull the headlight lens assembly out of the housing.

5. Disconnect the electrical connector (**Figure 23**) from the headlight bulb.

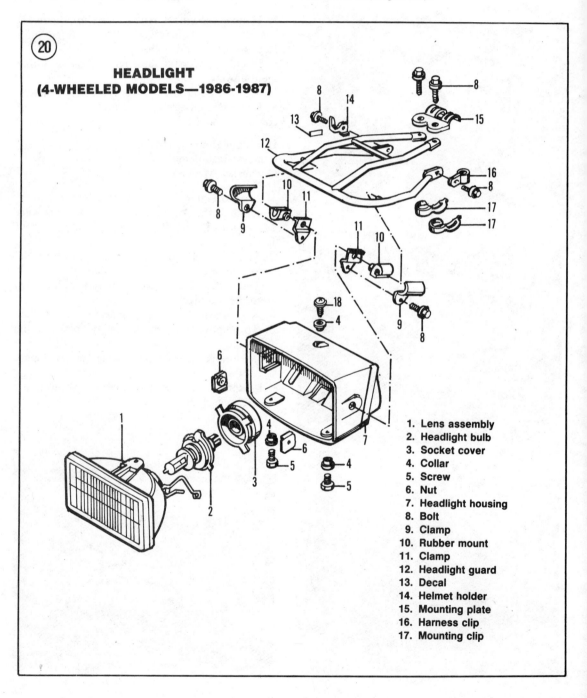

(20)

**HEADLIGHT
(4-WHEELED MODELS—1986-1987)**

1. Lens assembly
2. Headlight bulb
3. Socket cover
4. Collar
5. Screw
6. Nut
7. Headlight housing
8. Bolt
9. Clamp
10. Rubber mount
11. Clamp
12. Headlight guard
13. Decal
14. Helmet holder
15. Mounting plate
16. Harness clip
17. Mounting clip

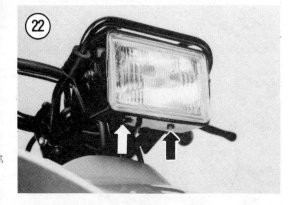

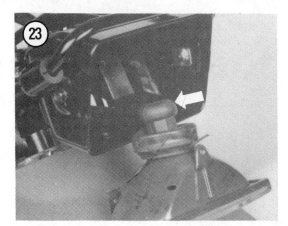

6. Remove the socket cover (**Figure 24**).

7. Unhook bulb retaining clip (**Figure 25**).

CAUTION
Carefully read all instructions shipped with the replacement quartz bulb. Do not touch the bulb glass with your fingers. Wear cotton gloves. Any traces of skin oil on the quartz halogen bulb will drastically reduce bulb life. Clean any traces of oil from the bulb with a cloth moistened in alcohol or lacquer thinner.

8. Remove the bulb (**Figure 26**) from the lens unit and replace with a new bulb.

9. Install by reversing these removal steps, noting the following.

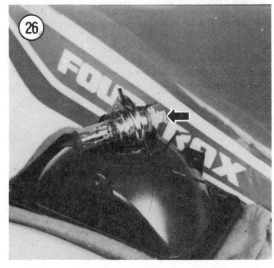

7

10. Be sure to use the collars with the bolts on each side securing the headlight lens assembly into the housing.

Headlight Bulb Replacement
(4-Wheeled Models—1988-on)

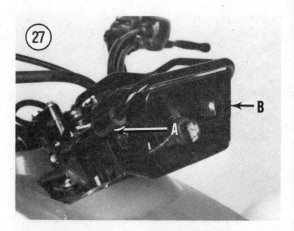

> *NOTE*
> *It may be easier to perform this procedure with the front fender removed. It is possible, but difficult, to work in the area under the front fender for bulb replacement. First try the procedure with the front fender in place, then remove it if necessary.*

1. If necessary, remove the front fender as described in Chapter Twelve.
2. Disconnect the electrical connector from the headlight bulb.
3. Remove the socket cover.
4. Unhook bulb retaining clip.

> *CAUTION*
> *Carefully read all instructions shipped with the replacement quartz halogen bulb. Do not touch the bulb glass with your fingers. Wear cotton gloves. Any traces of skin oil on the quartz halogen bulb will drastically reduce bulb life. Clean any traces of oil from the bulb with a cloth moistened in alcohol or lacquer thinner.*

5. Remove the bulb from the lens unit and replace with a new bulb.
6. Install by reversing these removal steps while noting the following.
7. Make sure the electrical connector is free of corrosion and is tight.

Headlight Housing
Removal/Installation
(4-Wheeled Models—1986-1987)

Refer to **Figure 20** for this procedure.
1. On models equipped with the optional headlight guard, remove the guard.
2. Remove the screw (**Figure 21**) on top of the headlight housing.
3. Remove the screws (**Figure 22**) on the bottom of the headlight housing securing the headlight assembly into the housing.
4. Carefully pull the headlight lens assembly out of the housing.

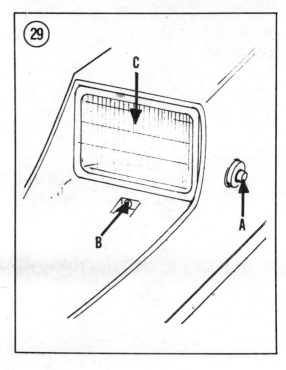

5. Disconnect the electrical connector (**Figure 23**) from the headlight bulb and remove the headlight lens assembly.

6. Carefully withdraw the electrical wires out of the rear of the headlight housing.

7. Remove the attachment bolt, mounting plates and rubber cushion (A, **Figure 27**) securing the headlight housing to the mounting bracket (B, **Figure 27**). Don't lose the rubber cushion within the mounting plates.

8. To remove the mounting bracket, remove the bolts (**Figure 28**) securing the bracket to the side and top of the steering column.

9. Install by reversing these removal steps. Make sure all electrical connections are free of corrosion and are tight.

10. Align the index mark on the headlight case with the punch mark on the mounting bracket.

Headlight Housing
Removal/Installation
(4-Wheeled Models—1988-on)

1. Disconnect the electrical connector from the headlight bulb.

2. Remove the bolt and collar (A, **Figure 29**) securing the headlight assembly to the front fender.

3. Unhook the adjust screw (B, **Figure 29**) from the front fender clip.

4. Remove the headlight assembly (C, **Figure 29**) from the front fender.

5. Install by reversing these removal steps. Note the following during installation.

6. Make sure the rubber grommet is in place on each side where the headlight mounts in the front fender.

7. Make sure the electrical connector is free of corrosion and is tight.

Taillight Bulb Replacement
and Housing Removal/Installation
(1985-1986 Models)

Refer to **Figure 30** for this procedure.

1. Remove the screws (**Figure 31**), nuts and collars securing the lens and the housing and remove the lens and gasket. Let the housing hang down by the electrical wires.

2. Wash out the inside and outside of the lens with a mild detergent and wipe dry.

3. Inspect the lens gasket and replace it if damaged or deteriorated.

4. Replace the bulb and install the lens. Do not overtighten the screws as the lens may crack.

7

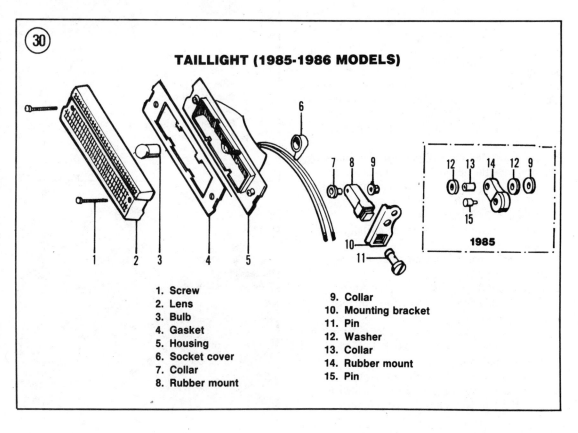

TAILLIGHT (1985-1986 MODELS)

1. Screw
2. Lens
3. Bulb
4. Gasket
5. Housing
6. Socket cover
7. Collar
8. Rubber mount
9. Collar
10. Mounting bracket
11. Pin
12. Washer
13. Collar
14. Rubber mount
15. Pin

1985

5. To remove the housing, disconnect the electrical connectors going to the wiring harness.
6. Install by reversing these removal steps.

Taillight Bulb Replacement and Housing Removal/Installation (1987-on Models)

Refer to **Figure 32** for this procedure.
1. Carefully pull the taillight assembly out of the rubber mounts on each side.
2. Rotate the bulb socket assembly 1/4 turn *counterclockwise* and remove the socket from the lens unit.
3. Carefully withdraw the bulb from the socket assembly.
4. Replace the bulb and install the socket assembly into the lens unit.
5. Rotate the bulb socket assembly 1/4 turn *clockwise* and install the socket into the lens unit.
6. If necessary, disconnect the electrical connectors going to the wiring harness.
7. Install by reversing these removal steps.

AC REGULATOR

Testing

1. Place the ATV on level ground and set the parking brake.
2A. On 3-wheeled models, perform the following.
  a. Remove the headlight lens as described under *Headlight Bulb Replacement* in this chapter.
  b. Disconnect the 6-pin lighting switch electrical connector.
2B. On 4-wheeled models, perform the following.
  a. Remove the headlight lens as described under *Headlight Bulb Replacement* in this chapter.
  b. Remove the front fenders as described in Chapter Twelve.
  c. Disconnect the 3-pin lighting switch electrical connector.
3. Connect a portable tachometer following the manufacturer's instructions.
4. Locate, but do not disconnect, the AC regulator 2-pin electrical connector to perform the following steps.
5A. On 3-wheeled models, the AC regulator 2-pin electrical connector (**Figure 33**) is located on the right-hand side of the steering stem.
5B. On 4-wheeled models, the AC regulator 2-pin electrical connector (**Figure 34**) is located just in front of the fuel tank on the left-hand side.

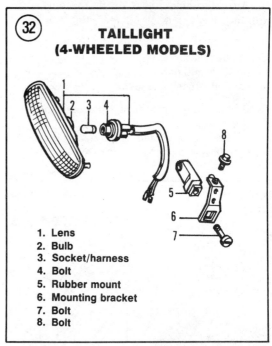

TAILLIGHT (4-WHEELED MODELS)

1. Lens
2. Bulb
3. Socket/harness
4. Bolt
5. Rubber mount
6. Mounting bracket
7. Bolt
8. Bolt

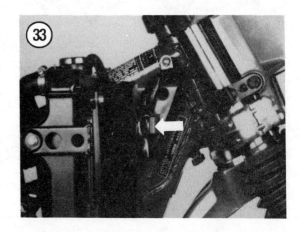

NOTE
Push the voltmeter's test probes into the electrical connector so they touch the bare wire of the terminal—not the wire's insulation. If a good electrical contact is not made you will get a false voltmeter reading.

6. Connect an AC voltmeter to the wiring harness side of the electrical connector's white/yellow and green wire terminals.

7. Start the engine and increase engine speed to the rpm listed in **Table 4**. Take voltage readings at the specified engine speed. The specified voltage readings are also listed in **Table 4**.

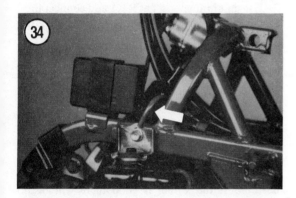

8. If the readings are either under or over the specified voltage, perform the following.
  a. Shut the engine off.
  b. Check the AC generator 2-pin electrical connector for loose wires and/or corroded terminals. Tighten or clean the terminals.
  c. Check the alternator lighting coil as described in this chapter.
  d. Check the wiring harness for a short or open circuit.

9. If all items check out okay in Step 8, the AC regulator is faulty and must be replaced as described in this chapter.

10. Disconnect the portable tachometer.

11. Install all items removed.

Removal/Installation

1. Place the ATV on level ground and set the parking brake.

2A. On 3-wheeled models, remove the headlight housing as described in this chapter.

2B. On 4-wheeled models, remove the front fenders as described in Chapter Twelve.

3. Disconnect the 2-pin electrical connector to the AC regulator.

4. Withdraw the AC regulator from the rubber mount on the frame. Refer to **Figure 35** for 3-wheeled models or **Figure 36** for 4-wheeled models.

5. Install a new AC regulator onto the rubber mount on the frame and attach the electrical connector to it.

6. Install all parts removed.

SWITCHES

Combination Lighting/Engine Kill Switch Testing

NOTE
If any portion of the combination switch is faulty, the entire switch assembly must be replaced.

1. Remove the headlight lens as described under *Headlight Bulb Replacement* in this chapter.

2A. On 3-wheeled models, disconnect the 5-pin electrical connector and single electrical connector from the combination lighting/engine kill switch. These are inside the headlight housing.

2B. On 4-wheeled models, disconnect the 3-pin electrical connector and single electrical connector from the combination lighting/engine kill switch. These are inside the headlight housing.

3. To test the lighting switch, perform the following.

a. Use an ohmmeter set at $R \times 1$ and connect the 2 leads of the ohmmeter to the brown and white/yellow wires.

b. Turn the lighting switch to the ON position. If the switch is good, there will be continuity (very low resistance).

c. Turn the lighting switch to the OFF position. There should be no continuity (infinite resistance).

4. To test the dimmer switch, perform the following.

a. Turn the dimmer switch to the HI position. Use an ohmmeter set at $R \times 1$ and connect the 2 leads of the ohmmeter to the brown and blue wires. If the switch is good there will be continuity (very low resistance).

b. Turn the dimmer switch to the LO position. Use an ohmmeter set at $R \times 1$ and connect the 2 leads of the ohmmeter to the brown and white wires. If the switch is good there will be continuity (very low resistance).

c. Turn the dimmer switch to the N (neutral) position. Use an ohmmeter set at $R \times 1$ and connect the 2 leads of the ohmmeter first to the brown and blue wires, then to the brown and white wires, then to the blue and white wires. If the switch is good, there will be continuity (very low resistance).

5. To test the engine kill switch, perform the following.

a. Use an ohmmeter set at $R \times 1$ and connect the 2 leads of the ohmmeter to the black/white and green wires.

b. Turn the kill switch button to the OFF position. If the switch is good there will be continuity (very low resistance).

c. Turn the kill switch button to the RUN position. If the switch is good there will be no continuity (infinite resistance).

6. If the switch fails to pass any of these tests, the switch assembly is faulty and must be replaced.

7. Install the headlight lens assembly as described in this chapter.

Ignition Switch Testing
(Models So Equipped)

1. Behind the ignition switch, disconnect the black/white and the green electrical connectors from the ignition switch.

2. Use an ohmmeter set at $R \times 1$ and connect the 2 leads of the ohmmeter to the black/white and green wires.

NOTE
The ignition switch grounds the ignition circuit in the OFF position.

3. Turn the ignition switch button to the OFF position. If the switch is good there will be continuity (very low resistance).

4. Turn the ignition switch button to the ON position. If the switch is good there will be no continuity (infinite resistance).

5. If the switch fails to pass any of these tests, the switch is faulty and must be replaced.

WIRING DIAGRAMS

Wiring diagrams are located at the end of this book.

Table 1 CDI TROUBLESHOOTING

Symptoms	Probable cause
Weak spark	Poor connections in circuit (clean and retighten all connections)
	High voltage leak (replace defective wire)
	Defective ignition coil (replace coil)
No spark	Broken wire (replace wire)
	Defective ignition coil (replace coil)
	Defective pulse generator (replace alternator stator assembly)
	Defective CDI unit (replace CDI unit)
	Faulty engine kill switch (replace switch)
	Defective ignition switch (models so equipped) (replace ignition switch)

Table 2 IGNITION SYSTEM TEST POINTS

Item	Terminal	Standard resistance values
Ignition coil primary circuit	Green and black/yellow wires	0.1-0.3 ohms*
Ignition coil secondary circuit with spark plug cap installed	Green wire and spark plug cap	7.4-11K ohms*
Alternator exciter coil	Black/red and green wires	50-250 ohms*
Pulse generator	Green/white and blue/yellow wires	50-200 ohms*
Engine stop switch (in RUN position)	Black/white and green wires	Infinity
Ignition switch (in ON position)	Black/white and green wires	Infinity

*For accurate readings the components must be at approximate temperature of 20° C (68° F).

Table 3 REPLACEMENT BULBS

Item/model	Voltage/wattage
Headlight	
ATC250R	
1985	12V 45/45W
1986	12V 60/55W
TRX250R/Fourtrax 250R	12V 45/45W
Taillight	
ATC250R	12V 5W
TRX250R/Fourtrax 250R	
1986	12V 8W
1987-on	12V 5W

Table 4 AC REGULATOR TEST

Model/year	Engine speed	Voltage
ATC250R	N.A.*	13.4-14.5
TRX250R/Fourtrax 250R		
1986	5,000 rpm	13.0-15.0
1987-on	3,000 rpm	12.0-14.0

*N.A.—Information not available from Honda.

COOLING SYSTEM

The pressurized cooling system consists of a radiator and a water pump. The water pump requires no routine maintenance and if found defective, replacement parts are available.

The 3-wheeled models are equipped with 2 radiators while the 4-wheeled models have a single radiator.

It is important to keep the coolant level up to the radiator inlet neck.

CAUTION
*Drain and flush the cooling system at least every 2 years. Refill with a mixture of ethylene glycol antifreeze (formulated for aluminum engines) and distilled water. Do not reuse the old coolant as it deteriorates with use. Do **not** operate the cooling system with only distilled water even in climates where antifreeze protection is not required. This is important because the engine is all aluminum. It will not rust but it will oxidize internally and have to be replaced. Refer to **Coolant Change** in Chapter Three.*

This chapter describes repair and replacement of cooling system components. **Table 1** at the end of this chapter lists all of the cooling system specifications. For routine maintenance of the system, refer to Chapter Three.

WARNING
Do not remove the radiator fill cap when the engine is hot. The coolant is very hot and is under pressure. Severe scalding could result if hot coolant comes in contact with your skin.

WARNING
The cooling system must be cool before removing any component of the system. Severe scalding could result if hot coolant comes in contact with your skin.

COOLING SYSTEM CHECK

Two checks should be made before disassembly if a cooling system fault is suspected.

1. Run the engine until it reaches operating temperature. While the engine is running a pressure surge should be felt when the lower radiator hose is squeezed.

2. If a substantial coolant loss is noted, the head gasket may be blown. In extreme cases coolant will leak into the crankcase when the bike is left standing for several hours. Sometimes sufficient coolant will leak in so the engine cannot be turned

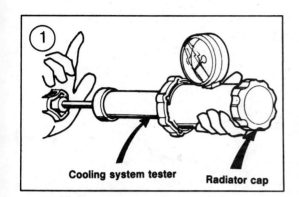

Cooling system tester   **Radiator cap**

over with the kickstarter. White smoke (vapor) might also be observed at the muffler when the engine is running. Coolant may also find its way into the transmission/clutch oil. If coolant has leaked into the crankcase or transmission/clutch oil cavity, correct the cooling system immediately and disassemble the engine as described in Chapter Four to remove all coolant residue.

PRESSURE CHECK

If the cooling system requires repeated refilling, there is probably a leak somewhere in the system and the following items should be checked. If you do not have the test equipment, the tests can be done by a Honda dealer, automobile dealer, radiator shop or service station.
1. Have the radiator cap pressure tested (**Figure 1**). The specified radiator cap relief pressure is listed in **Table 1**. The cap must be able to sustain this pressure for 6 seconds. Replace the radiator cap if it does not hold pressure or if the relief pressure is too high or too low.

CAUTION
If test pressure exceeds the specifications the radiator may be damaged.

2. Leave the radiator cap off and have the entire cooling system pressure tested. The entire cooling system should be pressurized up to, but not exceeding, 196 kPa (28.4 psi). The system must be able to sustain this pressure for 6 seconds. Replace or repair any components that fail this test.
3. Check all cooling system hoses for damage or deterioration. Replace any hose that is questionable. Make sure all hose clamps are tight.
4. Carefully clean any road dirt, bugs, mud, etc. from the radiator core(s). Use a whisk broom, compressed air or low-pressure water. If the radiator(s) has been hit by a small rock or other item, *carefully* straighten out the fins with a screwdriver.

NOTE
If the radiator has been damaged across approximately 20 percent or more of the frontal area, the radiator should be recored or replaced.

RADIATOR

Removal/Installation
(3-wheeled Models)

Refer to **Figure 2** for this procedure.
1. Place the ATV on level ground and set the parking brake. Block the rear wheels so the vehicle will not roll in either direction.
2. Remove the seat/rear fender assembly as described in Chapter Twelve.
3. Drain the cooling system as described in Chapter Three.
4. Remove the fuel tank as described in Chapter Six.
5. Disconnect the overflow tube from the filler neck (A, **Figure 3**).
6. Disconnect the joint tube (B, **Figure 3**) from each radiator and remove the joint tube.
7. Loosen the clamping screws on all radiator hose clamps. Move the clamps back onto the hose and off of their attachment points.
8. Remove the radiator-to-cylinder head hose (A, **Figure 4**).
9. Remove the radiator-to-water pump hose (B, **Figure 4**).
10. Remove the right-hand-to-left-hand radiator connector hose (C, **Figure 4**).
11. Remove the bolts securing the left-hand radiator grille (**Figure 5**) and remove the grille.
12. Remove the bolts (**Figure 6**) securing the left-hand radiator to the frame. Remove the left-hand radiator assembly from the frame.
13. Repeat Step 11 and Step 12 for the right-hand radiator assembly and remove the assembly.
14. Install by reversing these removal steps, noting the following.
15. Replace all radiator hoses if any are starting to deteriorate or are damaged.
16. Refill the cooling system with the recommended type and quantity of coolant as described in Chapter Three.

Removal/Installation
(4-wheeled Models)

Refer to **Figure 7** for this procedure.
1. Place the ATV on level ground and set the parking brake. Block the rear wheels so the vehicle will not roll in either direction.

8

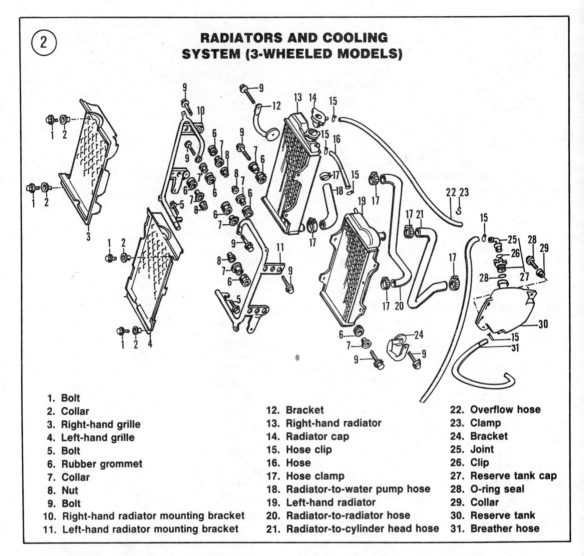

RADIATORS AND COOLING SYSTEM (3-WHEELED MODELS)

1. Bolt
2. Collar
3. Right-hand grille
4. Left-hand grille
5. Bolt
6. Rubber grommet
7. Collar
8. Nut
9. Bolt
10. Right-hand radiator mounting bracket
11. Left-hand radiator mounting bracket
12. Bracket
13. Right-hand radiator
14. Radiator cap
15. Hose clip
16. Hose
17. Hose clamp
18. Radiator-to-water pump hose
19. Left-hand radiator
20. Radiator-to-radiator hose
21. Radiator-to-cylinder head hose
22. Overflow hose
23. Clamp
24. Bracket
25. Joint
26. Clip
27. Reserve tank cap
28. O-ring seal
29. Collar
30. Reserve tank
31. Breather hose

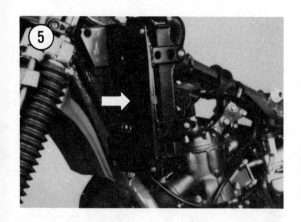

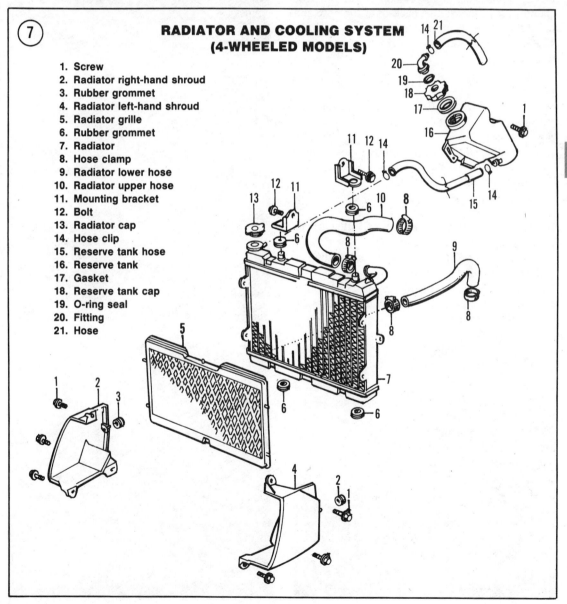

RADIATOR AND COOLING SYSTEM
(4-WHEELED MODELS)

1. Screw
2. Radiator right-hand shroud
3. Rubber grommet
4. Radiator left-hand shroud
5. Radiator grille
6. Rubber grommet
7. Radiator
8. Hose clamp
9. Radiator lower hose
10. Radiator upper hose
11. Mounting bracket
12. Bolt
13. Radiator cap
14. Hose clip
15. Reserve tank hose
16. Reserve tank
17. Gasket
18. Reserve tank cap
19. O-ring seal
20. Fitting
21. Hose

8

2. Remove the front fenders as described in Chapter Twelve.

3. Drain the cooling system as described in Chapter Three.

4. Remove the bolts (**Figure 8**) securing the radiator right-hand and left-hand shrouds and remove both shrouds.

5. Remove the AC regulator (**Figure 9**) from the front air inlet pipe.

6. Remove the bolts securing the front air inlet pipe and remove the pipe (**Figure 10**).

7. Disconnect the overflow tube from the filler neck (A, **Figure 11**).

8. Loosen the clamping screws on all radiator hose clamps. Move the clamps back onto the hose and off of their attachment points.

9. Remove the radiator-to-cylinder head hose (**Figure 12**).

10. Remove the radiator-to-water pump hose (B, **Figure 11**).

11. Remove the bolts (**Figure 13**) securing the radiator mounting brackets and remove the brackets.

12. Carefully pull the radiator up to release it from the mounting posts at the base of the radiator. Remove the radiator assembly from the frame.

13. Install by reversing these removal steps, noting the following.

14. Make sure the radiator shroud is attached to the radiator at the rear (**Figure 14**).

15. Replace all radiator hoses if any are starting to deteriorate or are damaged.

16. Refill the cooling system with the recommended type and quantity of coolant as described in Chapter Three.

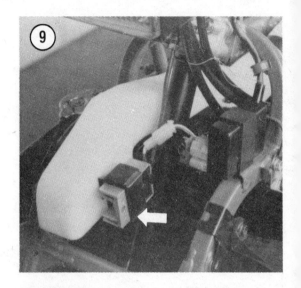

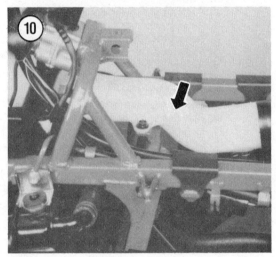

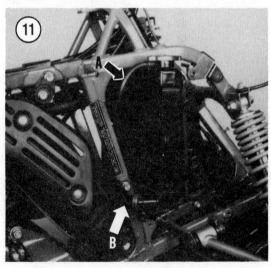

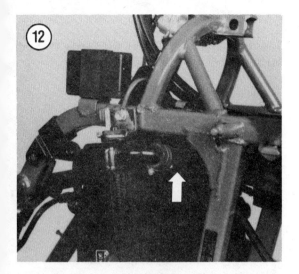

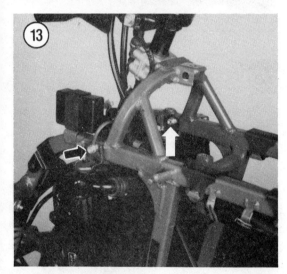

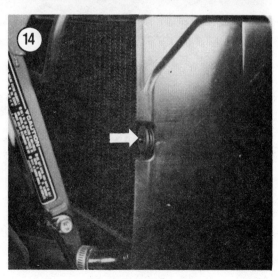

Cleaning and Inspection

1. If compressed air is available, use short spurts of air directed to the backside of the radiator and blow out dirt and bugs.

CAUTION
When using a whisk broom or stiff paint brush, do not press too hard or the cooling fins and tubes may be damaged, causing a leak.

2. Flush off the exterior of the radiator with a garden hose on low pressure. Spray both the front and the back to remove all road dirt and bugs. Carefully use a whisk broom or stiff paint brush to remove any stubborn dirt.

3. Carefully straighten out any bent cooling fins with a broad-tipped screwdriver or putty knife.

4. Check for cracks or leakage (usually a moss-green colored residue) at the filler neck, the inlet and outlet hose fittings and the upper and lower tank seams.

5. If the condition of the radiator is doubtful, have it checked as described under *Pressure Check* in this chapter. The radiator can be pressure checked while removed or installed on the bike.

6. To prevent oxidation to the radiator, touch up any area where the black paint is worn off. Use a good quality spray paint and apply several *light* coats of paint. Do not apply heavy coats as this will cut down on the cooling efficiency of the radiator.

8

WATER PUMP

Mechanical Seal Inspection

Inspect the small hole at the base of water pump on the right-hand crankcase cover (clutch cover) for signs of coolant leakage. If evident, replace the mechanical seal as described in this chapter.

Removal/Disassembly

Refer to **Figure 15** for this procedure.

1. Drain the cooling system as described in Chapter Three.

2. Drain the transmission/clutch oil as described in Chapter Three.

3. Remove the bolt (**Figure 16**) securing the kickstarter lever and remove the kickstarter lever.

4. On 3-wheeled models, perform the following.
   a. Remove the rear brake pedal assembly as described in Chapter Eleven.
   b. Remove the exhaust chamber as described in Chapter Six.

5. Loosen the clamping band screws (**Figure 17**) and disconnect the coolant hoses from the clutch cover.

6. Remove the bolts securing the water pump cover (**Figure 18**) and remove the cover, outer gasket, cover plate and inner gasket from the clutch cover. Discard the gaskets but don't lose the cover plate or locating dowels.

7. Shift the transmission into gear and have an assistant apply the rear brake.

8A. On 1985-1988 models, perform the following:
  a. Loosen the cap nut (A, **Figure 19**) securing the impeller. Remove the cap nut and sealing washer.
  b. Remove the impeller (B, **Figure 19**) and other washer.

> *NOTE*
> *On 1989 models, the cap nut is an integral part of the impeller.*

8B. On 1989 models, perform the following:
  a. Loosen the impeller.

b. Remove the impeller and washer.

9. Remove the bolts securing the clutch cover (**Figure 20**) and remove the cover and gasket. Discard the gasket but don't lose the locating dowels.

10. Turn the clutch cover over and withdraw the water pump drive shaft (**Figure 21**).

11. Inspect all components as described in this chapter.

Assembly/Installation

1. Install the water pump drive shaft (**Figure 21**) into the inner surface of the clutch cover.

2. Install a new clutch cover gasket (A, **Figure 22**) and make sure the locating dowels (B, **Figure 22**) are in place.

3. Align the groove water pump drive shaft (**Figure 21**) with the raised tab on the water pump drive (part of the balancer gear). See **Figure 23**.

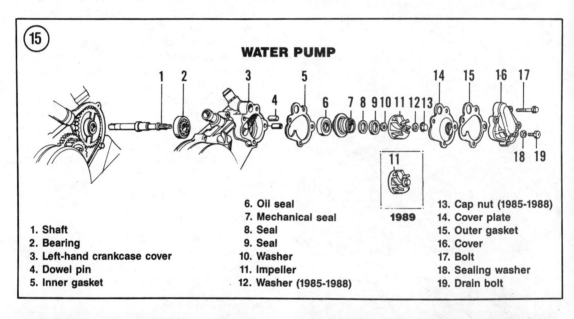

(15) **WATER PUMP**

1. Shaft
2. Bearing
3. Left-hand crankcase cover
4. Dowel pin
5. Inner gasket
6. Oil seal
7. Mechanical seal
8. Seal
9. Seal
10. Washer
11. Impeller
12. Washer (1985-1988)
13. Cap nut (1985-1988)
14. Cover plate
15. Outer gasket
16. Cover
17. Bolt
18. Sealing washer
19. Drain bolt

1989

CAUTION
*The clutch cover should fit snugly against the crankcase without force. In Step 4, if the water pump drive shaft and water pump drive are **not** properly meshed, the front portion of the clutch cover will not fit snugly against the crankcase. Remove the clutch cover and realign the 2 parts, then reinstall the clutch cover. Do not try to force the cover against the crankcase with the* cover bolts as the cover will be damaged.

4. Install the clutch cover and make sure the water pump drive shaft is properly meshed with the water pump drive. If necessary, slightly rotate the water pump shaft to align the shaft to the water pump drive. When the clutch cover fits properly against the crankcase, install the cover bolts and tighten all bolts securely.

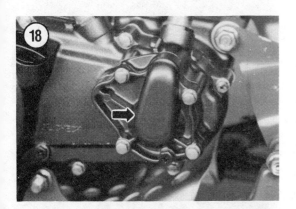

8

5. Connect the coolant hose onto the clutch cover and tighten the hose clamp securely.

> *NOTE*
> *On 1989 models, the cap nut is an integral part of the impeller. This new type of impeller can be installed on all other older models. This will solve the coolant leakage problem where coolant has leaked past the impeller threads. The new type of impeller is available from a Honda dealer in a set that includes the new impeller, drive shaft and washer.*

6A. On 1985-1988 models, perform the following:
  a. Install the washer and impeller (B, **Figure 19**).
  b. Install the sealing washer and cap nut (A, **Figure 19**).
  c. Tighten the cap nut to the torque specification listed in **Table 2.**
6B. On 1989 models, perform the following:
  a. Install the washer and impeller.
  b. Tighten the impeller to the torque specification listed in **Table 2.**
7. Shift the transmission into gear and have an assistant apply the rear brake.
8A. On 1985-1988 models, tighten the cap nut to the torque specification listed in **Table 2.**
8B. On 1989 models, tighten the impeller to the torque specification listed in **Table 2.**
9. Install the new inner gasket (**Figure 24**), cover plate and outer gasket (A, **Figure 25**).
10. Make sure the locating dowels (B, **Figure 25**) are in place.
11. Install the water pump cover (**Figure 18**) and the bolts. Tighten the bolts securely.
12. Install the kickstarter lever and pinch bolt. Tighten the bolt to the torque specification listed in Chapter Five.
13. On 3-wheeled models perform the following.
  a. Install the exhaust chamber as described in Chapter Six.
  b. Install the rear brake pedal assembly as described in Chapter Eleven.
14. Refill the cooling system as described in Chapter Three.
15. Refill the transmission/clutch with the recommended type and quantity of engine oil as described in Chapter Three.
16. Start the ATV and check for leaks.

Inspection

1. Inspect the water pump shaft for wear or damage. Replace if worn or damaged.
2. Rotate the bearing (**Figure 26**) in the clutch cover to make sure the bearing is not worn or

damaged. If the bearing is worn or damaged, replace it as described in this chapter.

3. Check the impeller blades (**Figure 27**). Replace the impeller if any blades are bent, chipped or missing.

4. Inspect the mechanical seal for wear or damage. Replace if necessary as described in this chapter.

5. Inspect the oil seal for wear or damage. Replace if necessary as described in this chapter.

Mechanical Seal, Bearing and Oil Seal Replacement

The following procedure requires special tools that are expensive and can be used only for this specific job. It may be less expensive to have these items replaced by a Honda dealer than to purchase the special tools. This procedure is included in case you choose to perform this task yourself.

1. Insert the 12 mm bearing spindle assembly (Honda part No. 07936-1660100) through the inner race of the bearing and onto the backside of the bearing.

2. Attach the remover weight (**Figure 28**) (Honda part No. 07741-0010201 or 07936-3710200) to the bearing spindle assembly.

3. Have an assistant hold onto the clutch cover and slide the weight back and forth on the remover. Withdraw the bearing from the clutch cover.

4. Carefully pry out the oil seal. Discard the oil seal.

5. From the backside of the clutch cover, carefully drive the mechanical seal from the clutch cover.

6. Set the clutch cover on a piece of soft wood to protect the sealing surface where it mates with the crankcase.

8

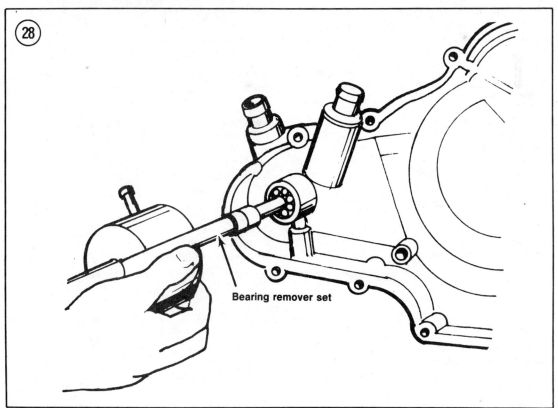

Bearing remover set

7. Use special tool, Mechanical Seal Installer (Honda part No. GH-AH-065-415) and carefully install the mechanical seal into the clutch cover (**Figure 29**).

8. Carefully install the oil seal into the clutch cover (**Figure 30**). Use special tools:

    a. Driver: Honda part No. 07749-0010000.

    b. Attachment, 28×30 mm: Honda part No. 07946-1870100.

    c. Pilot, 12 mm: Honda part No. 07946-0040200.

HOSES

Hoses deteriorate with age and should be replaced periodically or whenever they show signs of cracking or leakage. To be safe, replace the hoses every 2 years. The spray of hot coolant from a cracked hose can injure the rider and passenger. Loss of coolant can also cause the engine to overheat, causing damage.

Whenever any component of the cooling system is removed, inspect the hose and determine if replacement is necessary.

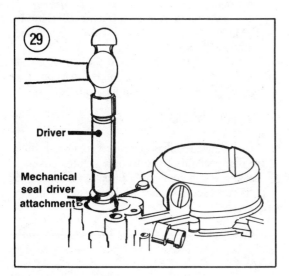

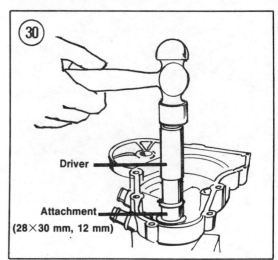

Table 1 COOLING SYSTEM SPECIFICATIONS

Coolant capacity (total system)	
ATC250R	
Coolant change	0.91 liters (0.97 U.S. qt., 0.802 Imp. qt.)
Disassembly	1.32 liters (1.4 U.S. qt., 1.632 Imp. qt.)
Fourtrax 250R	
Coolant change	1.16 liters (1.23 U.S. qt., 1.02 Imp. qt.)
Disassembly	1.52 liters (1.61 U.S. qt., 1.34 Imp. qt.)
Freezing point (hydrometer test)	
Water-to-antifreeze ratio	
55:45	−32° C (−25° F)
50:50	−27° C (−34° F)
45:55	−44.5° C (−48° F)
Radiator cap relief pressure	108-137 kPa (16-20 psi)

Table 2 COOLING SYSTEM TORQUE SPECIFICATIONS

Item	N·m	ft.-lb.
Water pump impeller cap nut (1985-1988)	8-12	6-9
Water pump impeller (1989)	10-14	7-10

CHAPTER NINE

FRONT SUSPENSION AND STEERING

This chapter describes repair and maintenance of the front wheel(s), hubs, forks and steering components.

Refer to **Table 1** for torque specifications for the front suspension components. **Tables 1-4** are located at the end of this chapter.

FRONT WHEEL
(3-WHEELED MODELS)

Removal

1. Place the ATV on level ground and set the parking brake. Block the rear wheels so the vehicle will not roll in either direction.

2. Jack up the front of the vehicle with a small hydraulic or scissor jack. Place the jack under the skid plate with a piece of wood between the jack and the skid plate.

3. Place wood block(s) under the skid plate to support the ATV securely with the front wheel off the ground.

4. Remove the bolts securing the brake hose clamp (**Figure 1**) to the fork slider. Remove the clamp and the brake hose.

5. Completely unscrew the lug nuts (**Figure 2**) securing the front wheel to the front hub.

6. On the right-hand side, loosen the nuts securing the front axle holder (**Figure 3**). It is not necessary to remove the axle holder.

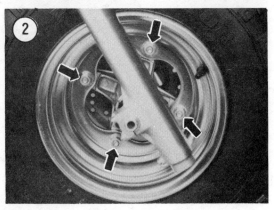

7. Unscrew the axle (**Figure 4**) from the left-hand fork leg.

8. Withdraw the axle from the right-hand side. Don't lose the axle spacers.

9. Slightly move the wheel to the right-hand side.

10. Remove the bolts (**Figure 5**) securing the front brake caliper assembly to the left-hand fork slider. Don't lose the brake hose guide plate on the upper mounting bolt.

11. Carefully slide the caliper assembly off of the brake disc. Tie the caliper to the handlebar with a bunji cord or piece of wire to take the strain off the brake hose.

12. Roll the wheel forward and hold onto the hub assembly as it is no longer attached to the wheel. Remove the wheel and the hub assembly.

> *NOTE*
> *Insert a piece of wood or vinyl tubing in the caliper in place of the brake disc. That way if the brake lever is inadvertently squeezed, the pistons will not be forced out of the cylinders. If this does happen the caliper might have to be disassembled to reseat the pistons and the system will have to be bled. By using the wood or vinyl tubing, bleeding the system is not necessary when installing the wheel.*

Installation

1. Make sure the axle bearing surfaces of the fork slider are free from burrs and nicks.

2. Clean the axle in solvent and thoroughly dry. Make sure all surfaces that the axle comes in contact with are clean and free from road dirt and old grease before installation.

3. Make sure that the axle spacers are in place on each side of the hub. Refer to **Figure 6** and **Figure 7**.

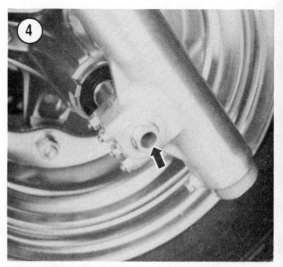

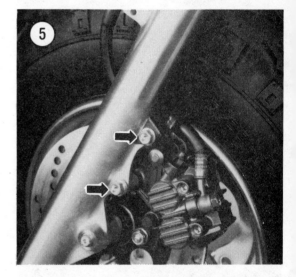

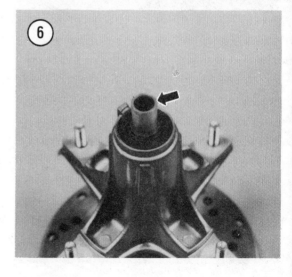

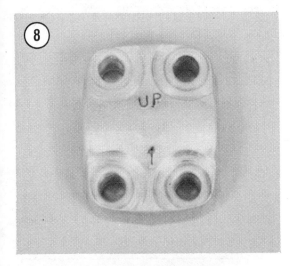

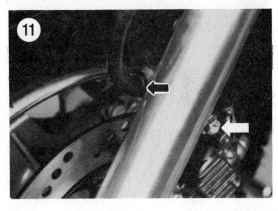

4. If removed, install the front axle holder with the UP mark and arrow facing up (**Figure 8**). Do not tighten the nuts at this time.

5. Position the wheel so the valve stem is on the right-hand side (**Figure 9**). Install the front hub assembly into the front wheel from the left-hand side with the brake disc on the left-hand side.

6. Position the front wheel/front hub assembly into place.

7. Carefully install the brake caliper assembly onto the brake disc. Be careful not to damage the leading edge of the brake pads during installation.

8. Install the caliper lower mounting bolt (**Figure 10**) and tighten only finger-tight at this time.

9. Install the caliper upper mounting bolt and brake hose guide plate (**Figure 11**). The brake hose guide plate must be installed as shown to keep the brake hose away from the front wheel.

10. Tighten the caliper mounting bolts to the torque specification listed in **Table 1**.

11. Move the front wheel into position and install the front axle (**Figure 4**) from the right-hand side through the wheel hub.

12. Screw the front axle into the left-hand fork leg and tighten to the torque specification listed in **Table 1**.

13. Tighten the upper front axle holder nuts first and then the lower nuts to the torque specification listed in **Table 1**.

14. Place the front wheel onto the front hub studs. Install the wheel lug nuts with the tapered side (**Figure 12**) going on first. Finger-tighten the nuts at this time; do *not* tighten them until the wheel is positioned correctly onto the wheel studs and the front wheel is on the ground.

15. Remove the wood blocks from under the skid plate.

WARNING
Always tighten the lug nuts to the correct torque specification or the lug nuts may work loose. •

16. Use a torque wrench and tighten the lug nuts to the torque specification listed in **Table 1**.

17. Raise the front wheel off the ground.

18. After the wheel is installed completely, rotate it. Apply the brake several times to make sure that the wheel rotates freely and that the brake is operating correctly.

FRONT WHEEL
(4-WHEELED MODELS)

Removal/Installation

1. Place the ATV on level ground and set the parking brake. Block the rear wheels so the vehicle will not roll in either direction.

2. Jack up the front of the vehicle with a small hydraulic or scissor jack. Place the jack under the frame with a piece of wood between the jack and the frame.

3. Place wood block(s) under the frame to support the ATV securely with the front wheels off the ground.

NOTE
This note relates to factory original equipped tires (after market tires may have a non-directional tread pattern). Note the direction of the front tire "V" tread prior to removal. The "V," or arrow, is facing in the direction of rotation on 1986 models. On 1987-on models, the "V," or arrow, is facing in the opposite direction of rotation. Prior to removing the wheel, mark the tire sidewall or the wheel indicating the direction of rotation and be sure to install the wheel on the correct side of the ATV. The tire must rotate in the correct direction.

4. Remove the lug nuts (**Figure 13**) securing the wheel to the hub/brake disc. Remove the front wheel.

5. Place the front wheel onto the front hub studs. Install the wheel lug nuts with the tapered side (**Figure 12**) going on first. Finger-tighten the nuts at this time. Do *not* tighten them until the wheel is positioned correctly onto the wheel studs and the front wheel is on the ground.

6. Remove the wood blocks from under the frame and lower the ATV.

WARNING
Always tighten the lug nuts to the correct torque specification or the lug nuts may work loose, resulting in the loss of the wheel.

7. Use a torque wrench and tighten the lug nuts to the torque specification listed in **Table 1**.

8. Raise the front wheel off the ground.

9. After the wheel is installed completely, rotate it. Apply the brake several times to make sure that the wheel rotates freely and that the brake is operating correctly.

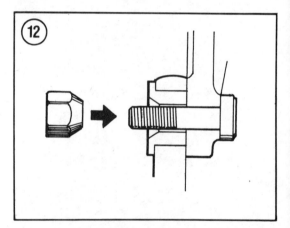

TIRES AND WHEELS

The ATV is equipped with tubeless, low pressure tires designed specifically for off-road use only. Rapid tire wear will occur if the ATV is ridden on paved surfaces. Due to their low pressure requirements, they should be inflated only with a hand-operated air pump instead of using an air compressor or the air available at service stations.

CAUTION
*Do not overinflate the stock tires as they will be permanently distorted and damaged. If overinflated they will bulge out similar to an inner tube that is not within the constraints of a tire and will **not** return to their original contour.*

NOTE
Additional inflation pressure in the stock tires will not improve the ride or the handling characteristics of the ATV. For improved handling, aftermarket tires will have to be installed.

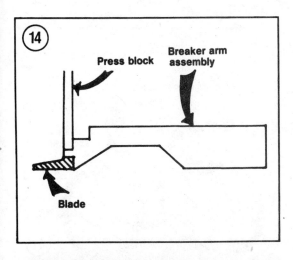

To guard against punctures from *small* objects install a commercially available liquid tire sealer into all tires though the valve stem. It's a good idea to carry a cold patch tire repair kit and hand held pump in the tow vehicle. ATV tire removal is different than on a motorcycle or automobile wheel.

CAUTION
*Do **not** use conventional motorcycle tire irons for tire removal as the tire sealing bead will be damaged when forced away from the rim flange.*

Tire Changing

The rims used on all models, front and rear, are of the 1-piece type and have a very deep built-in ridge to keep the tire bead seated on the rim under severe riding conditions. Unfortunately it also tends to keep the tire on the rim during tire removal.

A special tool is *required* for tire changing on these models and is shown in use in this procedure. The special tool from Honda is the Universal Bead Breaker (part No. GN-AH-958-BB1). The use of this specific tool is necessary as it exerts all of the applied pressure to a very small section of the tire bead at a time. Most other aftermarket bead breakers spread out the applied pressure over a larger section of the tire bead and therefore are unable to break the bead loose from this type of rim.

If you are going to purchase this bead breaker and also have other ATV's with different rim sizes, the blade length (**Figure 14**) is important and the following blades are recommended:

a. Short blade for 7 in. and 8 in. rims.
b. Long blade for 9 in. and 11 in. rims.

CAUTION
Use of the improper size blade may damge the rim, tire or the blade.

NOTE
*One aftermarket bead breaker, called the "Bead Buster" (**Figure 15**) works very well on this type of rim and is less expensive than the Honda special tool. It is available from Jenco Products, P.O. Box 610, Glide, Oregon 97443.*

1. On the front wheel of 3-wheeled models, the hub/disc must be removed from the rim for this procedure.
2. Remove the valve stem cap and core and deflate the tire. Do not reinstall the core at this time.

3. Install the correct size adapter onto the threaded shaft and place the wheel over this assembly (**Figure 16**).

4. Lubricate the tire bead and rim flanges with a liquid dish detergent or any rubber lubricant. Press the tire sidewall/bead down to allow the liquid to run into and around the bead area. Also apply lubricant to the area where the bead breaker arm will come in contact with the tire sidewall.

5. Hold the breaker arm at about 45° to the tire and insert the blade between the tire bead and the rim.

6. Push the breaker arm inward and downward until it is horizontal with the press block against the rim outer surface (**Figure 16**).

> *NOTE*
> *To completely seat the breaker arm, hold it horizontal and tap the end of the breaker arm with soft faced mallet to position the press block **completely** against the rim outer surface. This is necessary for the tool to work properly.*

7. With the breaker arm positioned correctly, place the breaker press head assembly over the press block of the breaker arm. Make sure the press head bolt is backed out all the way (**Figure 17**).

8. Position the nylon buttons on the press head against the inside edge of the rim.

9. Pull the threaded shaft and adapter assembly up and insert it into the breaker press head assembly. Install the bolts through the rim holes and the adapter to correctly position the adapter assembly to the center of the rim.

10. Slowly tighten the lever nut until both ends of the breaker press head assembly are in firm contact with the rim.

11. Slowly tighten the press head bolt until the reference mark on the press block is aligned with the top edge of the press head (**Figure 18**). At this point the tire bead *should* break away from the rim.

12. Using your hands, press down on the tire on either side of the breaker arm assembly and try to break the rest of the bead free from the rim.

13. If the rest of the tire bead cannot be broken loose, loosen the press head bolt and lever nut. Rotate the press head assembly about 1/8 to 1/4 of the way around the rim.

14. Repeat Steps 5-12 until the entire bead is broken loose from the rim.

15. Remove the tool assembly from the rim assembly. Turn the wheel over and repeat Steps 3-14 for the other rim flange.

16. Remove the tire from the rim using tire irons and rim protectors.

17. Inspect the rim sealing surface of the rim. If the rim has been severely hit, it will probably cause an air leak. Repair or replace any damaged rim.

18. Inspect the tire for cuts, tears, abrasions or any other defects.

19. Wipe the tire beads and rims free from any lubricating agent used in Step 4.

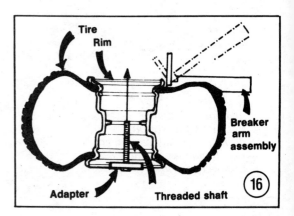

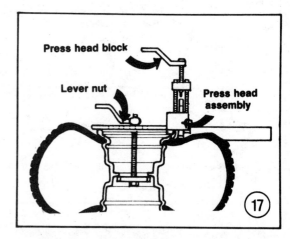

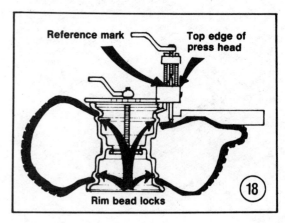

20. Apply clean water to the rim flanges, tire rim beads and onto the outer rim.

NOTE
Use only clean water and make sure the rim flange is clean. Wipe with a lint-free cloth before wetting down.

21. Install the tire onto the rim, starting with the side opposite the valve stem. Use tire irons and rim protectors and install the tire onto the rim.

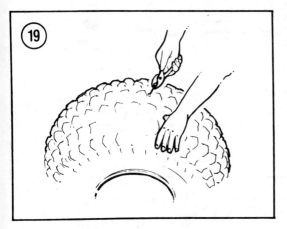

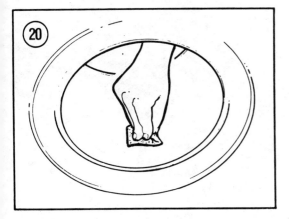

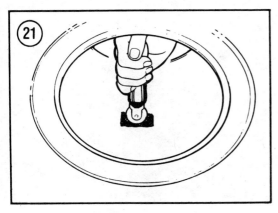

22. Install the valve stem core.

CAUTION
Do not use any mounting lubricant that contains silicone.

CAUTION
*Do not inflate the tire past the maximum inflation pressure listed in **Table 3**.*

23. Apply tire mounting lubricant or a liquid dish detergent to the tire bead and inflate the tire to the recommended tire pressure.

24. Deflate the tire and let it sit for about one hour.

25. Inflate the tire to the recommended air pressure (**Table 3**). Also check the tire circumference with a tape measure and compare to dimension given in **Table 3**.

26. Check for air leaks and install the valve cap.

Cold Patch Repair

This is the method that Honda recommends for patching a tire. The rubber plug type of repair is recommended only for an emergency repair, or until the tire can be patched correctly with the cold patch method.

1. Remove the tire as described in this chapter.

2. Before removing the object that punctured the tire, mark the location of the puncture with chalk or crayon on the outside of the tire. Remove the object (**Figure 19**).

3. On the inside of the tire, roughen the area around the hole slightly larger than the patch (**Figure 20**). Use the cap from the tire repair kit or pocket knife. Do not scrape too vigorously or you may cause additional damage.

4. Clean the area with a non-flammable solvent. Do not use an oil base solvent as it will leave a residue rendering the patch useless.

5. Apply a small amount of special cement to the puncture and spread it with your finger.

6. Allow the cement to dry until tacky—usually 30 seconds or so is sufficient.

7. Remove the backing from the patch.

CAUTION
Do not touch the newly exposed rubber with your fingers or the patch will not stick firmly.

8. Center the patch over the hole. Hold the patch firmly in place for about 30 seconds to allow the cement to dry. If you have a roller, use it to help press the patch into place (**Figure 21**).

9. Dust the area with talcum powder.

9

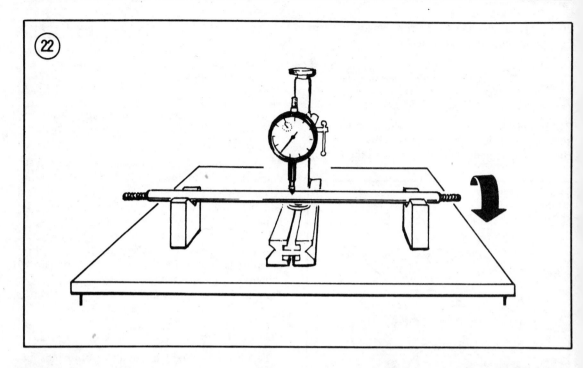

FRONT HUB/BRAKE DISC AND AXLE (3-WHEELED MODELS)

Inspection

Inspect each wheel bearing before removing it from the wheel hub.

> **CAUTION**
> *Do not remove the hub bearings for inspection as they will be damaged during the removal process. Remove the wheel bearings only if they are to be replaced.*

1. Perform Steps 1-5 of *Front Hub/Brake Disc and Axle Disassembly* in the following section.

2. Turn each bearing by hand. Make sure each bearing turns smoothly.

> **NOTE**
> *Some axial play (end play) is normal, but radial play (side play) should be negligible. The bearing should turn smoothly.*

3. On non-sealed bearings, check the balls for evidence of wear, pitting or excessive heat (bluish tint). Replace bearings if necessary; always replace as a complete set. When replacing, be sure to take your old bearings along to ensure a perfect matchup.

> **NOTE**
> *Fully sealed bearings are available from many good bearing specialty*

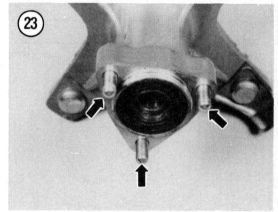

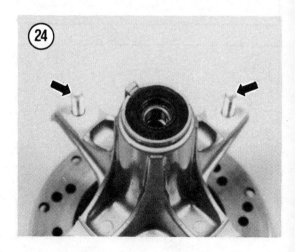

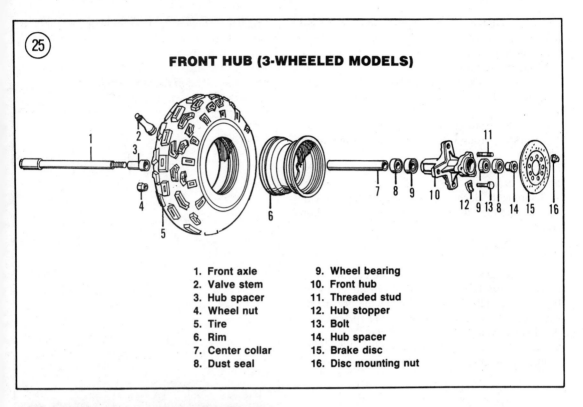

FRONT HUB (3-WHEELED MODELS)

1. Front axle
2. Valve stem
3. Hub spacer
4. Wheel nut
5. Tire
6. Rim
7. Center collar
8. Dust seal
9. Wheel bearing
10. Front hub
11. Threaded stud
12. Hub stopper
13. Bolt
14. Hub spacer
15. Brake disc
16. Disc mounting nut

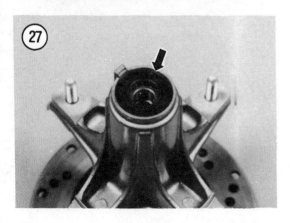

shops. Fully sealed bearings provide better protection from dirt and moisture that may get into the hub.

4. Check the axle for signs of fatigue, fractures and straightness. Use V-blocks and a dial indicator as shown in **Figure 22**. If the runout exceeds the service limit listed in **Table 2** or greater, the axle should be replaced.

5. Inspect the grease seals. Replace if they are deteriorating or starting to harden.

6. Check the brake disc threaded studs (**Figure 23**) and wheel lug studs (**Figure 24**) for wear or damage. Replace studs as necessary.

Disassembly

Refer to **Figure 25** for this procedure.

1. Remove the front wheel as described in this chapter.

2. If not already removed, remove front hub from the wheel.

3. Remove the nuts (**Figure 26**) securing the brake disc and remove the disc.

4. On the right-hand side, remove the axle spacer (**Figure 6**) and the grease seal (**Figure 27**).

5. On the left-hand side, remove the axle spacer and the grease seal (**Figure 28**).

6. Before proceeding any further, inspect the wheel bearings as described in this chapter.

7. To remove the left- and right-hand bearings and distance collar, perform the following.
   a. Insert a soft aluminum or brass drift into one side of the hub.
   b. Push the distance collar over to one side and place the drift on the inner race of the lower bearing.
   c. Tap the bearing out of the hub with a hammer working around the perimeter of the inner race.
8. Remove the center collar and tap out the opposite bearing.
9. Thoroughly clean out the inside of the hub with solvent and dry with compressed air or a shop cloth.

Assembly

1. On non-sealed bearings, pack the bearings with a good quality bearing grease. Work the grease in between the balls thoroughly. Turn the bearing by hand a couple of times to make sure the grease is distributed evenly inside the bearing.
2. Pack the wheel hub and distance collar with multipurpose grease.

> *CAUTION*
> *Install the wheel bearings with the sealed side facing out. During installation, tap the bearings squarely into place and tap on the outer race only. Use a socket (**Figure 29**) that matches the outer race diameter. Do not tap on the inner race or the bearing may be damaged. Be sure that the bearings are completely seated.*

3. Install the left-hand bearing.
4. Install the distance collar and the right-hand bearing.
5. Apply a light coat of multipurpose grease to the lips of both grease seals.
6. Install the grease seal onto each side of the hub.

7. Install the axle spacer on each side of the hub.
8. Install the brake disc with the DRIVE mark (**Figure 30**) facing toward the hub.
9. Install the disc nuts and tighten the nuts to the torque specification listed in **Table 1**.

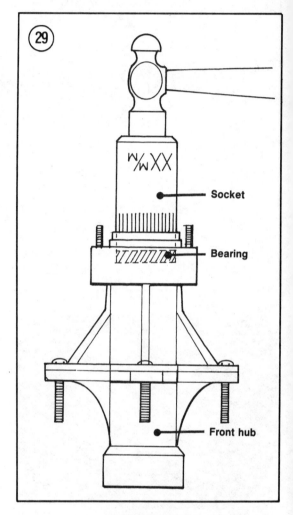

Socket

Bearing

Front hub

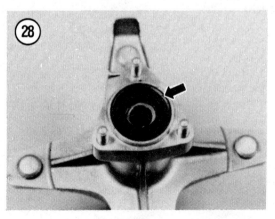

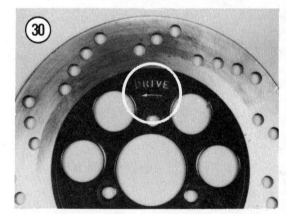

10. Install the front wheel as described in this chapter.

FRONT HUB/BRAKE DISC (4-WHEELED MODELS)

Inspection

Inspect each wheel bearing before removing it from the wheel hub.

> *CAUTION*
> *Do not remove the wheel bearings for inspection as they will be damaged during the removal process. Remove the wheel bearings only if they are to be replaced.*

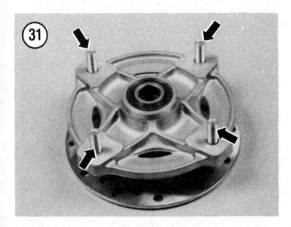

1. Perform Steps 1-7 of *Front Hub/Brake Disc Disassembly* in the following section.
2. Turn each bearing by hand. Make sure each bearing turns smoothly.

> *NOTE*
> *Some axial play (end play) is normal, but radial play (side play) should be negligible. The bearing should turn smoothly.*

3. On non-sealed bearings, check the balls for evidence of wear, pitting or excessive heat (bluish tint). Replace bearings if necessary; always replace as a complete set. When replacing, be sure to take your old bearings along to ensure a perfect matchup.

> *NOTE*
> *Fully sealed bearings are available from many good bearing specialty shops. Fully sealed bearings provide better protection from dirt and moisture that may get into the hub.*

4. Inspect the grease seals. Replace if they are deteriorating or starting to harden.
5. Inspect the threaded studs on the front hub/brake disc assembly (**Figure 31**) for wear or damage. Replace studs as necessary.

Disassembly

Refer to **Figure 32** for this procedure.

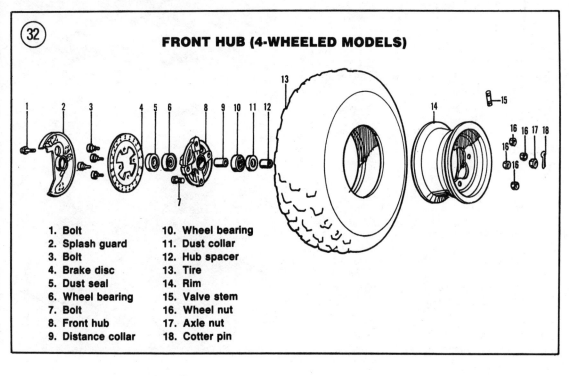

FRONT HUB (4-WHEELED MODELS)

1. Bolt
2. Splash guard
3. Bolt
4. Brake disc
5. Dust seal
6. Wheel bearing
7. Bolt
8. Front hub
9. Distance collar
10. Wheel bearing
11. Dust collar
12. Hub spacer
13. Tire
14. Rim
15. Valve stem
16. Wheel nut
17. Axle nut
18. Cotter pin

1. Remove the front wheel as described in this chapter.

2. Remove the front brake caliper assembly as described in Chapter Eleven.

3. On 1988-on models, remove the bolts securing the brake disc guard and remove the guard.

4. Remove the cotter pin and hub nut (**Figure 33**) securing the front hub/brake disc assembly.

5. Remove the collar (A, **Figure 34**) from the outside surface of the hub/brake disc.

6. Remove the bolts (A, **Figure 35**) securing the brake disc to the front hub and remove the brake disc.

7. Remove the grease seal (B, **Figure 34**) from the outside surface of the hub/brake disc.

8. Remove the grease seal (B, **Figure 35**) from the inside surface of the hub/brake disc.

9. Before proceeding any further, inspect the wheel bearings as described in this chapter.

10. To remove the inner and outer bearings and distance collar, perform the following:

   a. Insert a soft aluminum or brass drift into one side of the hub.

   b. Push the distance collar over to one side and place the drift on the inner race of the outer bearing.

   c. Tap the bearing out of the hub with a hammer working around the perimeter of the inner race.

   d. Remove the distance collar and tap out the inner bearing.

11. Thoroughly clean out the inside of the hub with solvent and dry with compressed air or a shop cloth.

Assembly

1. On non-sealed bearings, pack the bearings with a good quality bearing grease. Work the grease in between the balls thoroughly. Turn the bearing by hand a couple of times to make sure the grease is distributed evenly inside the bearing.

2. Pack the wheel hub and distance collar with multipurpose grease.

> *CAUTION*
> *Install the wheel bearings with the sealed side facing out. During installation, tap the bearings squarely into place and tap on the outer race only. Use a socket that matches the outer race diameter (**Figure 29**). Do not tap on the inner race or the bearing may be damaged. Be sure that the bearings are completely seated.*

3. Install the outer bearing.

4. Install the distance collar and the inner bearing.

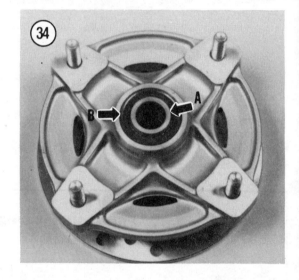

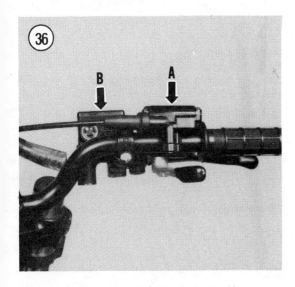

5. Apply a light coat of multipurpose grease to both grease seals.

6. Install the grease seal onto each side of the hub.

7. Install the collar (A, **Figure 34**) onto the outside surface of the hub/brake disc.

8. Install the front brake disc and bolts. Tighten the bolts to the torque specification listed in **Table 1.**

9. Install the front hub/brake disc onto the steering knuckle.

10. Install the hub nut and tighten to the torque specification listed in **Table 1.**

WARNING
Always install new cotter pins. Never reuse an old one as it may break and fall out.

11. Install a new cotter pin and bend the ends over completely.

12. Install the front brake caliper assembly as described in Chapter Eleven.

13. Install the front wheel as described in this chapter.

HANDLEBAR
(3-WHEELED MODELS)

Removal

CAUTION
Cover the fuel tank and front fender with a heavy cloth or plastic tarp to protect it from the accidental spilling of brake fluid. Wash spilled brake fluid off any painted, plated or plastic surface immediately as it will destroy the finish. Use soapy water and rinse thoroughly.

1. Remove the screws and clamp securing the throttle assembly (A, **Figure 36**) to the handlebar and remove the assembly.

2. Remove the screws (B, **Figure 36**) and clamp securing the front master cylider assembly to the handlebar. Remove the assembly and lay it over the front fender or fuel tank. Keep the reservoir in the upright position to minimize the loss of brake fluid and to keep air from entering the brake system. It is not necessary to remove the hydraulic brake line from the master cylinder.

3. Remove the screws securing the left-hand switch assembly (A, **Figure 37**) and remove the switch assembly.

4. Remove the wire clamps securing the electrical wires to the handlebar.

5. Remove the screws (B, **Figure 37**) and clamp securing the clutch/parking brake lever and remove the assembly.

6. Remove the bolts (**Figure 38**) securing the handlebar upper holders and remove the holders.

7. Remove the handlebar.

8. To maintain a good grip on the handlebar and to prevent it from slipping down, clean the knurled section of the handlebar with a wire brush. It should be kept rough so it will be held securely by the holders. The holders should also be kept clean and free of any metal that may have been gouged loose by handlebar slippage.

Installation

1. Position the handlebar on the handlebar lower holders so the punch mark on the handlebar is aligned with the top surface of the handlebar lower holders (**Figure 39**).

2. Install the handlebar upper holders with the punch mark facing toward the front.

3. Install the handlebar holder bolts. Tighten the forward bolts first, then the rear bolts. Tighten the bolts securely.

4. After installation is complete, recheck the alignment of the punch mark on the handlebar; readjust if necessary.

5. Install the left-hand switch assembly onto the handlebar. Install the screws and tighten the upper screw first, then the lower screw. Tighten the screws securely.

6. Install the clutch/parking brake lever assembly. Position the clamp with the UP mark toward the top and install the screws. Align the split mark of the housing with the punch mark on the handlebar. Tighten the upper screw first, then the lower screw. Tighten the screws securely.

7. Install the front brake master cylinder assembly. Position the clamp with the UP mark toward the top and install the screws. Align the split mark of the housing with the punch mark on the handlebar. Tighten the upper screw first, then the lower screw. Tighten the screws securely.

8. Place the throttle housing onto the handlebar and loosely install the holder and screws. Align the punch mark on the housing with the mating surface of the master cylinder holder. Tighten the forward screw first and then the rear screw. Tighten the screws securely.

9. After all assemblies have been installed, test each one to make sure it operates correctly with no binding. Correct any problem at this time.

STEERING STEM (3-WHEELED MODELS)

The steering stem is equipped with assembled roller bearings at the top and bottom. Refer to **Figure 40** for this procedure.

Disassembly

1. Remove the front wheel as described in this chapter.

2. Remove the headlight housing (A, **Figure 41**) as described in Chapter Seven.

3. Remove the bolts securing the front fender and remove the fender (B, **Figure 41**).

4. Remove the front forks (A, **Figure 42**) as described in this chapter.

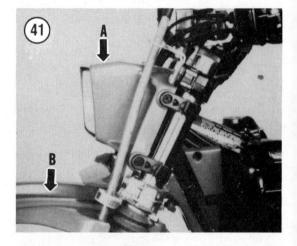

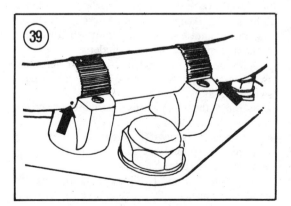

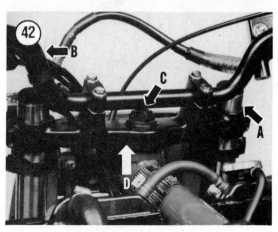

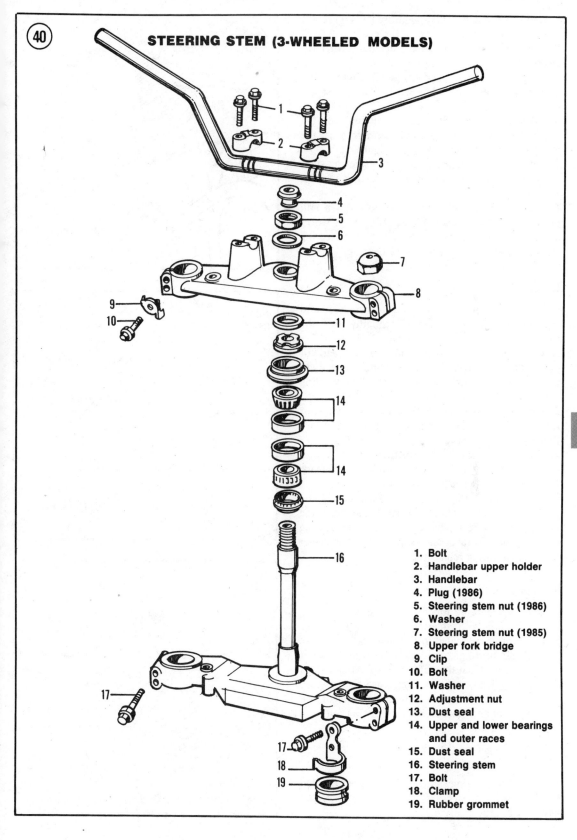

STEERING STEM (3-WHEELED MODELS)

1. Bolt
2. Handlebar upper holder
3. Handlebar
4. Plug (1986)
5. Steering stem nut (1986)
6. Washer
7. Steering stem nut (1985)
8. Upper fork bridge
9. Clip
10. Bolt
11. Washer
12. Adjustment nut
13. Dust seal
14. Upper and lower bearings
    and outer races
15. Dust seal
16. Steering stem
17. Bolt
18. Clamp
19. Rubber grommet

5. Remove the handlebar assembly (B, **Figure 42**) as described in this chapter.

6. Remove the steering stem nut and washer (C, **Figure 42**).

7. Remove the upper fork bridge (D, **Figure 42**).

8. Remove the washer (A, **Figure 43**) and dust seal (B, **Figure 43**).

9. Loosen the steering stem adjusting nut (C, **Figure 43**). Use a large drift and hammer or use the easily improvised tool shown in **Figure 44**.

10. Have an assistant hold onto the steering stem and remove the steering stem adjusting nut (C, **Figure 43**).

11. Lower the steering stem assembly down and out of the steering head (**Figure 45**). Don't worry about catching any loose steel balls as the steering stem is equipped with assembled bearings.

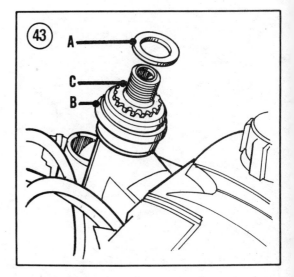

Inspection

1. Clean the bearing races in the steering head and the bearings with solvent. Throughly dry the bearings.

2. Check the welds around the steering head for cracks and fractures. If any are found, have them repaired by a competent frame shop or welding service.

3. Check the bearings for pitting, scratches or discoloration indicating wear or corrosion. Replace them in sets if any are bad.

4. Check the races for pitting, galling and corrosion. If any of these conditions exist, replace the races as described in this chapter.

5. Check the steering stem for cracks and check the lower bearing for damage or wear. If damaged, the bearing should be replaced as a complete bearing set. Take the old races and bearings to your dealer to ensure accurate replacement.

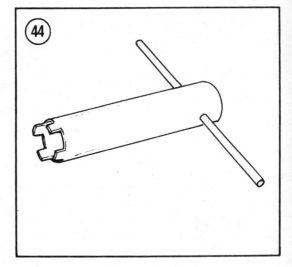

Assembly

Refer to **Figure 40** for this procedure.

1. Make sure both steering head bearing outer races are properly seated in the steering head tube.

2. Pack the bearing cavities of both bearings with bearing grease. Coat the outer bearing races, within the steering head, with bearing grease also.

3. Apply a coat of grease to the threads of the steering stem and steering stem adjusting nut.

NOTE
The upper and lower bearings are the same size.

4. Install the steering stem, with the lower bearing in place, into the steering head tube and have an assistant hold it firmly in place.

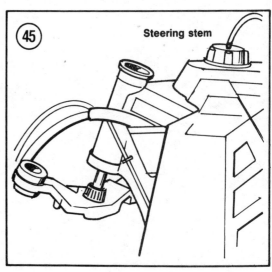

Steering stem

5. Install the upper bearing into the steering head tube (**Figure 46**).

6. Position the steering stem adjusting nut with the stepped side facing down. Install the steering stem adjusting nut and tighten it to the preliminary torque specification listed in **Table 1**.

7. Turn the steering stem from lock-to-lock 5-6 times to seat the bearings. Loosen the steering stem adjusting nut.

8. Tighten the steering stem adjusting nut to the final torque specification listed in **Table 1**.

9. Install the dust seal and washer.

10. Temporarily install the fork tubes in the lower fork bridge far enough so that the upper fork bridge will fit onto them when installed in the next step. Tighten the lower fork bridge bolts just tight enough to hold the forks in place.

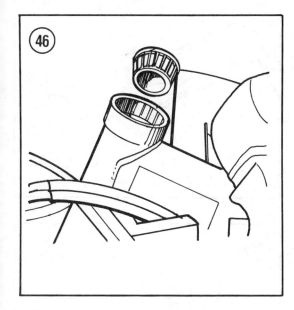

NOTE
Steps 11-13 must be performed in this order to assure proper upper and lower fork bridge-to-fork alignment.

11. Install the upper fork bridge, washer and steering stem nut. Tighten the steering stem only finger-tight at this time.

12. Loosen the lower fork bridge bolts and position the fork tubes so the alignment line is flush with the top surface of the upper fork bridge (**Figure 47**).

13. Tighten these items in the following order.

   a. Lower fork bridge bolts.

   b. Steering stem nut.

   c. Upper fork bridge bolts.

Tighten all items to the torque specification listed in **Table 1**.

14. Install the handlebar as described in this chapter.

15. Install the front fender.

16. Install the headlight housing assembly as described in Chapter Nine.

17. Install the front wheel as described in this chapter.

STEERING HEAD BEARING RACE

The headset and steering stem bearing races are pressed into place. Because they are easily bent, do not remove them unless they are worn and require replacement.

Steering Head Bearing Outer Race Replacement

NOTE
The top and bottom bearing races are the same size.

To remove the headset race, insert a hardwood stick or soft punch into the head tube and carefully tap the race out from the inside (**Figure 48**). After it is started, tap around the race so that neither the race nor the head tube is damaged.

To install the headset race, tap it in slowly with a block of wood, a suitable size socket or piece of pipe (**Figure 49**). Make sure that the race is squarely seated in the headset race bore before tapping it into place. Tap the race in until it is flush with the steering head surface.

Steering Stem Lower Bearing Assembly and Dust Seal Removal/Installation

NOTE
Do not remove the steering stem lower bearing assembly unless it is going to be

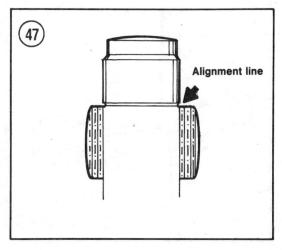

Alignment line

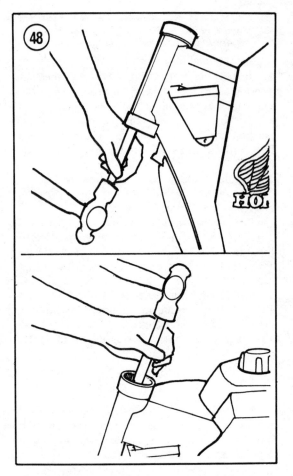

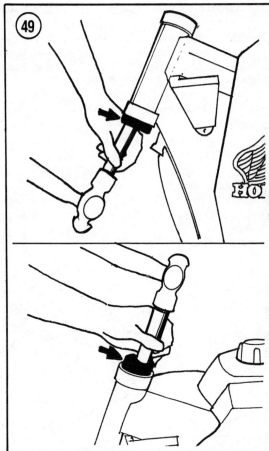

replaced with a new bearing. Do not install a bearing that has been removed as it is no longer true to alignment.

1. Install the steering stem adjusting nut (A, **Figure 50**) to the steering stem to protect the threads during this procedure.

2. To remove the steering stem lower bearing assembly (B, **Figure 50**), carefully pry it up with a screwdriver. Work around in a circle, prying a little at a time. If a screwdriver will not work, use a cold chisel and hammer.

3. Remove the steering stem adjusting nut.

4. Remove the lower bearing assembly and dust seal from the steering stem.

5. Slide a new dust seal over the steering stem.

NOTE
The lower bearing assembly should be pressed into place with a hydraulic press and a special tool. This is best entrusted to a dealer or machine shop.

6. If a press and special tool are not available, the lower bearing assembly can be installed as follows.

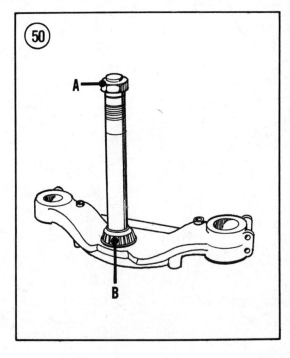

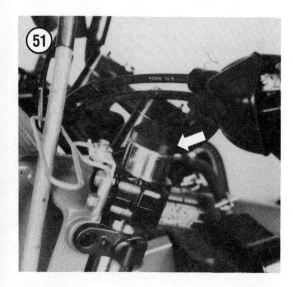

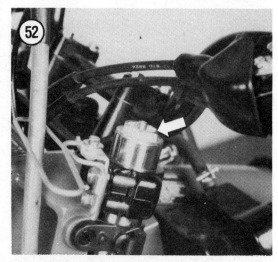

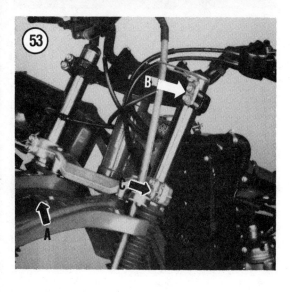

a. Slide the lower bearing assembly over the steering stem.

b. Tap the lower bearing assembly down with a long piece of metal pipe that fits the inner race diameter or use a piece of hardwood. Work around in a circle so the race will not be bent. Make sure it is seated squarely and is all the way down.

FRONT FORKS
(3-WHEELED MODELS)

The front suspension uses a spring controlled, hydraulically damped, telescopic fork.

Before suspecting major trouble, drain the front fork oil and refill with the proper type and quantity. Refer to *Front Fork Oil Change* in Chapter Three. If you still have trouble, such as poor damping, a tendency to bottom or top out or leakage around the rubber seals, follow the service procedures in this section.

To simplify fork service and to prevent the mixing of parts, the fork legs should be removed, serviced and installed individually.

Removal/Installation

NOTE
*Perform Step 1 **only** if the front forks are going to be disassembled. For fork removal only, start with Step 2.*

NOTE
The Allen screw in the base of the slider has been secured with Loctite and is often very difficult to remove because the damper rod will turn inside the slider. It sometimes can be removed with an air impact driver. If you are unable to remove it, take the fork tubes to a dealer and have the screws removed.

1. If the fork assembly is going to be disassembled, perform the following.
   a. Remove the top cap cover (**Figure 51**).
   b. Using a small screwdriver, depress the air valve and release all fork air pressure.
   c. Slightly loosen the Allen bolt at the base of the slider. If the bolt is loosened too much, fork oil may start to drain out of the slider.
   d. Loosen the fork top bolt (**Figure 52**).
2. Remove the front wheel as described in this chapter.
3. Remove the headlight housing as described in Chapter Seven.
4. Remove the bolts securing the front fender and remove the fender (A, **Figure 53**).

5. Loosen the upper (B, **Figure 53**) and lower fork bridge bolts (C, **Figure 53**).

6. Remove the fork tube. It may be necessary to slightly rotate the fork tube while pulling it down and out.

7. Install by reversing these removal steps, noting the following.

8. Position the fork tubes so the alignment line is flush with the top surface of the upper fork bridge (**Figure 54**).

9. Tighten the upper and lower fork bridge bolts to the torque specification listed in **Table 1**.

10. Remove the wood blocks from under the engine skid plate. Apply the front brake and pump the forks several times.

Disassembly

WARNING
*If disassembling a fork assembly that has been bent and damaged, take precautions when removing the fork top cap bolt. If the fork assembly is compressed, the fork spring(s) is compressed and is exerting more than normal force on the fork top cap bolt. The spring(s) will **shoot** out with considerable force when the fork top cap bolt is removed. If you choose to disassemble a fork in this condition, protect youself and anyone around you at the time of disassembly accordingly.*

Refer to **Figure 55** during the disassembly and assembly procedures.

1. Loosen the clamping screw at the top of the rubber boot. Remove the rubber boot from the groove in the top of the slider. Slide the rubber boot off of the fork tube.

2. Clamp the slider in a vise with soft jaws.

3. If not loosened in Step 1 of *Removal/Installation,* loosen the Allen head screw in the bottom of the slider.

NOTE
This screw has been secured with Loctite and is often very difficult to remove because the damper rod will turn inside the slider. It sometimes can be removed with an air impact driver. If you are unable to remove it, take the fork tubes to a dealer and have the screws removed.

4. Remove the Allen head screw and washer.

5. If not loosened in Step 1 of *Removal/Installation,* hold the upper fork tube in a vise with soft jaws and loosen the fork top cap bolt.

WARNING
Be careful when removing the fork top cap bolt as the spring(s) is under pressure.

6. Remove the fork top cap bolt from the fork.

7A. On 1985 models, remove the upper short spring "A," the spring seat and the lower long spring "B."

7B. On 1986 models, remove the fork spring.

8. Remove the fork from the vise, pour the fork oil out and discard it. Pump the fork several times by hand to expel most of the remaining oil.

9. Install the fork slider in a vise with soft jaws.

10. Remove the dust seal and the circlip from the slider.

NOTE
It may be necessary to slightly heat the area on the slider around the oil seal

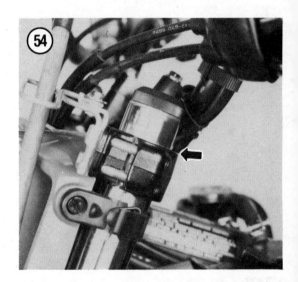

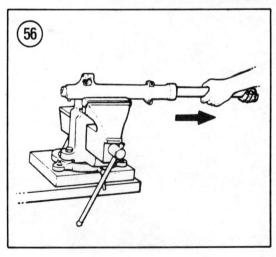

before removal. Use a rag soaked in hot water. Do not apply a flame directly to the fork slider.

11. There is an interference fit between the bushing in the fork slider and the bushing on the fork tube. In order to separate them, perform the following.

a. Place the fork slider in a vise with soft jaws.

b. To remove the fork tube from the slider, pull hard on the fork tube using quick in and out strokes (**Figure 56**). Doing this will withdraw the bushing, backup ring, oil seal and fork tube from the slider.

c. Withdraw the fork tube from the slider.

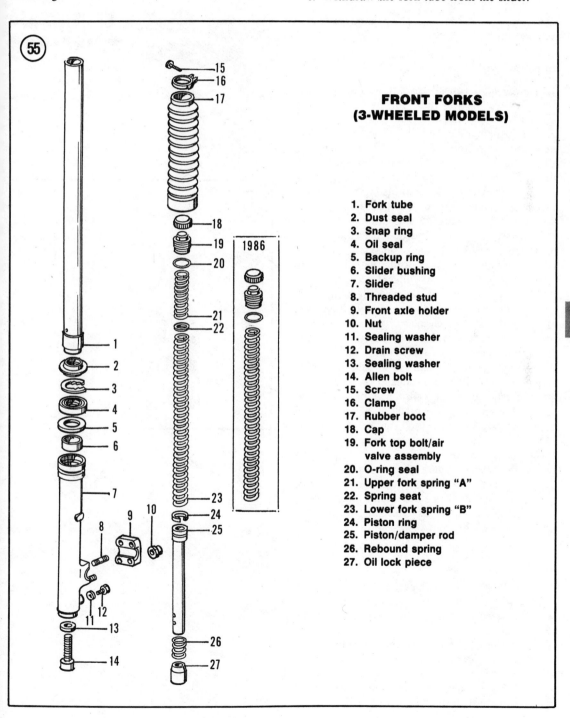

FRONT FORKS (3-WHEELED MODELS)

1. Fork tube
2. Dust seal
3. Snap ring
4. Oil seal
5. Backup ring
6. Slider bushing
7. Slider
8. Threaded stud
9. Front axle holder
10. Nut
11. Sealing washer
12. Drain screw
13. Sealing washer
14. Allen bolt
15. Screw
16. Clamp
17. Rubber boot
18. Cap
19. Fork top bolt/air valve assembly
20. O-ring seal
21. Upper fork spring "A"
22. Spring seat
23. Lower fork spring "B"
24. Piston ring
25. Piston/damper rod
26. Rebound spring
27. Oil lock piece

1986

9

12. Turn the fork tube upside down and slide off the oil seal and backup ring and bushing from the fork tube (**Figure 57**).

> *NOTE*
> *Do not discard the fork slider bushing at this time. It will be used during the installation procedure.*

13. Remove the oil lockpiece, the damper rod and rebound spring.

Inspection

1. Thoroughly clean all parts in solvent and dry them. Check the fork tube for signs of wear or scratches.

2. Check the damper rod for straightness. **Figure 58** shows one method. The rod should be replaced if the runout is warped to the service limit dimension in **Table 2** or greater.

3. Check the damper rod and piston ring for wear or damage (**Figure 59**); replace if necessary.

4. Check the fork tube for straightness. If bent or severely scratched, it should be replaced.

5. Check the slider for dents or exterior damage that may cause the upper fork tube to hang up during riding. Replace the slider if necessary.

6. Measure the uncompressed length of the fork springs (not rebound spring) as shown in **Figure 60**. If the spring(s) has sagged to the service limit dimension listed in **Table 2** or less, the spring(s) must be replaced.

7. Inspect the slider and fork tube bushings (**Figure 61**). If either is scratched or scored they must be replaced. If the Teflon coating is worn off so that the copper base material is showing on approximately 3/4 of the total surface, the bushing must be replaced. Also check for distortion on each check point of the backup ring; replace as necessary. Refer to **Figure 62**.

8. Any parts that are worn or damaged should be replaced. Simply cleaning and reinstalling unserviceable components will not improve the performance of the front suspension.

Assembly

1. Coat all parts with fresh automatic transmission fluid or fork oil before installation.

2. If removed, install a new fork tube bushing (**Figure 63**).

3. Install the rebound spring onto the damper rod and insert this assembly into the fork tube (**Figure 64**).

4A. On 1985 models, to hold the damper rod in place, temporarily install the lower long fork spring

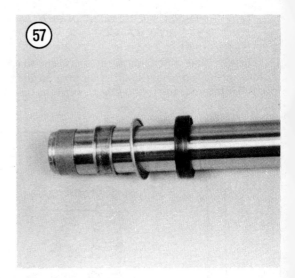

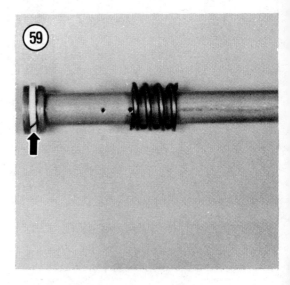

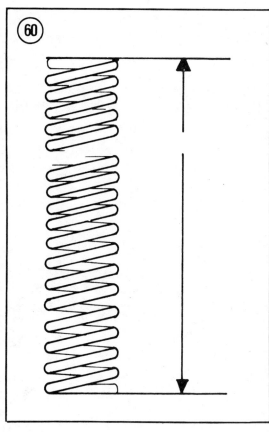

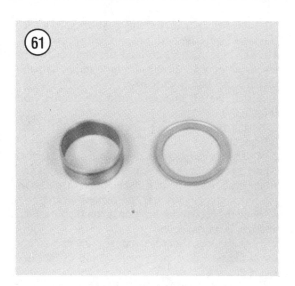

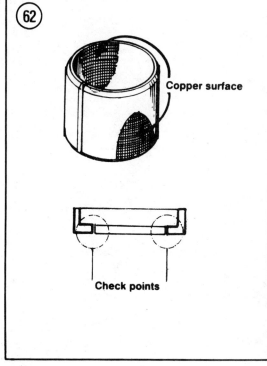

Copper surface

Check points

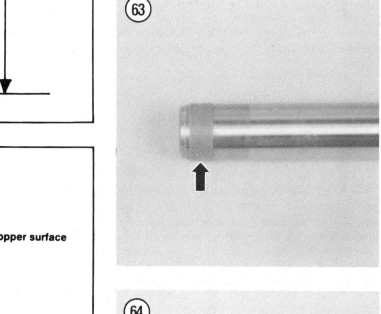

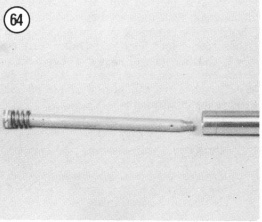

9

"B," the spring seat, the upper short spring "A" (**Figure 65**) and the fork top cap bolt (**Figure 66**).

4B. On 1986 models, to hold the damper rod in place, temporarily install the fork spring and the fork top cap bolt (**Figure 66**).

5. Install the oil lockpiece onto the damper rod (**Figure 67**).

6. Install the upper fork assembly into the slider (**Figure 68**).

7. Make sure the gasket is on the Allen head screw. Apply Loctite Lock N' Seal to the threads of the Allen head screw before installation. Install it in the fork slider (**Figure 69**) and tighten securely.

8. Slide the fork slider bushing down the fork tube and rest it on the slider.

9. Slide the fork slider backup ring (flange side up) down the fork tube and rest it on top of the fork slider bushing.

10. Place the old fork slider bushing on top of the backup ring. Drive the bushing into the fork slider with Honda special tool Fork Seal Driver part No. 07947-4630100. Drive the bushing into place until it seats completely in the recess in the slider. Remove the installation tool and the old fork slider bushing.

> *NOTE*
> *A piece of 2 in. galvanized pipe may also work as a tool. If both ends are threaded (a close nipple pipe fitting), wrap one end with duct tape to prevent the threads from damaging the interior of the slider.*

11. To prevent damage to the inside of the new fork seal during installation, wrap the alignment groove in the top of the fork tube with smooth, unabrasive, clear tape; do *not* use duct or masking tape.

12. Coat the new seal with automatic transmission fluid. Position the seal with the marking facing upward and slide it down onto the fork tube (**Figure 70**). Drive the seal into the fork slider with Honda special tool Fork Seal Driver (part No. 07947-4630100); refer to **Figure 71**. Drive the oil seal in until the snap ring groove in the slider can be seen above the top surface of the oil seal. Remove the installation tool.

> *NOTE*
> *A piece of 2 in. galvanized pipe may also work as a tool. If both ends are threaded (a close nipple pipe fitting), wrap one end with duct tape to prevent the threads from damaging the interior of the slider.*

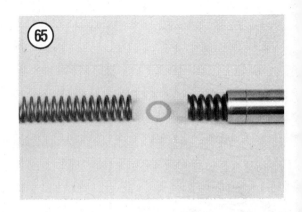

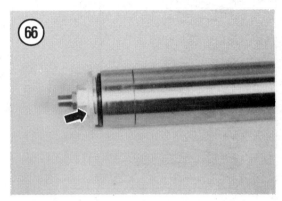

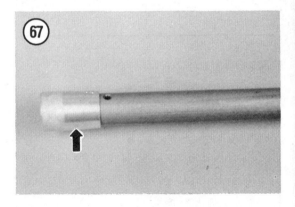

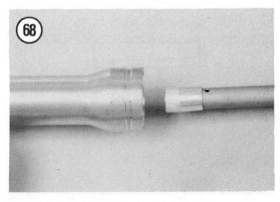

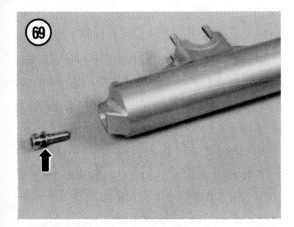

13. Install the circlip (**Figure 72**) with the sharp side facing up. Make sure the circlip is completely seated in the groove in the fork slider.

14. Install the dust seal (**Figure 73**).

15. Remove the fork top cap bolt.

16A. On 1985 models, remove the upper short fork spring "A," the spring seat and the lower long spring "B."

16B. On 1986 models, remove the fork spring.

17. Fill the fork tube with DEXRON automatic transmission fluid (ATF). Refer to **Table 4** for the specific quantity for each fork leg.

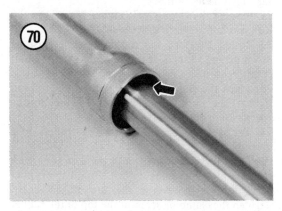

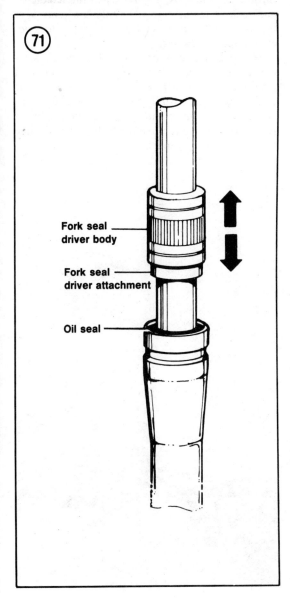

Fork seal
driver body

Fork seal
driver attachment

Oil seal

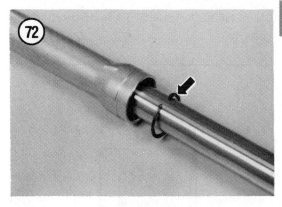

9

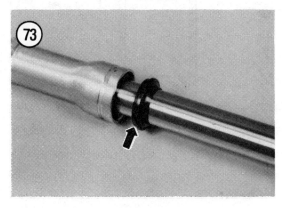

18. Hold the fork assembly upright and compress the fork several times to distribute the ATF. Completely compress the fork and measure the ATF fluid level from the top surface of the fork tube (**Figure 74**). Refer to **Table 4** for the specified level and adjust the level as necessary.

19. Completely clean the fork spring(s) by wiping with a clean, lint-free cloth.

20A. On 1985 models, install the lower long fork spring "B" (tapered end in first), the spring seat, and the upper short spring "A."

20B. On 1986 models, install the fork spring with the tapered end in first.

21. Inspect the O-ring seal (**Figure 75**) on the top fork cap bolt; replace if necessary.

22. Install the fork top cap bolt while pushing down on the spring(s). Start the bolt slowly; don't crossthread it.

23. Place the slider in a vise with soft jaws and tighten the fork top cap bolt to the torque specifications listed in **Table 1**.

24. Perform Steps 2-23 for the other fork assembly.

25. Slide the rubber boot onto the fork tube with the clamping end going on last. Install the rubber boot into the groove in the top of the slider. Tighten the clamping screw at the top of the rubber boot.

26. Install the fork assemblies as described in this chapter.

HANDLEBAR
(4-WHEELED MODELS)

Removal

Refer to **Figure 76** for this procedure.

> *CAUTION*
> *Cover the seat, fuel tank cover and front fender with a heavy cloth or plastic tarp to protect it from the accidental spilling of brake fluid. Wash any spilled brake fluid off any painted or plated surface immediately as it will destroy the finish. Use soapy water and rinse thoroughly.*

1. Remove the screws and clamp securing the throttle assembly (A, **Figure 77**) to the handlebar and remove the assembly. Lay the assembly over the front fender. Be careful that the cable does not get crimped or damaged.

2. Remove the screws securing the front master cylinder (B, **Figure 77**) to the handlebar and lay it over the front fender. Keep the reservoir in the upright position to minimize loss of brake fluid and to keep air from entering the brake system. It is not necessary to remove the hydraulic brake line from the master cylinder.

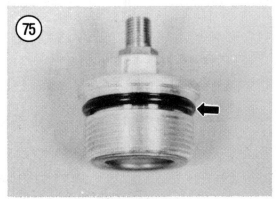

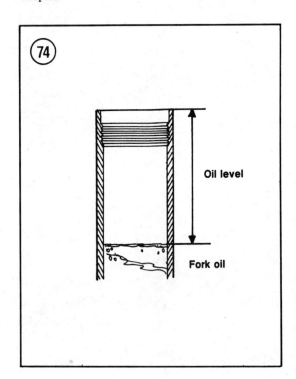

Oil level

Fork oil

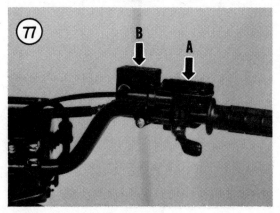

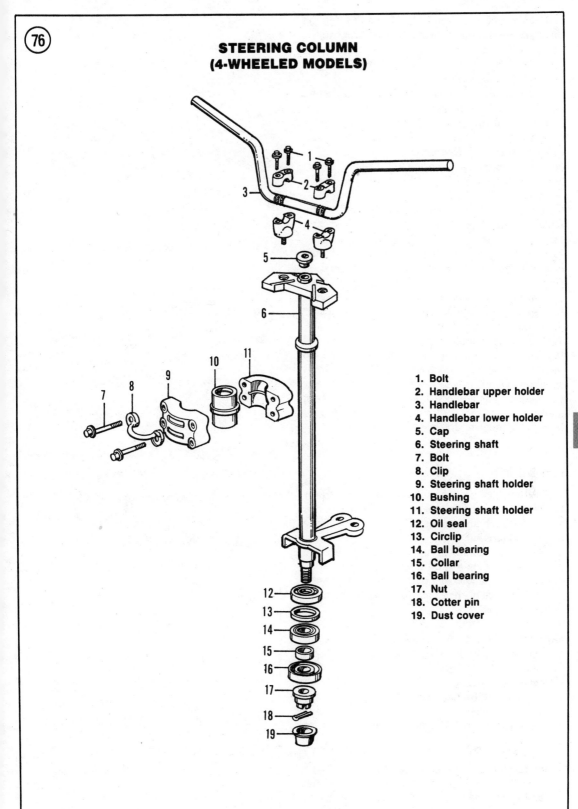

**STEERING COLUMN
(4-WHEELED MODELS)**

1. Bolt
2. Handlebar upper holder
3. Handlebar
4. Handlebar lower holder
5. Cap
6. Steering shaft
7. Bolt
8. Clip
9. Steering shaft holder
10. Bushing
11. Steering shaft holder
12. Oil seal
13. Circlip
14. Ball bearing
15. Collar
16. Ball bearing
17. Nut
18. Cotter pin
19. Dust cover

9

3. Remove the wire band (A, **Figure 78**) holding the brake and left-hand switch housing wires to the handlebar.

4. On models equipped with an ignition switch, perform the following.

    a. Disconnect the electrical wire connectors from the ignition switch.

    b. Remove the screws securing the ignition switch cover and remove the cover and ignition switch assembly.

5. Remove the screws securing the left-hand switch assembly (B, **Figure 78**) and remove the switch assembly.

6. Remove the screws (C, **Figure 78**) and clamp securing the clutch/parking brake lever and remove the assembly.

7. Remove the headlight housing and the headlight guard (A, **Figure 79**) as described in Chapter Seven.

8. Remove the bolts (B, **Figure 79**) securing the handlebar upper holders and remove the holders.

9. Remove the handlebar (C, **Figure 79**).

10. To maintain a good grip on the handlebar and to prevent it from slipping down, clean the knurled section of the handlebar with a wire brush. It should be kept rough so it will be held securely by the holders. The holders should also be kept clean and free of any metal that may have been gouged loose by handlebar slippage.

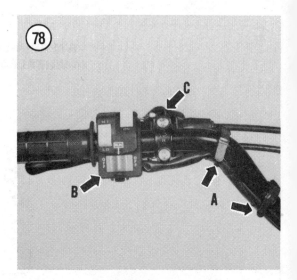

Installation

1. Position the handlebar on the handlebar lower holders so the punch mark on the handlebar is aligned with the top surface of the handlebar lower holders (**Figure 80**).

2. Install the handlebar upper holders with the punch mark facing toward the front.

3. Install the handlebar holder bolts. Tighten the forward bolts first, then the rear bolts. Tighten the bolts securely.

4. After installation is complete, recheck the alignment of the punch mark on the handlebar. Realign the punch mark if necessary.

5. Install the headlight guard bolt and tighten securely.

6. Install the left-hand switch assembly onto the handlebar and align the locating pin on the housing with the hole in the handlebar. Install the screws and tighten the upper screw first, then the lower screw. Tighten the screws securely.

7. Install the clutch/parking brake lever assembly. Position the clamp with the UP mark toward the top and install the screws. Align the split mark of the housing with the punch mark on the handlebar.

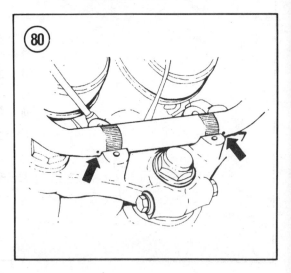

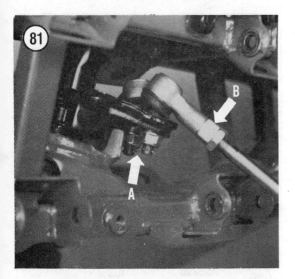

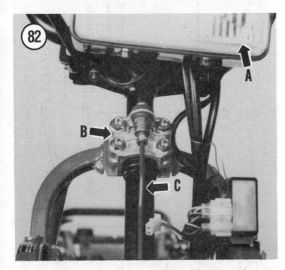

Tighten the upper screw first, then the lower screw. Tighten the screws securely.

8. Install the wire band holding the brake and left-hand switch housing wires to the handlebar.

9. On models equipped with an ignition switch, perform the following.

   a. Install the ignition switch cover and ignition switch assembly. Install the screws and tighten securely.

   b. Connect the electrical wire connectors to the ignition switch.

10. Install the front master cylinder as follows.

   a. Place the master cylinder on the handlebar.

   b. Install the holder clamp with the UP mark pointing up and install the screws.

   c. Tighten the upper screw first, then the lower screw. Tighten the screws to the torque specification listed in **Table 1**.

11. Install the throttle housing as follows.

   a. Place the throttle housing on the handlebar and install the holder. Loosely install the screws.

   b. Align the punch mark on the housing with the mating surface of the master cylinder holder.

   c. Tighten the forward screw first, then tighten the rear screw. Tighten the screws securely.

12. After all assemblies have been installed, test each one to make sure it operates correctly with no binding. Correct any problem at this time.

STEERING SHAFT

Removal

Refer to **Figure 76** for this procedure.

1. Place the ATV on level ground and set the parking brake. Block the rear wheels so the vehicle will not roll in either direction.

2. Remove the front fenders as described in Chapter Twelve.

3. Remove both front wheels as described in this chapter.

4. Disconnect both tie rods (A, **Figure 81**) from the steering shaft end as described in this chapter.

5. Remove the handlebar as described in this chapter.

6. Remove the bolts securing the headlight guard and headlight housing (A, **Figure 82**) as described in Chapter Seven. Move the headlight housing out of the way. It is not necessary to remove the headlight assembly.

7. Remove the dust cover from the lower end of the steering shaft.

8. Remove the cotter pin and nut (**Figure 83**) securing the lower end of the steering shaft to the bearing in the frame. Discard the cotter pin.

9. Remove the bolts securing the steering shaft holders at the top (B, **Figure 82**). Remove the clip, brake hose (C, **Figure 82**) and the steering shaft holders.

10. Pull the steering shaft up and out of the bearing at the lower end and remove the steering shaft from the frame.

11. Remove the steering shaft holder bearing from the steering shaft.

Inspection

1. Carefully inspect the entire steering shaft assembly, especially if the vehicle has been involved in a collision or spill. The shaft must be straight. If it is bent or twisted in any way it must be replaced. If a damaged shaft is installed in the vehicle, it will cause rapid and excessive wear to the bearings as well as place undue stress on other components in the frame and steering system.

2. Inspect the lower bearing in the frame. Rotate the inner race with your fingers. The bearing should move freely and smoothly. If the bearing is worn, it must be replaced. The bearing outer race must also be held tightly in place in the frame. If the outer race is loose, replace the bearing as described in this chapter.

3. Examine the steering shaft holders and bearing for wear or damage; replace as necessary.

Installation

1. Apply a coat of waterproof grease to the bearing and grease seals in the frame where the lower end of the steering shaft rides.

2. Apply a coat of waterproof grease to the inside surface of the steering shaft holder bearing. Install the bearing onto the steering shaft.

3. Install the steering shaft into the frame and into the lower end bearing.

4. The steering shaft holders are marked with an IN or OUT (**Figure 84**) and must be installed as follows.

   a. Position the IN steering shaft holder between the frame and the steering shaft and the OUT steering shaft holder onto the steering shaft.

   b. Align the groove in each holder with the ridge on the steering shaft bearing (**Figure 85**) and install both holders.

   c. Position the brake hose and clip onto the outer holder upper bolt holes.

   d. Loosely install the bolts securing the steering shaft holders.

5. Install the steering shaft lower nut and tighten to the torque specification listed in **Table 1**. Install a new cotter pin and bend the ends over completely.

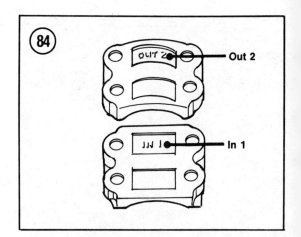

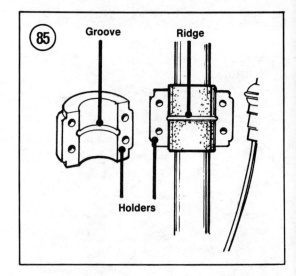

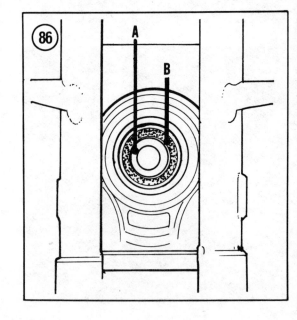

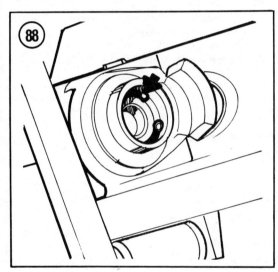

6. Don't forget to install the dust cover. This cover protects the lower bearing from dirt and moisture and should always be reinstalled.

7. Connect both tie rods to the steering shaft end as described in this chapter.

8. Tighten the steering shaft holder bolts in 2-3 steps in a crisscross pattern to the torque specification listed in **Table 1**.

9. Install the handlebar as described in this chapter.

10. Install the headlight housing and guard and tighten the bolts securely.

11. Install both front wheels as described in this chapter.

12. Install the front fenders as described in Chapter Twelve.

Steering Shaft Bearing
Replacement

1. Remove the collar (A, **Figure 86**) from the lower side of the bearing.

2. Remove the dust seal from the upper (**Figure 87**) and lower (B, **Figure 86**) side of the bearing.

3. Remove the snap ring (**Figure 88**) from the upper surface of the bearing.

4. Tap the bearing out of the frame from the lower side.

5. Install a new bearing into the frame as follows.
   a. Use a socket that matches the outer race diameter.
   b. Tap the bearing squarely into place. Tap on the outer race only.
   c. Do not tap on the inner race or the bearing may be damaged. Make sure the bearing is completely seated in the receptacle in the frame.

6. Install a new circlip into the groove in the frame. Make sure the circlip is completely seated.

7. Install new grease seals and coat the lips with multipurpose grease.

8. Install the collar into the lower side of the bearing.

TIE ROD

Removal

Both tie rod assemblies are the same. Refer to **Figure 89** and **Figure 90** for this procedure.

1. Place the ATV on level ground and set the parking brake. Block the rear wheels so the vehicle will not roll in either direction.

NOTE
Front fender removal is not necessary but it does allow more working room.

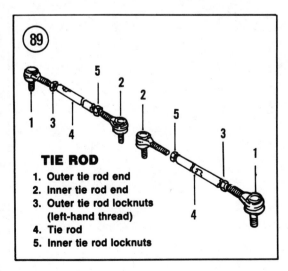

TIE ROD
1. Outer tie rod end
2. Inner tie rod end
3. Outer tie rod locknuts (left-hand thread)
4. Tie rod
5. Inner tie rod locknuts

2. Remove the front fenders as described in Chapter Twelve.

3. Remove both front wheels as described in this chapter.

4. Remove the cotter pin and nut (**Figure 91**) securing the tie rod end to the steering knuckle arm. Discard the cotter pin as a new pin must be installed.

> *CAUTION*
> *If the tie rod is difficult to remove from the steering knuckle, do not attempt to pry it out as the tie rod seal may be damaged.*

5. Carefully disconnect the tie rod from the steering knuckle arm. If the tie rod end is difficult to remove, install the nut just enough to cover the threads on tie rod end and tap the tie rod end out of the steering knuckle with a soft-faced mallet.

6. Remove the cotter pin and nut (A, **Figure 81**) securing the tie rod end to the steering shaft end. Discard the cotter pin as a new pin must be installed.

7. Carefully disconnect the tie rod from the steering shaft end and remove the tie rod assembly.

8. Repeat Steps 4-7 for the other tie rod.

Inspection/Disassembly/Assembly

1. Inspect the rubber boot at each end of the tie rod end swivel joint. The swivel joints are permanently packed with grease. If the rubber boot is damaged, dirt and moisture can enter the swivel joint and destroy it. If the boot is damaged in any way, disassemble the tie rod assembly and replace the rod end(s) as they can be replaced separately.

2. If the tie rod ends (swivel joints) are to be replaced, refer to **Figure 89** and perform the following.

  a. Carefully measure and write down the overall length of the tie rod assembly before removing the worn tie rod ends.

  b. Loosen the locknuts securing the tie rod ends. The locknut securing the outside tie rod end (golden color) has *left-hand* threads (unscrews clockwise).

  c. Unscrew the damaged tie rod end(s).

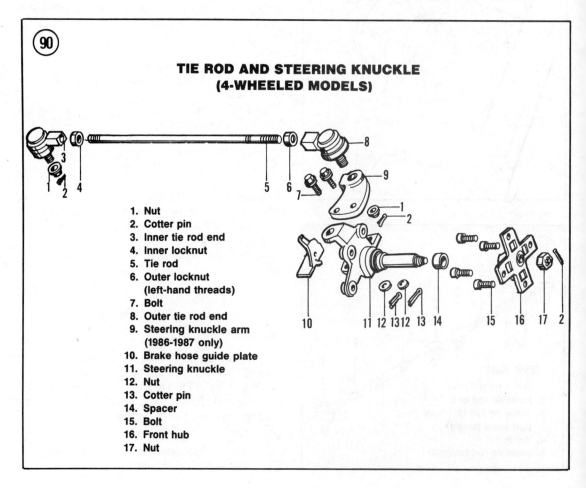

(90)

TIE ROD AND STEERING KNUCKLE
(4-WHEELED MODELS)

1. Nut
2. Cotter pin
3. Inner tie rod end
4. Inner locknut
5. Tie rod
6. Outer locknut
   (left-hand threads)
7. Bolt
8. Outer tie rod end
9. Steering knuckle arm
   (1986-1987 only)
10. Brake hose guide plate
11. Steering knuckle
12. Nut
13. Cotter pin
14. Spacer
15. Bolt
16. Front hub
17. Nut

NOTE

If installing a completely new tie rod assembly, turn the tie rod ends to obtain the overall dimension listed in **Table 2** *for a preliminary setting. Leave the locknuts loose at this time. They will be tightened after the wheel alignment is adjusted.*

d. Install the new tie rod end and turn it in or out until the overall length of the tie rod assembly is the same as that measured in Step 2a. Leave the locknuts loose at this time. They will be tightened after the wheel alignment is adjusted.

Installation

1. Position the tie rod assembly so the silver colored tie rod end (B, **Figure 81**) is attached to the steering shaft.
2. Attach the tie rod assembly to the steering shaft and to the steering knuckle. Install the ball-joint nuts and tighten to the torque specification listed in **Table 1**.

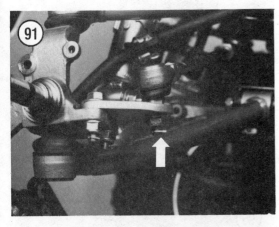

3. Install a new cotter pin at each location and bend the ends over completely.
4. Install both front wheels as described in this chapter.
5. Align the toe-in adjustment of the front wheels as described in Chapter Three.
6. Tighten the tie rod end locknuts to the torque specification listed in **Table 1**.
7. If removed, install the front fenders as described in Chapter Twelve.

STEERING KNUCKLE

Removal/Installation

Refer to **Figure 90** for this procedure.
1. Place the ATV on level ground and set the parking brake. Block the rear wheels so the vehicle will not roll in either direction.
2. Remove the front fenders as described in Chapter Twelve.
3. Remove both front wheels as described in this chapter.
4. Remove the front brake caliper assembly as described in Chapter Eleven. Move the caliper assembly out of the way.
5. Remove the bolts securing the splash guard (**Figure 92**) to the steering knuckle and remove the splash guard.
6. Remove the tie rod assembly (**Figure 91**) from the steering knuckle as described in this chapter.

NOTE

The following steps are shown with the suspension arms and steering knuckle removed from the frame for clarity. It is not necessary to remove the suspension arms for this procedure.

7. Remove the cotter pins and castellated nuts (A, **Figure 93**) securing the upper and lower suspension arms to the steering knuckle.

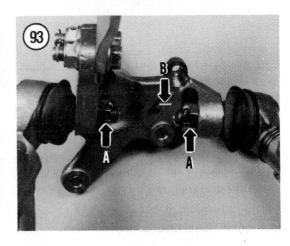

8. Remove the lower bolt and nut securing the shock absorber to the lower suspension arm. It is not necessary to completely remove the shock absorber.

9. Install the Honda special tool, Ball Joint Remover part No. 07941-6920003 between the upper suspension arm and the steering knuckle (**Figure 94**) and separate the steering knuckle from the upper suspension arm.

10. Repeat Step 9 for the lower suspension arm.

11. Remove the steering knuckle. The steering knuckles are different and must be installed on the correct side. Each steering knuckle is marked either "R" (right-hand side) or "L" (left-hand side) (B, **Figure 93**).

12. Install by reversing these removal steps, noting the following.

13. Apply a coat of waterproof grease to all pivot areas before installing any components.

14. Tighten all bolts and nuts to the torque specification listed in **Table 1**.

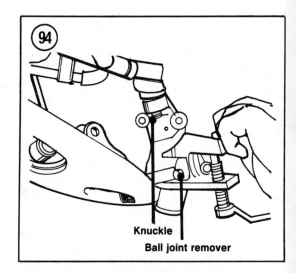

Knuckle
Ball joint remover

Inspection

1. Inspect the spindle portion of the steering knuckle (**Figure 95**) for wear or damage. A hard spill or collision may cause the spindle portion to bend or fracture. If the spindle is damaged in any way, replace the steering knuckle as described in this chapter.

2. Check the hole (**Figure 96**) at the end of the steering knuckle where the cotter pin fits. Make sure there are no fractures or cracks leading out toward the end of the steering knuckle. If any are present, replace the steering knuckle.

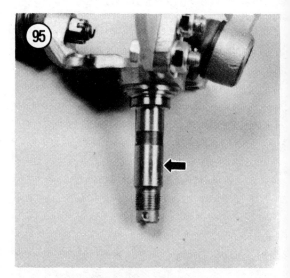

NOTE
On 1988-on models, the steering knuckle arm is an integral part of the steering knuckle and is not removable.

3. On 1986-1987 models, inspect the steering knuckle arm (**Figure 97**) for wear or damage. To replace, perform the following:

  a. Remove the bolts and nuts (**Figure 98**) securing the arm to the knuckle.

  b. The steering knuckle arms are different and must be installed on the correct side. Each arm is marked either "R" (right-hand side) or "L" (left-hand side) (**Figure 99**).

  c. Tighten the bolts and nuts to the torque specification listed in **Table 1**.

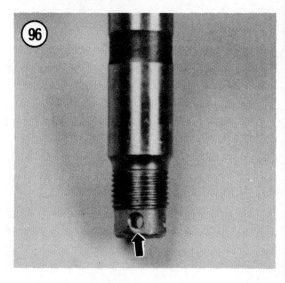

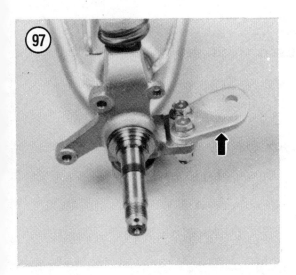

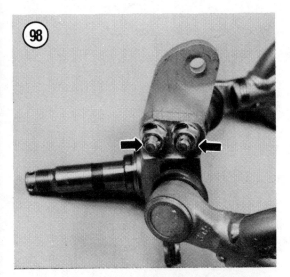

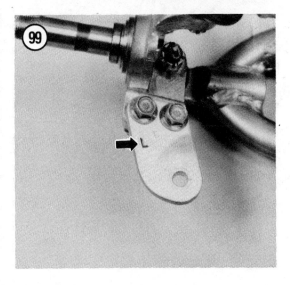

SUSPENSION ARMS

Removal/Installation

Refer to **Figure 100** (1986-1987 models) or **Figure 101** (1988-on models) for this procedure.

NOTE
This procedure is shown on a 1986-1987 model. On 1988-on models, the steering knuckle arm is an integral part of the steering knuckle and is not removable. Also, the upper ball joint is an integral part of the upper arm similar to the lower arm.

1. Place the ATV on level ground and set the parking brake. Block the rear wheels so the vehicle will not roll in either direction.
2. Remove the front fenders as described in Chapter Twelve.
3. Remove both front wheels as described in this chapter.
4. Remove the front hub assemblies as described in this chapter.
5. Disconnect the hydraulic brake line from the mounting bracket on the upper suspension arm.
6. Remove the front brake caliper assembly as described in Chapter Eleven. Move the caliper assembly out of the way. It is not necessary to disconnect the hydraulic brake line from the caliper.
7. Remove the shock absorber as described in this chapter.
8. Remove the tie rod end (**Figure 91**) from the steering knuckle as described in this chapter.
9. Remove the rear bolts (A, **Figure 102**) securing the skid plate to the frame.
10. Loosen the upper bolts (B, **Figure 102**) and remove the lower bolts (C, **Figure 102**) securing the front skid plate and front carry handle to the frame. Hinge the assembly up and secure it with a bunji cord (**Figure 103**) to the frame or handlebar.
11. Remove the bolts and nuts (**Figure 104**) securing the upper and lower suspension arms to the frame and remove the suspension arm assembly.
12. Install the Honda special tool, Ball Joint Remover part No. 07941-6920003 between the upper suspension arm and the steering knuckle (**Figure 94**). Separate the steering knuckle from the upper suspension arm.
13. Repeat Step 12 for the lower suspension arm.

9

FRONT SUSPENSION ARMS
(4-WHEELED MODELS—1986-1987)

1986 MODELS

1. Bolt
2. Pivot thrust bushing
3. Nut
4. Dust seal
5. Upper suspension arm
6. Lower suspension arm
7. Collar
8. Nut
9. Camber collar
10. Upper ball joint
11. Nut
12. Cotter pin

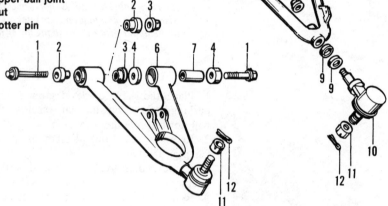

1987 MODELS

1. Bolt
2. Pivot thrust bushing
3. Dust seal
4. Stopper ring
5. Spherical bearing
6. Nut
7. Upper suspension arm
8. Lower suspension arm
9. Nut
10. Camber collar
11. Upper ball joint
12. Nut
13. Cotter pin

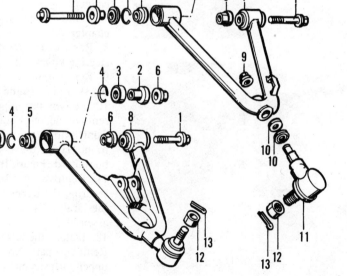

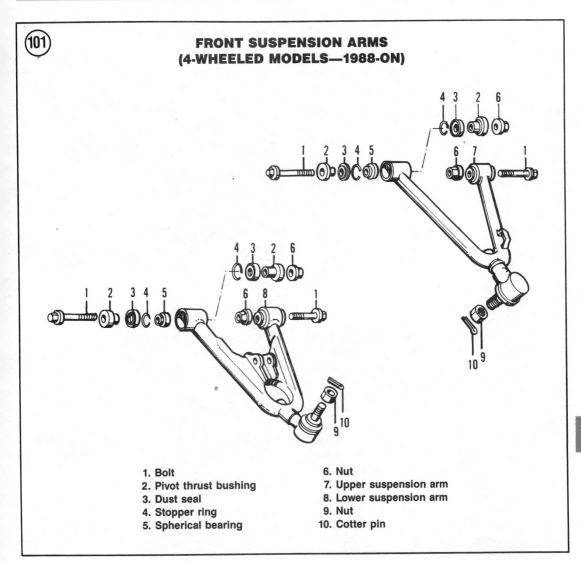

101

**FRONT SUSPENSION ARMS
(4-WHEELED MODELS—1988-ON)**

1. Bolt
2. Pivot thrust bushing
3. Dust seal
4. Stopper ring
5. Spherical bearing
6. Nut
7. Upper suspension arm
8. Lower suspension arm
9. Nut
10. Cotter pin

102

103

14. Install by reversing these removal steps, noting the following.

15. The suspension arms are different and must be installed on the correct side. Each arm is marked either "R" (right-hand side) or "L" (left-hand side) (**Figure 105**).

16A. On 1986 models, make sure the grease seals (**Figure 106**) are in place on each side of the pivot areas of each suspension arm.

16B. On 1987-on models, make sure the pivot collars are in place on each side of the pivot areas of each suspension arm.

17. Apply a coat of waterproof grease to all pivot areas and to all grease seals (1986 models) before installing any components.

18. Tighten all bolts and nuts to the torque specifications listed in **Table 1**.

Inspection (1986 Models)

Refer to **Figure 107** for this procedure.

1. Remove the grease seal (**Figure 108**) from each side of the pivot portion of the suspension arm.

2. Turn the pivot collar with your finger. Make sure it rotates freely with no binding. If worn or damaged, push the pivot collar (**Figure 109**) out of the pivot portion of the suspension arm and replace it.

3. If the pivot collar is worn or damaged, it is a good idea to replace the pivot bushings at the same time. Remove the pivot bushing from each side of the pivot portion of the suspension arm and install new pivot bushings.

4. Apply a coat coat of waterproof grease to the pivot bushings and pivot shafts (A, **Figure 110**) before installation.

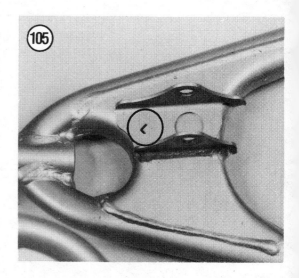

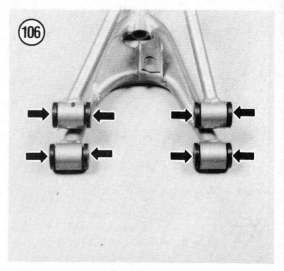

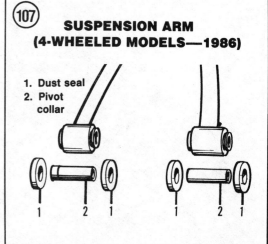

**SUSPENSION ARM
(4-WHEELED MODELS—1986)**

1. Dust seal
2. Pivot collar

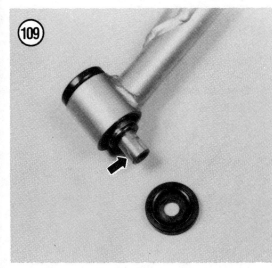

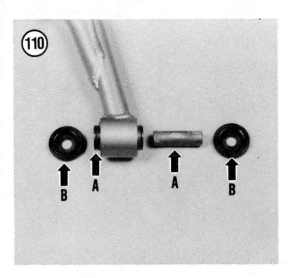

5. Apply a coat of waterproof grease to the lips of the grease seals (B, **Figure 110**) before installation.

Inspection and Spherical Bearing Replacement (1987-on Models)

Refer to **Figure 111** for this procedure.

NOTE
The following procedure requires special tools that are expensive and can be used only for this specific job. It may be less expensive to have the spherical bearings replaced by a Honda dealer than to purchase the special tools and locate a hydraulic press that can be used or rented. This procedure is included in case you choose to perform this task yourself.

1. Remove the pivot collar from each side of the pivot portion of the suspension arm.
2. Check the grease seals for wear or damage; replace if necessary.
3. Turn the spherical bearing inside the pivot portion with your finger. Make sure it rotates freely with no binding. If worn or damaged, it must be replaced.
4. Remove the grease seal from each side of the pivot portion of the suspension arm.
5. Remove the stopper ring from each side of the spherical bearing.

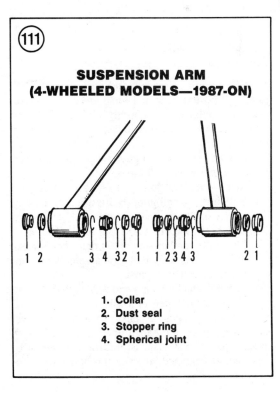

**SUSPENSION ARM
(4-WHEELED MODELS—1987-ON)**

1. Collar
2. Dust seal
3. Stopper ring
4. Spherical joint

6. Insert the spherical bearing driver (Honda part No. 07HMF-HC00100) (A, **Figure 112**) into the pivot portion of the suspension arm. Make a mark (B, **Figure 112**) on the side of the bearing driver where it is flush with the top surface of the pivot portion of the suspension arm. This mark will be used as a reference mark for installing the new bearing.

7. Press the spherical bearing (C, **Figure 112**) out of the pivot portion of the suspension arm.

8. Thoroughly clean out the inner surface of the pivot portion of the suspension arm with solvent and dry with compressed air.

9. Use the same special tools used in removal and press the new spherical bearing into place. Use the mark made in Step 6 as a reference point for how far to press in the new bearing. The correct distance is 12.75 mm (0.502 in.) from the top surface.

10. Install a new stopper ring on each side of the spherical bearing.

11. Apply a coat of waterproof grease to new grease seals and install on each side of the pivot portion of the suspension arm. Press the grease seal in until it is flush with the outside surface (**Figure 113**).

12. Install the pivot collar into each side of the pivot portion of the suspension arm.

Ball Joint Inspection
(All Models)

1. Hold onto the threaded stud portion of the ball joint and move it back and forth and from side-to-side. It should move smoothly and freely. If the movement is rough or very loose, the ball joint must be replaced.

2. On 1986-1987 model upper suspension arm, replace the ball joint as follows.

   a. Remove the ball joint nut (A, **Figure 114**).

   b. Withdraw the ball joint (B, **Figure 114**) from the suspension arm and remove the camber set collars (C, **Figure 114**) from the ball joint.

   c. Install the camber set collars onto the new ball joint and install the ball joint assembly onto the upper suspension arm.

   d. Install the ball joint nut and tighten to the torque specification listed in **Table 1**.

3. On 1988-on upper suspension arm and all lower suspension arms, the ball joint (**Figure 115**) is an integral part of the suspension arm and cannot be replaced. If damaged, replace the upper or lower suspension arm.

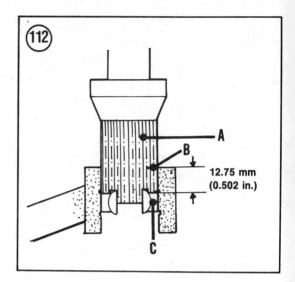

12.75 mm (0.502 in.)

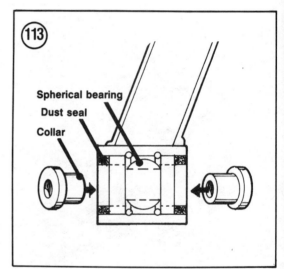

Spherical bearing
Dust seal
Collar

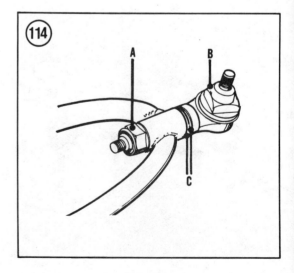

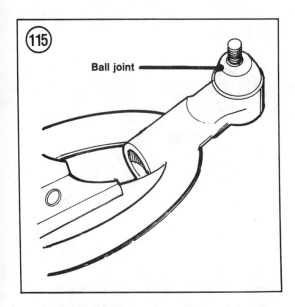

Ball joint

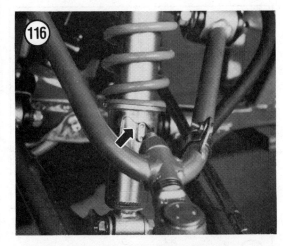

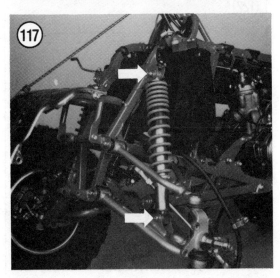

SHOCK ABSORBER

Spring Preload Adjustment

To compensate for ride weight and track conditions the shock can be adjusted. The spring preload can be adjusted to 5 positions by rotating the cam ring at the base of the spring (**Figure 116**). Rotate the cam ring *clockwise* to increase preload or *counterclockwise* to decrease preload.

NOTE
Use the spanner wrench furnished in the factory tool kit for this adjustment.

Both cams must be indexed to the same detent or it will result in an unsafe riding condition.

Removal/Installation

1. Place the ATV on level ground and set the parking brake. Block the rear wheels so the vehicle will not roll in either direction.
2. Jack up the front of the vehicle with a small hydraulic or scissor jack. Place the jack under the frame with a piece of wood between the frame and the jack.
3. Place wood block(s) under the frame to support the ATV securely with the front wheels off the ground.
4. Remove the upper and lower mounting bolts and nuts (**Figure 117**) securing the shock absorber to the frame and lower suspension arm and remove the shock absorber.
5. Repeat for the other side if necessary.
6. Installation is the reverse of these steps. Keep the following points in mind.
   a. Apply a light coat of multipurpose grease to the pivot points on the frame and suspension arm where the shock absorber is attached and the pivot points on the shock absorber (A, **Figure 118**).
   b. Tighten the bolts to the torque specification listed in **Table 1**.

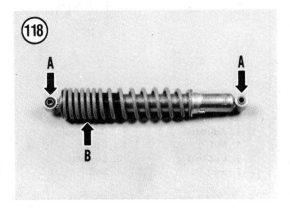

**FRONT SHOCK ABSORBER
(4-WHEELED MODELS)**

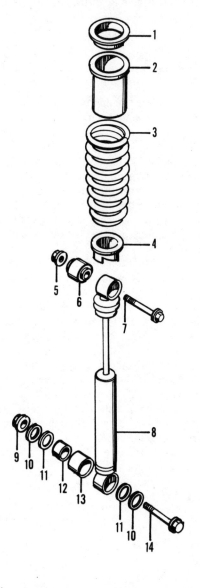

1. Spring seat
2. Spring guide
3. Spring
4. Adjuster
5. Nut
6. Bushing
7. Bolt
8. Damper unit
9. Nut
10. Dust seal cap
11. Dust seal
12. Collar
13. Bushing
14. Bolt

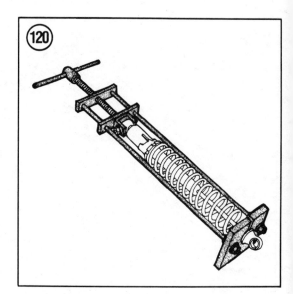

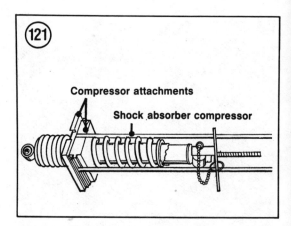

Compressor attachments

Shock absorber compressor

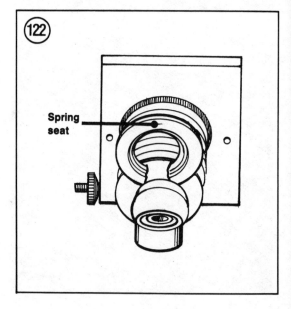

Spring
seat

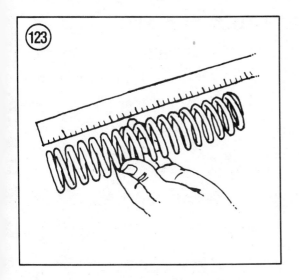

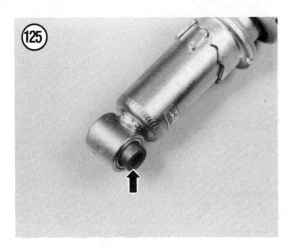

Disassembly/Inspection/Assembly

Refer to **Figure 119** for this procedure.

The shock is spring-controlled and hydraulically damped. The shock damper unit is sealed and cannot be serviced. Service is limited to removal and replacement of the damper unit and the spring.

A special tool and 2 additional items are needed for disassembly and assembly of the shock absorber. These tools are available from a Honda dealer and are as follows.

    a. Shock absorber compressor (Honda part No. 07959-3290001).

    b. Spring compressor attachment (Honda part No. 07959-MB51000).

WARNING
Without the proper tools, this procedure can be dangerous. The spring can fly loose, causing injury. For a small bench fee, a dealer can do the job for you.

1. Install the collar into the spring compressor.
2. Install the shock absorber into a compression tool as shown in **Figure 120**.
3. Install the attachment onto the shock absorber spring and into the upper portion of the spring compressor (**Figure 121**). Tighten the clamp securing the adaptor.
4. Compress the shock spring just enough to gain access to the spring seat.
5. Remove the spring seat (**Figure 122**).
6. Release the spring tension and remove the shock from the compression tool.
7. Remove the spring guide, spring and spring adjuster from the damper unit.
8. Measure the spring free length (**Figure 123**). The spring must be replaced if it has sagged to the service limit listed in **Table 2** or less.
9. Check the damper unit for leakage and make sure the damper rod is straight.

NOTE
The damper unit cannot be rebuilt. It must be replaced as a unit.

10. Inspect the rubber bushings in the upper (**Figure 124**) and lower joints (**Figure 125**); replace if necessary.
11. Assembly is the reverse of these disassembly steps, noting the following.
12. Install the spring with the closer wound coils toward the top (B, **Figure 118**).

9

Tables are on the following pages.

Table 1 FRONT SUSPENSION TORQUE SPECIFICATIONS

ATC250R		
Item	N·m	ft.-lb.
Front axle	70-110	51-80
Front axle holder nuts	10-14	7-10
Wheel lug nuts	60-70	43-51
Front brake caliper		
mounting bolts	24-30	17-22
Fork bridge bolts		
(upper and lower)	18-25	13-18
Steering stem nut	80-120	58-87
Steering stem adjust nut		
Preliminary torque value	36-45	26-33
Final torque value	36-58	26-42
Brake disc nuts	25-30	18-22
Front fork		
Top cap bolt	15-30	11-22
Socket bolt	15-25	11-18
TRX250R/FOURTRAX 250R		
Item	N·m	ft.-lb.
Front hub nut		
1986-1987	80-120	58-87
1988-on	60-80	43-58
Steering shaft		
Nut	60-80	43-58
Holder bolts	25-30	18-22
Tie rods		
Ball-joint nuts	40-50	29-36
Locknuts	50-60	36-43
Front master cylinder		
clamp screws	10-14	7-10
Steering knuckle		
To suspension arm nuts	50-60	36-43
To steering arm nuts	60-70	43-51
To tie rod ends	40-50	29-36
Suspension arm pivot bolt		
and nut (upper and lower)		
1986 and 1988-on	35-45	25-33
1987	50-60	36-43
Upper ball joint-to-		
suspension arm nut		
(1986-1987 only)	60-80	43-58
Shock absorber upper and lower		
mounting bolts and nuts	40-50	29-36

Table 2 FRONT SUSPENSION SPECIFICATIONS

ATC250R		
Item	Standard	Wear limit
Front axle runout	0.3 mm (0.01 in.)	0.5 mm (0.02 in.)
Front wheel bearing play		
Radial	—	0.05 mm (0.002 in.)
Axial	—	0.10 mm (0.004 in.)
	(continued)	

Table 2 FRONT SUSPENSION SPECIFICATIONS (continued)

Item	Standard	Wear limit
ATC250R (continued)		
Damper rod runout	—	0.2 mm (0.008 in.)
Front fork spring free length		
1985		
Upper spring A	76.2-82.2 mm (3.00-3.24 in.)	75.4 mm (2.97 in.)
Lower spring B	498.2-508.2 mm (19.61-20.01 in.)	493.1 mm (19.41 in.)
1986	575.2-586.8 mm (22.65-23.10 in.)	569.4 mm (22.42 in.)
Front wheel rim runout		
Radial and axial	1.0 mm (0.04 in.)	4.0 mm (0.16 in.)
TRX250R/FOURTRAX 250R		
Front shock absorber spring free length	271-277 mm (10.7-10.9 in.)	268 mm (10.6 in.)
Toe-in	10 ±10 mm (0.4 ±0.4 in.)	—
Camber	0°	—
Caster	0°	—
Tie rod length between tie rod ends		
1986-1987	273 mm (10.7 in.)	—
1988-on	271 mm (10.67 in.)	—

9

Table 3 TIRE INFLATION PRESSURE (COLD)*

Model	Tire pressure				Circumference	
	Minimum		Maximum			
	kPa	psi	kPa	psi	mm	in.
ATC250R						
Front	27	3.9	33	4.7	1,844	72.6
Rear	22	3.2	28	4.0	1,565	61.6
TRX250R/ Fourtrax 250R						
1986-1987						
Front	24.5	3.6	30.5	4.4	—	—
Rear	17	2.5	23	3.3	—	—
1988-on						
Front	24.5	3.6	30.5	4.4	—	—
Rear	19.5	2.9	25.5	3.7	—	—

*Tire inflation pressure for factory equipped tires. Aftermarket tires may require different inflation pressure.

Table 4 FRONT FORK OIL CAPACITY AND DIMENSION (3-WHEELED MODELS)

Model	Capacity		Dimension	
	cc	oz.	mm	in.
ATC250R				
1985	400	13.56	186	7.3
1986	465	15.5	113	4.4

REAR AXLE AND SUSPENSION

This chapter contains repair and replacement procedures for the rear wheel, rear hub and rear suspension. Service to the rear suspension consists of:

a. Periodically checking bolt tightness.

b. Replacing swing arm bearings and checking the condition of the rear shock absorber and replacing it as necessary. Tire removal and repair are covered in Chapter Nine.

Refer to **Table 1** for rear suspension torque specifications. **Table 1** and **Table 2** are located at the end of this chapter.

REAR WHEEL

Removal/Installation

1. Set the ATV on level ground and set the parking brake. Also block the front wheels so the vehicle will not roll in either direction.

2. Place wood blocks under the frame to support the ATV securely with the rear wheel off the ground.

3A. To remove the tire/wheel assembly only, remove the lug nuts (**Figure 1**). Remove the tire/wheel assembly from the rear hub.

3B. To remove the tire/wheel and hub, remove the cotter pin (**Figure 2**), hub nut (**Figure 3**) and collar (**Figure 4**) securing the tire/wheel assembly and

hub to the rear axle. Remove the tire/wheel and hub assembly from the rear axle.

4. Install by reversing these removal steps, noting the following.

5A. If only the tire/wheel assembly was removed, perform the following.

a. Place the tire/wheel assembly onto the rear hub studs. Install the wheel lug nuts with the

tapered side (**Figure 5**) going on first. Finger tighten the nuts at this time. Do *not* tighten them until the wheel is positioned correctly onto the wheel studs and the rear wheel is on the ground.

b. Remove the wood blocks from under the frame.

> *WARNING*
> *Always tighten the lug nuts to the correct torque specification or the lug nuts may work loose resulting in the loss of the wheel.*

c. Use a torque wrench and tighten the lug nuts to the torque specification listed in **Table 1**.

5B. If the tire/wheel assembly and hub were removed, perform the following.

a. Place the tire/wheel assembly and hub onto the rear axle.

b. Install the axle nut and tighten to the torque specification listed in **Table 1**.

c. Install a new cotter pin and bend the ends over completely. Never reuse a cotter pin as it may break and fall out.

REAR AXLE, DRIVEN SPROCKET AND BRAKE DISC

Removal

Refer to **Figure 6** for this procedure.

1. Place the ATV on level ground and set the parking brake.

2. Shift the transmission into NEUTRAL.

3. Remove the seat/rear fender as described in Chapter Twelve.

4A. On 3-wheeled models and 1985 4-wheeled models, release the drive chain tension as follows.

a. Loosen the rear axle bearing holder clamping bolts (**Figure 7**).

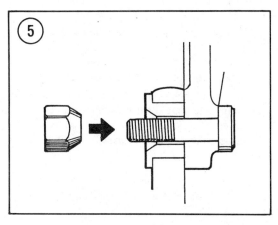

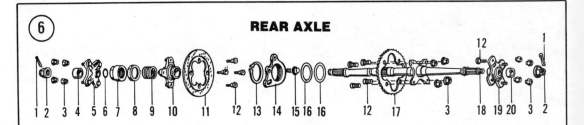

REAR AXLE

1. Cotter pin
2. Axle nut
3. Nut
4. Collar
5. Rear hub
6. Snap ring
7. Outer locknut
8. Inner locknut
9. Internal thread
10. Brake disc carrier
11. Brake disc
12. Bolts
13. Circlip
14. Brake caliper carrier
15. Bolt
16. O-ring seal
17. Driven sprocket
18. Rear axle
19. Rear hub
20. Collar

b. Attach the spanner wrench, furnished in the factory tool kit, to the axle adjuster.
c. Push spanner wrench toward the front of the vehicle, rotating the top of the axle holder toward the front. Rotate the axle holder until the maximum amount of drive chain slack is achieved.

4B. On 1986-on 4-wheeled models, release the drive chain tension as follows:

a. Loosen the rear axle bearing holder clamping bolts. The 1986-1987 models have one bolt on each side (**Figure 7**) and the 1988-on models have 2 bolts on each side.
b. Insert a drift or punch into one of the receptacles in the rear axle bearing holder adjuster (**Figure 8**).
c. Push the drift or punch toward the front of the vehicle, rotating the top of the axle holder toward the front. Rotate the axle holder until the maximum amount of drive chain slack is achieved.

5. Remove both rear tire/wheel and hub assemblies as described in this chapter.
6. Remove the drive chain master link assembly (A, **Figure 9**) from the drive chain. Don't lose the O-rings on each side of the drive chain link assembly. Remove the drive chain from the driven sprocket.
7. Inspect the rear axle bearings' condition at this time.

a. Pull in and out on the end of the axle.
b. Move the axle up and down and from side to side.

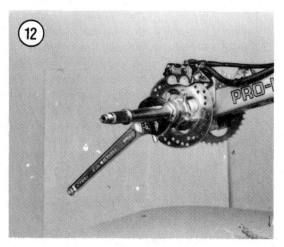

c. If there is any excessive play in any of these directions, replace the rear axle bearings as described in this chapter.

8. If the driven sprocket is going to be removed, perform the following.

a. Have an assistant apply the rear brake.

b. Loosen the bolts and nuts (B, **Figure 9**) securing the drive sprocket to the sprocket flange.

9. Remove the bolts securing the swing arm skid plate (**Figure 10**) and remove the skid plate.

10. Place a 56 mm open end wrench (Honda special tool part No. 07916-HA20000 or 07916-HA2010A) or large adjustable wrench on the inner locknut (A, **Figure 11**).

11. Place a 45 mm open end wrench or large adjustable wrench on the outer locknut (B, **Figure 11**) as shown in **Figure 12**.

> *CAUTION*
> *The rear axle locknuts have **left-hand** threads. The wrench must be rotated **clockwise** to loosen the locknuts.*

12. Hold onto the *outer* locknut and loosen the *inner* locknut on the right-hand side of the axle. It may be necessary to tap on the end of the wrench with a soft faced mallet to break the inner locknut loose. Remove the locknut.

> *CAUTION*
> *The locknut and inner nut have had Loctite applied during assembly and are tightened to a large torque value. They are very hard to remove even with the correct size tool and a lot of force. Do **not** apply heat to the area in order to try to loosen the locknut and inner nut, as this will ruin the heat-treated hardness of the axle.*

10

NOTE
Special flame cut wrenches are available from Honda dealers or mail order houses.

13. Have an assistant apply the rear brake.

CAUTION
*The rear axle locknuts have **left-hand** threads. The wrench must be rotated **clockwise** to loosen both locknuts.*

14. Loosen the outer locknut (A, **Figure 13**) and screw it *in* toward the brake disc until the snap ring is visible.

15. Remove the snap ring (B, **Figure 13**) from the rear axle.

16. Release the parking brake and remove the disc brake caliper assembly as described in Chapter Eleven. Tie the caliper assembly up to the frame with a wire or bunji cord.

17. On 3-wheeled models, slide off the snap ring collar.

18. Slide the outer and inner locknuts and the internal thread assembly off the right-hand end of the rear axle.

19. Slide the brake disc/hub assembly (**Figure 14**) off the right-hand end of the axle. Remove the O-ring seal (**Figure 15**) from the brake disc hub. The O-ring must be replaced every time the hub is removed.

20. Screw the rear hub nut onto the right-hand end of the axle. Using a soft faced mallet, tap on the right-hand end of the rear axle, then pull the rear axle assembly out of the swing arm from the left-hand side.

21. Remove the O-ring seal from the driven sprocket flange on the rear axle. The O-ring must be replaced every time the rear axle is removed.

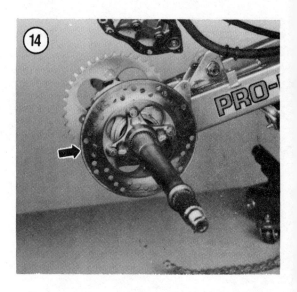

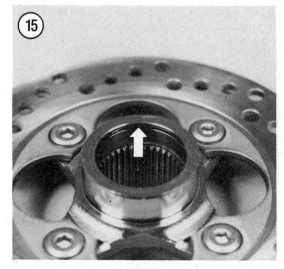

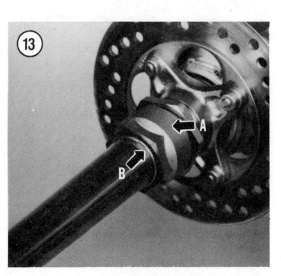

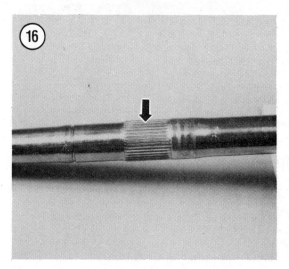

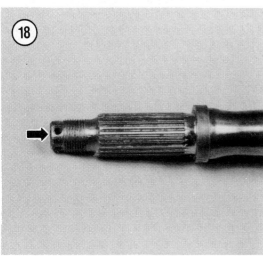

22. Inspect the rear axle as described in this chapter.

Inspection

1. Inspect the rear axle for signs of fatigue, fractures or damage. Inspect the splines (**Figure 16**) for wear or damage.

2. Inspect the splines (**Figure 17**) where the driven sprocket attaches. Inspect the holes in the sprocket flange and the driven sprocket for wear or damage; replace as necessary.

3. Check the hole at each end of the axle (**Figure 18**) where the cotter pin fits. Make sure there are no fractures or cracks leading out toward the end of the axle. If any are found, replace the axle.

4. Check the axle for straightness. Use V-blocks and a dial indicator as shown in **Figure 19**. Check the runout in the center of the axle and remember that the actual runout is 1/2 of the total indicator runout reading from the dial indicator. If the runout is 3.0 mm (0.12 in.) or greater the axle must be replaced.

5. Inspect the inner and outer locknuts and internal thread assembly (**Figure 20**) for wear or damage. Inspect the internal splines (**Figure 21**) of the internal thread assembly for wear or damage; replace as necessary.

6. Disassemble the internal thread assembly and clean off all Loctite residue from the threads on the assembly and both lockuts.

Installation

1. Make sure the axle bearing oil seals are in place on each side of the axle bearing holder. Apply a light coat of multipurpose grease to the lips of both seals.

10

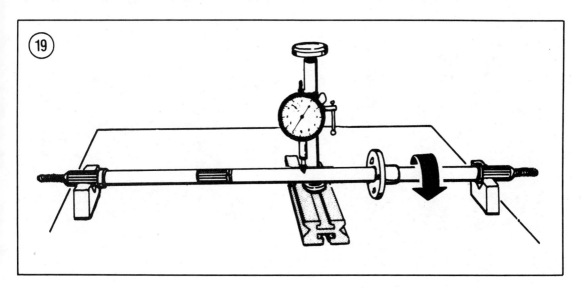

2. Install a new O-ring seal onto the driven sprocket flange on the rear axle.

3. Install the rear axle assembly into the swing arm from the left-hand side. Carefully tap into place until it completely seats in the rear axle bearing housing.

4. Install a new O-ring seal (**Figure 15**) into the brake disc/hub assembly.

5. Position the brake disc/hub with the disc mounting bolts toward the inside and slide the brake disc/hub assembly onto the rear axle.

6. Apply blue Loctite (Lock N' Seal No. 2114) to the threads of the *inner* locknut.

7. Slide the inner thread and the inner and outer locknut assembly onto the rear axle.

8. On 3-wheeled models, slide on the snap ring collar.

9. Install the snap ring (B, **Figure 13**) into the groove in the rear axle.

10. Install the parking brake/disc brake caliper assembly as described in Chapter Eleven.

11. Apply the parking brake.

NOTE
In the following steps, use the same tools used during the removal sequence.

NOTE
*The Honda special tool locknut wrenches have a receptacle for a 1/2 in. drive torque wrench. Use a 20 in. deflecting beam type torque wrench. The Honda special tool locknut wrench increases the torque wrench's leverage, so the torque wrench reading must be less than the torque actually applied. The 2 different torque specifications are listed in **Table 1** as "actual" and "indicated" on the torque wrench scale.*

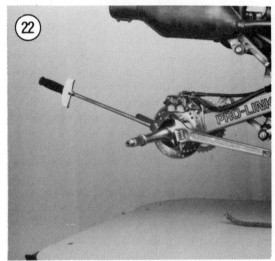

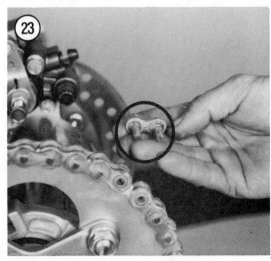

> *CAUTION*
> *The rear axle locknuts have **left-hand** threads. The wrench must be rotated **counterclockwise** to tighten the locknuts.*

12. Using the 45 mm locknut wrench, tighten the *outer* locknut against the snap ring in the rear axle. Tighten the locknut to the torque specification listed in **Table 1**.

13. Hold onto the outer locknut with the 45 mm locknut wrench and place a 56 mm locknut wrench on the inner locknut.

> *CAUTION*
> *The rear axle locknuts have **left-hand** threads. The wrench must be rotated **clockwise** to loosen the locknuts.*

14. Hold onto the *outer* locknut and tighten the *inner* locknut (**Figure 22**). See NOTE preceding Step 12 regarding torque specification and tighten the inner locknut to the torque specification listed in **Table 1**.

15. Install the driven sprocket onto the sprocket hub.

16. Apply blue Loctite (Lock N' Seal No. 2114) to the sprocket bolt threads. Install the bolts from the inside then install the nuts. Tighten to the torque specification listed in **Table 1**.

17. Install the drive chain onto the driven sprocket. Assemble the master link as follows.

   a. Install the O-rings onto the master link (**Figure 23**), then install the master link through the drive chain (**Figure 24**).

   b. Install the O-rings (**Figure 25**) and plate (**Figure 26**).

   c. Install the clip (A, **Figure 9**) so the closed end is facing in the direction of chain travel (**Figure 27**).

10

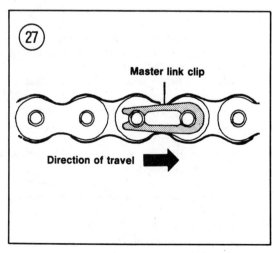

Master link clip

Direction of travel ▶

d. After the master link is completely assembled, there should be no gap between the master link plate and clip as shown in **Figure 28**. If there is a gap, one or more of the O-rings was not installed.

18. Install the skid plate and bolts. Tighten the bolts securely.

19. Apply multipurpose grease to the splines of the rear axle.

20. Install both rear tire/wheel and hub assemblies as described in this chapter.

21. Adjust the drive chain as described in Chapter Three.

22. Install the seat/rear fender.

DRIVEN SPROCKET

Refer to **Figure 6** for this procedure.

Removal

1. Place the ATV on level ground and set the parking brake.

2. Shift the transmission into NEUTRAL.

3. Remove the seat/rear fender as described in Chapter Twelve.

4A. On 3-wheeled models and 1985 4-wheeled models, release the drive chain tension as follows.

a. Loosen the rear axle bearing holder clamping bolts (**Figure 7**).

b. Attach the spanner wrench, furnished in the factory tool kit, to the axle adjuster.

c. Push spanner wrench toward the front of the vehicle, rotating the top of the axle holder toward the front. Rotate the axle holder until the maximum amount of drive chain slack is achieved.

4B. On 1986-on 4-wheeled models, release the drive chain tension as follows.

a. Loosen the rear axle bearing holder clamping bolts (**Figure 7**).

b. Insert a drift or punch into one of the receptacles in the rear axle bearing holder adjuster (**Figure 8**).

c. Push the drift or punch toward the front of the vehicle, rotating the top of the axle holder toward the front. Rotate the axle holder until the maximum amount of drive chain slack is achieved.

5. Remove the left-hand rear tire/wheel assembly as described in this chapter.

6. Remove the drive chain master link assembly (A, **Figure 9**) from the drive chain. Don't lose the O-rings from the clip. Remove the drive chain from the driven sprocket.

7. Have an assistant apply the rear brake.

8. Loosen the bolts and nuts (B, **Figure 9**) securing the drive sprocket to the sprocket flange.

9. Remove the bolts and nuts.

10. Slide the sprocket off the axle.

Installation

1. Install the driven sprocket onto the sprocket hub.

2. Apply blue Loctite (Lock N' Seal No. 2114) to the sprocket bolt threads. Install the bolts from the inside, then install the nuts. Tighten to the torque specification listed in **Table 1**.

3. Install the drive chain onto the driven sprocket. Assemble the master link as follows.

a. Install the O-rings onto the master link (**Figure 23**), then install the master link through the drive chain (**Figure 24**).

b. Install the O-rings (**Figure 25**) and plate (**Figure 26**).

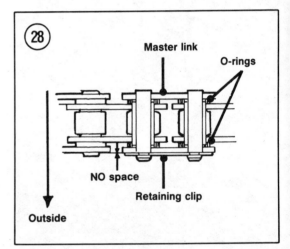

28

Master link

O-rings

NO space

Retaining clip

Outside

29

c. Install the clip (A, **Figure 9**) so the closed end is facing in the direction of chain travel (**Figure 27**).

d. After the master link is completely assembled, there should be no gap between the master link plate and clip as shown in **Figure 28**. If there is a gap, one or more of the O-rings was not installed.

4. Apply multipurpose grease to the splines of the rear axle.

5. Install the left-hand wheel hub and the collar onto the axle.

6. Install the axle nut onto the axle and tighten to the torque specification listed in **Table 1**.

7. Install a new cotter pin and bend the ends completely. Never reuse an old cotter pin.

8. Install the left-hand rear tire/wheel assembly as described in this chapter.

9. Adjust the drive chain as described in Chapter Three.

10. Install the seat/rear fender.

DRIVE SPROCKET AND DRIVE CHAIN

Removal

1. Place the ATV on level ground and set the parking brake.

2. Shift the transmission into NEUTRAL.

3. Remove the seat/rear fender as described in Chapter Twelve.

4. Remove the clamping bolt on the gearshift lever (**Figure 29**) and remove the lever.

5. Remove the bolts securing the drive sprocket cover (**Figure 30**) and remove the sprocket cover and backing plate.

6. Have an assistant apply the rear brake.

7. Loosen then remove the drive sprocket bolt and washer (**Figure 31**).

8A. On 3-wheeled models and 1985 4-wheeled models, release the drive chain tension as follows.

a. Loosen the rear axle bearing holder clamping bolts (**Figure 7**).

b. Attach the spanner wrench, furnished in the factory tool kit, to the axle adjuster.

c. Push spanner wrench toward the front of the vehicle, rotating the top of the axle holder toward the front. Rotate the axle holder until the maximum amount of drive chain slack is achieved.

8B. On 1986-on 4-wheeled models, release the drive chain tension as follows.

a. Loosen the rear axle bearing holder clamping bolts (**Figure 7**).

b. Insert a drift or punch into one of the receptacles in the rear axle bearing holder adjuster (**Figure 8**).

c. Push the drift or punch toward the front of the vehicle, rotating the top of the axle holder toward the front. Rotate the axle holder until the maximum amount of drive chain slack is achieved.

9. Remove the left-hand rear tire/wheel assembly as described in this chapter.

10. Remove the drive chain master link assembly (A, **Figure 9**) from the drive chain. Don't lose the O-rings from the clip. Remove the drive chain from the driven sprocket.

11. Remove the drive chain and drive sprocket.

12. Clean and inspect the drive chain as described in this chapter.

10

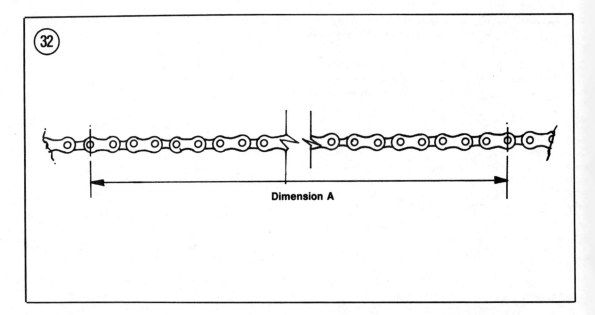

Dimension A

Installation

1. Feed the drive chain through the swing arm and the frame.

2. Install the drive sprocket.

3. Install the drive chain onto the drive sprocket and the driven sprocket.

4. Position the lockwasher with the OUTSIDE mark facing out and install the lockwasher and nut (**Figure 31**). Tighten the nut to the torque specification listed in **Table 1**.

5. Install the drive chain onto the driven sprocket. Assemble the master link as follows.

    a. Install the O-rings onto the master link (**Figure 23**), then install the master link through the drive chain (**Figure 24**).

    b. Install the O-rings (**Figure 25**) and plate (**Figure 26**).

    c. Install the clip (A, **Figure 9**) so the closed end is facing in the direction of chain travel (**Figure 27**).

    d. After the master link is completely assembled, there should be no gap between the master link plate and clip as shown in **Figure 28**. If there is a gap, one or more of the O-rings was not installed.

6. Install the backing plate, drive sprocket cover and bolts. Tighten the bolts securely.

7. Install the gearshift lever and clamping bolt. Tighten the bolt securely.

8. Install the left-hand rear tire/wheel assembly as described in this chapter.

9. Adjust the drive chain as described in Chapter Three.

10. Install the seat/rear fender.

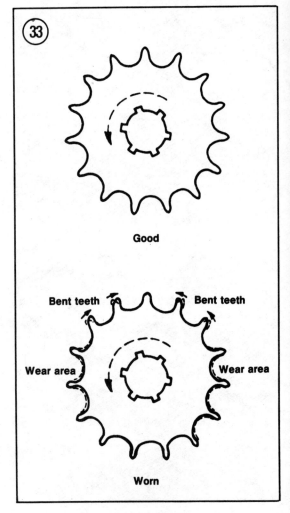

Good

Bent teeth   Bent teeth

Wear area   Wear area

Worn

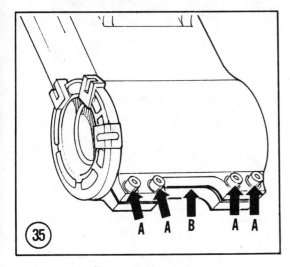

Drive Chain
Cleaning/Inspection/Lubrication

CAUTION
The drive chain is equipped with O-rings. These rubber O-rings can easily be damaged. Do not use a steam cleaner, a high-pressure washer or any solvent that may damage the rubber O-rings.

1. Remove the drive chain as described in this chapter.
2. Immerse the chain in a pan of kerosene or non-flammable solvent and allow it to soak for about half an hour. Move it around and flex it during this period so that the dirt between the links, pins, rollers and O-rings may work its way out.

CAUTION
In the next step, do not use a wire brush or the O-rings will be damaged and the drive chain must be replaced.

3. Scrub the rollers and side plates with a medium soft brush and rinse away loosened dirt. Do not scrub hard as the O-rings may be damaged. Rinse it a couple of times to make sure all dirt and grit are washed out. Dry the chain with a shop cloth then hang it up and allow the chain to thoroughly dry.
4. After cleaning the chain, examine it carefully for wear or damage. Replace the chain if worn or damaged.
5A. On 1985-1987 models, lay the drive chain alongside a ruler and pull the chain taut. Measure the distance between 95 pins; refer to dimension "A" in **Figure 32**. The standard new dimension "A" is 1,508 mm (59.4 in.). Replace the drive chain if it has stretched to 1,515 mm (59.6 in.).
5B. On 1988-on models, lay the drive chain alongside a ruler and pull the chain taut. Measure the distance between 91 pins; refer to dimension "A" in **Figure 32**. The standard new dimension "A" is 1,429 mm (56.3 in.). Replace the drive chain if it has stretched to 1,436 mm (56.5 in.).

NOTE
*Always check both sprockets every time the chain is removed. If any wear is visible on the teeth (**Figure 33**), replace both sprockets. Never install a new chain over worn sprockets or a worn chain over new sprockets.*

6. Lubricate the chain with SAE 80 or 90 weight gear oil or a good grade of chain lubricant specifically formulated for O-ring chains, following the manufacturer's instructions.
7. Reinstall the chain as described in this chapter.

REAR AXLE
BEARING HOUSING

The rear axle bearing housing is attached to the rear of the swing arm and contains the rear axle bearings and grease seals.

Removal

1. Loosen the rear axle bearing holder clamping bolts. Refer to **Figure 34** for 1985-1987 models or A, **Figure 35** for 1988-on models.
2. Remove the circlip (**Figure 36**) securing the rear brake caliper mounting plate. Do not remove the plate at this time.
3. Remove the rear axle as described in this chapter.
4A. On 1985-1987 models, remove the bolts and rubber seals (**Figure 37**).

10

4B. On 1988-on models, remove the bolts and rubber seal (B, **Figure 35**) that runs from side-to-side at the joint line.

> *CAUTION*
> *Be careful not to damage the inner surfaces of the swing arm where the rear axle bearing housing rides. These surfaces must remain smooth so the rear axle bearing housing can rotate freely for drive chain adjustment.*

5. Before removing the rear axle bearing housing, perform *Bearing Preliminary Inspection* as described in this chapter.

6. Remove the rear caliper mounting plate (**Figure 38**) and remove the O-ring seal (**Figure 39**) from the plate. The O-ring seal must be replaced every time the plate is removed.

> *NOTE*
> *The 1988-on models are not equipped with a stopper bolt.*

7. On 1985-1987 models, remove the stopper bolt and washer (**Figure 40**) from the swing arm.

8. On 4-wheeled models, remove the O-ring seal (**Figure 41**) from the bearing holder. The O-ring seal must be replaced every time the bearing holder is removed.

9. Using a soft-faced mallet, carefully tap the rear axle bearing holder out of the swing arm from the left-hand side. Note that the flanged side of the holder is on the left-hand side.

10. Thoroughly clean out the inside surface of the swing arm where the bearing holder rides (**Figure 42**). Apply a light coat of waterproof grease to the inner surfaces.

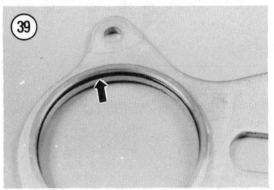

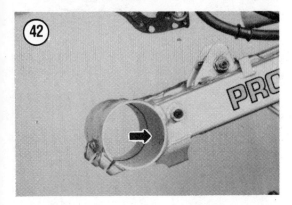

Inspection

1. Remove and discard the O-ring seals on the bearing holder. Refer to **Figure 43** and **Figure 44**. The O-rings must be replaced every time the bearing holder is removed.

2. Inspect the rubber seal(s) for wear or deterioration. On 1985-1987 models, replace the seals as a set even if only one is damaged.

3. Inspect the bearing housing (**Figure 45**) for cracks or damage. Replace if necessary.

Installation

> *CAUTION*
> *Be sure to install **new** O-rings where indicated. The O-rings are relative inexpensive and protect parts within the bearing holder assembly. If new O-rings are not installed, water, sand and other foreign matter will find its way into the bearing holder and cause expensive damage.*

1. Apply a coat of multipurpose grease to the O-ring seals. Install new O-ring seals on the rear axle bearing holder. Refer to **Figure 43** and **Figure 44**.

2. Apply a coat of waterproof grease to the outside surface of the bearing holder.

> *NOTE*
> *The 1988-on models are not equipped with a stopper bolt.*

3. On 1985-1987 models, position the bearing holder so the stopper bolt tab (A, **Figure 46**) is positioned lower than the stopper bolt hole (B, **Figure 46**) in the swing arm. This tab is used to control the rotation of the bearing holder.

10

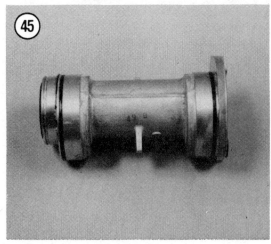

4. Install the bearing holder into the swing arm from the left-hand side (**Figure 47**). Carefully tap it in until it is completely seated.

5. On 1986 3-wheeled models and 1986-1987 4-wheeled models, align the center tang with the punch mark (**Figure 48**) on the swing arm.

6. On 1985-1987 models, install the stopper bolt and washer (**Figure 40**) into the swing arm.

7A. On 1985-1987 models, install the bolts and rubber seals (**Figure 37**).

7B. On 1988-on models, install the rubber seal (B, **Figure 35**) that runs from side-to-side at the joint line and the bolts.

8. Temporarily tighten one of the clamping bolts at this time to hold the bearing holder in place.

9. On 4-wheeled models, perform the following:

    a. Install a new O-ring seal on the right-hand side of the bearing holder (**Figure 41**).

    b. Install a new O-ring seal into the recess in the caliper mounting plate (**Figure 39**).

10. Install the caliper mounting plate.

11. Position the circlip with the OUTSIDE mark facing out. Refer to the following:

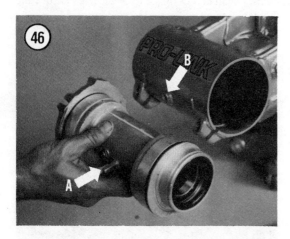

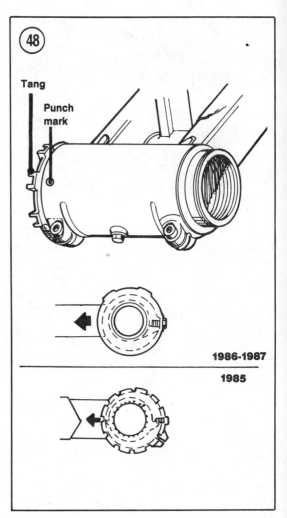

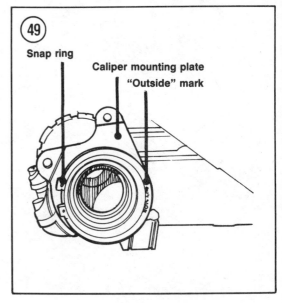

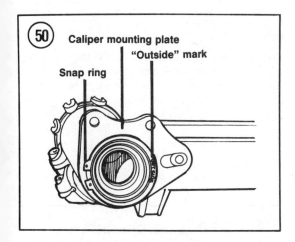

a. 1985 3-wheeled models (**Figure 49**).
b. 1986 3-wheeled models (**Figure 50**).
c. All 4-wheeled models (**Figure 36**).

12. Install the circlip with the open end facing toward the rear. Make sure the circlip is correctly seated in the groove in the bearing holder.

13A. On 1985-1987 models, perform the following:
  a. Install the rear axle as described in this chapter.
  b. Adjust the rear brake and drive chain as described in Chapter Three.

13B. On 1988-on models, perform the following:
  a. Loosen the clamping bolt that was tightened in Step 8.
  b. Insert a drift or punch into the middle receptacle in the rear axle bearing holder adjuster (A, **Figure 51**).
  c. Rotate the axle holder until there is a clearance of 8 mm (0.30 in.) between the top surface of the swing arm and the bottom of the caliper mounting bolt hole (B, **Figure 51**). Remove the drift or punch.
  d. Install the rear axle as described in this chapter.
  e. Insert a drift or punch into the middle receptacle in the rear axle bearing holder adjuster.
  f. Rotate the axle holder until the rear receptacle aligns with the punch mark on the swing arm (**Figure 52**).
  g. Temporarily retighten one of the clamping bolts at this time to hold the bearing holder in this position.
  h. Install the rear axle as described in this chapter.
  i. Adjust the rear brake and drive chain as described in Chapter Three.

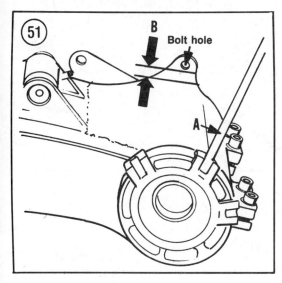

10

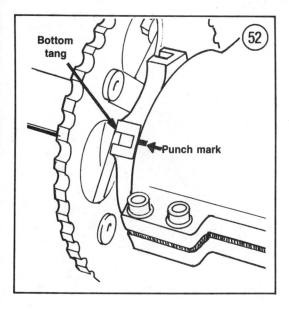

Bearing Preliminary Inspection

Before removing the rear axle bearing housing, perform the following.

1. Remove the rear axle as described in this chapter.
2. Wipe off all excessive grease from both bearings.
3. Turn each bearing by hand. Make sure the bearings turn smoothly. Check for roughness and free play. Some axial play (end play) is normal, but radial play (side play) should be negligible.
4. Replace the bearings, if necessary, as described in this chapter.
5. Inspect the grease seals. Replace if they are deteriorating or starting to harden.

Bearing Removal

Refer to the following exploded view drawings for this procedure.

a. 1985 3-wheeled models (**Figure 53**).
b. 1986 3-wheeled and 4-wheeled models (**Figure 54**).

1. Remove the rear axle bearing housing as described in this chapter.
2. Carefully remove the right-hand (**Figure 55**) and left-hand (**Figure 56**) grease seal from the rear axle bearing housing.
3. To remove the left- and right-hand bearings and center collar, perform the following.

a. Insert a soft aluminum or brass drift into one side of the bearing housing.
b. Push the center collar over to one side and place the drift on the inner race of the opposite bearing.
c. Tap the bearing out of the hub with a hammer, working around the perimeter of the inner race.
d. Remove that bearing and the center collar and spacer on each side of the center collar, on models so equipped, and tap out the opposite bearing.

Bearing Inspection and Lubrication

1. On non-sealed bearings, check the balls for evidence of wear, pitting or excessive heat (bluish tint). Replace bearings, if necessary, but always replace as a complete set. When replacing, be sure to take your old bearings along to ensure a perfect matchup.

NOTE
Fully sealed bearings are available from many bearing specialty shops.

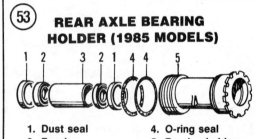

(53)

REAR AXLE BEARING HOLDER (1985 MODELS)

1. Dust seal
2. Bearing
3. Center spacer
4. O-ring seal
5. Bearing holder

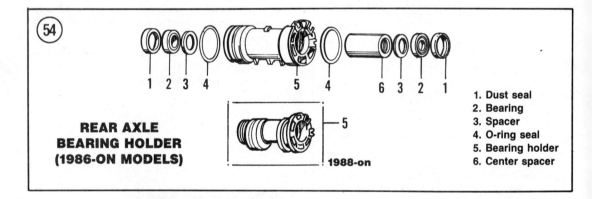

(54)

REAR AXLE BEARING HOLDER (1986-ON MODELS)

1988-on

1. Dust seal
2. Bearing
3. Spacer
4. O-ring seal
5. Bearing holder
6. Center spacer

(55)

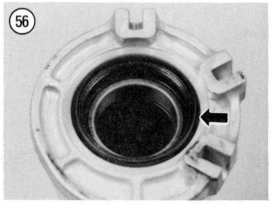

(56)

Fully sealed bearings provide better protection from dirt and moisture that may get into the housing.

2. Thoroughly clean the inside of the rear axle bearing housing with solvent and dry with compressed air or a shop cloth.

3. Do not clean sealed bearings. If non-sealed bearings are installed, thoroughly clean them in solvent and thoroughly dry with compressed air. Do not let the bearing spin while drying.

4. If non-sealed bearings are to be reinstalled, pack the bearings with a good grade of waterproof grease, such as boat trailer wheel bearing grease, as follows.

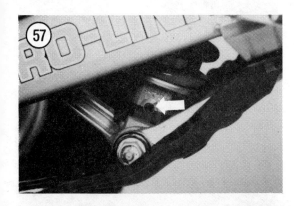

a. Spread some grease in the palm of your hand and scrape the open end of the bearing across your palm. Continue to add grease until the bearing is packed completely full of grease.

b. Slowly turn the bearing a few times to determine if there are any areas that are empty of grease. Thoroughly work the grease in between the balls.

c. Turn the bearing by hand a couple more times to make sure the grease is distributed evenly inside the bearing.

Bearing Installation

1. Coat the outside of the both bearings and inside of the rear axle bearing housing and the center collar with multipurpose grease.

CAUTION
During installation, tap the bearings squarely into place and tap on the outer race only. Use a socket that matches the outer race diameter. Do not tap on the inner race or the bearing may be damaged. Be sure that the bearings are completely seated.

2. On non-sealed bearings, position the bearing with the sealed surface facing outward. Non-sealed bearings have one sealed surface and this surface must face toward the outside.

3. Install the right-hand bearing.

4A. On 1985 3-wheeled models, turn the bearing housing over and install the center collar.

4B. On 1986 3-wheeled and 4-wheeled models, turn the bearing housing over and install a spacer, the center collar and another spacer.

5. Install the left-hand bearing.

6. Apply a light coat of multipurpose grease to the grease seals.

7. Install a grease seal onto each side of the bearing housing until it is flush with the outside surface of the bearing holder.

8. Install the rear axle bearing housing and rear axle as described in this chapter.

SHOCK ABSORBER

The shock absorber can be adjusted for rebound and compression damping to compensate for rider weight and track conditions.

To adjust the rebound damping, use a small screwdriver and turn the adjuster (**Figure 57**) to one of the 3 settings.

To adjust the compression damping, turn the knob on the remote reservoir to either "S" (soft) or "H" (hard). Refer to **Figure 58** for 3-wheeled models or **Figure 59** for 4-wheeled models.

10

Removal/Installation
(3-Wheeled Models)

1. Place the ATV on level ground and set the parking brake.

2. Remove the bolts securing the swing arm skid plate (A, **Figure 60**) and remove the skid plate.

3. Place wood block(s) under the frame to support the ATV securely with the rear wheels off of the ground.

4. Remove the air filter case as described in Chapter Six.

5. Remove the clamping bolts securing the remote reservoir (**Figure 61**) to the frame and remove the remote reservoir from the frame.

6. Remove the upper (B, **Figure 60**) and lower (C, **Figure 60**) mounting bolts and nuts securing the shock absorber to the frame and linkage.

7. Remove the shock absorber assembly from the frame. Be careful not to damage the remote reservoir hose during removal.

8. Install by reversing these removal steps, noting the following.

9. Apply a coat of molybdenum disulfide grease to the upper mounting bushing on the shock absorber and to the lower mounting bolt.

10. Position the shock absorber assembly in the frame and install the shock absorber upper mounting bolt and nut. Tighten the nut to the torque specification listed in **Table 1**.

11. Align the bolt mounting holes in the shock arm, shock link and shock absorber. Install the shock absorber lower mounting bolt and nut. Tighten the nut to the torque specification listed in **Table 1**.

12. Position the remote reservoir so that the boss aligns with the hole in the bracket on the frame, then tighten the clamping bolts securely.

13. Remove the wood blocks from under the frame.

14. Push down on the rear of the ATV and make sure the rear suspension is operating properly.

Removal/Installation
(4-wheeled Models)

1. Place the ATV on level ground and set the parking brake.

2. Remove the bolts securing the swing arm skid plate and remove the skid plate.

3. Place wood block(s) under the frame to support the ATV securely with the rear wheels off of the ground.

4. Remove the seat/rear fender assembly as described in Chapter Twelve.

5. On 1987 models remove the nut and washer securing the air filter case resonator to the frame.

6. Loosen the clamping screws on the air filter carburetor-to-air filter case connecting tube (**Figure 62**) and remove the tube.

7. Remove the bolt (**Figure 63**) securing the remote reservoir hose guide and remove the hose guide.

8. Remove the clamping bolts and clamps securing the remote reservoir (**Figure 64**) to the frame and remove the remote reservoir from the frame.

9. Remove the lower (**Figure 65**) and upper (**Figure 66**) mounting bolts and nuts securing the shock absorber to the frame and linkage.

10. Remove the shock absorber assembly from the frame. Be careful not to damage the remote reservoir hose during removal.

11. Install by reversing these removal steps, noting the following.

12. On the upper mounting portion of the shock absorber, perform the following.

   a. Remove the grease seal (**Figure 67**) on each side of the upper mounting bushing.

   b. Withdraw the collar (**Figure 68**) from the upper mounting bushing.

10

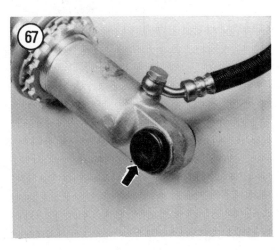

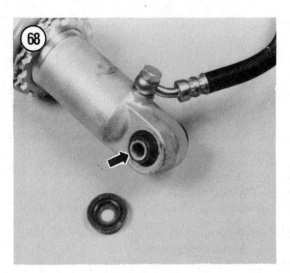

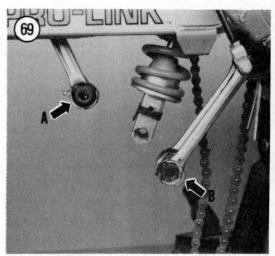

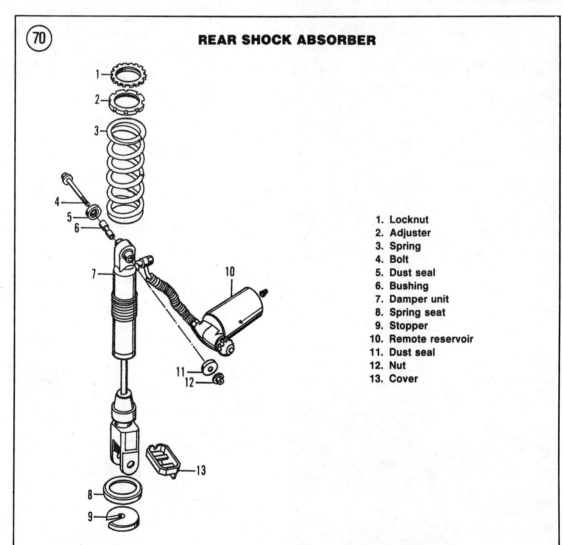

REAR SHOCK ABSORBER

1. Locknut
2. Adjuster
3. Spring
4. Bolt
5. Dust seal
6. Bushing
7. Damper unit
8. Spring seat
9. Stopper
10. Remote reservoir
11. Dust seal
12. Nut
13. Cover

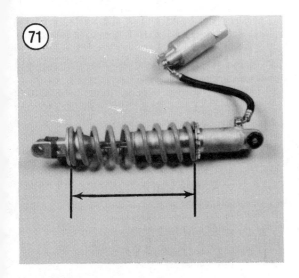

c. Apply a coat of molybdenum disulfide grease to the upper mounting bushing and the inside and outside surfaces of the collar.

d. Reinstall the collar and the grease seals.

13. Apply a coat of molybdenum disulfide grease to the lower mounting bolt and lower bolt holes in the shock absorber.

14. Position the shock absorber assembly in the frame.

15. Install the shock absorber upper mounting bolt and nut (**Figure 66**). Tighten the nut to the torque specification listed in **Table 1**.

16. Align the shock absorber lower mounting hole with the mounting hole of the shock arm (A, **Figure 69**) and shock link (B, **Figure 69**) then install the shock absorber lower mounting bolt from the left-hand side. Install the nut and tighten to the torque specification listed in **Table 1**.

17. Remove the wood blocks from under the frame.

18. Push down on the rear of the ATV and make sure the rear suspension is operating properly.

Disassembly/Inspection/Assembly (All Models)

Refer to **Figure 70** for this procedure.

Service by the home mechanic is limited to removal and installation of the spring. Under no circumstances should you attempt to disconnect the reservoir hose or disassemble the shock absorber unit or reservoir due to the high internal pressure of the nitrogen. If you are satisfied with the existing spring pre-load setting and want to maintain it, measure the spring length (**Figure 71**) before disassembly.

1. Secure the lower end of the shock absorber in a vise with soft jaws. Be careful not to kink or damage the remote reservoir hose.

NOTE
Special tools are required to loosen the locknut and the adjuster. These are pin spanners, Honda part No. 89201-KA4-820 and 89202-KA4-820.

2. Use special tools to loosen the locknut and spring adjuster (**Figure 72**) to almost the end of the threads. Do not completely unscrew either nut.

3. Remove the shock absorber from the vise.

4. From the lower portion of the shock absorber assembly, compress the spring and slide out the spring stopper (A, **Figure 73**) and remove the spring seat (B, **Figure 73**).

5. Slide off the spring (C, **Figure 73**).

10

6. Measure the free length of the spring. Replace the spring if it has sagged to the service limit listed in **Table 2** or less.

7. On the upper mounting portion of the shock absorber, perform the following.

   a. Remove the grease seal (**Figure 67**) on each side of the upper mounting bushing.

   b. Withdraw the collar (**Figure 68**) from the upper mounting bushing.

   c. Inspect the collar for wear or damage and replace, if necessary.

   d. Apply a coat of molybdenum disulfide grease to the upper mounting bushing and the inside and outside surfaces of the collar.

   e. Reinstall the collar and the grease seals.

8. Check the remote reservoir hose (**Figure 74**) for deterioration or damage. If damaged, have it replaced by a dealer.

9. Check the damper unit for dents, oil leakage or other damage. Make sure the damper rod is straight.

10. Place the lower end of the shock absorber on a scale (**Figure 75**) and measure the required force to compress the damper unit 10 mm (0.14 in.). Refer to **Table 2** for specified force. If the force required is less than specified in **Table 2**, some of the nitrogen gas has has leaked out and must be serviced by a dealer.

NOTE
The damper unit cannot be rebuilt. It can be recharged with gas, the fluid replaced or the entire unit can be replaced.

WARNING
The shock absorber damper unit and remote reservoir contain nitrogen gas compressed to between 284-327 psi (20-23 kg/cm²). Pressure varies depending on year and model. Do not tamper with or attempt to open the damper unit or disconnect the reservoir hose from either unit. Do not place it near an open flame or other extreme heat. Do not dispose of the damper assembly yourself. Take it to a dealer where it can be deactivated and disposed of properly. Never attempt to remove the valve core from the base of the reservoir.

11. Install the spring onto the damper unit.

12. Position the spring seat with the flange side toward the spring and install the spring seat and spring stopper.

13. Secure the lower end of the shock in a vise with soft jaws. Be careful not to damage the reservoir hose.

14. Screw the adjuster and locknut by hand until they contact the spring.

15. Use the special Honda tools used during disassembly and tighten the adjuster to the dimension taken before disassembly or to the standard spring length indicated in **Table 2**.

16. Hold onto the adjuster and tighten the locknut to the torque specification listed in **Table 1**.

SUSPENSION LINKAGE

Removal

Refer to **Figure 76** for this procedure.

1. Place the ATV on level ground and set the parking brake.

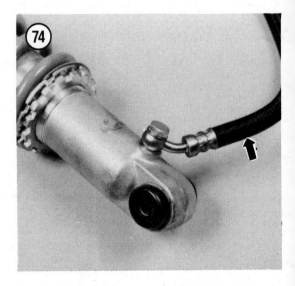

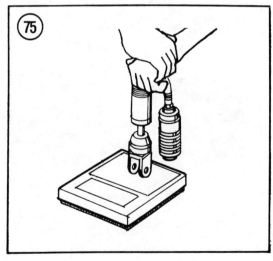

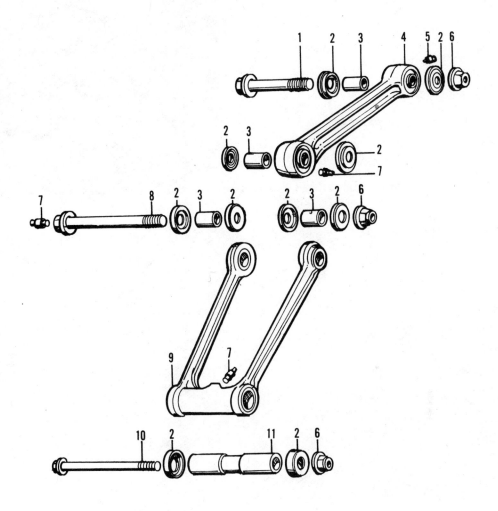

SUSPENSION LINKAGE

1. Pivot bolt
2. Dust seal
3. Pivot collar
4. Shock arm
5. Grease fitting
6. Nut
7. Grease fitting
8. Pivot bolt
9. Shock link
10. Pivot bolt
11. Pivot collar

10

2. Remove the bolts securing the swing arm skid plate and remove the skid plate (**Figure 77**).

3. Place wood block(s) under the frame to support the ATV securely with the rear wheels off of the ground.

4. Remove the seat/rear fender assembly as described in Chapter Twelve.

5. Remove the shock absorber lower mounting bolt and nut (**Figure 63**).

> *NOTE*
> *In the following steps the rear axle is removed for clarity. Rear axle removal is not necessary for this procedure.*

6. Remove the bolt and nut (A, **Figure 78**) securing the shock arm (B, **Figure 78**) to the swing arm and remove the shock arm. Don't lose the grease seal on each side of the mounting hole.

7. Remove the bolt and nut (A, **Figure 79**) securing the shock link (B, **Figure 79**) to the frame and remove the shock link from the frame. Don't lose the grease seal on each side of the mounting hole.

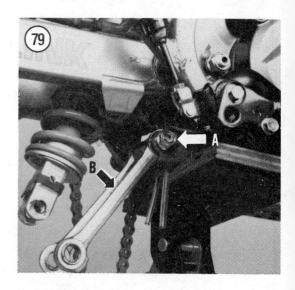

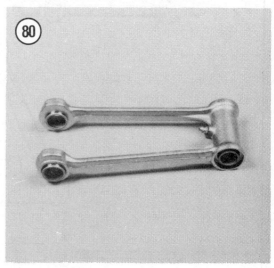

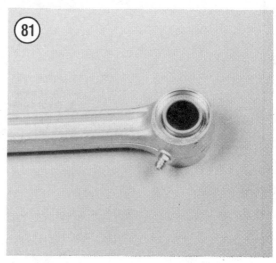

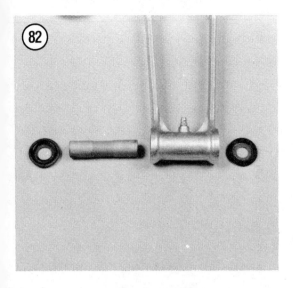

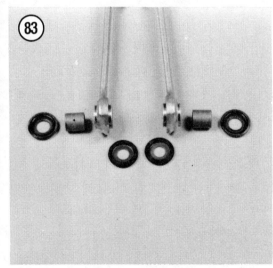

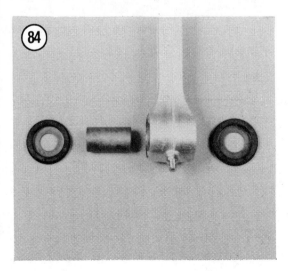

Inspection

1. Inspect the shock link (**Figure 80**) and arm (**Figure 81**) for cracks or damage; replace as necessary.

2. Remove the grease seals at all pivot points and push out the bushings from the following.

   a. Shock link: **Figure 82** and **Figure 83**.

   b. Shock arm: **Figure 84**.

3. Clean all parts in solvent and dry thoroughly with compressed air.

4. Inspect the bushings for scratches, abrasion or abnormal wear; replace as necessary.

5. Inspect the grease seals. Replace all of them as a set if any are worn or starting to deteriorate. If the grease seals are in poor condition, they will allow dirt to enter into the pivot areas and cause the bushings to wear.

6. Check that the grease fittings are not damaged or plugged. Refer to the following.

   a. Shock link (**Figure 85**).

   b. Shock arm (**Figure 86**).

   c. Shock absorber lower mounting bolt (**Figure 87**).

Replace the fittings if necessary.

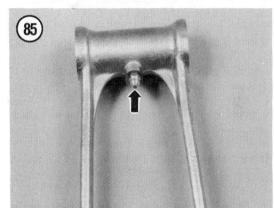

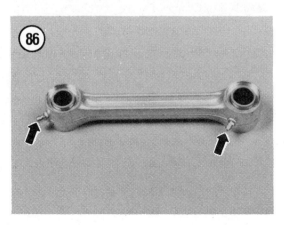

10

7. Coat all surfaces of the pivot receptacles, the bushings and the inside of the grease seals with molybdenum disulfide paste grease. Insert the bushings into both ends of the shock link (A, **Figure 88**) and the shock arm (A, **Figure 89**). Insert the grease seals onto both ends of the shock link (B, **Figure 88**) and the shock arm (B, **Figure 89**).

NOTE
Make sure the grease seal lips seat correctly. If not, they will allow dirt and moisture into the bushing areas and cause wear.

8. Coat the inside surfaces of the pivot bushings with molybdenum disulfide paste grease.

Installation

1. Position the shock link onto the mounting bracket on the frame. Make sure the grease seals are in place on each side of the mounting holes.
2. Push the flange bolt (A, **Figure 79**) all the way through from the left-hand side. Install the nut but do not tighten at this time.
3. Position the shock arm with the UP mark (**Figure 90**) onto the mounting bracket on the swing arm. Make sure the grease seals are in place on each side of the mounting holes.
4. Push the flange bolt (A, **Figure 79**) all the way through from the left-hand side and install the nut.
5. Tighten the bolts and nuts securing the shock arm and shock link to the torque specifications listed in **Table 1**.
6. Align the shock absorber lower mounting hole with the mounting hole of the shock link and shock arm, then install the shock absorber lower mounting bolt (**Figure 63**) from the left-hand side. Install the nut and tighten to the torque specification listed in **Table 1**.
7. Remove the swing arm skid plate and tighten the bolts securely.
8. Install the seat/rear fender assembly as described in Chapter Twelve.

SWING ARM

In time, the pivot needle bearings will wear and will have to be replaced. The condition of the pivot needle bearings can greatly affect handling performance and if worn parts are not replaced they can produce erratic and dangerous handling. Common symptoms are wheel hop, pulling to one side during acceleration and pulling to the other side during braking.

Removal

1. Place the ATV on level ground and set the parking brake.

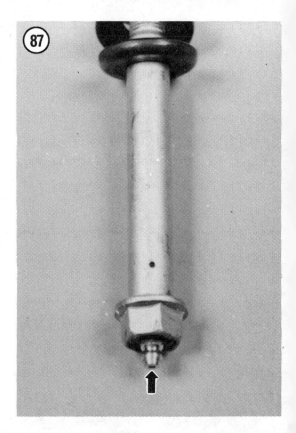

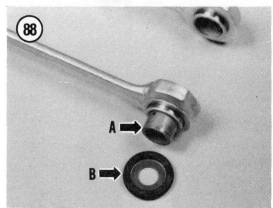

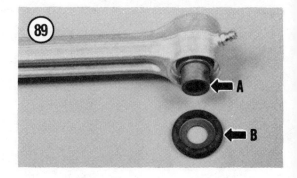

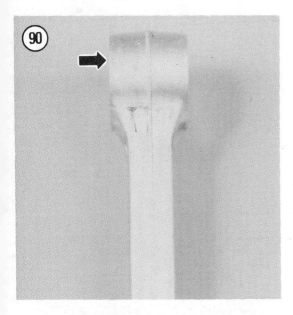

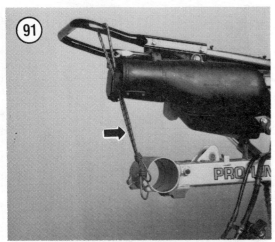

2. Remove the bolts securing the swing arm skid plate and remove the skid plate.

3. Place wood block(s) under the frame to support the ATV securely with the rear wheels off of the ground.

4. Remove the seat/rear fender assembly as described in Chapter Twelve.

5. Remove the rear wheels and rear axle as described in this chapter.

6. Remove the shock absorber as described in this chapter.

7. Remove the suspension linkage as described in this chapter.

8. Remove the rear brake caliper assembly and brake hose from the swing arm as described in Chapter Eleven.

9. On 3-wheeled models remove the rear brake pedal assembly as described in Chapter Eleven.

10. Grasp the rear end of the swing arm and try to move it from side to side in a horizontal arc. There should be no noticeable side play. If play is evident and the pivot bolt nut is tightened correctly, the bearings should be replaced.

11. Secure the rear of the swing arm to the frame with a bunji cord (**Figure 91**).

12. Remove the pivot bolt self-locking nut (**Figure 92**).

13. Using a drift and hammer, tap the pivot bolt out of the frame and swing arm. Withdraw the pivot bolt from the left-hand side.

14. Pull back on the swing arm and remove the swing arm from the frame.

10

NOTE
Don't lose the dust seal on each side of both pivot points on 1985-1987 models. On 1988-on models, don't lose the dust seal on the outer side of the pivot points. They will usually fall off when the swing arm is removed.

Disassembly/Inspection/Assembly

Refer to **Figure 93A** for 1985-1987 models or **Figure 93B** for 1988-on models.

1. Remove the swing arm as described in this chapter.

2. If necessary, remove the bolt and set plate securing the drive chain slider and remove the slider.

3A. On 1985-1987 models, remove the dust seal on each side of both pivot points, if they have not already fallen off when the swing arm was removed.

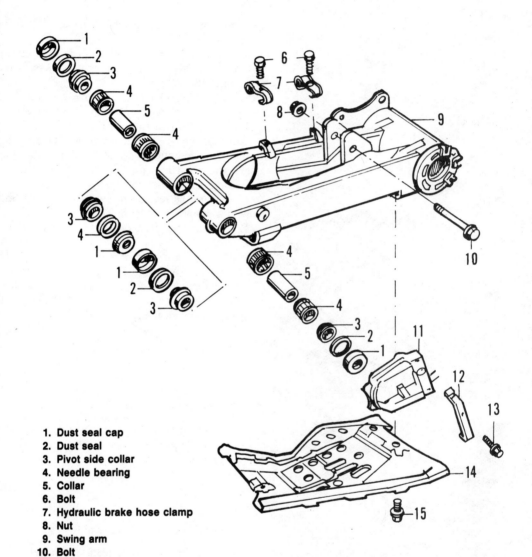

SWING ARM (1985-1987)

1. Dust seal cap
2. Dust seal
3. Pivot side collar
4. Needle bearing
5. Collar
6. Bolt
7. Hydraulic brake hose clamp
8. Nut
9. Swing arm
10. Bolt
11. Drive chain slider
12. Set plate
13. Bolt
14. Skid plate
15. Bolt

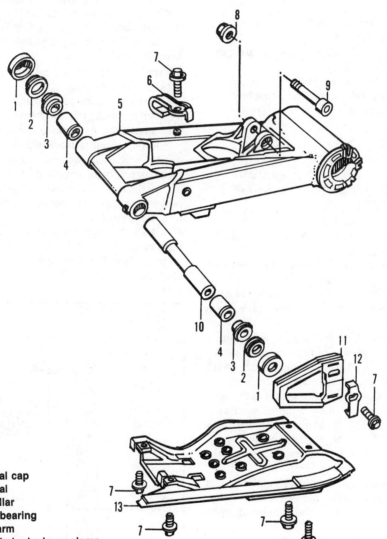

SWING ARM (1988-ON)

1. Dust seal cap
2. Dust seal
3. Side collar
4. Needle bearing
5. Swing arm
6. Hydraulic brake hose clamp
7. Bolt
8. Nut
9. Bolt
10. Long pivot collar
11. Drive chain slider
12. Set plate
13. Skid plate

10

3B. On 1988-on models, remove the dust seal on the outer side of the pivot points, if they have not already fallen off when the swing arm was removed.

4A. On 1985-1987 models, remove the short pivot collar from the inner surface of each pivot point.

4B. On 1988-on models, remove the long pivot collar from the inner surface of both pivot points.

5. Wipe off any excess grease from the needle bearing within each pivot area of the swing arm. Inspect them as follows:

   a. The needle bearings wear very slowly and wear is very difficult to measure.

   b. Turn each bearing with your fingers; make sure they rotate smoothly.

   c. Check the rollers for evidence of wear, pitting, or color change (bluish tint) indicating heat from lack of lubrication.

> *NOTE*
> *Always replace **all** needle bearings as a set even though only one may show signs of wear or damage.*

6. Replace the needle bearings, if necessary, as described in this chapter.

7. Coat the inner surface of all needle bearings with molybdenum disulfide grease.

8A. On 1985-1987 models, coat the inner and outer surface of both short pivot collars with molybdenum disulfide grease.

8B. On 1988-on models, perform the following:

   a. Coat the outer surface of the long pivot collar, where the needle bearings ride, with molybdenum disulfide grease.

   b. Apply molybdenum disulfide grease to the inner surface of the long pivot collar at each end. Apply grease in as far as you can reach.

9A. On 1985-1987 models, perform the following:

   a. Install a pivot collar into the inner surface of the pivot areas of the swing arm.

   b. Coat the lips of all dust seals with molybdenum disulfide grease. Position the dust seals as shown in **Figure 95** and install them into both pivot areas.

9B. On 1988-on models, perform the following:

   a. Coat the lips of both dust seals with molybdenum disulfide grease.

   b. Install them into both pivot areas.

10. Coat the inside surface of the dust seal caps with molybdenum disulfide grease and install them over the dust seals.

11. If removed, install the drive chain slider, set plate and bolt. Tighten the bolt securely.

12. Inspect the attachment points on the swing arm where the shock absorber is attached. If worn or damaged, the swing arm must be replaced.

13. Install the swing arm as described in this chapter.

Installation

1. Make sure that all dust seal caps are in position.

2. Place the swing arm through the drive chain and position the swing arm into the mounting area. Align the holes in the swing arm with the holes in the frame. To help align the holes, insert a drift in from the left-hand side.

3. Apply a light coat of grease to the pivot bolt and perform the following.

   a. After all holes are aligned, insert the pivot bolt from the left-hand side.

   b. Install the self-locking nut and tighten to the torque specification listed in **Table 1**.

4. On 3-wheeled models, install the rear brake pedal assembly as described in Chapter Eleven.

5. Install the rear brake caliper assembly and brake hose onto the swing arm as described in Chapter Eleven.

6. Install the suspension linkage as described in this chapter.

7. Install the shock absorber as described in this chapter.

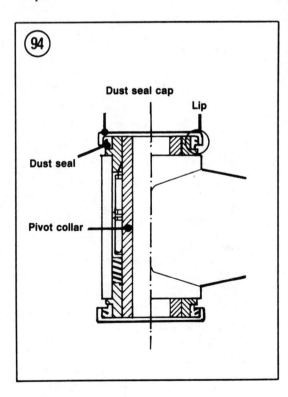

94

Dust seal cap

Lip

Dust seal

Pivot collar

8. Install the rear wheels and rear axle as described in this chapter.

9. Install the seat/rear fender assembly as described in Chapter Twelve.

10. Install the bolts securing the swing arm skid plate and remove the skid plate.

Needle Bearing Replacement (1985-1987)

The following procedure requires a special tool that is expensive and can be used only for this

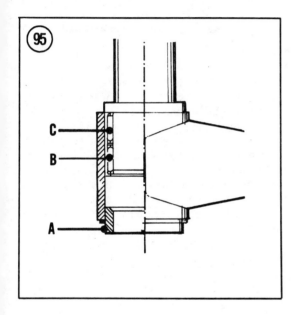

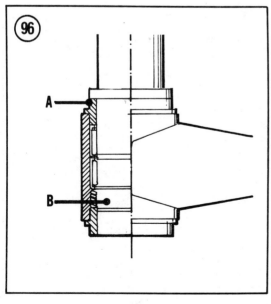

specific job. It may be less expensive to have the needle bearings replaced by a Honda dealer than to purchase the special tool and locate a hydraulic press that you can use. This procedure is included in case you choose to perform this task yourself.

The needle bearings will be damaged when removed, so remove them for replacement purposes only.

1. Remove the swing arm as described in this chapter.

2. Remove the dust seal caps and dust seals from each side of both pivot points.

3. To remove the inner side collar, perform the following.

    a. Insert a soft aluminum or brass drift from the outside surface of the pivot area and onto the inner side collar.

    b. Using a hammer, tap the inner side collar out of the pivot area, working around the perimeter of the collar.

4. To remove the needle bearings and outer side collar, perform the following.

    a. Insert a soft aluminum or brass drift from the inside surface of the pivot area and onto the needle bearings.

    b. Using a hammer, tap the needle bearings and outer side collar out of the pivot area working around the perimeter of the needle bearings.

5. Install the needle bearing remover (Honda part No. 07946-KA50000) into the hydraulic press.

6. Using the Honda special tool and press, press the inner side collar (A, **Figure 95**) into place in the pivot area.

7. Press the needle bearings and outer side collar as follows.

    a. Position the needle bearings with their markings facing toward the outside of the swing arm.

    b. Using the Honda special tool and press, press the inner needle bearing (B, **Figure 95**) into place in the pivot area.

    c. Using the special tool and press, press the outer needle bearing (C, **Figure 95**) into place in the pivot area until it is just past the outer edge of the pivot area.

    d. Place the outer collar (A, **Figure 96**) into the pivot area and press the collar and needle bearings into place.

    e. Pack the space between the inner needle bearing and inner collar with grease (B, **Figure 96**).

8. Install the dust seal caps and dust seals onto each side of both pivot points.

9. Install the swing arm as described in this chapter.

10

Needle Bearing Replacement
(1988-on)

The following procedure requires several special tools that are expensive and can be used only for this specific job. It may be less expensive to have the needle bearings replaced by a Honda dealer than to purchase the special tools and locate a hydraulic press that you can use. This procedure is included in case you choose to perform this task yourself.

The needle bearings will be damaged when removed, so remove them for replacement purposes only.

1. Remove the swing arm as described in this chapter.
2. Remove the dust seal caps and dust seals from each side of the pivot points.
3. To remove the collars, perform the follow:
   a. Install Honda special tool (20 mm bearing remover head, part No. 07746-0050600) into the collar to be removed.
   b. From the other side of the swing arm, install the Honda special tool (bearing remover shaft, part No. 07GGD-0010100) into the bearing remover head on the opposite side.
   c. Using a hammer, tap on the end of the bearing remover and carefully tap the collar out of the pivot point.
   d. Remove the special tools and repeat for the collar on the other side.
4. To remove the needle bearings, perform the follow:

   a. Insert a long soft-aluminum or brass drift into one side of the swing arm and against the backside of the needle bearing on the opposite side.
   b. Using a hammer, tap the needle bearing out of the pivot area working around the perimeter of the needle bearing.
5. The following Honda special tools are required to install the needle bearing and collar on each side:
   a. Driver (part No. 07749-0010000).
   b. 20 × 30 mm attachment, (part No. 07946-1870100).
   c. 20 mm pilot, (part No. 07746-0040500).

   NOTE
   The needle bearing and collar are installed at the same time.

6. Install the needle bearing and collar as follows:
   a. Position the needle bearing with the markings facing toward the outside of the swing arm.
   b. Using the Honda special tools and press, press the needle bearing and collar into the pivot area of the swing arm. Press the collar in until it bottoms out.
   c. Remove the special tools and repeat for the collar and needle bearing on the other side.
7. Pack the needle bearings with molybdenum disulfide grease.
8. Install the swing arm as described in this chapter.

Table 1 REAR SUSPENSION TORQUE SPECIFICATIONS

Item	N·m	ft.-lb.
Rear wheel lug nut	60-70	43-51
Rear axle nut		
3-wheeled models		
1985	100-120	72-87
1986	120-170	87-123
4-wheeled models	120-170	87-123
Rear axle locknuts		
Outer		
Actual	80-100	58-72
Indicated	73-91	53-66
Inner		
Actual	120-140	87-101
Indicated	109-127	79-92
Driven sprocket		
bolts and nuts	47-55 (continued)	34-40

Table 1 REAR SUSPENSION TORQUE SPECIFICATIONS (continued)

Item	N·m	ft.-lb.
Drive sprocket nut	30-34	22-24
Rear axle bearing		
holder clamp bolts	19-23	14-17
Shock absorber mounting		
Upper bolt and nut	45-55	32-40
Lower bolt and nut	70-80	51-58
Shock absorber spring locknut	80-100	58-72
Suspension linkage		
Shock link bolt and nut	70-80	51-58
Shock arm bolt and nut	70-80	51-58
Swing arm pivot bolt and nut	70-110	51-80

Table 2 REAR SUSPENSION SPECIFICATIONS

Item	Standard	Service limit
Rear axle runout	1.0 mm (0.04 in.)	3.0 mm (0.12 in.)
Rear wheel rim runout		
Axial and radial	1.0 mm (0.04 in.)	4.0 mm (0.16 in.)
Rear shock spring free length		
ATC250R	254.7-260.7 mm (10.028-10.264 in.)	252.1 mm (9.93 in.)
TRX250R/Fourtrax 250R		
1986	247-253 mm (9.7-10.0 in.)	244 mm (9.6 in.)
1987	225.7-231.7 mm (8.89-9.12 in.)	224 mm (8.8 in.)
1988-on	233.6-239.6 mm (9.20-9.43 in.)	231 mm (9.1 in.)
Rear shock damper unit specified force for 10 mm (0.14 in.) of travel		
ATC250R		
1985	15-25 kg (33-55 lb.)	—
1986	23.1-38.5 kg (51-85 lb.)	—
TRX250R/Fourtrax 250R		
1986	23.1-38.5 kg (51-85 lb.)	—
1987	11.6-19.2 kg (26-43 lb.)	—
1988-on	10.9-15.6 kg (24-34 lb.)	—

	Standard	Minimum-maximum
Rear shock spring length installed		
ATC250R	241.7 mm (9.52 in.)	236.7-248.7 mm (9.319-9.791 in.)
TRX250R/Fourtrax 250R		
1986	241.3 mm (9.50 in.)	236.3-241.3 mm (9.30-9.50 in.)
1987	220.7 mm (8.69 in.)	215.7-220.7 mm (8.49-8.69 in.)
1988-on	225 mm (8.86 in.)	220-225 mm (8.66-8.86 in.)

10

BRAKES

Both the front and rear wheels are equipped with disc brakes.

The ATV is equipped with a parking brake that is cable operated and is integrated into the rear brake assembly. The parking brake is activated by the hand lever on the left-hand side of the handlebar that is integral with the clutch lever.

WARNING
When working on the brake system, do ***not*** *inhale brake dust. It may contain asbestos, which can cause lung injury and cancer.*

DISC BRAKES

The front disc brakes are actuated by hydraulic fluid and are controlled by a hand lever on the handlebar-mounted master cylinder. The rear disc brake is actuated by hydraulic fluid and is controlled by a foot-operated brake pedal and master cylinder. As the brake pads wear, the piston extends further from the caliper bore and brake fluid fills the larger space which this leaves in the caliper. The brake fluid level drops in the reservoir and automatically adjusts for wear.

When working on hydraulic brake systems, it is necessary that the work area and all tools be absolutely clean. Any tiny particles of foreign matter and grit in the caliper assembly or the master cylinder can damage the components. Also, sharp tools must not be used inside the caliper or on the piston. If there is any doubt about your ability to correctly and safely carry out major service on the brake components, take the job to a dealer or brake specialist.

There is no recommended mileage interval for changing the friction pads in the disc brake. Pad wear depends greatly on riding habits and conditions. The pads should be checked for wear every 6 months and replaced when worn to the service limit dimension (or less) listed in **Table 1**. To maintain an even brake pressure on the disc always replace both pads in the caliper at the same time.

CAUTION
Watch the pads more closely when the pads wear close to the wear limit dimension. If pad wear happens to be uneven for some reason the backing plate may come in contact with the disc and cause damage.

FRONT BRAKE PAD REPLACEMENT (3-WHEELED MODELS)

Removal

Refer to **Figure 1** for this procedure.

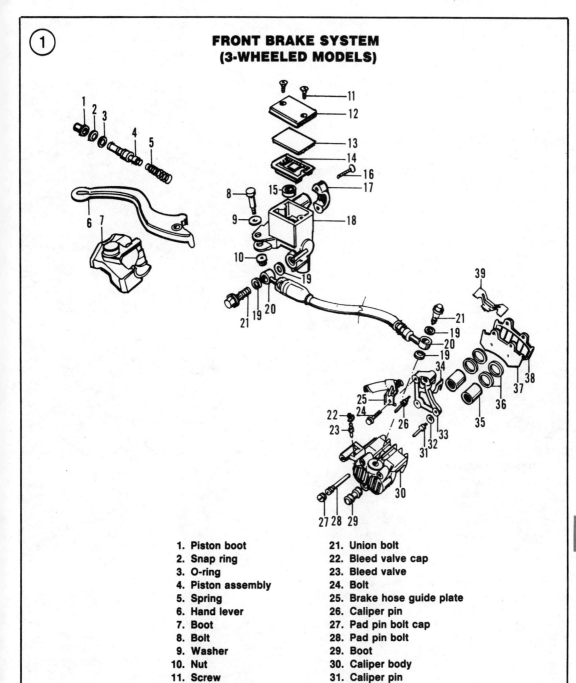

FRONT BRAKE SYSTEM (3-WHEELED MODELS)

1. Piston boot
2. Snap ring
3. O-ring
4. Piston assembly
5. Spring
6. Hand lever
7. Boot
8. Bolt
9. Washer
10. Nut
11. Screw
12. Top cover
13. Diaphragm plate
14. Diaphragm
15. Separator
16. Bolt
17. Clamp
18. Master cylinder body
19. Sealing washer
20. Upper brake hose
21. Union bolt
22. Bleed valve cap
23. Bleed valve
24. Bolt
25. Brake hose guide plate
26. Caliper pin
27. Pad pin bolt cap
28. Pad pin bolt
29. Boot
30. Caliper body
31. Caliper pin
32. Seal
33. Caliper bracket
34. Retainer clip
35. Piston
36. Dust and piston seals
37. Outboard brake pad
38. Inboard brake pad
39. Anti-rattle spring

11

1. Place the ATV on level ground and set the parking brake. Block the rear wheels so the vehicle will not roll in either direction.

2. Jack up the front of the vehicle with a small hydraulic or scissor jack. Place the jack under the skid plate with a piece of wood between the jack and the skid plate.

3. Place wood block(s) under the skid plate to support the ATV securely with the front wheel off the ground.

4. Remove the bolts securing the brake hose clamp (**Figure 2**) to the fork slider. Remove the clamp and the brake hose.

5. Completely unscrew the lug nuts (**Figure 3**) securing the front wheel to the front hub.

6. Slightly move the wheel to the right-hand side.

7. Unscrew the pad pin bolt caps (**Figure 4**).

8. Loosen, but do not remove, the pad pin bolts (**Figure 5**).

9. Remove the bolts (**Figure 6**) securing the caliper assembly to the left-hand fork slider. Don't lose the brake hose clip on the upper bolt.

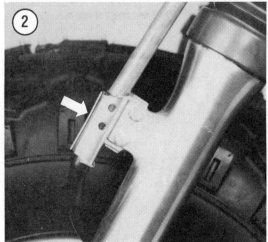

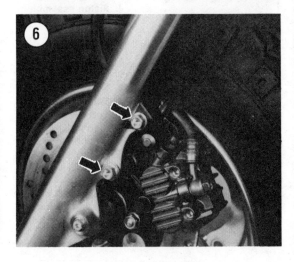

10. Slide the caliper assembly off the brake disc.
11. Unscrew the pad pin bolts.
12. Remove both brake pads and the pad spring.

13. Clean the pad recess and the end of the piston (**Figure 7**) with a soft brush. Do not use solvent, wire brush or any hard tool which would damage the cylinder or the piston.
14. Carefully remove any rust or corrosion from the disc.

Installation

1. Lightly coat the end of the piston and the backs of the new pads, *not* the friction material, with disc brake lubricant.

> *NOTE*
> *When purchasing new pads, check with your dealer to make sure the friction compound of the new pad is compatible with the disc material. Remove any roughness from the backs of the new pads with a fine cut file. Blow them clean with compressed air.*

2. When new pads are installed in the caliper, the master cylinder brake fluid level will rise as the caliper piston is repositioned. Perform the following.

    a. Clean the top of the master cylinder of all dirt and foreign matter.
    b. Remove the screws securing the cover (**Figure 8**) and remove the cover, the plate and the diaphragm from the master cylinder.
    c. slowly push the caliper pistons into the caliper.
    d. Constantly check the reservoir to make sure brake fluid does not overflow. Remove fluid, if necessary, before it overflows.
    e. The caliper pistons should move freely. If they don't, and there is evidence of them

11

sticking in the cylinders, the caliper should be removed and serviced as described under *Caliper Rebuilding* in this chapter.

3. Push the caliper pistons in all the way (**Figure 7**) to allow room for the new pads.

4. Install the brake pad spring (**Figure 9**).

5. Install the outboard pad (**Figure 10**). Align the holes in the outboard pad with the pad pin and partially install one of the pad pins.

6. Install the inboard pad (**Figure 11**) into the caliper, then push the pad pin through this pad and screw it into the caliper assembly. Do not tighten at this time.

7. Install the remaining pad pin (**Figure 12**) and screw it into the caliper assembly. Do not tighten at this time.

8. Carefully separate the brake pads so there is room for the brake disc.

9. Carefully install the caliper assembly onto the disc. Be careful not to damage the leading edges of the pads during installation.

10. Install the caliper lower mounting bolt (**Figure 13**).

11. Install brake hose guide plate and caliper upper mounting bolt (**Figure 14**). The guide plate must be installed over the brake hose to keep the hose away from the front wheel.

12. Tighten the caliper mounting bolts to the torque specification listed in **Table 2**.

13. Tighten the pad pin bolts (**Figure 5**) to the torque specification listed in **Table 2**.

14. Tighten the pad pin bolt caps (**Figure 4**) to the torque specification listed in **Table 2**.

15. Install the clamp and bolts securing the brake line to the front fork (**Figure 2**). Tighten the bolts securely.

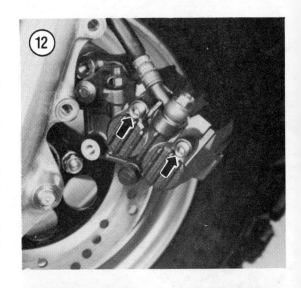

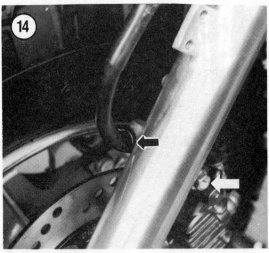

16. Place the front wheel onto the front hub studs. Install the wheel lug nuts with the tapered side (**Figure 15**) going on first. Finger tighten the nuts at this time. Do *not* tighten them until the wheel is positioned correctly onto the wheel studs and the front wheel is on the ground.

17. Remove the wood blocks from under the skid plate.

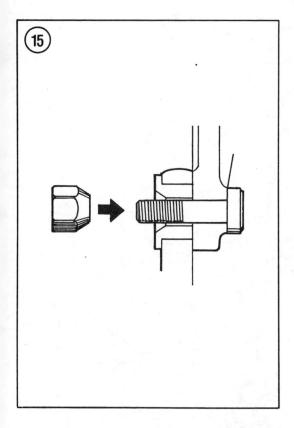

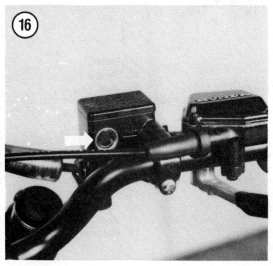

WARNING
Always tighten the lug nuts to the correct torque specification or the lug nuts may work loose.

18. Use a torque wrench and tighten the lug nuts to the torque specification listed in **Table 2**.

19. Raise the front wheel off the ground.

20. Spin the front wheel and activate the brake lever as many times as it takes to refill the cylinder in the caliper and correctly locate the pads.

WARNING
*Use brake fluid from a sealed container marked DOT 3 or DOT 4 **only** and specified for disc brakes. Other types may vaporize and cause brake failure. Do not intermix different brands or types as they may not be compatible. Do not intermix a silicone based (DOT 5) brake fluid as it can cause brake component damage leading to brake system failure.*

21. Refill the master cylinder reservoir, if necessary, to maintain the correct fluid level (**Figure 16**). Install the diaphragm, plate and cover. Tighten the screws securely.

WARNING
Do not ride the ATV until you are sure the brakes are operating correctly with full hydraulic advantage. If necessary, bleed the brake as described in this chapter.

22. Bed the pads in gradually for the first 10 days of riding by using only light pressure as much as possible. Immediate hard application will glaze the new friction pads and greatly reduce the effectiveness of the brake.

FRONT BRAKE PAD REPLACEMENT (4-WHEELED MODELS)

Removal

Refer to **Figure 17** for 1986-1987 models or **Figure 18** for 1988-on models.

1. Place the ATV on level ground and set the parking brake.

2. Loosen the bolts (A, **Figure 19**) securing the caliper assembly and brake hose guide plate (B, **Figure 19**) to the steering knuckle.

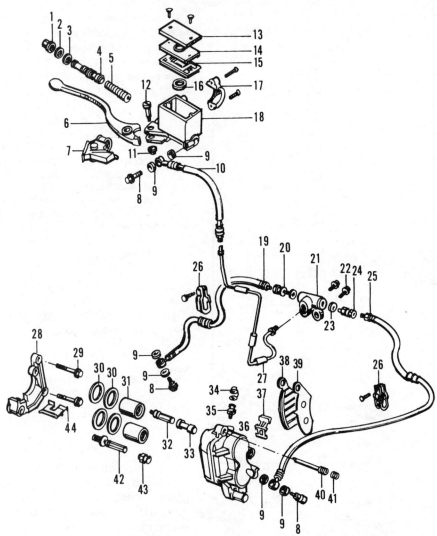

**FRONT BRAKE SYSTEM
(4-WHEELED MODELS—1986-1987)**

1. Piston boot
2. Snap ring
3. O-ring
4. Piston assembly
5. Spring
6. Hand lever
7. Boot
8. Union bolt
9. Sealing washer
10. Upper flexible brake hose
11. Nut
12. Bolt
13. Top cover
14. Diaphragm plate
15. Diaphragm
16. Separator
17. Clamp
18. Master cylinder body
19. Right-hand lower flexible brake hose
20. Hose fitting
21. 3-way fitting
22. Bolt
23. Sealing washer
24. Hose fitting
25. Left-hand lower flexible brake hose
26. Brake hose clamp
27. Metal brake line
28. Caliper bracket
29. Bolt
30. Dust and piston seals
31. Piston
32. Caliper pin
33. Boot
34. Bleed valve cap
35. Bleed valve
36. Caliper body
37. Anti-rattle spring
38. Inboard brake pad
39. Outboard brake pad
40. Pad pin bolt
41. Pad pin bolt cap
42. Caliper pin
43. Boot
44. Retainer clip

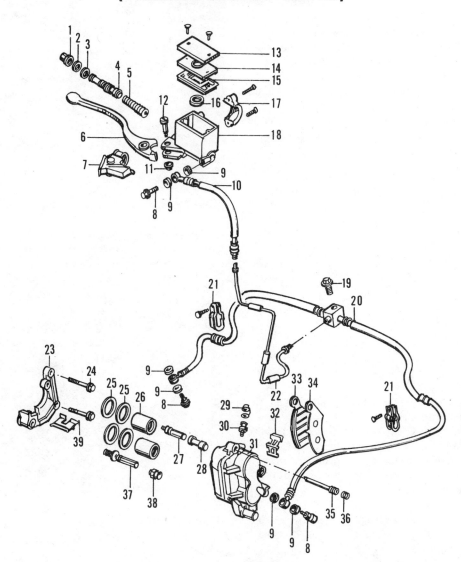

⑱

FRONT BRAKE SYSTEM
(4-WHEELED MODELS—1988-ON)

1. Piston boot	14. Diaphragm plate	27. Caliper pin
2. Snap ring	15. Diaphragm	28. Boot
3. O-ring	16. Separator	29. Bleed valve cap
4. Piston assembly	17. Clamp	30. Bleed valve
5. Spring	18. Master cylinder body	31. Caliper body
6. Hand lever	19. Bolt	32. Anti-rattle spring
7. Boot	20. Lower flexible hose	33. Inboard brake pad
8. Union bolt	21. Brake hose clamp	34. Outboard brake pad
9. Sealing washer	22. Metal brake line	35. Pad pin bolt
10. Upper flexible brake hose	23. Caliper bracket	36. Pad pin bolt cap
11. Nut	24. Bolt	37. Caliper pin
12. Bolt	25. Dust and piston seals	38. Boot
13. Top cover	26. Piston	39. Retainer clip

11

3. Remove the front wheels as described in Chapter Nine.

4. Remove the caliper assembly from the brake disc.

5. Unscrew the pad pin bolt cap.

6. Unscrew the pad pin bolt (**Figure 20**).

7. Remove both brake pads and the pad spring.

8. Clean the pad recess and the end of the piston (**Figure 21**) with a soft brush. Do not use solvent, wire brush or any hard tool which would damage the cylinder or the piston.

9. Carefully remove any rust or corrosion from the disc.

Installation

1. Lightly coat the end of the piston and the backs of the new pads, *not* the friction material, with disc brake lubricant.

> *NOTE*
> *When purchasing new pads, check with your dealer to make sure the friction compound of the new pad is compatible with the disc material. Remove any roughness from the backs of the new pads with a fine cut file. Blow them clean with compressed air.*

2. When new pads are installed in the caliper, the master cylinder brake fluid level will rise as the caliper piston is repositioned. Perform the following.

  a. Clean the top of the master cylinder of all dirt and foreign matter.

  b. Remove the screws securing the cover (**Figure 22**) and remove the cover, the plate and the diaphragm from the master cylinder.

  c. Slowly push the caliper pistons into the caliper.

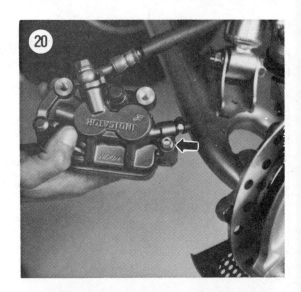

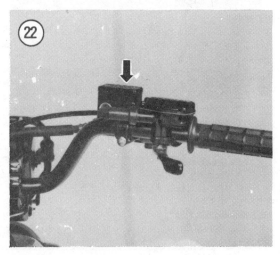

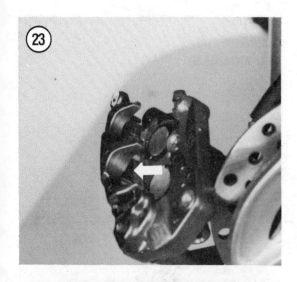

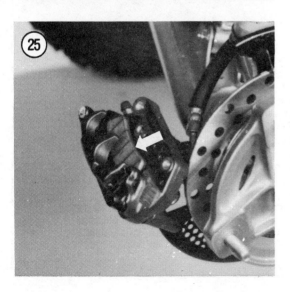

d. Constantly check the reservoir to make sure brake fluid does not overflow. Remove fluid, if necessary, before it overflows.

e. The caliper pistons should move freely. If they don't, and there is evidence of them sticking in the cylinders, the caliper should be removed and serviced as described under *Caliper Rebuilding* in this chapter.

3. Push the caliper piston in all the way (**Figure 21**) to allow room for the new pads.

4. Install the brake pad spring (**Figure 23**) and if removed, the retainer clip (**Figure 24**).

5. Install the outboard pad (**Figure 25**) and the inboard pad (**Figure 26**).

6. Press both brake pads against the brake pad spring. Align the pad pin holes in both pads and in the caliper.

7. Install the pad pin (**Figure 20**) and tighten to the torque specification listed in **Table 2**.

8. Install the pad pin bolt cap (**Figure 19**) and tighten to the torque specification listed in **Table 2**.

9. Carefully separate the brake pads so there is room for the brake disc.

10. Carefully install the caliper assembly onto the disc. Be careful not to damage the leading edge of the pads during installation.

> *WARNING*
> *The brake hose guide plate must be installed **as shown**. The guide plate protects the brake hose from rubbing against the moving parts of the steering knuckle. If the guide plate is not installed, the brake hose may wear through, resulting in a complete loss of brake fluid. This could cause a serious accident.*

11. Install the front caliper assembly onto the steering knuckle.

12. Install the front wheels as described in Chapter Nine.

13. Be sure to install the brake hose guide plate as shown in B, **Figure 18**.

11

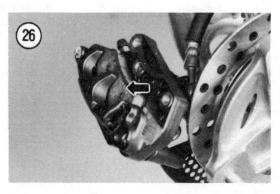

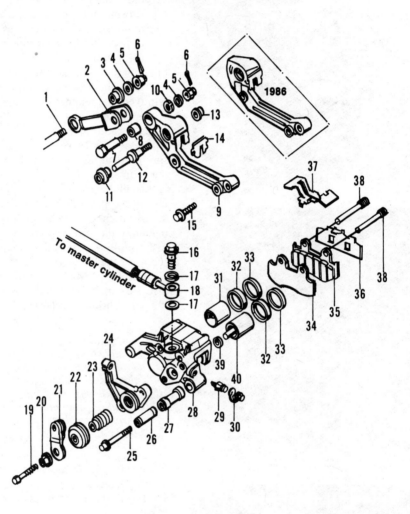

REAR CALIPER (ALL MODELS)

1. Torque link
2. Torque link arm
3. Collar
4. Washer
5. Nut
6. Cotter pin
7. Bolt
8. Collar
9. Caliper mounting bracket
10. Washer
11. Boot
12. Caliper pin
13. Nut
14. Retainer clip
15. Bolt
16. Union bolt
17. Sealing washer
18. Flexible brake hose
19. Parking brake adjust bolt
20. Locknut
21. Parking brake arm
22. Boot
23. Parking brake shaft
24. Parking brake base
25. Caliper mounting bolt
26. Caliper pivot collar
27. Collar
28. Caliper
29. Bleed valve
30. Bleed valve cap
31. Piston
32. Piston seal
33. Dust seal
34. Inboard brake pad
35. Outboard brake pad
36. Shim
37. Anti-rattle spring
38. Pad pin bolts
39. O-ring seal
40. Piston

14. Tighten the front caliper mounting bolts (A, **Figure 18**) to the torque specification listed in **Table 2**.

15. Spin the front wheel and activate the brake lever as many times as it takes to refill the cylinders in the caliper and correctly locate the pads.

> *WARNING*
> *Use brake fluid specified for disc brakes from a sealed container marked DOT 3 or DOT 4 **only**. Other types may vaporize and cause brake failure. Do not intermix different brands or types as they may not be compatible. Do not intermix a silicone based (DOT 5) brake fluid as it can cause brake component damage leading to brake system failure.*

16. Refill the master cylinder reservoir, if necessary, to maintain the correct fluid level. Install the diaphragm, the plate and the cover. Tighten the screws securely.

> *WARNING*
> *Do not ride the ATV until you are sure the brakes are operating correctly with full hydraulic advantage. If necessary, bleed the brake as described in this chapter.*

17. Bed the pads in gradually for the first 10 days of riding by using only light pressure as much as possible. Immediate hard application will glaze the new friction pads and greatly reduce the effectiveness of the brake.

REAR BRAKE PAD REPLACEMENT

Removal

Refer to **Figure 27** for this procedure.

1. Place the ATV on level ground. Block the front wheel(s) so the ATV cannot move in either direction.

2. Remove the seat/rear fender assembly as described in Chapter Twelve.

3. Unscrew the pad pin bolt caps (**Figure 28**).

4. Loosen the pad pin bolts (**Figure 29**). Do not remove at this time.

5. Remove the bolt and clip (**Figure 30**) securing the hydraulic brake line to the locating tab on the swing arm.

6. Remove the bolt (**Figure 31**) securing the caliper assembly to the caliper bracket.

7. Pivot the caliper assembly and torque link up and off the disc.

8. Unscrew the pad pin bolts.

9A. On 3-wheeled models, remove both brake pads, the shim and the brake spring.

9B. On 4-wheeled models, remove both brake pads and the brake spring.

10. Clean the ends of the piston (**Figure 32**) and surrounding area of the caliper with a soft brush. Do not use solvent, wire brush or any hard tool which would damage the cylinders or pistons.

11. Carefully remove any rust or corrosion from the disc.

Installation

1. Lightly coat the ends of the pistons and the backs of the new pads, *not* the friction material, with disc brake lubricant.

> *NOTE*
> *When purchasing new pads, check with your dealer to make sure the friction compound of the new pad is compatible with the disc material. Remove any roughness from the backs of the new pads with a fine cut file. Blow them clean with compressed air.*

2. When new pads are installed in the caliper the master cylinder brake fluid level will rise as the caliper pistons are repositioned. Perform the following.

   a. Clean the top of the master cylinder of all dirt and foreign matter.

   b. Remove the screws securing the cover and remove the cover, the plate and the diaphragm from the master cylinder. Refer to **Figure 33** for 3-wheeled models or **Figure 34** for 4-wheeled models.

   c. Slowly push the caliper pistons into the caliper.

   d. Constantly check the reservoir to make sure brake fluid does not overflow. Remove fluid, if necessary, before it overflows.

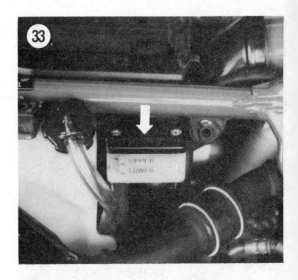

e. The caliper pistons should move freely. If they don't, and there is evidence of them sticking in the cylinders, the caliper should be removed and serviced as described under *Caliper Rebuilding* in this chapter.

3. Push the caliper pistons (**Figure 32**) in all the way to allow room for the new pads.

4. Install the pad spring (A, **Figure 35**) and the retainer (B, **Figure 35**) into the caliper.

5. Install the shim (**Figure 36**).

6. Install the outboard pad (**Figure 37**).

7. Install the inboard pad (A, **Figure 38**) into the caliper.

8. Align the holes in both brake pads with the pad pin holes in the caliper and partially install one of the pad pins (B, **Figure 38**).

9. Install the remaining pad pin and screw it into the caliper assembly. Do not tighten at this time.

10. Apply a light coat of silicone grease to the caliper pin (**Figure 39**).

11. Carefully separate the brake pads so there is room for the brake disc.

12. Install the caliper assembly onto the caliper pin and carefully install the caliper assembly onto the disc (**Figure 40**). Be careful not to damage the leading edge of the pads during installation.

11

13. Install the caliper mounting bolt (**Figure 31**) and tighten to the torque specification listed in **Table 2**.

14. Tighten the pad pin bolts (**Figure 29**) to the torque specification listed in **Table 2**.

15. Install the pad pin bolt caps (**Figure 28**) and tighten to the torque specification listed in **Table 2**.

16. Install the clamp and bolt (**Figure 30**) securing the hydraulic brake hose under the locating tab on the swing arm. Tighten the bolt securely.

17. Shift the transmission into NEUTRAL.

18. Jack up the rear of the vehicle with a small hydraulic or scissor jack. Place the jack under the skid plate with a piece of wood between the jack and the skid plate.

19. Place wood block(s) under the skid plate to support the ATV securely with the rear wheels off the ground.

20. Spin the rear wheels and activate the brake pedal as many times as it takes to refill the cylinder in the caliper and correctly locate the pads.

WARNING
*Use brake fluid from a sealed container marked DOT 3 or DOT 4 **only** and specified for disc brakes. Other types may vaporize and cause brake failure. Do not intermix different brands or types as they may not be compatible. Do not intermix a silicone based (DOT 5) brake fluid as it can cause brake component damage leading to brake system failure.*

21. Refill the master cylinder reservoir, if necessary, to maintain the correct fluid level. Refer to **Figure 41** for 3-wheeled models or **Figure 42** for 4-wheeled models. Install the diaphragm, the plate and top cover. Tighten the screws securely.

WARNING
Do not ride the ATV until you are sure the brake is operating correctly with full hydraulic advantage. If necessary, bleed the brake as described in this chapter.

22. Bed the pads in gradually for the first 10 days of riding by using only light pressure as much as possible. Immediate hard application will glaze the new friction pads and greatly reduce the effectiveness of the brake.

FRONT MASTER CYLINDER

Removal/Installation

1. Place the ATV on level ground and set the parking brake. Block the rear wheels so the vechicle will not roll in either direction.

CAUTION
Cover the front fender with a heavy cloth or plastic tarp to protect it from accidental brake fluid spills. Wash any brake fluid off any plastic, painted or plated surfaces immediately, as it will destroy the finish. Use soapy water and rinse completely.

2. Drain the front brake system of all brake fluid as described in this chapter.

3. Remove the union bolt (**Figure 43**) securing the brake hose to the master cylinder and remove the brake hose and sealing washers. Tie the brake hose up and cap the end to prevent the entry of foreign matter.

4. Remove the bolt and nut securing the brake lever to the master cylinder body and remove the lever.

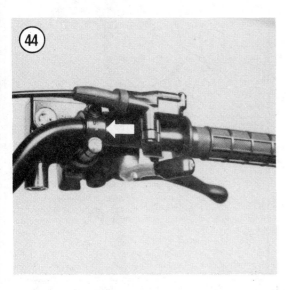

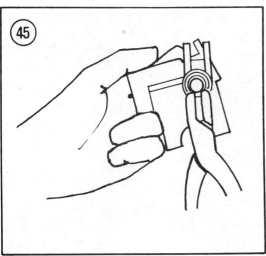

5. Remove the throttle housing as described in Chapter Six.

6. Remove the clamping screws and clamp (**Figure 44**) securing the master cylinder to the handlebar and remove the master cylinder.

7. Install by reversing these removal steps, noting the following.

8. Align the end of the clamp with the punch mark on the handlebar.

9. Tighten the upper screw first, then the lower screw to the torque specification listed in **Table 2**.

10. Install the brake hose onto the master cylinder as follows.

    a. Position the hose in the stopper in the master cylinder body.

    b. Be sure to place a sealing washer on each side of the fitting and install the union bolt.

    c. Tighten the union bolt to the torque specification listed in **Table 2**.

11. Bleed the brake as described in this chapter.

Disassembly

Refer to **Figure 1** for 3-wheeled models or **Figure 17** for 4-wheeled models for for this procedure.

1. Remove the master cylinder as described in this chapter.

2. Remove the screws securing the cover and remove the cover, the plate and diaphragm. Pour out the brake fluid and discard it. *Never* reuse brake fluid.

3. Remove the rubber boot from the area where the hand lever actuates the internal piston.

4. Using circlip pliers, remove the internal circlip from the body (**Figure 45**).

5. Remove the piston and cup as an assembly.

6. Remove the spring.

Inspection

1. Clean all parts in denatured alcohol or fresh brake fluid. Inspect the cylinder bore and piston contact surfaces for signs of wear and damage. If either part is less than perfect, replace it.

2. Check the end of the piston for wear caused by the hand lever. Replace the piston if necessary.

3. Replace the piston assembly if either cup is worn or damaged.

4. Inspect the pivot hole in the hand lever. If worn or elongated, replace the hand lever.

5. Make sure the passages in the bottom of the brake fluid reservoir are clear. Check the reservoir cover and diaphragm for damage and deterioration and replace as necessary.

6. Inspect the brake line bore threads in the body. If worn or damaged, replace the body.

7. Check the front hand-lever pivot lug for cracks.

11

8. Measure the cylinder bore (**Figure 46**). Replace the master cylinder if the bore exceeds the service limit listed in **Table 1**.

9. Measure the outside diameter of the piston assembly as shown in **Figure 47** with a micrometer. Replace the piston assembly if it is less than the service limit listed in **Table 1**.

Assembly

1. Soak the new piston assembly in fresh brake fluid for at least 15 minutes to make the cups pliable. Coat the inside of the cylinder with fresh brake fluid before assembling parts.

> *CAUTION*
> *When installing the piston assembly, do not allow the cups to turn inside out as they will be damaged and allow brake fluid leakage within the cylinder bore.*

2. Position the spring with the narrow end facing toward the piston assembly.

3. Install the spring, the piston and cup set into the cylinder together.

4. Install the circlip, then slide on the rubber boot.

5. Install the diaphragm, the plate and cover. Do not tighten the cover screws at this time as fluid will have to be added during the bleeding procedure.

6. Install the brake lever onto the master cylinder body.

7. Install the master cylinder as described in this chapter.

REAR MASTER CYLINDER

Removal/Installation
(3-wheeled Models)

1. Place the ATV on level ground and set the parking brake. Block the front wheel so the vehicle will not roll in either direction.

2. Remove the seat/rear fender assembly as described in Chapter Twelve.

> *CAUTION*
> *Cover the surrounding frame with a heavy cloth or plastic tarp to protect it from accidental brake fluid spills. Wash any brake fluid off any plastic, painted or plated surfaces immediately, as it will destroy the finish. Use soapy water and rinse completely.*

3. Drain the rear brake system of all brake fluid as described in this chapter.

4. Remove the union bolt (A, **Figure 48**) securing the brake hose to the backside of the master

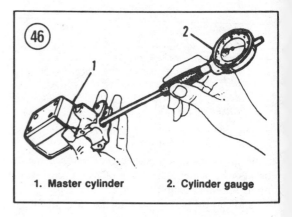

1. **Master cylinder**   2. **Cylinder gauge**

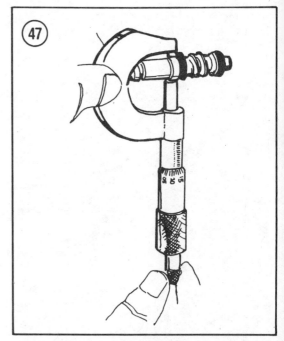

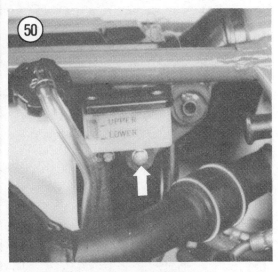

cylinder and remove the brake hose. Don't lose the sealing washers on each side of the brake hose fitting.

5. Remove the hose clamp (B, **Figure 48**) securing the reservoir brake hose to the master cylinder.

6. Remove the cotter pin and washer and remove the pivot pin (**Figure 49**) from the rod eye at the bottom of the master cylinder.

7. Remove the bolts (C, **Figure 48**) securing the master cylinder to the frame and remove the master cylinder.

8. To remove the reservoir, remove the flange bolt and washer (**Figure 50**) securing it to the frame and remove the reservoir.

9. Install by reversing these removal steps, noting the following.

10. Inspect the brake actuating rod boot on the bottom of the master cylinder. Replace boot if it is cracked or deteriorated.

11. Install the washer and a new cotter pin on the pivot pin and bend the ends over completely. Never reuse an old cotter pin.

12. Install the brake hose onto the master cylinder. Be sure to place a sealing washer on each side of the fitting and install the union bolt. Tighten the union bolt to the torque specification listed in **Table 2**.

13. Attach the master cylinder to the frame and tighten the mounting bolts to the torque specification listed in **Table 2**.

14. Bleed the brake as described in this chapter.

Removal/Installation (4-wheeled Models)

1. Place the ATV on level ground and set the parking brake. Block the rear wheels so the vehicle will not roll in either direction.

2. Remove the seat/rear fender assembly as described in Chapter Twelve.

CAUTION
Cover the surrounding frame with a heavy cloth or plastic tarp to protect it from accidental brake fluid spills. Wash any brake fluid off any plastic, painted or plated surfaces immediately, as it will destroy the finish. Use soapy water and rinse completely.

3. Drain the rear brake system of all brake fluid as described in this chapter.

4. Remove the union bolt (A, **Figure 51**) securing the brake hose to the backside of the master cylinder and remove the brake hose. Don't lose the sealing washers on each side of the brake hose fitting.

11

5. Remove the hose clamp (B, **Figure 51**) securing the reservoir brake hose to the master cylinder.

NOTE
*Drain the fluid from the hose and discard it. **Never** reuse brake fluid. Contaminated brake fluid may cause brake failure.*

6. Remove the cotter pin and washer and remove the pivot pin (**Figure 52**) from the rod eye at the bottom of the master cylinder.

7. Remove the bolts (C, **Figure 51**) securing the master cylinder to the frame and remove the master cylinder.

8. To remove the reservoir, remove the flange bolt and collar (**Figure 53**) securing it to the frame and remove the reservoir.

9. Install by reversing these removal steps, noting the following.

10. Inspect the brake actuating rod boot on the bottom of the master cylinder. Replace boot if it is cracked or deteriorated.

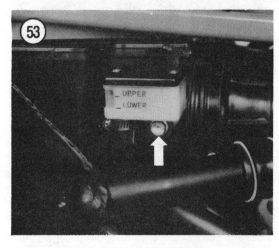

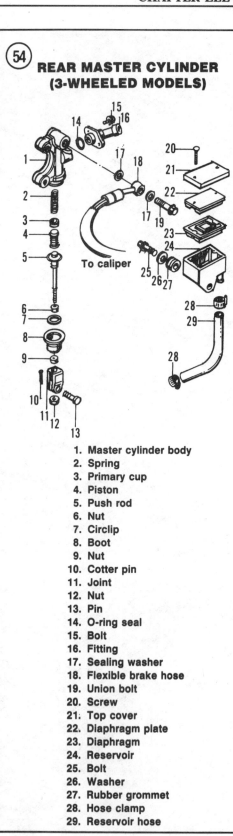

REAR MASTER CYLINDER (3-WHEELED MODELS)

To caliper

1. Master cylinder body
2. Spring
3. Primary cup
4. Piston
5. Push rod
6. Nut
7. Circlip
8. Boot
9. Nut
10. Cotter pin
11. Joint
12. Nut
13. Pin
14. O-ring seal
15. Bolt
16. Fitting
17. Sealing washer
18. Flexible brake hose
19. Union bolt
20. Screw
21. Top cover
22. Diaphragm plate
23. Diaphragm
24. Reservoir
25. Bolt
26. Washer
27. Rubber grommet
28. Hose clamp
29. Reservoir hose

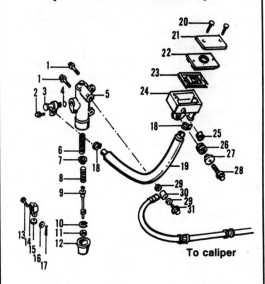

**REAR MASTER CYLINDER
(4-WHEELED MODELS)**

To caliper

1. Bolt
2. Screw
3. Fitting
4. O-ring seal
5. Master cylinder body
6. Spring
7. Primary cup
8. Piston
9. Push rod
10. Circlip
11. Nut
12. Boot
13. Pin
14. Joint
15. Nut
16. Washer
17. Cotter pin
18. Hose clamp
19. Reservoir hose
20. Screw
21. Top cover
22. Diaphragm plate
23. Diaphragm
24. Reservoir
25. Collar
26. Rubber grommet
27. Collar
28. Bolt
29. Sealing washer
30. Flexible brake hose
31. Union bolt

11. Install the washer and a new cotter pin on the pivot pin and bend the ends over completely. Never reuse an old cotter pin.

12. Install the brake hose onto the master cylinder. Be sure to place a sealing washer on each side of the fitting and install the union bolt. Tighten the union bolt to the torque specification listed in **Table 2**.

13. Attach the master cylinder to the frame and tighten the mounting bolts to the torque specification listed in **Table 2**.

14. Bleed the brake as described in this chapter.

Disassembly

Refer to **Figure 54** for 3-wheeled models or **Figure 55** for 4-wheeled models for this procedure.

1. Remove the master cylinder as described in this chapter.

2. Slide the rubber boot down the master cylinder piston rod.

3. Using circlip pliers, remove the internal circlip from the body (**Figure 56**).

4. Remove the pushrod, the piston and cup set and the spring from the body (**Figure 57**).

NOTE
*If the piston assembly is difficult to remove from the body, apply a **small** amount of air pressure to the brake hose receptacle in the body. Point the opening in the end of the body at a pile of shop rags or into a cardboard box. Catch the piston assembly and spring as they are forced out by the air pressure.*

11

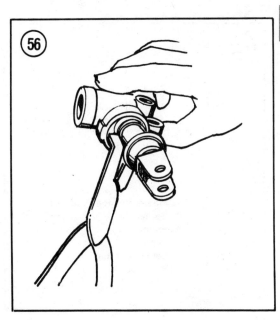

5. Remove the screw securing the brake hose connector to the master cylinder body. Remove the brake hose connector and the O-ring seal. Discard the O-ring seal.

Inspection

1. Clean all parts in denatured alcohol or fresh brake fluid. Inspect the cylinder bore and piston contact surfaces for signs of wear and damage. If either part is less than perfect, replace it.

2. Check the end of the piston for wear caused by the pushrod. Replace the piston assembly if worn or damaged.

3. Make sure the passages in the bottom of the brake fluid reservoir are clear. Check the reservoir cover and diaphragm for damage and deterioration and replace as necessary.

4. Inspect the threads in the brakeline bore.

5. Measure the cylinder bore (A, **Figure 58**). Replace the master cylinder if the bore exceeds the service limit listed in **Table 1**.

6. Measure the outside diameter of the piston assembly (B, **Figure 58**) with a micrometer. Replace the piston assembly if the diameter is less than the service limit listed in **Table 1**.

Assembly

1. Install a new O-ring seal and the brake hose connector onto the master cylinder body. Install the screw and tighten securely.

2. Soak the new piston assembly in fresh brake fluid for at least 15 minutes to make the cups pliable. Coat the inside of the cylinder with fresh brake fluid before the assembly of parts.

CAUTION
When installing the piston assembly, do not allow the cups to turn inside out as they will be damaged and allow brake fluid leakage within the cylinder bore.

3. Install the spring and the piston assembly into the cylinder together. The spring's tapered end faces toward the piston assembly.

4. Install the piston rod assembly and install the circlip. Slide the rubber boot into position.

5. Install the master cylinder as described in this chapter.

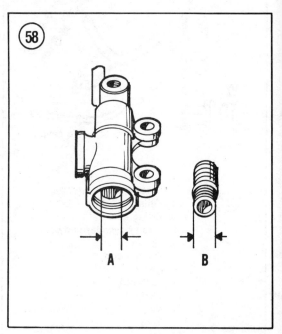

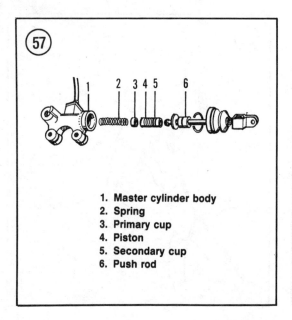

1. Master cylinder body
2. Spring
3. Primary cup
4. Piston
5. Secondary cup
6. Push rod

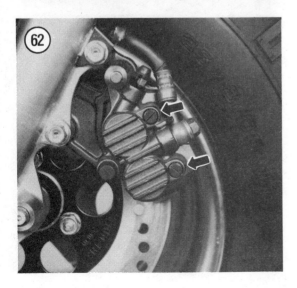

FRONT CALIPER

**Removal/Installation
(3-wheeled Models)**

Refer to **Figure 1** for this procedure.

> *CAUTION*
> *Do not spill any brake fluid on the painted portion of the front wheel. Wash any spilled brake fluid immediately as it will destroy the finish. Use soapy water and rinse completely.*

1. Place the ATV on level ground and set the parking brake. Block the rear wheels so the vehicle will not roll in either direction.
2. Jack up the front of the vehicle with a small hydraulic or scissor jack. Place the jack under the skid plate with a piece of wood between the jack and the skid plate.
3. Place wood block(s) under the skid plate to support the ATV securely with the front wheel off the ground.
4. Drain the front brake system of all brake fluid as described in this chapter.
5. Remove the bolts securing the brake hose clamp (**Figure 59**) to the fork slider. Remove the clamp and the brake hose.
6. Completely unscrew the lug nuts (**Figure 60**) securing the front wheel to the front hub.
7. Slightly move the wheel to the right-hand side.
8. Place a container under the brake line at the caliper.
9. Remove the union bolt and sealing washers (A, **Figure 61**) securing the brake line to the caliper assembly.
10. Remove the brake line and let the brake fluid drain out into the container. Dispose of this brake fluid. *Never* reuse brake fluid. To prevent the entry of moisture and dirt, cap the end of the brake line and tie the loose end up to the front fork.
11. Unscrew the pad pin bolt caps (**Figure 62**).
12. Loosen, but do not remove, the pad pin bolts (**Figure 63**).

11

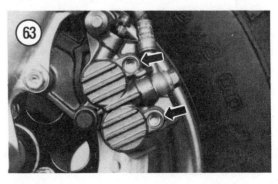

13. Remove the bolts (B, **Figure 61**) securing the caliper assembly to the left-hand fork slider.

14. Slide the caliper assembly off the brake disc.

15. Remove both brake pads and the pad spring as described in this chapter.

16. Install by reversing these removal steps, noting the following.

17. Carefully install the caliper assembly onto the disc. Be careful not to damage the leading edges of the pads during installation.

18. Install the caliper lower mounting bolt (**Figure 64**).

19. Install the caliper upper mounting bolt and brake hose guide plate (**Figure 65**). The guide plate must be installed to keep the brake hose away from the wheel.

20. Tighten the front caliper mounting bolts to the torque specification listed in **Table 2**.

21. Install the brake hose, with a sealing washer on each side of the fitting, onto the caliper. Install the union bolt and tighten to the torque specification listed in **Table 2**.

22. Bleed the brake as described in this chapter.

23. Place the front wheel onto the front hub studs. Install the wheel lug nuts with the tapered side (**Figure 15**) going on first. Finger tighten the nuts at this time. Do *not* tighten them until the wheel is positioned correctly onto the wheel studs and the front wheel is on the ground.

24. Remove the wood blocks from under the skid plate.

> *WARNING*
> *Always tighten the lug nuts to the correct torque specification or the lug nuts may work loose.*

25. Use a torque wrench and tighten the lug nuts to the torque specification listed in **Table 2**.

> *WARNING*
> *Do not ride the ATV until you are sure that the brakes are operating properly.*

Removal/Installation
(4-wheeled Models)

Refer to **Figure 17** for this procedure.

> *CAUTION*
> *Do not spill any brake fluid on the painted portion of the steering knuckle or front wishbone. Wash off any spilled brake fluid immediately as it will destroy the finish. Use soapy water and rinse completely.*

1. Place the ATV on level ground and set the parking brake.

2. Loosen the bolts (A, **Figure 66**) securing the caliper assembly and the brake hose guide plate (B, **Figure 66**) to the steering knuckle.

3. Remove the front wheels as described in Chapter Nine.

4. Drain the front brake system of all brake fluid as described in this chapter.

5. Place a container under the brake line at the caliper.

6. Remove the union bolt and sealing washers (C, **Figure 66**) securing the brake line to the caliper assembly.

7. Remove the brake line and let the brake fluid drain out into the container. Dispose of this brake fluid. *Never* reuse brake fluid. To prevent the entry of moisture and dirt, cap the end of the brake line and tie the loose end up to the front fork.

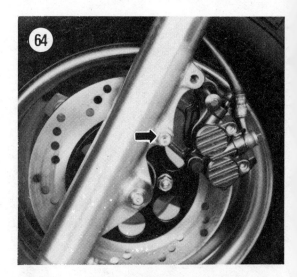

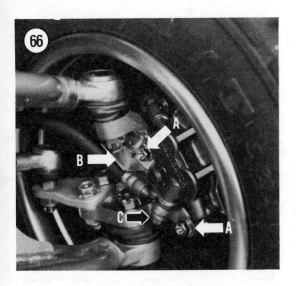

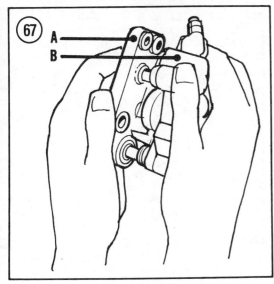

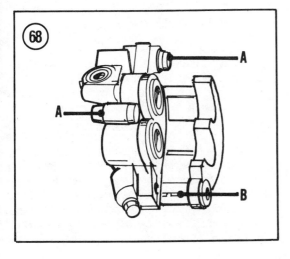

8. Remove the bolts (A, **Figure 66**) securing the caliper assembly and the brake hose guide plate (B, **Figure 66**) to the steering knuckle.

9. Slide the caliper assembly off the brake disc.

10. Remove the brake pads and spring as described in this chapter.

11. Install by reversing these removal steps, noting the following.

12. Carefully separate the brake pads so there is room for the brake disc.

13. Carefully install the caliper assembly onto the disc. Be careful not to damage the leading edges of the pads during installation.

WARNING
*The brake hose guide plate must be installed **as shown**. The guide plate protects the brake hose from rubbing against the moving parts of the steering knuckle. If the guide plate is not installed, the brake hose may wear through, resulting in a complete loss of brake fluid. This could cause a serious accident.*

14. Install the front caliper assembly onto the steering knuckle. Be sure to install the brake hose guide plate as shown.

15. Tighten the front caliper mounting bolts to the torque specification listed in **Table 2**.

16. Tighten the pad pin bolt to the torque specification listed in **Table 2**.

17. Tighten the pad pin bolt cap to the torque specification listed in **Table 2**.

18. Install the brake hose, with a sealing washer on each side of the fitting, onto the caliper. Install the union bolt and tighten to the torque specification listed in **Table 2**.

19. Bleed the brake as described in this chapter.

20. Install the front wheels as described in Chapter Nine.

WARNING
Do not ride the ATV until you are sure the brakes are operating correctly with full hydraulic advantage. If necessary, bleed the brake as described in this chapter.

Caliper Rebuilding
(3- and 4-wheeled Models)

1. Remove the caliper and brake pads as described in this chapter.

2. Separate the caliper bracket (A, **Figure 67**) from the caliper body (B, **Figure 67**).

3. Remove the caliper pivot boots (A, **Figure 68**).

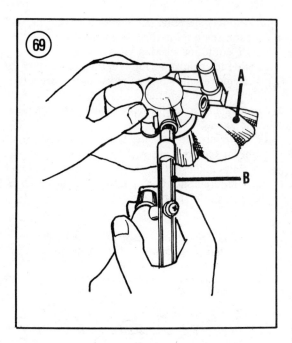

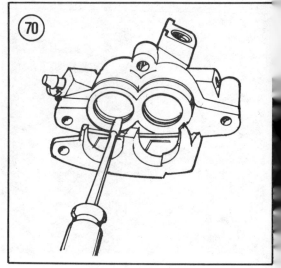

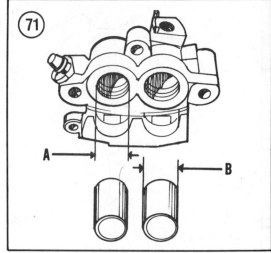

4. If not already removed, remove the brake pad spring (B, **Figure 68**).

5. Place a shop cloth (A, **Figure 69**) or piece of soft wood in the area normally occupied by the brake pads.

6. Place the caliper assembly on the workbench with the pistons facing down.

> *WARNING*
> *In the next step, the pistons may shoot out of the caliper body like bullets. Do not point the cylinder at your face. Keep your fingers out of the way. Wear shop gloves and apply air pressure gradually. Do **not** use high pressure air or place the air hose nozzle directly against the hydraulic line fitting inlet in the caliper body. Hold the air nozzle away from the inlet, allowing some of the air to escape.*

7. Apply the air pressure in short spurts to the hydraulic line fitting inlet (B, **Figure 69**) and force both pistons out. Use a service station air hose if you don't have a compressor.

> *CAUTION*
> *In the following step, do not use a sharp tool to remove the dust and piston seals from the caliper cylinders. Do not damage the cylinder surface.*

8. Use a piece of plastic or wood and carefully push the dust and piston seals in toward the caliper cylinder and out of their grooves (**Figure 70**).

Remove the dust and piston seals from both cylinders and discard all seals.

9. Inspect the caliper body for damage. Replace the caliper body if necessary.

10. Inspect the cylinders and the pistons for scratches, scoring or other damage. Light dirt may be removed with a cloth dipped in clean brake fluid. If rust is severe, replace the caliper body. Replace the caliper body if necessary.

11. If serviceable, clean the caliper body with rubbing alcohol and rinse with clean brake fluid.

12. Measure the inside diameter of both caliper cylinders (A, **Figure 71**) with an inside micrometer. If worn to the service limit dimension listed in **Table 1**, or greater, replace the caliper assembly.

13. Measure the outside diameter of the pistons (B, **Figure 71**) with a micrometer. If worn to the

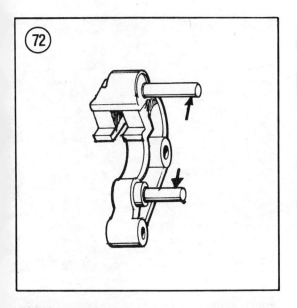

service limit dimension listed in **Table 1**, or less, replace the pistons.

> *NOTE*
> *Never reuse the old dust seals and piston seals. Very minor damage or age deterioration can make the seals useless.*

14. Coat the new dust seals and piston seals with fresh DOT 3 or DOT 4 brake fluid.

15. Carefully install the new dust seals and piston seals in the grooves in each caliper cylinder. Make sure the seals are properly seated in their respective grooves.

16. Coat the pistons and caliper cylinders with fresh DOT 3 or DOT 4 brake fluid.

17. Position the pistons with the flush side facing out toward the brake pads and install the pistons into the caliper cylinders. Push the pistons in until they bottom out.

18. Apply silicone grease to the caliper pivot boots and install the boots into the caliper body (B, **Figure 68**). Make sure the boots are properly seated in the caliper body grooves.

19. Apply silicone grease to the pins on the caliper bracket (A, **Figure 72**).

20. Install the caliper bracket onto the caliper body (**Figure 67**). Push it on until it bottoms out.

21. Install the brake pads and the caliper as described in this chapter.

REAR CALIPER
(3- AND 4-WHEELED MODELS)

Removal/Installation

Refer to **Figure 27** for this procedure.

> *CAUTION*
> *Do not spill any brake fluid on the painted portion of the swing arm or axle bearing housing. Wash off any spilled brake fluid immediately, as it will destroy the finish. Use soapy water and rinse completely.*

1. Place the ATV on level ground. Block the front wheel(s) so the ATV cannot move in either direction.

2. Remove the seat/rear fender assembly as described in Chapter Twelve.

3. Drain the rear brake system of all brake fluid as described in this chapter.

4. Unscrew the pad pin bolt caps (**Figure 73**).

5. Loosen the pad pin bolts (**Figure 74**). Do not remove at this time.

11

6. Remove the bolt and clamp (A, **Figure 75**) securing the hydraulic brake line from the locating tab on the swing arm.

7. Loosen the parking brake adjusting bolt locknut (A, **Figure 76**).

8. Unscrew the parking brake adjusting bolt (B, **Figure 76**) and locknut.

9. Remove the parking brake arm (B, **Figure 75**) from the rear caliper. Move the parking brake cable and arm out of the way.

10. Remove the union bolt and sealing washers (C, **Figure 75**) securing the brake line to the caliper assembly. Remove the brake line and let any residual brake fluid drain out. To prevent the entry of moisture and dirt, cap the end of the brake line and tie the loose end up to the frame.

11. Remove the bolt (**Figure 31**) securing the caliper assembly to the caliper bracket.

12. Pivot the caliper assembly up and off the disc.

13. Pull the caliper assembly off the caliper carrier pivot pin on the rear axle and remove the caliper assembly.

14. Remove both brake pads and the brake spring as described in this chapter.

15. Install by reversing these removal steps, noting the following.

16. Make sure the retaining clip (A, **Figure 77**) is in place.

17. Apply a coat of silicone grease to the caliper pin (B, **Figure 77**) on the caliper carrier.

18. Carefully install the caliper assembly onto the disc. Be careful not to damage the leading edges of the pads during installation.

19. Tighten the caliper mounting bolt to the torque specification listed in **Table 2**.

20. Install the brake hose, with a sealing washer on each side of the fitting, onto the caliper. Install the union bolt and tighten to the torque specification listed in **Table 2**.

21. Adjust the parking brake as described in Chapter Three.

22. Bleed the brake as described in this chapter.

Caliper Rebuilding

1. Remove the caliper and brake pads as described in this chapter.

2. If not already removed, remove the brake pad spring (A, **Figure 78**).

3. Remove the caliper pivot boot collar (B, **Figure 78**) and the boots (C, **Figure 78**).

4. Place a shop cloth or piece of soft wood in the area normally occupied by the brake pads.

5. Place the caliper assembly on the workbench with the pistons facing down.

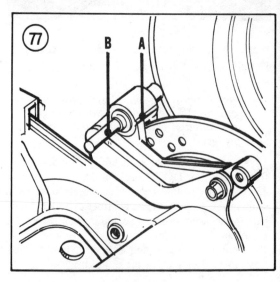

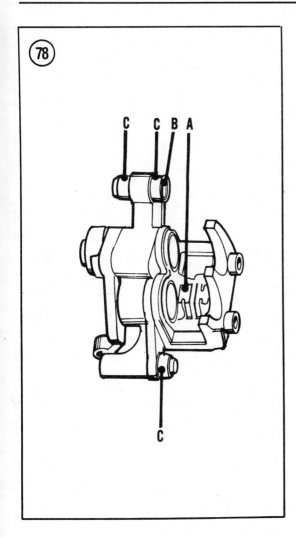

WARNING
*In the next step, the pistons may shoot out of the caliper body like bullets. Keep your fingers out of the way. Wear shop gloves and apply air pressure gradually. Do **not** use high pressure air or place the air hose nozzle directly against the hydraulic line fitting inlet in the caliper body. Hold the air nozzle away from the inlet allowing some of the air to escape.*

6. Apply the air pressure in short spurts to the hydraulic line fitting inlet (**Figure 79**) and force both pistons out. Use a service station air hose if you don't have a compressor.

CAUTION
In the following step, do not use a sharp tool to remove the dust and piston seals from the caliper cylinders. Do not damage the cylinder surface.

7. Use a piece of plastic or wood and carefully push the dust and piston seals in toward the caliper cylinder and out of their grooves (**Figure 80**). Remove the dust and piston seals from both cylinders and discard all seals.
8. Inspect the caliper body for damage; replace the caliper body if necessary.
9. Inspect the cylinders and the pistons for scratches, scoring or other damage. Light dirt may be removed with a cloth dipped in clean brake fluid. If rust is severe, replace the caliper body. Replace the caliper body if necessary.
10. If serviceable, clean the caliper body with rubbing alcohol and rinse with clean brake fluid.

11

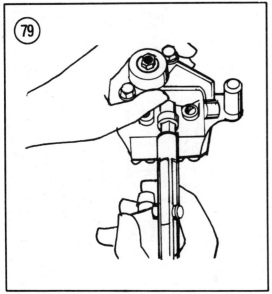

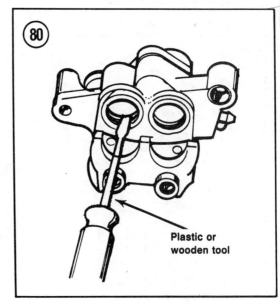

Plastic or wooden tool

11. Measure the inside diameter of both caliper cylinders (A, **Figure 81**) with a inside micrometer. If worn to the service limit dimension listed in **Table 1**, or greater, replace the caliper assembly.

12. Measure the outside diameter of the pistons (B, **Figure 81**) with a micrometer. If worn to the service limit dimension listed in **Table 1**, or less, replace the pistons.

NOTE
Never reuse the old dust seals and piston seals. Very minor damage or age deterioration can make the seals useless.

13. Coat the new dust seals and piston seals with fresh DOT 3 or DOT 4 brake fluid.

14. Carefully install the new dust seals and piston seals in the grooves in each caliper cylinder. Make sure the seals are properly seated in their respective grooves.

15. Coat the pistons and caliper cylinders with fresh DOT 3 or DOT 4 brake fluid.

16. Position the pistons with the flush side facing out toward the brake pads and install the pistons into the caliper cylinders. Push the pistons in until they bottom out.

17. Apply silicone grease to the caliper pivot boots and collar. Install the boots (C, **Figure 78**) and collar (B, **Figure 78**) into the caliper body. Make sure the boots are properly seated in the caliper body grooves.

18. If necessary, remove the parking brake mechanism from the caliper as described in this chapter.

19. Make sure the retaining clip (A, **Figure 77**) is in place.

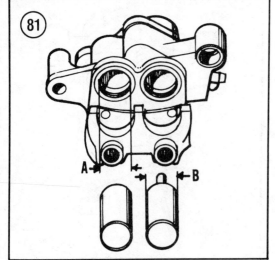

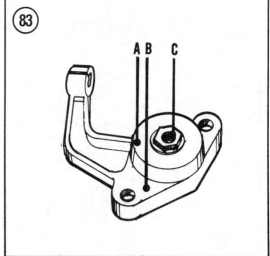

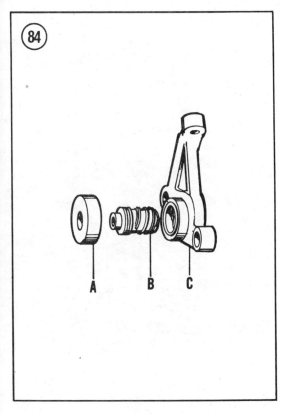

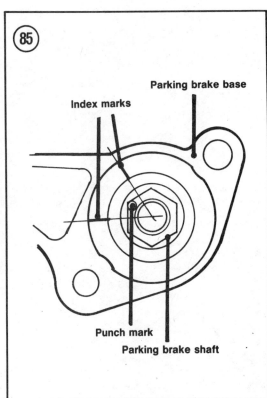

Parking brake base

Index marks

Punch mark

Parking brake shaft

20. Apply a coat of silicone grease to the caliper pin (B, **Figure 77**) on the caliper carrier.

21. Install the brake pads and the caliper as described in this chapter.

Parking Brake Mechanism
Disassembly/Assembly

1. Remove the rear brake caliper assembly as described in this chapter.

2. Remove the bolts (**Figure 82**) securing the parking brake assembly to the caliper and remove the assembly. Discard the gasket.

3. Remove the rubber boot (A, **Figure 83**) from the parking brake base (B, **Figure 83**).

NOTE
*The shaft is equipped with **left-hand**
threads.*

4. Unscrew the shaft (C, **Figure 83**) from the parking brake base.

5. Inspect the rubber boot (A, **Figure 84**) for wear or deterioration and replace as necessary.

6. Inspect the shaft threads (B, **Figure 84**) for wear or damage. Replace the shaft if necessary.

7. Inspect the shaft threads in the base (C, **Figure 84**) for wear or damage; replace as necessary.

8. Apply a coat of grease to the threads of the shaft.

9. Screw the shaft into the parking brake base until it stops, then back it out 1/8 turn. At this point the index mark on the shaft must be within the index marks on the parking brake base (**Figure 85**). If the marks are not aligned correctly, unscrew the shaft, rotate it slightly and screw the shaft back into the parking brake base. Recheck the index mark alignment.

10. Install the rubber boot over the shaft. Make sure it is completely seated on the base.

11. Install a new gasket (**Figure 86**) onto the parking brake base and install onto the caliper assembly.

11

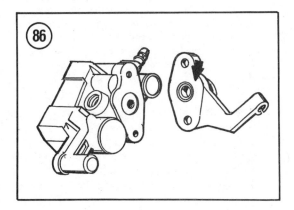

12. Install the bolts and tighten to the torque specification listed in **Table 2**.

13. Install the rear caliper assembly as described in this chapter.

FRONT BRAKE DISC

Inspection

It is not necessary to remove the disc from the hub to inspect it. Small marks on the disc are not important, but deep radial scratches, deep enough to snag a fingernail, reduce braking effectiveness and increase brake pad wear. If these grooves are found, the disc should be replaced.

1. Measure the thickness of the disc at several locations around the disc with vernier calipers or a micrometer.

2. The disc must be replaced if the thickness, in any area, is worn to the service limit listed in **Table 1** (or less) .

3. Clean the disc of any rust or corrosion and wipe clean with lacquer thinner. Never use an oil-based solvent that may leave an oil residue on the disc.

4A. On 3-wheeled models, replace the brake disc as follows:

    a. Remove the front wheel and hub as described in Chapter Nine.

    b. Remove the nuts (**Figure 87**) securing the brake disc to the front hub. Remove the brake disc from the threaded studs on the front hub.

    c. Install the brake disc onto the front hub.

    d. Apply blue Loctite (Lock N' Seal No. 2114) to the nuts and tighten to the torque specification listed in **Table 2**.

4B. On 4-wheeled models, replace the brake disc as follows:

    a. Remove the front wheel and hub as described in Chapter Nine.

NOTE
*The 1986-1987 models have 4 disc mounting bolts. The 1988-on models have 3 disc mounting bolts. **Figure 88** shows a 1987 model. The bolts are tightened to the same torque specification.*

    b. Remove the bolts (**Figure 88**) securing the brake disc to the front hub.

    c. Install the brake disc onto the front hub.

    d. Apply blue Loctite (Lock N' Seal No. 2114) to the bolts and install the bolts.

    e. Tighten the bolts to the torque specification listed in **Table 2**.

Removal/Installation

1A. On 3-wheeled models, perform the following.

    a. Inspect the disc before removing the front wheel.

    b. Remove the front wheel as described in Chapter Nine.

1B. On 4-wheeled models, remove the front wheels as described in Chapter Nine.

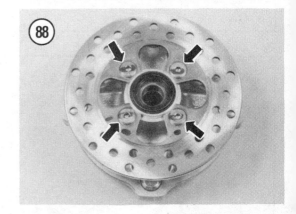

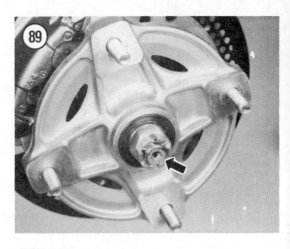

NOTE
Place a piece of wood or vinyl tube in each caliper in place of the disc. This way, if the brake lever is inadvertently squeezed, the piston will not be forced out of the cylinder. If this does happen, the caliper might have to be disassembled to reseat the piston and the system will have to be bled. By using the wood or vinyl tube, bleeding the

system is not necessary when installing the wheel.

2. On 4-wheeled models, perform the following.
   a. Before removing the front hub/brake disc, inspect the disc as described in this chapter.
   b. Remove the front caliper as described in this chapter.
   c. Remove the cotter pin and nut (**Figure 89**) securing the front hub/brake disc to the steering knuckle. Remove the front hub/brake disc assembly (**Figure 90**).

3. Install by reversing these removal steps, noting the following.

4. On 4-wheeled models, install the front hub/brake disc assembly and tighten the nut to the torque specification listed in **Table 2**. Install a new cotter pin and bend the ends over completely.

REAR BRAKE DISC

Inspection

It is not necessary to remove the disc from the wheel to inspect it. Small marks on the disc are not important, but deep radial scratches, deep enough to snag a fingernail, reduce braking effectiveness and increase brake pad wear. If these grooves are found, the disc should be replaced.

1. Measure the thickness of the disc at several locations around the disc with vernier calipers or micrometer (**Figure 91**). The disc must be replaced if the thickness, in any area, is worn to the service limit (or less) listed in **Table 1**.

2. Clean the disc of any rust or corrosion and wipe clean with lacquer thinner. Never use an oil-based solvent that may leave an oil residue on the disc.

Removal

Refer to **Figure 92** for this procedure.

11

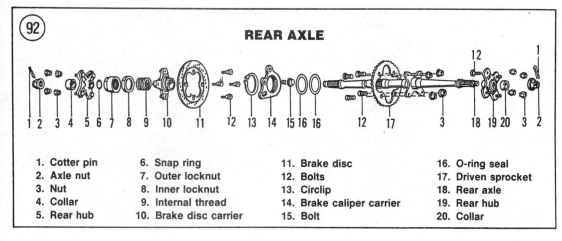

REAR AXLE

1. Cotter pin	6. Snap ring	11. Brake disc	16. O-ring seal
2. Axle nut	7. Outer locknut	12. Bolts	17. Driven sprocket
3. Nut	8. Inner locknut	13. Circlip	18. Rear axle
4. Collar	9. Internal thread	14. Brake caliper carrier	19. Rear hub
5. Rear hub	10. Brake disc carrier	15. Bolt	20. Collar

1. Place the ATV on level ground and set the parking brake.

2. Shift the transmission into NEUTRAL.

3. Remove the seat/rear fender as described in Chapter Twelve.

4. Remove the right-hand rear tire/wheel and hub assembly as described in Chapter Ten.

5. Remove the bolts securing the swing arm skid plate (**Figure 93**) and remove the skid plate.

6. Place a 56 mm open end wrench (Honda special tool part No. 07916-HA20000 or 07916-HA2010A) or large adjustable wrench on the inner locknut.

7. Place a 45 mm open end wrench (Honda special tool part No. 07916-1870101) or large adjustable wrench on the outer locknut (**Figure 94**).

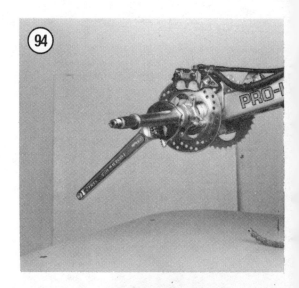

CAUTION
*The rear axle locknuts have **left-hand** threads. The wrench must be rotated **clockwise** to loosen the locknuts.*

8. Hold onto the *outer* locknut and loosen the *inner* locknut on the right-hand side of the axle. It may be necessary to tap on the end of the wrench with a soft faced mallet to break the inner locknut loose. Remove the locknut.

CAUTION
*The locknut and inner nut have had Loctite applied during assembly and are tightened to a large torque value. They are very hard to remove, even with the correct size tool and a lot of force. Do **not** apply heat to the area in order to try to loosen the locknut and inner nut as this will ruin the heat-treated hardness of the axle.*

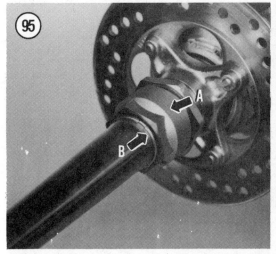

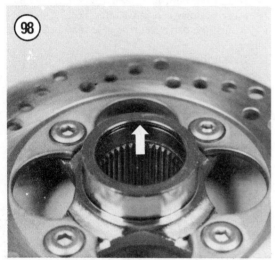

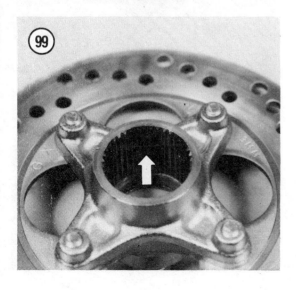

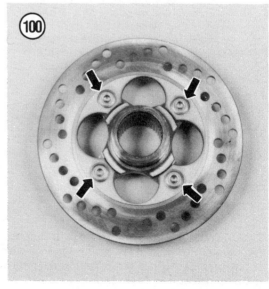

NOTE
Special flame cut wrenches are available from a Honda dealer or mail order house.

9. Have an assistant apply the rear brake.

CAUTION
The rear axle locknuts have left-hand threads. The wrench must be rotated clockwise to loosen both locknuts.

10. Loosen the outer locknut (A, **Figure 95**) and screw it *in* toward the brake disc until the snap ring is visible.

11. Remove the snap ring (B, **Figure 95**) from the rear axle.

12. Release the parking brake and remove the rear brake caliper assembly (**Figure 96**) as described in this chapter. Tie the caliper assembly up to the frame with a wire or bunji cord.

13. On 3-wheeled models slide off the snap ring collar.

14. Slide the outer and inner locknuts and the internal thread assembly off the right-hand end of the rear axle.

15. Slide the brake disc/hub assembly (**Figure 97**) off the right-hand end of the axle.

16. Remove the O-ring seal (**Figure 98**) from the brake disc hub. The O-ring must be replaced every time the hub is removed.

17. Inspect the splines (**Figure 99**) of the carrier for wear or damage. Replace if necessary.

18. To replace the brake disc, perform the following.

    a. Remove the Allen bolts (**Figure 100**) securing the disc to the carrier and remove the disc.

b. Position the brake disc with the DRIVE mark and arrow (**Figure 101**) on the side opposite the Allen bolts.

c. Install the Allen bolts and tighten to the torque specification listed in **Table 2**.

Installation

1. Make sure the axle bearing oil seal is in place on the right-hand side of the axle holder. Apply a light coat of multipurpose grease to the lips of the seal.

2. Install a new O-ring seal (**Figure 98**) onto the brake disc/hub assembly.

3. Position the brake disc/hub with the disc mounting bolts toward the inside and slide the brake disc/hub assembly onto the rear axle.

4. Clean off all Loctite residue from the threads on the internal thread and both locknuts.

5. Apply blue Loctite (Lock N' Seal No. 2114) to the threads of the *inner* locknut.

6. Slide the inner thread and the inner and outer locknut assembly (**Figure 102**) onto the rear axle.

7. On 3-wheeled models, slide on the snap ring collar.

8. Install the snap ring (B, **Figure 95**) into the groove in the rear axle.

9. Install the parking brake/disc brake caliper assembly as described in this chapter.

10. Apply the parking brake.

NOTE
In the following steps, use the same tools used during the removal sequence.

NOTE
The Honda special tool locknut wrenches have a receptacle for a 1/2 in. drive torque wrench. Use a 20 in. deflecting beam type torque wrench. The Honda special tool locknut wrench increases the torque wrench's leverage, so the torque wrench reading must be less than the torque actually applied. The 2 different torque specifications are listed in **Table 2** *as "actual" and "indicated" on the torque wrench scale.*

CAUTION
*The rear axle locknuts have **left-hand** threads. The wrench must be rotated **counterclockwise** to tighten the locknuts.*

11. Using the 45 mm locknut wrench, tighten the *outer* locknut (A, **Figure 95**) against the snap ring in the rear axle. Tighten the locknut to the torque specification listed in **Table 2**.

12. Place a 56 mm locknut wrench on the inner locknut (A, **Figure 103**) and hold onto the outer locknut (B, **Figure 103**) with the 45 mm locknut wrench.

CAUTION
*The rear axle locknuts have **left-hand** threads. The wrench must be rotated **clockwise** to loosen the locknuts.*

13. Hold onto the *outer* locknut and tighten the *inner* locknut (A, **Figure 103**). See the note preceeding Step 11 regarding torque specifications, then tighten the inner locknut to the torque specification listed in **Table 2**.

14. Install the skid plate and bolts. Tighten the bolts securely.

15. Apply multipurpose grease to the splines of the rear axle.

16. Install the right-hand rear tire/wheel and hub assembly as described in Chapter Ten.

17. Adjust the drive chain as described in Chapter Three.

18. Install the seat/rear fender.

FRONT BRAKE HOSE REPLACEMENT

There is no factory-recommended replacement interval but it is a good idea to replace the flexible

brake hoses every four years or when they show signs of cracking or damage.

3-wheeled Models

Refer to **Figure 104** for this procedure.

> *CAUTION*
> *Cover the front wheel, fender and fuel tank with a heavy cloth or plastic tarp to protect it from accidental spilling of brake fluid. Wash any brake fluid off of any plastic, painted or plated surface immediately, as it will destroy the finish. Use soapy water and rinse completely.*

1. Place the ATV on level ground and set the parking brake. Block the rear wheels so the vehicle will not roll in either direction.
2. Drain the front brake system of all brake fluid as described in this chapter.
3. Remove the union bolt and sealing washers (A, **Figure 105**) securing the lower flexible brake hose to the caliper assembly.
4. Remove the brake hose and let any residual brake fluid drain out.
5. To prevent the entry of moisture and dirt, cap the caliper assembly where the brake line attaches.
6. Remove the caliper upper mounting bolt (B, **Figure 105**) and brake hose guide plate. Remove the brake hose clamp (C, **Figure 105**).

> *NOTE*
> *In the following steps, remove the upper fork bridge bolts, then reinstall and tighten them securely. This must be done to maintain the correct front fork-to-fork bridge relationship. Do **not** loosen both the upper and lower fork bolts at the same time as the front fork may slide up or down in the fork bridges.*

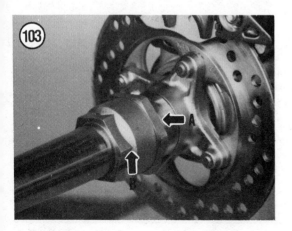

7. Remove the upper fork bridge bolts securing the brake hose clamp (A, **Figure 106**) on the left-hand side. Remove the brake hose clamp, then reinstall the bolts and tighten securely.
8. Remove the lower fork bridge bolts securing the brake hose clamp (B, **Figure 106**) on the left-hand side. Remove the brake hose clamp, then reinstall the bolts and tighten securely.
9. Remove the bolt and clamps (**Figure 59**) securing the front brake hose to the left-hand fork slider. Remove the clamps.
10. Move the brake hose out from the front fork slider and the receptacle in the front fender (C, **Figure 106**).
11. Note the orientation of the upper and lower brake hose clamps and slide them off of the brake hose. The clamps must be installed correctly on the brake hose.
12. Remove the union bolt and sealing washers (A, **Figure 107**) securing the upper flexible brake hose to the master cylinder and remove the hose (B, **Figure 107**).
13. Install a new flexible brake hose, sealing washers and union bolts in the reverse order of removal. Be sure to install new sealing washers in the correct positions; refer to **Figure 104**.
14. Correctly position the upper and lower brake hose clamps and slide them onto the brake hose. The clamps must be repositioned on the brake hose the correct way so the brake hose can be routed correctly through the frame.
15. Tighten the upper and lower fork bridge bolts and the caliper upper mounting bolt to the torque specifications listed in **Table 2**.
16. Tighten all union bolts to the torque specification listed in **Table 2**.

11

> *WARNING*
> *Use brake fluid from a sealed container marked DOT 3 or DOT 4 **only** and specified for disc brakes. Other types may vaporize and cause brake failure. Do not intermix different brands or types as they may not be compatible. Do not intermix a silicone based (DOT 5) brake fluid as it can cause brake component damage leading to brake system failure.*

17. Refill the master cylinder with fresh brake fluid marked DOT 3 or DOT 4 only. Bleed the brake as described in this chapter.

> *WARNING*
> *Do not ride the ATV until you are sure that the brakes are operating properly.*

FRONT BRAKE SYSTEM
(3-WHEELED MODELS)

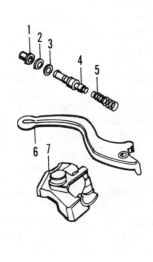

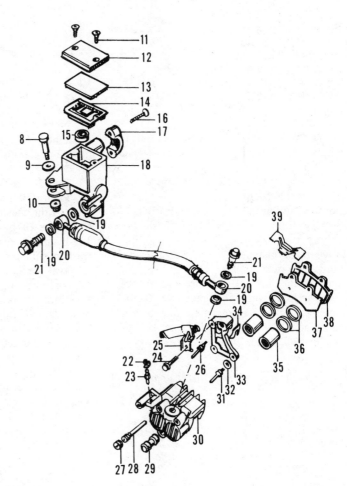

1. Piston boot	14. Diaphragm	27. Pad pin bolt cap
2. Snap ring	15. Separator	28. Pad pin bolt
3. O-ring	16. Bolt	29. Boot
4. Piston assembly	17. Clamp	30. Caliper body
5. Spring	18. Master cylinder body	31. Caliper pin
6. Hand lever	19. Sealing washer	32. Seal
7. Boot	20. Upper brake hose	33. Caliper bracket
8. Bolt	21. Union bolt	34. Retainer clip
9. Washer	22. Bleed valve cap	35. Piston
10. Nut	23. Bleed valve	36. Dust and piston seals
11. Screw	24. Bolt	37. Outboard brake pad
12. Top cover	25. Brake hose guide plate	38. Inboard brake pad
13. Diaphragm plate	26. Caliper pin	39. Anti-rattle spring

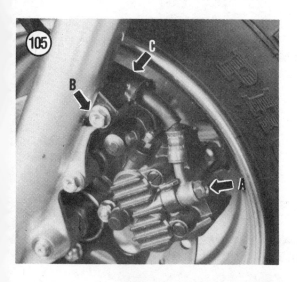

4-Wheeled Models

Refer to **Figure 108** for 1986-1987 models or **Figure 109** for 1988-on models.

> *CAUTION*
> *Cover the front wheel and fuel tank with a heavy cloth or plastic tarp to protect them from accidental spilling of brake fluid. Wash any brake fluid off of any plastic, painted or plated surface immediately, as it will destroy the finish. Use soapy water and rinse completely.*

1. Place the ATV on level ground and set the parking brake. Block the rear wheels so the vehicle will not roll in either direction.

2. Remove the front fenders as described in Chapter Twelve.

3. Drain the front brake system of all brake fluid as described in this chapter.

4. Remove the union bolt and sealing washers (A, **Figure 110**) securing the lower flexible brake hose to the caliper assembly on each side.

5. Remove the brake hoses and let any residual brake fluid drain out.

6. To prevent the entry of moisture and dirt, cap the caliper assemblies where the brake hoses attach.

7. Remove the caliper upper mounting bolt and hose guide plate (B, **Figure 110**) on each side.

8. Remove the front wheels as described in Chapter Three.

9. Remove the bolt and clamp securing the lower flexible brake hose to the upper suspension arm on each side.

10A. On 1986-1987 models, perform the following:
  a. Unscrew each lower flexible brake hose from the 3-way fitting on the frame (**Figure 111**).
  b. Remove the lower flexible brake hose from each side.
  c. Hold onto the metal brake line and unscrew the upper flexible brake hose from the upper connection of the metal brake line.

10B. On 1988-on models, perform the following:
  a. Unscrew the metal brake line lower connection from the center of the lower flexible brake hose.
  b. Remove the bolt securing the center of the lower flexible brake hose to the frame.
  c. Remove the lower flexible brake hose from the frame.
  d. Hold onto the metal brake line and unscrew the upper flexible brake hose from the metal brake line from the frame.
  e. Remove the bolts and clamps securing the metal brake line to the frame and remove the metal brake line.

11

11. Remove the union bolt and sealing washers (**Figure 113**) securing the upper flexible brake hose to the master cylinder and remove the hose.

12. On 1986-1987 models, to remove the 3-way joint and metal brake line, perform the following:

a. Unscrew the metal brake line (**Figure 114**) from the 3-way fitting.

b. Remove the bolts (**Figure 115**) securing the 3-way joint to the frame and remove the 3-way joint.

c. Remove the bolts and clamps securing the metal brake line to the frame. Refer to **Figure 116** and **Figure 117**.

d. Remove the metal brake line from the frame.

e. If necessary, unscrew the fittings and sealing washers from the 3-way joint.

13. Install new flexible brake hoses, new sealing washers and union bolts in the reverse order of removal. Be sure to install **new** sealing washers in the correct positions. Refer to **Figure 108** for 1986-1987 models or **Figure 109** for 1988-on models.

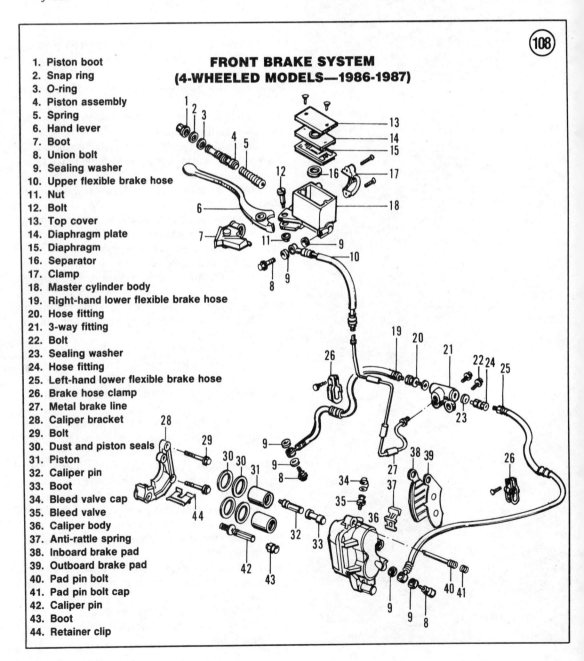

(108)

**FRONT BRAKE SYSTEM
(4-WHEELED MODELS—1986-1987)**

1. Piston boot
2. Snap ring
3. O-ring
4. Piston assembly
5. Spring
6. Hand lever
7. Boot
8. Union bolt
9. Sealing washer
10. Upper flexible brake hose
11. Nut
12. Bolt
13. Top cover
14. Diaphragm plate
15. Diaphragm
16. Separator
17. Clamp
18. Master cylinder body
19. Right-hand lower flexible brake hose
20. Hose fitting
21. 3-way fitting
22. Bolt
23. Sealing washer
24. Hose fitting
25. Left-hand lower flexible brake hose
26. Brake hose clamp
27. Metal brake line
28. Caliper bracket
29. Bolt
30. Dust and piston seals
31. Piston
32. Caliper pin
33. Boot
34. Bleed valve cap
35. Bleed valve
36. Caliper body
37. Anti-rattle spring
38. Inboard brake pad
39. Outboard brake pad
40. Pad pin bolt
41. Pad pin bolt cap
42. Caliper pin
43. Boot
44. Retainer clip

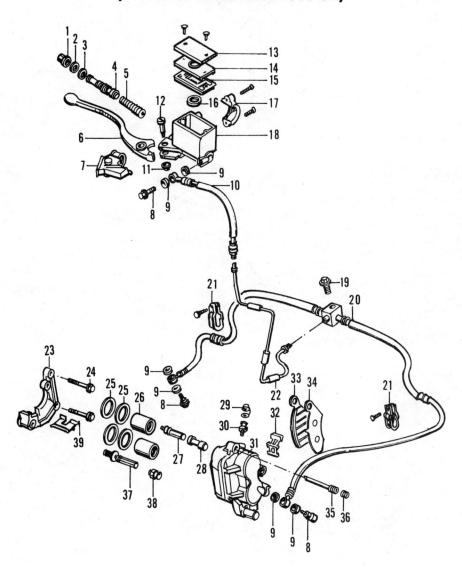

**FRONT BRAKE SYSTEM
(4-WHEELED MODELS—1988-ON)**

1. Piston boot
2. Snap ring
3. O-ring
4. Piston assembly
5. Spring
6. Hand lever
7. Boot
8. Union bolt
9. Sealing washer
10. Upper flexible brake hose
11. Nut
12. Bolt
13. Top cover

14. Diaphragm plate
15. Diaphragm
16. Separator
17. Clamp
18. Master cylinder body
19. Bolt
20. Lower flexible hose
21. Brake hose clamp
22. Metal brake line
23. Caliper bracket
24. Bolt
25. Dust and piston seals
26. Piston

27. Caliper pin
28. Boot
29. Bleed valve cap
30. Bleed valve
31. Caliper body
32. Anti-rattle spring
33. Inboard brake pad
34. Outboard brake pad
35. Pad pin bolt
36. Pad pin bolt cap
37. Caliper pin
38. Boot
39. Retainer clip

11

14. Tighten all union bolts and fittings on the metal brake lines to the torque specifications listed in **Table 2.**

> *WARNING*
> *Use brake fluid from a sealed container marked DOT 3 or DOT 4 **only** and specified for disc brakes. Other types may vaporize and cause brake failure. Do not intermix*

different brands or types as they may not be compatible. Do not intermix a silicone based (DOT 5) brake fluid as it can cause brake component damage leading to brake system failure.

15. Refill the master cylinder with fresh brake fluid marked DOT 3 or DOT 4 only. Bleed the brakes as described in this chapter.

> *WARNING*
> *Do not ride the ATV until you are sure that the brakes are operating properly.*

REAR BRAKE HOSE REPLACEMENT

There is no factory-recommended replacement interval but it is a good idea to replace all brake hoses every four years or when they show signs of cracking or damage.

Refer to **Figure 54** for 3-wheeled models or **Figure 55** for 4-wheeled models for this procedure.

> *CAUTION*
> *Cover the swing arm and axle bearing housing with a heavy cloth or plastic tarp to protect it from accidental spilling of brake fluid. Wash any brake fluid off of any plastic, painted or plated surface immediately, as it will destroy the finish. Use soapy water and rinse completely.*

1. Place the ATV on level ground and set the parking brake. Block the front wheel(s) so the vehicle will not roll in either direction.
2. Remove the seat/rear fender assembly as described in Chapter Twelve.
3. Place a wood block under the swing arm to support it in the up position.
4. Remove both rear wheels as described in Chapter Ten.
5. Drain the rear brake system of all brake fluid as described in this chapter.
6. Remove the union bolt and sealing washers (**Figure 118**) securing the flexible brake line to the caliper assembly.
7. Remove the bolt and clamp (**Figure 119**) securing the flexible brake hose to the swing arm and remove the hose from the frame.
8. Remove the brake line and let any residual brake fluid drain out.
9. Remove the union bolt and sealing washers securing the flexible brake hose to the master cylinder and remove the hose. Refer to **Figure 120**

11

for 3-wheeled models or **Figure 121** for 4-wheeled models.

10. Install a new flexible brake hose, sealing washers and union bolts in the reverse order of removal. Be sure to install new sealing washers on each side of the union bolts. Refer to **Figure 54** for 3-wheeled models or **Figure 55** for 4-wheeled models for this procedure.

11. Tighten all union bolts to the torque specification listed in **Table 2**.

> *WARNING*
> *Use brake fluid from a sealed container marked DOT 3 or DOT 4 **only** and specified for disc brakes. Other types may vaporize and cause brake failure. Do not intermix different brands or types as they may not be compatible. Do not intermix a silicone based (DOT 5) brake fluid as it can cause brake component damage leading to brake system failure.*

12. Refill the master cylinder with fresh brake fluid marked DOT 3 or DOT 4 only. Bleed the brake as described in this chapter.

> *WARNING*
> *Do not ride the ATV until you are sure that the brakes are operating properly.*

13. Install the rear wheels and seat/rear fender assembly.

DRAINING THE SYSTEM

Drain the brake system whenever a component is removed from either the front or rear brake system (except brake pad replacement). Doing this will help eliminate the accidental spilling of brake fluid on various components of the vehicle during the disassembly procedures. Care should still be taken during component removal as some residual brake fluid will still leak out when parts are removed.

Also drain the system whenever the brake fluid becomes contaminated or should be replaced. Never reuse the drained brake fluid even if it is not time to replace it. Brake fluid absorbs moisture from the air, which lowers its boiling point and can cause brake failure. Brake fluid is relatively inexpensive and should always be replaced.

1. Place the ATV on level ground and set the parking brake. Block the rear wheels so the vehicle will not roll in either direction.

2. On 4-wheeled models remove the front wheels as described in Chapter Nine.

3. Remove the dust cap from the bleed valve on the caliper assembly. Refer to the following.

    a. Front brake—3-wheeled models: **Figure 122**.

    b. Front brake—4-wheeled models: **Figure 123**.

    c. Rear brake—all models: **Figure 124**.

> *NOTE*
> *On 4-wheeled models, drain both front caliper assemblies at the same time.*

4. Connect the bleed hose to the bleed valve on the caliper assembly(ies). Refer to **Figure 125** for the front brake or **Figure 126** for the rear brake.

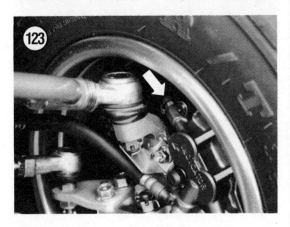

CAUTION
Cover the surrounding area with a heavy cloth or plastic tarp to protect it from the accidental spilling of brake fluid. Wash any brake fluid off of any plastic, painted or plated surface immediately as it will destroy the finish. Use soapy water and rinse completely.

5. Clean the top of the master cylinder of all dirt and foreign matter.

6. Remove the screws securing the reservoir top and remove the reservoir top, plate and diaphragm. Refer to **Figure 127** for front brake(s) or **Figure 128** for the rear brake.

7. Loosen the bleed valve and pump the front brake lever or rear brake pedal until no more brake fluid flows out of the bleed valve.

WARNING
*Dispose of this brake fluid properly. **Never** reuse brake fluid. Contaminated brake fluid can result in brake failure.*

8. Close the bleed valve and disconnect the bleed hose.

9. Refill and bleed the brake system as described in this chapter.

10. On 4-wheeled models install the front wheels as described in Chapter Nine.

BLEEDING THE SYSTEM

This procedure is not necessary unless the brakes feel spongy, there has been a leak in the system, a component has been replaced or the brake fluid has been replaced.

This procedure pertains to both the front and rear brake systems.

Brake Bleeder Process

This procedure uses a brake bleeder that is available from motorcycle or automotive supply stores or from mail order outlets.

1. Remove the dust cap from the bleed valve on the caliper assembly. Refer to the following.
   a. Front brake—3-wheeled models: **Figure 122**.
   b. Front brake—4-wheeled models: **Figure 123**.
   c. Rear brake—all models: **Figure 124**.

NOTE
On 4-wheeled models, bleed one front caliper at a time.

2. Connect the brake bleeder to the bleed valve on the caliper assembly. Refer to **Figure 129** for the front brake or **Figure 130** for the rear brake.

11

CAUTION
Cover the front suspension arms or the swing arm area with a heavy cloth or plastic tarp to protect it from the accidental spilling of brake fluid. Wash any brake fluid off of any plastic, painted or plated surface immediately as it will destroy the finish. Use soapy water and rinse completely.

3. Clean the top of the master cylinder of all dirt and foreign matter.

4. Remove the screws securing the reservoir top and remove the reservoir top, plate and diaphragm. Refer to **Figure 127** for front brake(s) or **Figure 128** for the rear brake.

5. Fill the reservoir almost to the top lip. Insert the diaphragm, plate and the top loosely. Leave the top in place during this procedure to prevent the entry of dirt.

WARNING
*Use brake fluid from a sealed container marked DOT 3 or DOT 4 **only** and specified for disc brakes. Other types may vaporize and cause brake failure. Do not intermix different brands or types as they may not be compatible. Do not intermix a silicone based (DOT 5) brake fluid as it can cause brake component damage leading to brake system failure.*

6. Open the bleed valve about one-half turn and pump the brake bleeder.

NOTE
If air is entering the brake bleeder hose from around the bleed valve, apply several layers of Teflon tape to the bleed valve. This should make a good seal between the bleed valve and the brake bleeder hose.

7. As the fluid enters the system and exits into the brake bleeder the level will drop in the reservoir. Maintain the level at about 3/8 inch from the top of the reservoir to prevent air from being drawn into the system.

8. Continue to pump the lever on the brake bleeder until the fluid emerging from the hose is completely free of bubbles. At this point, tighten the bleed valve.

NOTE
Do not allow the reservoir to empty during the bleeding operation or more air will enter the system. If this occurs, the entire procedure must be repeated.

9. When the brake fluid is free of bubbles, tighten the bleed valve, remove the brake bleeder tube and install the bleed valve dust cap.

10. On 4-wheeled models, repeat Steps 1-9 for the other wheel's brake assembly.

11. If necessary, add fluid to correct the level in the reservoir. It should be to the upper level line.

12. Install the diaphragm, plate and the reservoir top. Tighten the screws securely.

13. Test the feel of the brake lever or pedal. It should be firm and should offer the same resistance each time it's operated. If it feels spongy, it is likely that there is still air in the system and it must be bled again. When all air has been bled from the system and the fluid level is correct in the reservoir, double-check for leaks and tighten all fittings and connections.

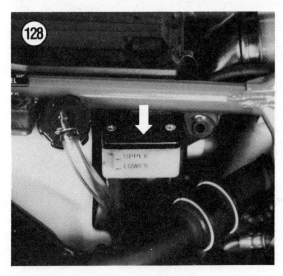

14. Test ride the ATV slowly at first to make sure that the brakes are operating properly.

Without a Brake Bleeder

1. Remove the dust cap from the bleed valve on the caliper assembly. Refer to the following.
   a. Front brake—3-wheeled models: **Figure 122**.
   b. Front brake—4-wheeled models: **Figure 123**.
   c. Rear brake—all models: **Figure 124**.
2. Connect the bleed hose to the bleed valve on the caliper assembly(ies). Refer to **Figure 125** for the front brake or **Figure 126** for the rear brake.

3. Place the other end of the tube into a clean container. Fill the container with enough fresh brake fluid to keep the end submerged. The tube should be long enough so that a loop can be made higher than the bleed valve to prevent air from being drawn into the caliper during bleeding.

4. Clean the top of the master cylinder of all dirt and foreign matter.
5. Remove the screws securing the reservoir top and remove the reservoir top, plate and diaphragm. Refer to **Figure 127** for front brake(s) or **Figure 128** for the rear brake.
6. Fill the reservoir almost to the top lip. Insert the diaphragm, plate and the top loosely. Leave the top in place during this procedure to prevent the entry of dirt.

7. Slowly apply the brake lever or pedal several times as follows.
   a. Pull the lever in or push the pedal down. Hold the lever or pedal in the applied position.
   b. Open the bleed valve about one-half turn. Allow the lever or pedal to travel to its limit.
   c. When this limit is reached, tighten the bleed screw.
8. As the fluid enters the system, the level will drop in the reservoir. Maintain the level at about 3/8 inch from the top of the reservoir to prevent air from being drawn into the system.
9. Continue to pump the lever or pedal and fill the reservoir until the fluid emerging from the hose is completely free of bubbles.

11

air will enter the system. If this occurs, the entire procedure must be repeated.

10. Hold the lever or pedal down, tighten the bleed valve, remove the bleed tube and install the bleed valve dust cap.

11. On 4-wheeled models, repeat Steps 1-10 for the other wheel's brake assembly.

12. If necessary, add fluid to correct the level in the reservoir. It should be to the upper level line.

13. Install the diaphragm, plate and reservoir top. Tighten the screws securely.

14. Test the feel of the brake lever or pedal. It should be firm and should offer the same resistance each time it's operated. If it feels spongy, it is likely that there is still air in the system and it must be bled again. When all air has been bled from the system and the fluid level is correct in the reservoir, double-check for leaks and tighten all fittings and connections.

> *WARNING*
> *Before riding the ATV, make certain that the brakes are operating correctly by operating the lever or pedal several times.*

15. Test ride the ATV slowly at first to make sure that the brakes are operating properly.

REAR BRAKE PEDAL

Removal (3-wheeled Models)

1. Place the ATV on level ground and set the parking brake.

2. Remove the seat and rear fender assembly as described in Chapter Twelve.

3. Using Vise Grips, unhook the brake pedal return spring (A, **Figure 131**) from the frame.

4. Remove the cotter pin, washer and pivot pin (B, **Figure 131**) securing the master cylinder brake rod to the brake pedal. Discard the cotter pin.

5. Remove the clamping bolt (C, **Figure 131**) on the actuating arm. Slide off the actuating arm from the pivot shaft on the backside of the brake pedal.

6. Withdraw the brake arm (D, **Figure 131**) from the frame.

7. Install by reversing these removal steps, noting the following.

8. Apply grease to the brake pedal pivot shaft before installing the brake pedal.

9. Position the actuating arm with the clamping bolt' facing up. Align the punch mark on the actuating arm with the pivot shaft and install the actuating arm onto the backside of the pivot shaft.

10. Tighten the clamping bolt securely.

11. Install a new cotter pin and bend the ends over completely. Never reuse an old cotter pin.

12. Adjust the rear brake height as described in Chapter Three.

Removal (4-wheeled Models)

1. Place the ATV on level ground and set the parking brake.

2. Remove the seat and rear fender assembly as described in Chapter Twelve.

3. Remove the cotter pin, washer and pivot pin (A, **Figure 132**) securing the master cylinder brake rod to the brake pedal. Discard the cotter pin.

4. Loosen, but do not remove, the bolts (B, **Figure 132**) securing the rear brake pedal and right-hand foot peg assembly to the frame.

5. Using Vise Grips, unhook the brake pedal return spring (C, **Figure 132**) from the frame while withdrawing the brake arm from the pivot shaft on the frame.

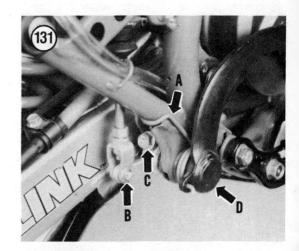

6. Remove the bolts (B, **Figure 132**) loosened in Step 4 and remove the rear brake pedal and right-hand foot peg assembly.

7. Install by reversing these removal steps, noting the following.

8. Apply grease to the brake pedal pivot shaft on the frame before installing the brake pedal.

9. Tighten the rear brake pedal and right-hand foot peg mounting bolts to the torque specification listed in **Table 2**.

10. Install a new cotter pin and bend the ends over completely. Never reuse an old cotter pin.

11. Adjust the rear brake height as described in Chapter Three.

Table 1 BRAKE SPECIFICATIONS

Item	Specification	Wear limit
Front master cylinder		
Cylinder bore I.D	12.700-12.743 mm	12.756 mm
	(0.500-0.5017 in.)	(0.5022 in.)
Piston O.D.	12.657-12.684 mm	12.645 mm
	(0.4983-0.4994 in.)	(0.4978 in.)
Front caliper		
Cylinder bore I.D.	25.40-25.45 mm	25.46 mm
	(1.000-1.002 in.)	(1.0023 in.)
Piston O.D.	25.30-25.35 mm	25.29 mm
	(0.996-0.998 in.)	(0.995 in.)
Front Disc		
Thickness	3.8-4.2 mm	3.0 mm
	(0.15-0.17 in.)	(0.12 in.)
Runout	—	0.30 mm (0.012 in.)
Rear Master Cylinder		
Cylinder bore I.D	14.000-14.043 mm	14.055 mm
	(0.5120-0.5529 in.)	(0.5533 in.)
Piston O.D.	13.957-13.984 mm	13.945 mm
	(0.5495-0.5506 in.)	(0.5490 in.)
Rear Caliper		
Cylinder bore I.D.	25.40-25.45 mm	25.46 mm
	(1.000-1.002 in.)	(1.0023 in.)
Piston O.D.	23.30-25.35 mm	25.29 mm
	(0.996-0.998 in.)	(0.996 in.)
Rear Disc		
Thickness	3.8-4.2 mm	3.0 mm
	(0.15-0.17 in.)	(0.12 in.)
Runout	—	0.30 mm (0.012 in.)

Table 2 BRAKE TORQUE SPECIFICATIONS

Front Brake		
Item	N•m	ft.-lb.
Front wheel lug nuts		
(3-wheeled models)	60-70	43-51
Front hub nut		
(4-wheeled models)	80-120	58-72
Front master cylinder		
Clamping screws	10-14	7-10
Union bolt	25-35	18-25
Front caliper		
Mounting bolts	24-30	17-22
Pad pin bolts	15-20	10-14
Pad pin bolt caps	10-20	7-14
Union bolt	25-35	18-25
(continued)		

11

Table 2 BRAKE TORQUE SPECIFICATIONS (continued)

Front Brake (continued)		
Item	N•m	ft.-lb.
Front brake disc		
Mounting nuts		
(3-wheeled models)	25-30	18-22
Mounting bolts		
(4-wheeled models)	14-16	10-12
3-way joint (4-wheeled models)		
Fitting	30-40	22-29
Mounting bolts	10-14	7-10
Flexible hose to fitting	12-15	9-11
Fork bridge bolts (3-wheeled models)		
Upper and lower	18-25	13-18
Rear Brake		
Item	N•m	ft.-lb.
Rear axle nut		
3-wheeled models		
1985	100-120	72-87
1986	120-170	87-123
4-wheeled models	120-170	87-123
Rear master cylinder		
3-wheeled models		
Mounting bolts	24-30	17-22
Union bolt	25-35	18-25
4-wheeled models		
Mounting bolts	25-35	18-25
Union bolt	25-35	18-25
Rear caliper		
Mounting bolts	20-25	14-18
Pad pin bolts	15-20	10-14
Pad pin bolt caps	10-20	7-14
Union bolt	25-35	18-25
Rear brake disc		
mounting bolts	35-40	25-29
Rear axle locknuts		
Outer		
Actual	80-100	58-72
Indicated	73-91	53-66
Inner		
Actual	120-140	87-101
Indicated	109-127	79-92
Parking brake base		
mounting bolts	20-25	14-18
Rear brake pedal and right-hand		
foot peg mounting bolts		
(4-wheeled models)	50-60	36-43

CHAPTER TWELVE

BODY AND FRAME

This chapter contains removal and installation procedures for front and rear fenders and front and rear hand grips.

This chapter also describes procedures for completely stripping the frame and recommendations for repainting the stripped frame.

FRONT FENDER
(4-WHEELED MODELS)

Removal/Installation
(1986-1987)

Refer to **Figure 1** for this procedure.

1. Remove the seat/rear fender as described in this chapter.
2. Unhook the rubber strap (**Figure 2**) securing the rear portion of the front fenders.
3. Remove the bolts (**Figure 3**) on each side securing the front fender to the frame.
4. Carefully pull the fender assembly free from the rubber grommets (**Figure 4**) on the locating pins at the front, side and rear.
5. Move the front fender up and toward the front. Spread the rear portion of the front fender out and pull the front fender toward the front and remove it from the frame.

6. Install by reversing these removal steps, noting the following.
7. Be sure to install the rubber grommets and tighten all bolts securely. Do not overtighten as the plastic fender may fracture.

Removal/Installation
(1988-on)

Refer to **Figure 5** for this procedure.

1. Remove the seat/rear fender as described in this chapter.
2. Disconnect the electrical connector from the backside of the headlight unit.
3. Unhook the rubber strap (**Figure 2**) securing the rear portion of the front fenders.
4. Remove the bolts (**Figure 3**) on each side securing the rear portion of the front fender to the frame.
5. Remove the bolts and metal washer on each side securing the front portion of the front fender to the frame.
6. Carefully pull the front fender assembly free from the rubber grommets on the locating pins at the side and rear.
7. Move the front fender up and toward the front. Spread the rear portion of the front fender out and pull the front fender toward the front and remove it from the frame.

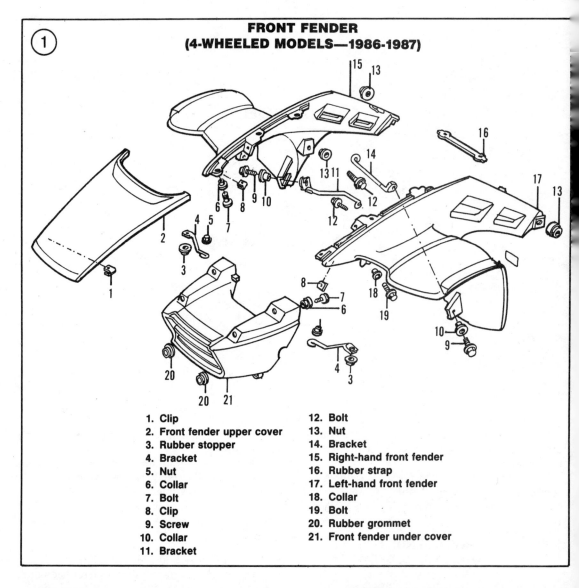

FRONT FENDER
(4-WHEELED MODELS—1986-1987)

1. Clip
2. Front fender upper cover
3. Rubber stopper
4. Bracket
5. Nut
6. Collar
7. Bolt
8. Clip
9. Screw
10. Collar
11. Bracket
12. Bolt
13. Nut
14. Bracket
15. Right-hand front fender
16. Rubber strap
17. Left-hand front fender
18. Collar
19. Bolt
20. Rubber grommet
21. Front fender under cover

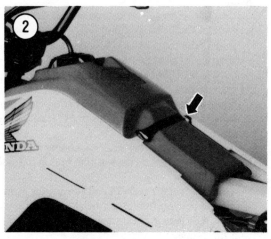

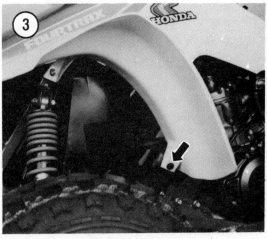

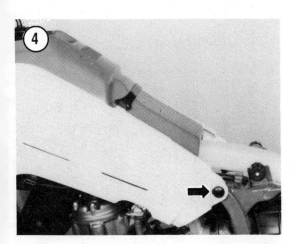

8. Install by reversing these removal steps while noting the following.

9. Be sure to install the rubber grommets and tighten all bolts securely. Do not overtighten as the plastic fender may fracture.

SEAT/REAR FENDER (ALL MODELS)

Removal/Installation

1. Move the seat lock toward the left. Refer to **Figure 6** for 3-wheeled models or **Figure 7** for 4-wheeled models.

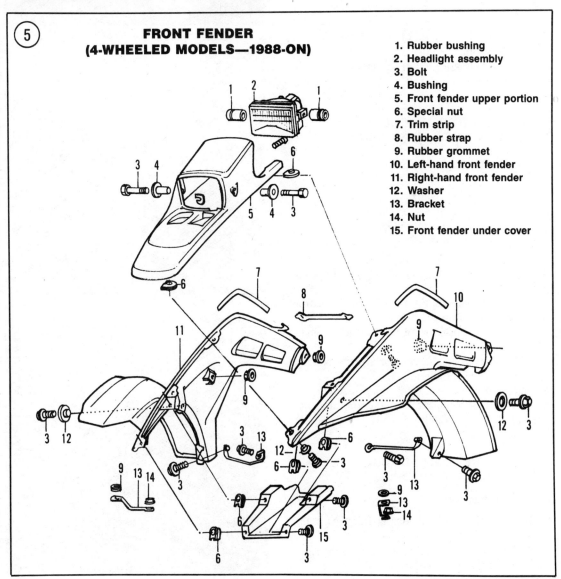

FRONT FENDER (4-WHEELED MODELS—1988-ON)

1. Rubber bushing
2. Headlight assembly
3. Bolt
4. Bushing
5. Front fender upper portion
6. Special nut
7. Trim strip
8. Rubber strap
9. Rubber grommet
10. Left-hand front fender
11. Right-hand front fender
12. Washer
13. Bracket
14. Nut
15. Front fender under cover

12

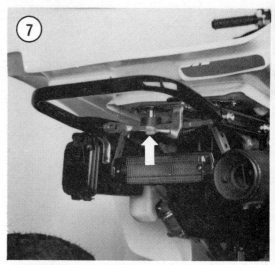

2. Pull the seat/rear fender toward the rear then straight up and off the frame.

3. Install by reversing these removal steps, noting the following.

4. Make sure the kickstarter lever is moved out into the START position (**Figure 8**). If the lever is placed back against the engine it will be trapped behind the rear fender.

FRONT HAND GRIP
(4-WHEELED MODELS)

Removal/Installation

> *NOTE*
> *On the 1988-on models, the front skid plate is an integral part of the hand grip and cannot be removed separately.*

1. On 1986-1987 models, remove the bolts (A, **Figure 9**) securing the skid plate and remove the skid plate.

2. Remove the bolts (B, **Figure 9**) securing the front hand grip to the frame.

3. Pull the hand grip forward and remove it from the frame.

4. Install by reversing these removal steps. Note the following during installation.

5. Tighten the front hand grip bolts securely.

6. On 1986-1987 models, tighten the front skid plate bolts to 28-34 N•m (20-25 ft.-lb.).

REAR HAND GRIP
(ALL MODELS)

Removal/Installation

1. Remove the seat/rear fender as described in this chapter.

2. Remove the bolts (**Figure 10**) securing the right-hand side of the rear hand grip to the frame.

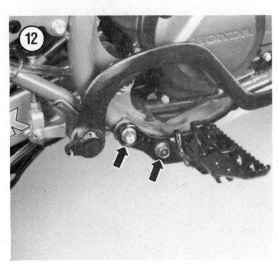

3. Remove the bolts (A, **Figure 11**) securing the left-hand side of the rear hand grip and the tool box to the frame. Remove the tool box and mounting brackets (B, **Figure 11**).

4. Pull the rear hand grip (C, **Figure 11**) to the rear and remove it from the frame.

5. Install by reversing these removal steps, noting the following.

6. Tighten all bolts and nuts securely. Don't forget the tool box mounting brackets on the left-hand side.

FOOTPEGS

Replacement

On 3-wheeled models remove the bolts (**Figure 12**) securing the foot peg to the frame and remove the footpeg assembly. Repeat for the other side.

On 4-wheeled models remove the bolts securing the left-hand foot peg (**Figure 13**) to the frame and remove the left-hand footpeg assembly.

On 4-wheeled models the right-hand foot peg is removed during rear brake pedal removal as described in Chapter Eleven.

On all models, tighten the mounting bolts to 50-60 N•m (36-43 ft.-lb.).

12

FRAME

The frame does not require routine maintenance. However, it should be inspected immediately after any accident or spill.

Component Removal/Installation

1. Remove the seat/rear fender and front fender(s) as described in this chapter.

2. Remove the engine as described in Chapter Four.

3A. On 3-wheeled models, remove the front wheel, steering head and front forks as described in Chapter Eight.

3B. On 4-wheeled models, remove the front wheels, steering shaft and front suspension arms as described in Chapter Eight.

4. Remove the rear wheels, shock absorber and swing arm as described in Chapter Nine.

5. Remove the electrical components and wiring harness.

6. Remove the footpegs as described in this chapter.

7. On 3-wheeled models, remove the steering head races from the steering head tube as described in Chapter Eight.

8. Inspect the frame for bends, cracks or other damage, especially around welded joints and areas that are rusted.

9. Assemble by reversing these removal steps.

Stripping and Painting

Remove all components from the frame. Thoroughly strip off all old paint. The best way is to have it sandblasted down to bare metal. If this is not possible, you can use a liquid paint remover and steel wool and a fine, hard wire brush.

> *CAUTION*
> *The fenders and air filter air box are molded plastic. If you wish to change the color of these parts, consult an automotive paint supplier for the proper procedure. Do not use any liquid paint remover on these components as it will damage the surface. The color is an integral part of these components and cannot be removed.*

When the frame is down to bare metal, have it inspected for hairline and internal cracks. Magnaflux is the most common and complete process.

Make sure that the primer is compatible with the type of paint you are going to use for the finish color. Spray on one or two coats of primer as smoothly as possible. Let it dry thoroughly and use a fine grade of wet sandpaper (400-600 grit) to remove any flaws. Carefully wipe the surface clean and then spray a couple of coats of the final color. Use either lacquer or enamel base paint and follow the manufacturer's instructions.

A shop specializing in painting will probably do the best job. However, you can do a surprisingly good job with a good grade of spray paint. Spend a few extra dollars and get a good grade of paint as it will make a difference in how good it looks and how long it will stand up. It's a good idea to shake the can and make sure the ball inside the can is loose when you purchase the can of paint. Shake the can as long as is stated on the can. Then immerse the can *upright* in a pot or bucket of *warm* water not over 120° F.

> *WARNING*
> *Higher temperatures could cause the can to burst. Do **not** place the can in direct contact with any flame or heat source.*

Leave the can in the water for several minutes. When thoroughly warmed, shake the can again and spray the frame. Be sure to get into all the crevices where there may be rust problems. Several light mist coats are better than one heavy coat. Spray painting is best done in temperatures of 70-80° F (21-26° C). Any temperature above or below this will give you problems.

After the final coat has dried completely, at least 48 hours, any overspray or orange peel may be removed with a *light* application of Dupont rubbing compound (red color) and finished with Dupont polishing compound (white color). Be careful not to rub too hard or you will go through the finish.

Finish off with a couple coats of good wax before reassembling all the components.

It's a good idea to keep the frame touched up with fresh paint if any minor rust spots or scratches appear.

An alternative to painting is powder coating. The process involves spraying electrically charged particles of pigment and resin on the object to be coated, which is negatively charged. The charged powder particles adhere to the electrically grounded object until heated and fused into a smooth coating in a curing oven. Powder coated surfaces are more resistant to chipping, scratching, fading and wearing than other finishes. A variety of colors and textures are available.

INDEX

13

13

13

1985 ATC 250R

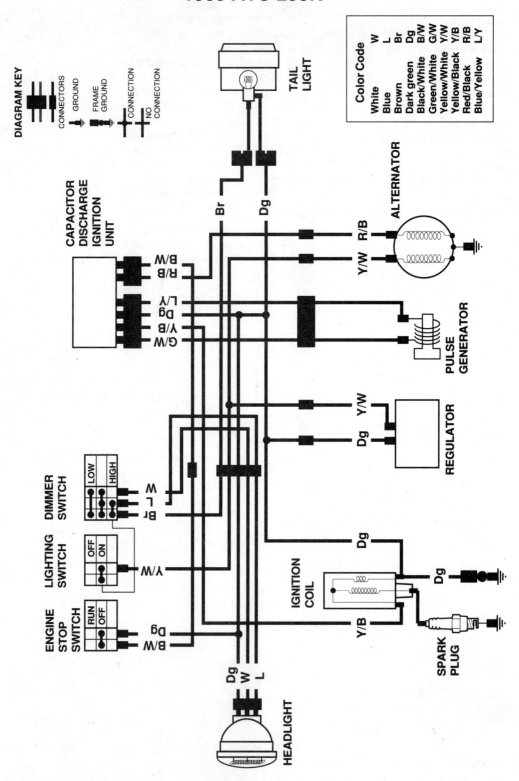

1986 ATC 250R

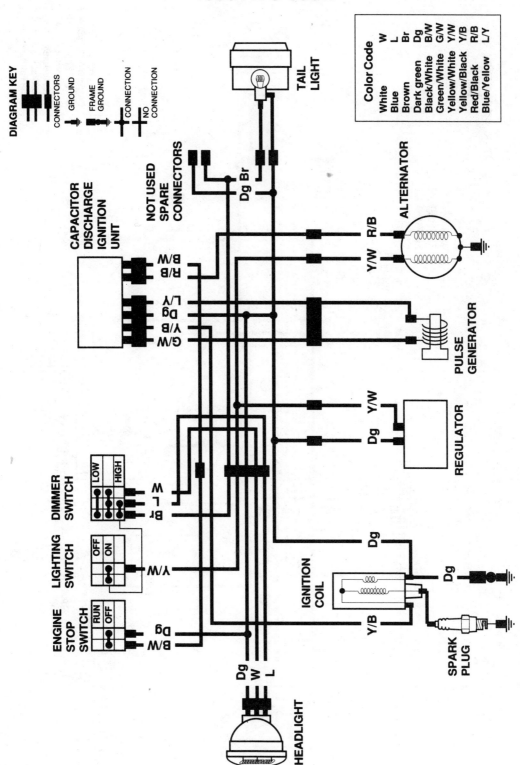

1986 TRX250R/FOURTRAX 250R

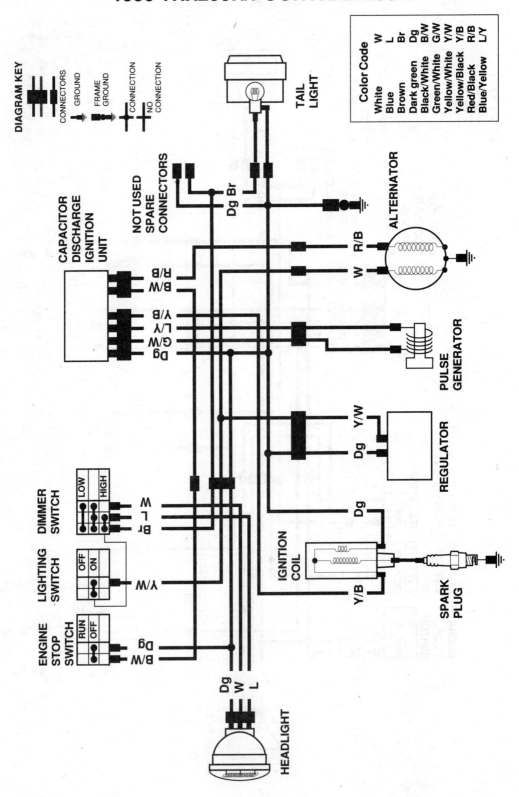

1987-1989 TRX250R/FOURTRAX 250R

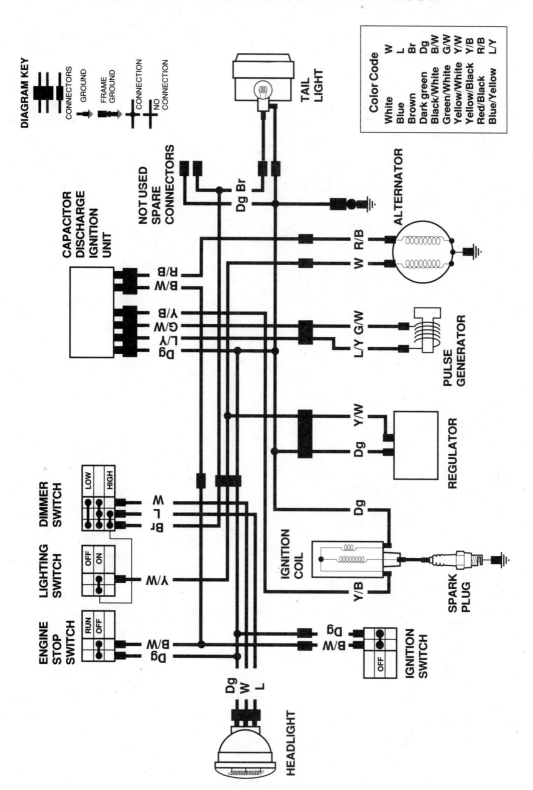

14

NOTES

NOTES

NOTES

NOTES

NOTES

NOTES

MAINTENANCE LOG

Service Performed	Mileage Reading				
Oil change (example)	2,836	5,782	8,601		